India Ever Independent

Why Only 50 Years

Devi Dayal Aggarwal

Foreword by

Dr. Lokesh Chandra

1999

Kaveri Books
New Delhi-110 002

First Published in 1999
ISBN: 81-7479-031-4

Published by : **Rakesh Goel**
Kaveri Books
4697/5-21A, Ansari Road,
New Delhi-110002 (India).
Tel : 3288140, Fax: 011-7198902
e-mail : kaveribooks@vsnl.com

Laser Typesetting by : **Delite Printers, Delhi-110035**

Printed at : **Chawla Offset Printers, Delhi-110052.**

PRINTED IN INDIA

Dedicated to my late son

Arvind Mohan

whose memory and words of doing something remarkable in the universe, inspired me to start writing books.

Foreword

Shri D.D. Aggarwal has raised the crucial question of the continuity of India beyond its legalistic and international definitions. Is India just an administration and a state constituted as the Government in continuity with the British regnum of two centuries, or beyond both of them is it also a Nation with several millennia of systems of governance, polity, and a pervading psychosphere. The Government of India derives its power and authority from the Constitution which has been explicitly stated to have been given by the people of India unto themselves. The British Parliament passed an Act for the Independence of India, and her official position is stated in the dozen fat volumes of the "Transfer of Power". Technically and officially, the Independence of India commences from the 15th of August, 1947, when British power was transferred to India and Pakistan. We, the people of India, have a Government, but the vast historic span of our existence as a Nation has been considered to be a bleak and blank silence. Both the concepts of our historicity and of our ecumene as a Nation, have been victims of secularism. The excavations at Mehargarh have been dated to the seventh millenium BC by the potassium-argon method. These archaeological remains show an urban civilization. Urbanism has been our inheritance of millennia, and its corollary should be sophisticated systems of governance. The English word *city* is derived from the Latin *civitas,* from *civis* 'citizen', which is cognate to Sanskrit *Shiva.* The essence of a city is its dimension of shiva 'the auspicious and propitious', happiness and prosperity, as opposed to the dense forest of ancient India with predatory animals on the prowl. The evolution of a proto-state and its imperative corollary of a hierarchy of administration goes back to the most ancient phase of Indian civilisation. But the millennia of India's history that live in our lives and languages, rites and practices, have been overlooked. We have been thinking of ourselves as an ancient nation but a young state. The de-recognition of India's eternity is derived from the five ems *(pancha-makara)* of colonial and post-colonial India. The five are Metcalfe, Mill (James Stuart Mill), Macaulay, Marx and Mahatmaism. The psychosphere that arose in the mind of the colonial rulers has become the viaticum of the post-colonial period. Founding fathers of the post-colonial era wandered eyeless among canvasses, imagining the beauty of each one. The canvasses are in the concrete crushers. Tears roll down the eyes of Eternity.

Shri D. D. Aggarwal discovers new images of India's polity. We stop breathless, to wonder what we really were, are and have to be. This book is a maiden attempt of Shri Aggarwal to elaborate the administration of India from the Vedic era onwards and its underlying value system which gave us such a long span of uninterrupted existence. The moral stature of the Ruler has been an important input in the political perceptions of Classical India. Franchise, cabinet system, espionage and vigilance, archaeological evidence of the socio-political context, and scores of other facts have been discussed by Shri Aggarwal. He has outlined the Rule of Law and the Law of Rulers from the pre-historic down to the Sindhu-Sarasvati period, Mauryas, Guptas, Mediaeval and British periods. He has dealt with the more recent events of British rule in India and our struggle for freedom culminating in independence in 1947. He discusses the negative effects of theocratic rule in the mediaeval period on the culture of India. It is a racy, readable and easy-to understand presentation of our political creativity for several millennia, as well as the blood, toil and tears of our culture and people under foreign domination. As India stands at the eve of the new century, she has to leave behind wolf-men, the *luperci,* to redesign her mindscape in keeping with her inner terrains. *Dharmo Akshati Rakshitah.* Thomas Babington Macaulay has found an obliging ally in the globalisation of economy. "Indians in blood and colour, but English in tastes, in opinions, in morals and in intellect" are against our deepest core. Intellectual domination is being fortified by an economic and political mosaic. The book of Shri Aggarwal is a caution against the storm of the world-flow of Europe.

(Lokesh Chandra)

Director,
International Academy of Indian Culture,
New Delhi-110016.

Preface

Having come across the country celebrating its 50th year of independence, it pinched my mind as to why we should term it country's 50th year of independence, when we have been an independent nation for lacs of years or according to Swami Dayanand crores of years. Ever since 'Vedic era' we have been independent except for the small period of British rule during which we wère ruled by the English as a colony under U.K. or a few years, when after Mohammed Ghori had conquered and left Qutab-ud-din Aibak as his lieutenant. Just after about a decade, Qutab-ud-din had declared himself a Sovereign King of India and the subsequent Kings of Slave Dynasty and further Muslim rulers had almost Indianised themselves. Similarly, if we take the annexation of Delhi (the seat of Indian Mughal Empire) by British in around 1810, we can say we were a colony for about 137 years upto 1947, when British left India. So except for a few years under Mohammed Ghori and 137 years under British, we have been a sovereign country as all other Muslim rulers had Indianised themselves and had ruled India as sovereign kings. It is, therefore, farce to say that India has been independent for only 50 years and thus annuling the entire existence of an Independent India for lacs of years.

Existence of India starts from the Vedic era or the start of mankind in the universe as vedas are considered to be in existence ever since the start of mankind, lacs of years back. The vedas, however, had not been brought into black and white as such was the belief to pass on the vedas by the guru to the pupil by heart only and for so many years, it had passed on like that. All brahmins remembered the vedas by heart and had been teaching the relevant Dharma to the people of other varnas as per their requirement i.e. the Kshatriya Dharma to a kshatriya and Vaish Dharma to a vaish. All rulers had been ruling as per vedic dharma as propounded by the Rajgurus. Manu had divided the mankind into four varnas viz. Brahmin, Kshatriya, Vaish and Shudra on functional basis with a view to see that all people lived peacefully in the kingdom doing their own job as per their respective Dharma.

As implied by the word 'varana', it was chosen by each person as per his volition and his capability and not by birth. After preliminary education, a person could continue further studies if he wanted to become a brahmin; could learn the tactics of warfare, if he wanted to become an kshatriya; or learn about the canons of trade, industry, agriculture, if he wanted to become a vaish and if one was not able to accommodate himself in any of the above three varnas, he became a shudra. Now since everyone opted the varna of his choice, he had no grudge on belonging to the particular varna and discharged his duties as per Dharma pertaining to his varna. The person was, as such, recognised as per his vocation. This is amply proved by 'Manas'-

कहि मृदुबचन विनीत तिन्ह बैठारे नर नारि,

उत्तम मध्यम नीच लघु निज निज थल अनुहारि ।

In Sita's svayamber and so in all functions, people were made to sit as per their position and not as per their respective varnas. Similarly in Bhagwat too people were recognised by their capability. It is only later on that this Vedic concept of varna was forgiven and strict caste system as per birth came into vogue, which resulted in the killing of our culture and dharma so much so that in case of any foreign invasion, it was for the kshatriyas only to defend and all other people remained aloof. In this way three fourth of the people were out from defending the country and the result was that Ghazni could wade through the entire country and looted it without any contest by anyone with a small force at his command and subsequently Ghori also came and conquered the country and then Muslim rulers could rule the country without any opposition from crores of people inspite of the tyranny let loose by them on Hindus. So there was no unity of purpose but adherence to strict casteism and tolerating what the kings commanded. After all the Muslims were initially in thousands only and they could be overpowered easily if the masses were united for the purpose of putting out the foreign rulers. It is at this time that Indians had lost the love for independence and their own rule although in strict sense of independence for the country, even the Muslim rulers were sovereign Indian Kings.

We treat the start of history from a date from which a verifiable proof of existence of any ruler is available. From that angle, we have only about 2600 years history but even Mahabharat has been considered to have taken place 5000 years before and taking another five thousand years when Ram existed and another ten thousand prior to that, we are atleast 20,000 years old civilisation. This has also been amply proved now by the excavation of Mohenjo Daro, Harappa and further by Dwarka and Mehargarh although the western historians have reckoned Mohenjo Daro too as only 6000 years old as they do not recognise the existence of mankind prior to that period. So the ancient civilisation of India and a period of over 20000 years of independent India has been taken out from any reckoning. From Bhagwat, we find the existence of Chakravarty Raja Puru, who was the ruler of the entire universe, comprising of seven oceans and seven continents, which is now a historical fact too, followed by another Chakravarty Raja Bharat, who also ruled entire universe and thus spread Arya civilisation in all countries, although it developed more in India in subsequent years. This also proves the exhaustive knowledge of our ancient people not only of this universe but also of all other stars. Hindu literature had been annihilated by the Muslim invaders, destroying all Hindu temples and universities, leaving us in dark about our past and it is unfortunate that we subsequently learnt about India's past only from the universities in Europe and not in India. Such a knowledge from a foreign country about our old civilisation could only be biased one, to suit the feelings of western philosophers, who were not interested in making us aware of the prehistoric period of this country and give Hindus a chance of feeling proud of the same.

After Vedic era, we enter the Ram period, Krishna period and then to Budha, Mauryas, Guptas. Upto that time, India was the only civilised country in the universe with maximum resources, maximum education, maximum knowledge of the universe and so on but Hindu rulers cared to remain sovereign in the country facing all foreign invaders only for the purpose of defending the country. They never thought of colonising the other countries. In Vedic dharma, even a conquered area was given back to be ruled by the defeated raja of that place after only taking some presents or compensation for battle from him, otherwise as per the illustration of their power, they could have been the rulers of entire universe. Such an attempt had once been made by Raja Kanishaka to conquer Central Asia but the Indian army, brought up with Indian pleasures, could not face the cold weather of Himalaya, when crossing it and most of the troops died. Another effort was made by Jaipal, a Rajput Raja of Punjab, but was defeated while crossing Hindukush. Except these two occasions, there is no mention of our rulers having tried to conquer foreign land in post-historic period. Of course in prehistoric period, as already indicated, we had ruled the entire universe as per Bhagwat. The decline of India started during Rajput period in about 9th or 10th century A.D. due to bifurcation of the country into small kingdoms; they too fighting within themselves and giving chance to the foreign invaders to invade and defeat the Indian rulers, one by one, and become the ruler of the country. Similarly having been spoiled by the pleasures of India, the Muslim rulers and Muslim chiefs too started fighting within themselves giving chance to English to conquer and rule the country without much of a force and resources. They fought with Indian rulers by help of Indians and with Indian resources. They made the country a dependent and their colony like their colonies of Africa, America etc. of that time and India too was branded like those negro countries as a barbaric nation, uneducated and uncivilised and Indians accepted these adjectives as they were neither aware of their past nor their civilisation except what they were groomed for by the English. So India as a country remained independent in pre-historic period; during Hindu period and also in Mohammedan period as all their rulers were sovereign Indian rulers but the British ruled India as a colony from England and exploited it economically, to such an extent that it became from the richest country of the world to the poorest one during British regime.

Even prior to Mohammedans, many invaders had come to India like Sungas, Huns etc but they also Indianised themselves and became part of inhabitants of this country-Aryavrat or Bharat. The term 'Hindu' would appear to have been coined by the Muslims for the inhabitants east of Sindh river, who were formerly known as 'Sindhus. The word 'Hindu' has subsequently got the effect of a religion as Muslims kept themselves aloof from them unlike Huns and Sungas, who had got amalgamated in Indians (Hindus). After the Muslims advent, India became a country of two religions-Hindus and Muslims - and this ultimately led to the coining of 'Two Nation Theory' by Muslim Fundamentalists culminating in the partition of the country on that basis. So Hindustan was named as the place of the inhabitants, east of Sindh river, and the inhabitants were called Hindus and so 'Hindutava' is the characteristic of a Hindu or the way of life of the people east of Sindhu river. In other words Hindustan or Hindu or Hindutava or Bhartiyata are all synonyms and calling ourselves as Hindu or Bhartiya should accordingly be the same. Rather than calling 'Hindutava', which has been linked with religion 'Hindu', if we call it Bhartiyata', it would be better even though it represents same nation living as per Hindu way of life or inhabitants of Bharat.

Now we have to see how we have been ruled in Vedic Era and by the rulers of foreign advent, who had Indianised themselves and ruled for the well-being of the inhabitants of this country i.e. the rule as 'Bhartiyata' and subsequently as we were ruled by British as a colony without Indianising themselves and thinking always for the well-being of United Kingdom and not of India as such. For this purpose we shall have to go through the past of the Bharat as per vedic, pauranic tenets and times, how it was always an Independent country, finding out what independence means as per vedas and then go on analysing the periods of various rulers. This would give a proper insight of the history of Independent India, which is lacs of years old if not crores of years old and treat India as an independent country for this much time except for about 140 years of British rule and not start the independence after the departure of British, which is cnly fifty years old, marring our entire independent period of thousands and lacs of years.

In this book I have tried to dig out how independence was understood and exercised in vedic era and post vedic era. Whenever we have performed as per vedic dharma, we progressed and whenever we got estrayed from vedic way of life or 'Bhartiyata', we have been doomed and forced to be ruled by Mohammedans first and by British later. Even now there is a need of the feeling of Bhartiyata in all our people to become a strong nation of the universe as we had been in our past period till about the advent of English. With emphasis on this theme, the book has come out as a mini history of India starting from the vedas to date.

I am thankful to the writers of works available, but for whose help I would not have been able to bring out this book, as indicated in the bibliography at the end of this book. I am also thankful for the inspiration and assistance provided by my wife, son, other members of family and my cousin Jagan Nath in bringing out this book.

H-13, Ashok Vihar, **Devi Dayal Aggarwal**
Delhi-110052.
Tel.: 7428669

Contents

Introduction

The year 1998 is being celebrated in the country as the fiftieth year of India's independence. It is correct that India attained independence from British yoke in 1947—fifty years back and so the fiftieth year of independence. But India has been independent ever since the advent of mankind, crores of years back and our vedas speak of the independence of the country, ruled by elected king with the assistance of elected representatives in the Samiti or Sabha and villages being administered by the elected body, called 'Panchayat'. This is the democratic way of governance of Independent India, where the say of the people was supreme in all matters of governance. India was so much caring for independence that even when within India, one raja conquered the other, the kingdom was returned to be ruled by the defeated raja, after payment of some presents or compensation and accepting the conquering raja's suzerainty; otherwise for all practical purposes the defeated raja was sovereign and autonomous ruler of the kingdom. How then a country, with such thinking and according importance to independence even for the defeated rajas, for such a long past, could be treated as independent for the last fifty years only. Correct that this period is relevant for getting independence from British rule, who infact ruled the country for about 140 years (taking the year of annexation of Delhi in British empire in India) only. Leaving, therefore, aside this black period of 140 years in the history of India, we should feel proud of having been independent eversince the advent of mankind or atleast after the coming up of Vedas/Manu Smṛiti, who taught us the importance of independence and the democratic way of governance and having been lived as such for such a long period. Infact the word 'colonialism' was unknown to India and British gave this form of governance to India, after having made so many colonies in Africa, America, Australia etc. So they bracketted India with the colonies of Africa etc (inhabited by Negros) inspite of her having been the most developed, most educated, most resourceful country of the universe with a very impressive past so much so that every country felt proud in extending the hand of friendship with Indian kings and people from various countries used to come for education to India after crossing a very tough competition for admission in Indian universities. From such a glorious past, it is a pity that, India had been termed by British as 'barbaric' during their rule and they considered it their duty to civilise the Indians. It is because Hindu literature etc. had all been destroyed by the Muslim rulers and the education centres eliminated. It is India's misfortune that whatever literature was left was interpreted by Europeans and to know India's past civilisation, Indians had to go to U.K., Germany, etc. or depend on what was written by Chinese visitors or Greek visitors and writings of Muslim historians, which were generally biased to please the Muslim rulers.

But the things have changed after the discovery of Mohenjo Daro, Harappa, Mehargarh and Dwarka towns as also by research conducted by Indians during the past one century starting from Maharishi Dayanand and Balgangadhar Tilak. The thinking has now come round the fact that Indian civilisation and Aryan civilisation are synonymous and Aryans had gone from India to other countries and that Indian civilisation is the oldest and most accomplished in the universe.

Taking advantage of the research already conducted by Indian philosophers, historians, religious leaders, I have tried to bring out some of the contents in this book and tried to establish that rather than calling India 50 years old independent nation, we have been ever independent for lacs of years and the concept of independence has been taught by us to the universe, demolishing the rhyme of India having been independent for fifty years only.

1 General View of Indian Polity

Like prehistoric Europe, Northern India (symbolising India as a whole) experienced ice ages and it was after the second of these, in the second interglacial period more than 100000 years before Christ, the man first left surviving traces in India. These are the palaeolithic pebble tool and Soan culture, so called from the little rivers of Panjab where they have been found in large numbers.

Then very recently in the perspective of geological time, great changes took place in man's way of living, certainly not much earlier than 15000 B.C. and perhaps as late as 6000 B.C., man developed what Prof. Gordon Childe calls "an aggressive attitude to his environment". The man learnt how to grow food crops, to tame domestic animals, to make pots and to weave garments. Developed agriculture and permanent villages, however, came into being probably in the 7000 B.C. The earliest remains of settled cultures are of little agricultural villages in Baluchistan and lower Sind. In the early part of 3000 B.C. civilisation in the sense of an organised system of government over a comparatively large area developed nearly simultaneously in the river valleys of the Nile and Indus. We know a great deal of Egypt and of Mesopotamia civilisations because they have left written material which has been satisfactorily deciphered. The Indian people, on the other hand, did not engrave long inscriptions on stone or place papyrus scrolls in the tombs of their dead. All that we know, is derived from the brief incriptions of their seals. Efforts have been made to read the Indus seals but none so far succeeded. Hence our knowledge of Indus civilisation is inadequate in many respects. The civilisation of the Indus is known to the archaeologists as the Harappa culture from the modern name of the site of one of its two great cities, on the left bank of river Ravi in the Panjab. Mohenjo Daro, the second city, is on the right bank of the Indus. Some recent revelations, which have come to notice, in the valley of old river Saraswati (since dried up) near border of India and Pakistan, is the third city almost as large as the two earlier known and designed on the same plan. A few smaller towns as also a large number of village sites from Ropar on the upper Satlej to Gujrat have been traced. The area covered by Harappa culture, therefore, extends for some 950 miles from north to south and the pattern of its civilisation was so uniform that even the bricks were usually of the same size and shape from one end to the other. This civilisation owed little to the middle east and there is no reason to believe that it was formed by the immigrants. The cities were built by the people, who had probably been in the Indus valley for several centuries. The Harappa people were already Indians when they planned their cities which hardly altered for about a thousand years. We cannot fix a precise date for the beginning of this civilisation but certain indications synchronise it roughly with the village culture of Baluchistan. As per hypothesis, the cities were oligarchic, commercial or republics, without sharp extremes of wealth and poverty and with only a weak repressive organisation but the excavations at Harappa in 1946 and further discoveries at Mohenjo Daro have shown that this idyllic picture is incorrect. Each city had a well justified citadel, which seems to have been used for both religious and governmental purposes. The regular planning of the streets and the strict uniformity throughout the area of the Harappa culture in such features as weights and measures, the size of bricks and even the layout of great cities suggest rather a single centralised state, than a number of free countries. The most striking feature of the culture was its intense conservatism. The two cities were built on a similar plan. To the west of each was a citadel and oblong artificial platform. This was defended by crenelated walls and on it were erected the public buildings.

Below it was the town proper atleast a square mile in area in each case. The main streets were quite straight and divided the city into large blocks, within which were net works of narrow planned lanes. In the houses, bath-rooms were provided with drains, which flowed into sewers under the main streets leading to soak pits. The sewers were covered throughout their length by large brick-slabs. The unique severage system of the Indus people must have been maintained by some municipal organisation, and is one of the most impressive of their achievements. No other ancient civilisation had so efficient a system of drains. Like the tank of a Hindu temple, it had a bathing pool of 39x23 ft. in area and 8 ft. depth, constructed of beautiful brick work made water tight with bitumen. It shows that like the later Hindus, they had a strong belief in the purificatory effects of water from a ritual point of view. The largest building so far excavated is one at Mohenjo Daro, with a superficial area of 230'x78' which may have been a palace. At Harappa a great granary has also been discovered to the north of the citadel. This was raised on a platform to save from flood and was divided in blocks to store corn, which was collected from peasants as land tax and we may assume that it had its counter-part at Mohenjo Daro. The main food crops were wheat, barley, peas, and sesamum. The main domestic animals known to modern India had already been tamed-humped and humpless cattle, buffaloes, goats, sheep, pigs, asses, dogs, and domestic fowls. Harappa people had known horse since a few horse's teeth have been found in the lowest stratum of the Baluchistan site of Rana Ghundai, probably dating from several centuries earlier than the foundation of Harappa. This would indicate existing of horse riding at that time. Latest excavations at Mehargarh have been dated to the seventh millenium B.C. by the potassium argon method.

Trade was also there in those days, whether by land or sea, the products of the traders reached Mesopotamia as a number of typical Indus seals and a few other objects from the Indus valley have been found in Sumer at levels dating between 2300-2000 B.C. and some authorities believe that the land of

Melukka reached by sea from Sumer and referred to in Sumerian documents was the Indus valley. Evidence of Sumerian exports to India is very scant and uncertain and we must assume that they were mainly precious metals and raw materials. The findings from Indus seals suggest that merchants from India actually resided in Mesopotamia; their chief merchandise were cotton, which has always been Indian staple export. Over 2000 seals have been discovered in the Indus cities and it would seem that every important citizen possessed one. Their purpose was to mark the ownership of property but they doubtless also served as amulets and were regularly carried on the persons of their owners.

The people were not on the whole artistic, no doubt they had a literature with religious epics, similar to those of Sumer and Babylon but these are forever lost to us. They also seem to have been using metal. The most striking of the figurines is the bronze "dancing girl' naked but for a necklace and a series of bangles almost covering one arm; her hair dressed in a complicated coiffure, standing in a provocative posture with one arm on the hips and one lanky leg half bent. This young woman has an air of lively pertness, quite unlike anything in the work of the other ancient civilisations. It has been suggested that the dancing girl is a representation of a class of temple dancers and prostitutes such as existed in contemporary middle eastern civilisation and were an important feature of later Hindu culture but this cannot be proved.

The religion of the Harappa people had some features suggesting those characteristics of later Hinduism which are not to be found in the earlier strata of Indian religious literature. The mother goddess for instance reappear only after a lapse of over a thousand years from the fall of Harappa. She probably was the divinity of the people. The most striking deity of the Harappa culture is the horned God of the seals. His posture is one well known to later Indian holymen, with the legs drawn up close to the body and the two heels touching, to position quite impossible to the average westerner without much practice.

This may be proto Shiv. Certain other sites in the western half of northern India also give evidence of Harappa culture influence on people at a lower cultural level. Material from places such as Hastinapur, Kaushambi and the very recently excavated Atranji Khere near Aligarh together with some Deccan sites like Newdutoli and Nevasa show that by the end of 2000 B. C. there were many settlements—whose inhabitants lived in reasonably comfortable conditions knowing the use of metal. Also ancient India made certain advances in husbandry for which the whole world owes her a debt. Cotton was first used by Harappa people. Wild rice was known to eastern Indian-Ganga valley.

After the barbarians had conquered the outlying villages, the ancient laws and rigid organization of the Indus cities must have suffered great strain. Hoards of jewellery were burried, evidently the city was over populated and law and order was less well kept perhaps because the barbarians were already raging the provinces and the city was full of newcomers, where the city fathers could not force into the age old patterns of its culture or frequent flooding too would have worsened the situation.

Among the many people, who inhabited India in about 5000 B.C. was a group of related tribes, whose priests had perfected a very advanced poetic technique, which they used for the composition of hymns in praise of their gods to be sung at sacrifices. These tribes, chief of which was that of Bharatas, settled mainly in east Panjab and in the region between Satlej and Yamuna, which later became known as Brahmvarta. The hymns composed by the priests were carefully handed down by word of mouth and early in 2000 B.C. were collected and arranged. They were still not committed to writing but looked on as so sacred that even minor alterations in the texts were not permitted and the priestly schools, which preserved them devised the most remarkable and effective system of checks and counter-checks to ensure their purity. The period of Vedas, Brahamanas and Upnishadas is a sort of transition from prehistory to history. If history as distinct from archaeology is the study of the human past from written sources then India's history begins with Aryans. The Rig Ved and the great body of oral religious literature, which followed it in the first half of 2000 B.C. belonged to the living Hindu traditions. The vedic hymns are still recited at weddings and funerals and the daily devotion of the brahmins.Thus they are part of historical India and do not belong only to the pre-historic period as made out by western thinkers.

No real synchronisms are contained in the Rig Ved itself to give any certain information on the date of its composition. Some authorities in the past claimed on exceedingly early date for it on the basis of the tradition and ambiguous astronomical references in the hymns themselves - it was even believed by our respected Indian scholars that it went back to over 6000 B.C. Of course they would not have composed before the end of Harappa. When the hymns were written, the focus of Aryan culture was the region between Yamuna and Satlej and along the upper course of river Saraswati (since dried up). Though many hymns refer to battles between one Aryan tribe and another, there is underlying this inter-tribal rivalry, a sense of solidarity against the Dasyus, who evidently represent the survivors of kindered (non-aryan) people of the Punjab and North-West. Other enemies of the Aryans were the Panis, who are described as wealthy people, who refused to patronise the vedic priests and who stole the cattle of Aryans. Hindu also find the mention of varnas in vedas. In the earliest hymns we read of the Kstra, the nobility and the Vis, the ordinary tribesmen and the records of several of the Indo-European people suggest that a tribal aristocracy was a feature of Indo-European society even before the tribes migrated from the original homes. The four classes—Priests (Brahmins), Warriors (Kshatriyas), Peasants (Vaish), and Serf (Sudras) were crystalising throughout the period of Rig Ved. They have survived to the present day. The Sanskrit word used for these "varnas", means "to opt" and suggest that initially out of the Aryans and non-Aryans, the people could opt for any of the varnas and those who did not opt for any of the four varnas, were Dasyus or non-Aryans. The Aryans followed a mixed pastoral and agricultural economy in which cattle played an important part. References are there of riding the horses and their use as motive power of chariots. The Aryans also loved music and played "flute", harp to the accompaniment of drums and cymbals. There is also reference of singing and dancing and dancing girls, who may have been professional. They also delighted in gambling. In the remains of Indus cities, numerous dices have been found and the Aryans have left their own record of the gambling properties in the beautiful "Gamester's lament", one of the few predominantly secular processes, which by lucky chance have found their way in Rig Ved. All these things refer to the civilisation during Mahabharat. Therefore, we can safely go back to over 3000 years B.C. as the time the Rig Ved would have been conceived as time of Mahabharat has been placed at that time. Specialised trade and crafts had appeared too. In place of few craftsmen in the Rig Ved, many are now referred to including jewellers, goldsmiths, metal-workers, basket-makers, rope-makers, weavers, dyers, carpenters and potters.

However, it is in the sixth century B.C. that Indian history emerges from legend and dubious tradition. Here, we read of great kings, whose history is certain and some of whose achievements are well known and political developments are clear. The age in which true history appears in India was one of great intellectual and spiritual firment. Mystics and sophists of all kinds roamed throughout the Ganga valley, all advocating some form of mental discipline and asceticism as a measure of salvation. But this is one part of the society. The other was that there were well established kingdoms of Kosala, Magadh, Vatsa and Avanti. Kosal, the house of Ram (10000 B.C.) was declining. Here King Prasenajit was still a mighty monarch but was inefficient and squandered his time and wealth on holymen. Bimbsar of Magadh, on the other hand, was a man of different stamp. He was a resolute and energetic organiser, ruthlessly dismissing inefficient officers, calling his village headmen together for conferences, building roads and causeways and travelling over kingdom on tours and inspection. A man of peace; had kept on good terms with kingdoms west of line, exchanging courtiers even upto Gandhara. His conquest was Anga (Bengal) and gained control over Kashi in dowry of his queen. He was killed by his son Ajat Shatru. He conquered Kosal, Vajji, Vaisali and annexed these lands. In his time, city of Taxila in north west was already a city of learning and trade. The existence of such a seat of learning and well established kingdom even in 600 BC, would indicate that the governance on vedic system or Bharatiyata would have been in existence even several thousand years BC. That can safely take us to Mahabharat or even Ramayan period, which though considered mythological period, could have been in existence in some shape.

Subsequently in 326 B.C., Alexander crossed the Hindukush and occupied the district of Kabul and reached Indus. Ambi, the king of Taxila submitted to him and helped him in defeating Raja Porus. It is here that the mutual jealousies of the kings of Indian sub-continent came to fore, giving a chance to the foreign aggressors to step on Indian soil for the first time. This has subsequently been repeatedly noticed leading to the occupation of part of India by Sungas, Huns, Mohammedans and finally the English. But all invaders before Mohammedans had got assimilated in Hinduism or Bhartiyata. Mohammedans not only kept their separate identity because of the greater fanaticism in them but also made a large number of Hindus converted to Islam. Still we have to be proud that whereas Mohammedans had converted the entire habitants of the East European and Middle East countries into Islam, Hindus had been able to keep their identity despite tyranny by Muslims on them. One good thing even in Muslims had been that they declared themselves as sovereign Indian kings and did not allow India to be a colony of any foreign ruler as had been the case under British.

History would, however, appear to be meaningless, if facts of the outstanding importance of Turkish and British rule are not viewed in their true perspective against a proper background of the theme of independent India.

स्वाधीनता वृत्ते साफल्यं नपराधीन वृत्तिता,
ये पराधीन कर्माणो जीवन्तोऽपि च ते मृता।

According to vedic tenets, independence is necessary for the mankind and those who are not independent are worse than the dead. This is how the Aryans valued well the fruits of freedom. In varnashrama institution too, an independent living has been kept in mind. A man lived independently during grihastha ashrama and when he was likely to be dependent, on the offspring coming of age, there is the provision of the older people resorting to banprastha and then to sanyas, again living freely in the solitudes of hills and dales rather than living as dependents of their children. So much so that vedic tenets even provide for the mankind to be independent of worldly attachments and it was with this background too that banprastha and sanyas have been provided. The struggle for political freedom, which we now enjoy, is the result of a mind—the state of mind which manifested itself also in the desire to conduct human affairs according to the dictates of reason. Markandey, centuries before the age of Rousseau, upheld liberty to be the basic right of humanity. Rousseau's views are incorporated in the famous declaration of the 'Rights of Man' (1789 AD). As per vedic dictates, an kshatriya aspired to live and die with honour without being sullied or slandered. Defeat and discomfiture distressed him and even denied status of human personality. Thus national patriotism rooted in vedas is elaborately expounded in the epics, purans, smritis, Ramayan etc. Mahabharat has one message to convey:

गृहे च राजानः स्वस्थ स्वस्य प्रियंकरा।
दक सर्वेषामेव भूतानां प्रिय भारत भारतः।

Nationalism implies—nation, national and nationalism. Nation is a land and aggregation of individuals on it. National is individuals forming part of a nation. Nationalism is the patriotic feeling or principles of efforts and policy of independence. In the beginning of the Indian history, it is only the vedic literature alone that provides us a faithful history of Indian culture and patriotism. Ramayan too extolls this country as a 'Karambhoomi', the land of pious acts. Hence it was ordained by the people and the princes alike. During Mahabharat period too, the need of national unity was felt as at that time, every village was ruled by a raja, like Gokul being ruled by Raja Nand and so on. So much so that in Mahabharat, thousands of rajas fought but still there were big kingdoms too like those of Hastinapur, Inderprastha, Mathura, Dwarka, Angdesh, etc. Hence Krishna felt the necessity of establishing a sole empire under the sovereignty of Yudhisthra and this task was well accomplished by him. After a few centuries, however, Hindus do not have any link and, therefore, they have to see the extent of Yudhisthra's territory. Hastinapur had vassal states under it. These petty states were governed by rajas, who had the authority of the suzerain king emperor to rule over vassal states. These vassal states used to pay annual tribute to the suzerain king and were not interfered with so far as they paid the tribute, acknowledging the suzerainty of the overall Lord. There is mention of one such raja Nand, who had gone to see Kans, the king of Mathura and suzerain of that area to pay his tirbute and Kansa did not interfere in the governance by such petty rajas so much so that even when Kansa had known through Narad that Krishna was the eighth child of Devki and Vasudeva, being brought up in Gokul, and who would kill him, Kansa did not attack or take any martial/police action to get hold of Krishna but had diplomatically been sending rakshasas to kill him and subsequently to bring him to Mathura to be killed by ferocious elephants etc. Similarly when Krishna's grand son Samb desired to be married with Duryodhan's daughter Lakshmana and Duryodhan did not like it, he asked Balram to divest himself of the regal authority bestowed on him by the rulers of Hastinapur confirming Dwarka as having been the vassal state under Hastinapur. Bharat is placed in puranas to the north of the ocean and to the south of Himalaya and mentioned as a matchless country styled 'karambhoomi', where the fruits of virtues and of vices as well as heaven and salvation could be attained so much so that it is mentioned that even gods yearned to be in India for their life leaving the life of swaraga. In the duties of the raja, even Ram had once called all his subjects and told them to attain salvation via his bhakti. So apart from a free, independent and comfortable living in the universe, rajas considered it their duty to wish for the salvation of their subjects by adopting banprastha/sanyas or even by living in the universe and resorting to Bhagwad bhakti. This was the Bhartiya way of living, where the people lived a life better than what can be assumed of living in Swaraga and how rajya and religion were one and also separate in as much as when Ram told his subjects the way of salvation through bhakti, he left it to them to abide by his advice or not as per their sweet will unlike in Mohammedan rule, when religion was enforced on all middle east countries and to a great extent on Hindus too.

Reverting back to the ancient period, even with the help granted by Raja Ambi of Taxila, Alexander could have victory over Porus, the raja of Sind and Punjab diplomatically after a surprise attack on his army. But even here the Bhartiya pride could be vindicated by an arrested Raja Porus, when he was produced before Alexander and on his asking the sort of behaviour to be meted to him, Porus had replied "As befits me like a king". Alexander was impressed by his reply and returned his kingdom to be kept as a vassal state, which again gained sovereignty on Alexander's death within an year. Then Alexander had advanced winning over petty kingdoms but after crossing Beas river, he had to face the strong king which his army was not prepared to and Alexander reversed back from there. There is no doubt that Alexander intended to retain control of his Indian conquests as he left garrisons behind him and appointed Satraps to govern that territory but revolts in Indian provinces after the sudden death of Alexander in 323

B.C., made the Macedonian position in India untenable and the last of Alexander's general Eudamus left north-west province in 317 B.C. It would indicate that even after Alexander's invasion and victory, India was able to retain sovereignty and independence.

Chandra Gupta Maurya overthrew the last of Nanda of Magadha and occupied Patliputra. He later added entire north-west area too in his kingdom driving out Greek garrison (314-313 B.C.). He was the architect of the greatest of India's ancient empires with the help of Chanakya. Greeks again appeared under Seleucus but he was defeated by the mighty force of Chandra Gupta, and was forced to yield Punjab and part of Afghanistan to him with marriage of his daughter. Ashoka succeeded the throne after a short period of rule by his father Bindusara. After Kalinga battle, he stopped further battles and adopted the "Path of Righteousness". He had the vastest kingdom in India, ever had by any ruler known to history, comprising of the present India, Pakistan, Bangladesh, Nepal, Bhutan and part of Afghanistan.

After decline of Mauryas, Kanishka came on the scene and then Guptas and Harsha. Harsha was the last important Hindu King having entire north India under him. India was subsequently divided into small kingdoms and all rajas had been fighting within themselves. It was at this time that Mohammendans under the affinity of Islam rose in middle east and overpowered most of Europe and entire middle east. Having heard of the richness of India, Mahmud Gazni invaded India seventeen times during 11th century and took away a lot of wealth. In 1191 Mohammed Ghori also, taking advantage of enmity with each other, amongst rajput rajas, invaded India and established a Muslim rule in India. Ghori had invaded several times and was defeated but was spared by Prithviraj, the king, as according to Bhartiya concept of dharma, the enemy is pardoned if he runs away from the field. But ultimately he succeeded and left Qutab-ud-din Aibak, as his lieutenant to rule Delhi (Prithviraj's kingdom). Then he defeated several other rajas and their territories annexed in Muslim kingdom. In 1206 Ghori was assassinated and Qutab-ud-din became the first Sultan of Delhi declaring himself sovereign. So India, on Muslims' invasion and conquest remained under foreign ruler Ghori for about fourteen years (1192 to 1206 AD). After that again it became sovereign and remained so during the entire period of Muslim rule till the advent of English.

In vedas, there is no mention/evidence of really longer Indian kingdoms existing at that time although in Bhagwat there is mention of universal kingdom of Raja Prithu. Small kingdoms were there and the attack on other's kingdom was generally:

1. To take wealth and allow the defeated raja to continue ruling; or
2. To take wealth and change the ruler, who was generally the relative of existing raja; or
3. To change the ruler if the existing one was not acting as per dharma as Ram had coronated Sugreev after killing Bali and Vibheesan after killing Ravan; or
4. To defeat and keep it a vassal state and not to interfere in their affairs if they continued to pay annual tribute and accepted suzerainty of the emperor; or
5. Conquer and annex with the main territory.

But in all cases the conquered territory got the autonomy either through the existing ruler or through the king emperor on annexation as after annexation, the conquerred territory got all the rights of the previous independent country. The institution of colonialism was infact unthinkable in vedic system of governance. So *Bhartiyata* lay in granting independent living to all people. In fact as per evolution of state, as per vedas starting from Manu or Adam or Noah in Hebrew tradition, there are different versions. The one in Bhagwat tells that at the beginning of this period of cosmic time, when greed and wrath disturbed human relation, man inflicted untold misery upon one another. As in the Buddhist legend, they agreed to respect each other's life and property but they had no confidence in their contacts and so they approached God Brahma to help them. He nominated Manu, apparently not as a man but as a god to be the first king. Though the king was an autocrat, not limited by constitutional controls, there were many practical checks on his sovereignty. The king's function was not conceived in terms of legislation as for that purpose vedas and samritis were there, but of protection only and this involved the protection not only of his subjects from invasions but also of the order of society the right way of life for all classes and ages as laid down in shastras. The raja had to work as per dharma, otherwise his fate was that of king Bain of Bhagwat, who was removed and killed by the brahmins on not governing as per tenets of his dharma. Thus ancient India had the supporters of passive obedience. Mahabharat expressly allows revolt against a wicked king although initially the dread of anarchy, in the absence of a king, was a potent factor in preserving even a weak and oppressive king on his throne.

Arth Shastra provides that : "A man should first choose his king, then his wife and only then amass wealth, for without a king in the world, where would wife and property be ? The king's pious vow is readiness in action, his sacrifice, and the discharge of his duty. In the happiness of his subjects, lies the king's happiness; in the welfare of his subjects, his welfare. The king's good is not that which pleases him, but that which pleases his subjects. Therefore, the king should be ever active and should strive for prosperity, for prosperity depends on effort and failure on the reverse".

This is as per vedas too and was followed in Maurya period and is applicable in all times but for the post-Mauryan kings, the idea of empire was something very different from vedas and akin to what the West is accustomed to.

As per Mahabharat: "A king should not attempt to gain the earth unrighteously, for, who reverses the king, who wins unrighteous victory, unrighteous conquest being impermanent, does not lead to Heaven".

As per vedas, therefore, the conquest for gaining earth was forbidden as it was encroachment on other's independence and gave rise to inter-state rivalries and jealousies and ultimately harmful for both. Therefore, the belief was that although, if a king suffers decisive defeat, he must submit, in the hope that he will be allowed to retain his throne as a vassal and will ultimately again achieve independence and conquer his former overlord. But from the point of view of Arthshastra, the main motive of war is gain and the building up of a great empire.

Position of Woman: Hindu society was monogamous. Only rarely and mostly kings only had polygamous life. In Muslim times, the Hindus of North India adopted the system of "Purdah" by which from puberty to old age, the women were carefully screened from the sight of all men except their husbands and close relations. Though such a system did not exist in ancient India, the freedom accorded to married women has often been exaggerated by authorities anxious to show that the more objectionable aspects of later Hindu customs had no place in India's ancient culture. Certainly the Rig Ved depicts young men and unmarried girls mixing freely and gives no evidence that married women were in any way secluded but this text belongs to a time which had long passed in the great days of Hindu culture. Though the early Indian mind prone to exaggeration, perhaps over-did the necessity of wifely obedience, her status was not without honour. The 'purdah' system had of necessity been adopted by Hindu girls and ladies during Muslim period as Muslim rulers ordained it and the Hindu girls and women were kidnapped by Muslims and to avoid it, the purdah had been adopted by Hindus too.

Habitations: India has since ancient times been an agricultural country. The people generally earned their livelihood from agriculture and the king's revenues were also from the agriculture products (a part was taken as tax by king). By the time of Buddha, there were villages and small towns all over north India and some towns such as Kashi, Kausambhi,

Taxila, Patliputra, had an antiquity of centuries. Even Buddha died in a small town of Kusinagar. Six cities were, however, important viz Saravasti, Champa, Rajgriha, Saket, Kausambhi and Kashi. In Maurya time, Patliputra came in limelight. In South there was Vijaynagar, which was larger and more populous than Rome and contained one lakh houses with a population of at least five lakh or more.

Industry: Though the basis of ancient Indian history was at all times the individual craftsman, aided chiefly by members of his own family, longer manufactories worked chiefly by hired labour, were by no means unknown. The Maurya State owned not only spinning and weaving workshops but also shops for the manufacture of weapons and other military supplies, employing salaried craftsmen. Also in Maurya times, prices of commodities in market were regulated by market officials. As a further effort at maintaining a just price, government officers used to buy from the open market when any staple commodity was cheap and plentiful and released stocks from government stores, when it was in short supply, thus bringing down the prices and making a profit for the king in the bargain. It is striking that ancient Indian political theorists anticipated by over 3000 years the plans put forward by the Food and Agriculture Organisation of UNO for maintaining a stable level of prices of staple commodities on a world-wide scale and control over minimum and maximum prices over the essential commodities in India too.

At all times the work of Indian craftsmen has been admired for its delicacy and skill and technical achievement of ancient India was far from negligible. Her spinners and weavers could produce semi transparent silks and muslins of extreme thinness which are clearly depicted in sculptures and which were much in demand in Roman empire. Ashoka's inscriptions in stone are further examples of craftsmanship at Sanchi etc. The columns weighing as much as fifty tons and measuring some forty ft. are carved from single block of stone, given a polish of wonderful hardness and lustre and often transported from many hundreds of miles to their present positions. It was, however, mostly lost after Maurya period. The iron pillar of Mehrauli near Delhi is even more remarkable, though of little antique value and less impressive than the Maurya columns. This, however, is the metallurgical achievement, not still been deciphered. The metallurgical skill of ancient India is further attested by the fact that this pillar, though it has weathered the torrential rains of over 2500 monsoons, shows no signs of rusting. Since the process of oxidisation demands a catalyst, it may be the great purity of the metal which has preserved the iron pillar so long as another memorial to India's technical skill.

Sea Trade: Whether or not the Aryans of vedic period knew the sea, by the time of Buddha or soon thereafter, Indian sailors had probably circumnavigated the sub-continent and perhaps made the first contacts with Burma, Ceylon, Malayasia, Islands of Indonesia and upto Rome in europe through Egypt. In early centries of A.D., maritime trade became most vigorous specially with the West, where Roman empire demanded the luxuries of East in great quantity. Contacts also existed with China and south east asian countries in Gupta period. The trade was flourishing with other countries via sea-route. The trade requirements of West were spices, perfumes, jewels, and fine textiles but lesser luxuries such as sugar, rice, *ghee* were exported as well as ivory—both raw and worked. Indian iron was much esteemed for its purity and hardness and dyestuffs such as lac and indigo were much in demand. In exchange, India took mostly gold, pottery and glass wares, and other wares, wire, tin, lead, coral and slave girls but the balance of trade was favourable to India, the balance being met by gold.

Library: Hinduism relying for its strength mainly on independent brahmins and ascetics and on domestic ceremonies, suffered from Muslim invasions. Buddhism by then mainly concentrating in large monasteries and already rapidly declining in influence, could not stand up to the change. In the first rush of the Muslim advance down the Ganga,

Nalanda and other great monastries of Bihar were sacked, libraries were burnt and other great monastries of Bihar and other places were sacked and monks were put to sword but some monastries still survived in Bihar and West Bengal, which throw light on how rich, intellect, technologically sound the knowledge of Indians had been as available in vedas and other remnant shastras, samritis etc.; the real matter of proud for Indians.

Mathematics and Science: Through the necessity of accurately laying out the open air site of a sacrifice, Indians very early evolved a simple system of geometry but in the sphere of practical knowledge, the world owes most to India in the realm of mathematics, which were developed in Gupta times to a stage more advanced than that reached by any other nation of antiquity. The success of Indian mathematics was mainly due to the fact that the Indians had a clear conception of abstract number as distinct from numerical quantity of objects or spatial extension. While Greek mathematical science was largely based on mensuration and geometry, India transcended these conceptions quite early and with the aid of a simple numeral notation, devised a rudimentary algebra, which allowed more complicated calculations than were possible to the Greeks and led to the study of number for its own sake. In the earliest inscriptions of India, dates and other numerals are written in a notation not unlike that of the Romans, Greeks and Hebrews, with separate symbols for the tens and hundreds. The earliest inscription recording the date by a system of nine digits and a zero with place notation for the tens and hundreds comes from Gujarat and is dated 595 A.D. Soon after it had been heard of in Syria and Vietnam. Evidently the system was known in India much before it was put in inscriptions -Aryabhatt in 499 A.D.

For long it was thought that the decimal system of numerals was invented by the Arabs but this is certainly not the case. The Arabs themselves called mathematics, "The Indian art (Hindisat)" and it appears that the decimal notation with other mathematical lore was learnt by the Muslim world either through merchants trading with the west coast of India or through the Arabs, who conquered Sind in 712 A.D. The debt of the western world to India in this respect cannot be over-estimated. Most of the great discoveries and inventions of which Europe is so proud would have been impossible without developed system of mathematics and this in turn would have been impossible if Europe had been shackled by the unwieldy system of Roman numerals. The unknown man, who devised the new system was from the world's point of view after the Buddha, the most important son of India. His achievement, though easily taken for granted, was the work of an analytical mind of the first order and he deserves much more honour than he has so far received. Medieval Indian Mathematicians such as Brahm Gupta (7th century A.D.) made several discoveries, which in Europe were unknown until the renaissance or later. They understood the import of positive and negative quantities evolved sound systems of extracting squares and cube roots and could solve quadratic and certain types of indeterminate equations.

In vedic era, universe was classified by elements, which of all schools admitted as earth, air, fire, water and ether. These five elements were thought of by the medium of sense impression—earth for smell, air for feeling, fire for vision, water for taste and ether (Akash) for sound. The vedic belief was that except akash, the other elements were atomic. Indian atomism was certainly independent of Greek influence, for an atomic theory was taught by Pakudha Katyayana, an older contemporary of the Buddha, and was, therefore, earlier than that of Democritus. The Jains believed that all atoms (anu) were identical, and that the differences of the character of the elements were due to the manner in which the atoms were combined. Most schools, however, maintained that there were as many types of atoms as there were elements.The atom was thought to be eternal but some Buddhists conceived it not only as a minutest object, capable of occupying space, but also as occupying the minutest possible duration of time coming into being and vanishing almost in an instant only to be succeeded by another atom, caused by the first. Then the atom of Buddhism, in some measure, resembles the quantum of Planck. The Vaisesika school (Buddhist era) which specially elaborated its atomic doctrines and was the school of atomism par excellence, maintained that before continuing to form material objects atoms made primary combinations of diads and triads. This doctrine of molecules was developed differently by the Buddhists and Ajivikas, who taught that in normal conditions no atoms exist in a pure state but only combined in different proportions in a molecule (samghata, kalapa). Indian atomic theories may not be based on experiment but on intuition and logic. They were not universally held. But the atomic theories of ancient India are brilliant, imaginative explanation of the physical structure of the world. Though it seems mere coincidence that they agree in part with the discoveries of modern physics, they must have been based on the knowledge of the people of ancient time and are nevertheless much to the credit of the intellect and imagination of the early Indian thinkers.

Medicines: System of ayurvedic treatment even now hold good. Indian authorities taught that the health was maintained through the even balance of the vital fluids of the body, viz wind, gall, and mucus. Such a balance could be maintained by ayurvedic medicines, yoga and mystical experience. The three fluids are also connected with three gunas or universal qualities and associated with virtue, passion and dullness respectively. Despite their inaccurate knowledge of physiology, which was by no means inferior to that of most ancient people, India evolved a developed empirical surgery. The caesarian section was known, bone-setting reached a high degree of skill and plastic surgery was developed beyond anything known elsewhere at that time.

Weights and Measures: In ancient India, perfect systems of weighment or measuring each thing—solid, liquid and cloth were there. This shows the perfectness achieved in these respects by the vaishas of that time. There is mention of government officials in existence in Maurya and Gupta periods to check that no short measurement or weight was adopted than standard. There were heavy punishments for such guilts. This could be possible only because of perfectness in mathematics even in pre-historic periods. In Ram rajya also there is mention of standard measures existing for all the commodities and traders were maintaining correct measurements and weights.

Indian Civilisation in Foreign Countries

During Maurya and Gupta periods, Indians had settled abroad in various south-east countries. Few are discussed:

1. **Bali:** This is the only Hindu colony in far East, which still retains its old culture and civilisation to a considerable extent. Vedas, Ramayan and Mahabharat are found there and Indian caste system prevails. It was ruled by the Hindu rulers, gone from India, and became sovereign rulers of that place. Buddhism had also spread there during Ashoka's period. Hindus and Buddhists are still found there.
2. **Cambodia or Kamboja:** Earliest Hindu settlement in Cambodia is known by the Chinese name of Funan starting from 5th century A.D. For sometime it was dependent of Jawa. However, it again became independent under Hindu ruler Jayavarman, who ruled from 802 A.D. to 825 A.D. The art of Kambuja is of Indian origin at Angkorvat built by King Surya Varman (1113-1145 A.D.). A great artistic worth of the world with perfect architecture and rare art is found there.
3. **Siam or Thailand:** Hindu civilisation spread in early second century A.D. Most important was Duaravati, ruled from Cambodia to the Bay of Bengal. Buddhism was spread there via Burma. The rulers of this place were from Sailender dynasty.
4. **Burma:** It was another Hindu kingdom with Srikshetra as the ruler. He subsequently became Buddhist. Both Hinduism and Buddhism are available there even now.

5. China: Cultural relations between India and China can be traced back to 2nd century B.C. It was through land route from Kashmir and Tibet. Buddhism was spread in China by Indian rulers. Chinese tourists frequently visited India. Fahien and Hiuen-Tsang are famous among them and have written very valuable books about India.

6. Tibet: Culture and civilisation are all from India. Regular contacts were developed from 6th century AD. Entire Tibet population is Buddhist with Dalai Lama as the head—political and religious.

The above description gives in general the idea of the Hindu rulers' regime in India and abroad, which had been most developed compared to other parts of universe in all fields and inspite of having been a staunch believer of rule of dharma and knowing the value of sovereignty, India succumbed to the Muslim invasions and subsequently had to bear the British rule due mainly to—

1. Iniquitous system of castes and the absence of contact with the outside world. It has been indicated in detail how the varna institution had come into being in our vedic period. The varna was actually chosen by each person according to his capability and taste and as such everyone acted as per dharma of that varna and since he himself had opted for it, he had no grouse but in course of time the varnas become caste-ridden and rigid. This resulted in fragmentation of Indian society into mutually exclusive classes, among whom the privileged minority preserved their vested interest by depriving the basis of many civic rights, specially of education and of free intercourse and association on equal basis with the fellowmen, who were in majority.

2. Hindus restricted themselves to inland Bharat as their dharma, they believed, did not allow crossing the seas or even the territorial limits of certain areas. This deprived them of the designs of alien invaders, their advancement in armaments, tricks of fighting and even the timing of the invasions.

3. There was lack of spying in the Indian rulers. Alexander's sudden attack on Porus is an example. Similarly Hindu rulers were taken unawares of the attacks by Mahmud Gazni and Mohammed Ghori.
4. No public upheaval greeted the invaders. Like a paralysed body, the Indian people helplessly looked on while the conqueror marched on their corpses, thinking this as the job of the king and his army only.
5. False ideals of kshatriya chivalery made the rajput princes paralyse one another by perpetual internecine conflicts and what was more fatal made them oblivious of a broad national vision and patriotic sentiment of Bhartiyata.
6. The enormous wealth of the country not only made the inhabitants, the rajas and nobles and warriors leasurely and luxury loving but also attracted the foreigners to invade, conquer and loot it and take to Ghazni, Ghori etc., rather than being used in creating new and modern armaments of war and preparing a disciplined army to quell the foreign invasion.
7. After Guptas had established the rule in India, defeating the foreign invaders - Huns at that time - and establishing Indian ruler's/army's superiority over foreigners, there was peace from foreign invaders upto 10th-11th century and the Indian rulers had resorted to luxuries when Ghazni/ Ghori appeared on the scene. The original academic idea of four varnas and taboos for food and drinking interse created a gulf in the army.
8. Disparity of wealth existed between the mercantile class and the ordinary villagers. Further, a regular bureaucracy costituted the structure of Indian government and that the Indian kingdom had been organised on a semi-military basis with large inefficient army.
9. Determination of caste by birth and the prohibition of inter-marriage and inter-dining among the castes, contrary to what was aimed at in the varna institution initially,

created water-tight compartmentisation amongst people. Brahmins consolidated their position by introducing the new elements comprehending the doctrine of impurity of shudras' food and touch and restricting the number of kshatriyas and vaishyas till they practically vanished from the Indian society and their descendents sank to the level of shudras.

10. There was complete lack of political unity and patriotic sense. Indian rulers had been fighting amongst themselves trying to snatch each other's territory, wealth, women etc. and developing quarrels amongst themselves. They did not even join together when the foreign invaders came and went straight upto the Somnath temple unchecked and looted lot of wealth, accumulated in temples which should have been used in organising the army to fight against the foreign invaders, rather than against oher Hindu rulers.
11. There was complete isolation of one raja from another and the rajas from foreign invaders.
12. There was lack of capable leadership among the Indians and they had worn out military system as well as the lack of cooperation between masses and their leaders.
13. The country was parcelled out into numerous independent states and there was political apathy of the masses and lack of patriotism.
14. Economic and military resources had been frittered away by Mohammedan invaders and an atmosphere of mutual distrust ensued amongst the contending states, which prevented the effective combination against the common foe. Even the crisis of the series of foreign invasions failed to produce a single leader of sufficiently commanding political and military talent to unite the Indians of his time—as Chandra Gupta Maurya had united long before, the people of Indus valley against the Macedonian garrison left behind by Alexander. Still the rajput rulers, even individually, were capable of beating back the enemy in the open battle field as proved by the crushing victories

over sultan of Ghori by Prithvi Raj in 1190-91 and by Bhim-II of Gujarat in 1178.

15. Unlike the armies of the invaders fighting under one undivided command, those of Indians largely consisted of contingents of feudatory chiefs fighting under their own leaders.

16. The invaders derived their will to victory from an unparallel religious enthusiasm. The Indian fighting classes were inclined as a rule to fight more for the exhibition of individual valour and vindication of personal honour than for collective success.

17. Rather than uniting together against the common foe, the Indian rulers like Jay Chand of Kanauj, on the contrary, invited Ghori against Prithvi Raj Chauhan and the fall of Chauhans heralded the fall of ancient Hindu India resulting in the fall of Jay Chand too.

18. The Chauhans adhered to shastras in fighting with the Muslim invaders, who had no scruples. Even the shastras permit fighting with maya if the other party adopted the same as enunciated in Mahabharat. But Prithvi Raj let the enemy go scot free even when defeated as permitted by shastras rather than killing such an enemy for good and creating terror amongst the Muslim invaders as they did in Hindus murdering lakhs of them.

19. Race for political superiority in northern India like in Jay Chand and Prithvi Raj and others, made the rulers weak in fighting within themselves and could not, therefore, give thrust to the invaders with full force.

20. Marriage of Sanyogita with Prithvi Raj was not only responsible for hostile relations and quarrel between the two great rulers of northern India viz Jay Chand and Prithvi Raj but the latter seems to have been passionately and intensely lost in love of the newly wedded queen at the cost of state and the government. Even Bhagwat asserts that woman was the root cause of mutual jealousy and

quarrel, for many people strive for one and the same woman.

सा त्वं नः स्पंघमानानामेक वस्तुनि मानिनि,
ज्ञातीनां बद्धवैराणां शं विधत्स्व सुमध्यमे।
(भागवत पुराण) 9-6

21. Tyranny by the rulers and officials led to maladministration and stirred the people's heart to agony and frustration, which further aggravated their feelings against the tyrant. It thus led to the people's opposition and dislike, popular confusion and anarchy as well as people's arrogance and rising against the ruler/nobles themselves. Even the kings were so morally degraded and sensuous that they did not hesitate in seizing by force the wives and daughters of their subjects. In such a situation one does look for a change, even if it eventually proved to be more disastrous.

22. India, again, lost her freedom not because the conquerors were strong but because the country was riven with dissensions.

2 Vedic Era

Vedas have a special position in Indian religion, culture and polity. By going through the vedas, we cannot reach any historical period when the vedas were written. They only speak of the passage of vedas by God to rishis in the beginning of the universe. According to Aryan shastras, the universe was created some 200 crore years back. So vedas should also be taken to be belonging to that period. Rishis did not consider vedas as having been created by human beings but believed that God had created the same at the time of the creation of the mankind for their benefit. These had never been brought in black and white but had only passed by heart from one teacher to his pupil and so on. It is only in and around the beginning of the Christian era that something of the vedas had been written too but all attempts had gone waste after the Indian libraries had been destroyed by Muslim invaders in 12th and 13th centuries AD.

Atharva Ved is considered to be a compilation of life, people, animals, wealth and their praise. This is considered to be an abstract of entire universe.

यस्मिन वेदानिहिता विश्वरूपा। (अथर्व)

Although vedas had been known in France from 18th century, yet the first study appears to have been conducted by Colebook. Subsequently Rozen, Langloya, Bugan, Maxmullar, Roath, Ludwig, Grassman, Whitwel, Wilson, Macdonell and Keath appear to have had deep study of vedas. Although they have appreciated the contents of vedas but still have at places made a mockery of the same indicating their ignorance about the real meaning of the contents. It is, however, unfortunate that the universe is guided by the interpretation of vedas given by western philosophers, who are unaware of the Hindu culture and have interpreted without knowing the correct theme and secondly in a biased way as they did not want to give credit to Indians of their illustrious ancient time, what they do not know even today.

The origin of Aryans is still disputed but in view of the origin of vedas, which is timed lakhs of years back, and as per the ancient Hindu mythology, Aryans can be said to have been belonging originally to India and have spread from here to other countries as is supported by the contents of Ramayan and Bhagwat, indicating that the rulers of India in ancient times had their kingdom spread throughout the universe. During Vedic era, since it was the start of the universe, the question of colonisation did not arise. Vedas, therefore, speak of small independent states. But such a state was firm like the mountain and centrally administered. In such a centrally administered state, it is natural that there would be some control over the liberty of individuals and society. The theories of sovereign states and the governance of such states prescribe some control of the government on individuals, corporates, communities etc. The duties of the public in such a state are to have a government and fill up government exchequer with a view to run the government and leave the liberal administration of the state and punishment to the criminals, to the government.

ध्रुवं ध्रुवेण ह विषाभि सोमं मृशामसि,
अथो त इंद्रः केवलीर्विशो बलिहृतस्करत। (ऋगवेद)

Rig Ved provides for the strength of the king in punishing the criminals in the state and to face the invaders from abroad. The kings, therefore, had to maintain army comprising of elephants, cavalry, chariots, and on foot. The international disputes were settled by mutual understanding or conciliation, peacefully through mediators or consultation and if it was not possible to settle the dispute in this way, then use of force was resorted to. Whatever was the result of the battle, the identity of the independent state continued except that after the battle, the defeated state used to agree to the terms of the victorious state and pay compensation for the war as presents and also accepted the suzerainty of the winning state. With this, the autonomy of the governance of the state even by the defeated state continued. In vedas, Indra has been considered as the king of the state, which is always independent and centrally administered; the strength of its people being reflected in the strength of the king. Ram, after killing Bali, retained his brother Sugreeva as the king of Kishkindha and Vibheeshan was coronated as king of Lanka after Ravan was killed and so on. In present days such a centralised, all powerful state is commended by Austin too. Force, therefore, was the arm of centrally administered states. Elsewhere too swaraj has been explained in Rig Ved as a thing of pride and all Indian kingdoms did have it.

स्वादोरित्था विषूवेता मधवा पिवन्ति शौर्यः।

This means that with a forceful independent Indian king, the subjects enjoyed the fruits of their lives. All sorts of luxuries were available in such a kingdom. In Atharva Ved too mention has been made of independent Indian kings viz.,

स्वराजमासते स्वराजं वृषभम

and विराट स्वराजमम्येति प चात

and यदजः प्रथमं सबभूव सह तत् स्वराज्यमियाय

यास्मान्नान्यत् परमस्ति भूतम

(अथ 10, 7, 31)

These indicate that king born in India, attained independence after which there is no creature stronger than him. There is detailed appreciation of independence in this context and there is nothing above such independence, has been explained. There is also mention that the public too accepted the supremacy of the independent sovereign king and offered their all for the sake of such askance to enable the king to keep the invaders away. The kingdom is considered to be superior not only to the people in that kingdom but also to all living beings. Such a kingdom is told to be ideal, sovereign, nationalistic and killer of the enemies. In such a centralised kingdom too, the subjects had their individuality, who were considered to be the participants of the governance. This made the nation very strong and ideal. The reference to Indra, Varuna, Agni, Vishnu etc. in vedas is to indicate a strong king with decentralised powers and a state for the well-being of the people. Vedas also speak of vassal states—

इन्द्रो जयाति न पराजयाता अधिराजो राजषु राजयातै।

The king cannot be won over by any one and all his vassals respect the king as such as an all powerful state. This would indicate that in vedic period the political organisation was furthering from simplicity to complicity in view of its having accepted on itself the job of well-being of the subjects and participation of the public at large indirectly in the governance of the state.

In Ram rajya, which was strictly the follower of vedas, it has been indicated that the king should rule as per principles laid down for him in the vedas. The king should, rather than feeling satisfied with the punishment of criminals, reform the subjects. Such a feeling had been held during Gupta's rule and holds good even today. Accordingly, in such a kingdom, there were no poor, no ailments, no premature deaths, no famines and so on. The king had to follow all vedic rituals, including yagyas, sacrificing pleasures and leading a tough life. A selfish king, it is indicated, cannot lead the nation to becoming a welfare state. A selfless state could only be stated as moral, ideal and spiritually upto the mark. Here independence has been indicated as not without controls but with checks as considered necessary to avoid the king from going stray. The king had to had control on self first and then only on the subjects. This can be possible when the king had no self interest and this could be possible when he had no belongings. This exactly is the theory of state prescribed by Plato too. A well ruled state, therefore, presupposes—

1. Peaceful living.
2. Contentment in life.
3. Working for the well-being of the subjects.
4. Killing of all devilish and animal addictions.
5. The subjects too have to be dutiful to the king selflessly.

Today we hear of independence in the entire universe. This has become more known after independence of states in Europe and colonialism resorted to by them. In the past all kingdoms in India were independent only but the independence of today is hollow as independence has converted into a luxurious, selfish and exploiting kingdom. As per Rig Ved, independence implied sacrifice of all possessions and violence and leading a contented and a morale life. The public had to follow the law not in view of the fear but considering this as their moral duty and taking the well-being of all into consideration. The king too considered such subjects as his real force apart from the army retained by him for the sake of checking invasions.

In the ideal independent king's rule, the vedas impliedly expect the say of the public too in the matter of governance of the state. Ram, Krishna, Bhishma, Bharat, Prithu, Yudhisthra, Parikshit etc. are the examples in Hindu mythology of the high morality combined with the kingly force. Similar spiritual force has been depicted by Chanakya too in his Arthshastra. But only the moral conduct does not help in the successful attainment in the universe and at the same time mere kingly force too only leads to demonstration of force as in the case of Alexander, Napoleon, Hitler etc. Vedas, therefore, have pleaded the independent sovereign king to be having spiritual force as well as worldly strength for being a successful ruler. Also equally important aspect is that governance should not be centralised in one individual or a group of individuals but should be delegated to divisions, sub-divisions etc. as per vedic pronouncements :

तं सभा च समिति च सेना च
सम्य सभा मे पाहि ये च सभ्याः सभासदः
त्वमिन्द्रा पुरुरुत वि वमर्युव्य नवत।।

(अथ 15-6-2)

Meaning thereby that there should be a Rajya Sabha and the members of the sabha should be learned and protectors of dharma. The king should rule as per dictates of vedas by imbibing in oneself completely in the job which leads to satisfaction in life.

On the contrary, the centralisation of power leads to exploitation of public and harrassment of public. As a meat eater is tempted to kill an animal on the very sight of the animal, so the dictator cannot tolerate the excellence of any individual and becomes whimsical in his conduct. It is, therefore, essential, in the interest of public that the governance should be by keeping the welfare and views of the subjects in view. Vedas, therefore, speak of—

'विशस्त्वा सर्वा वांछन्तु'।

Independence should, therefore, be a moral one, even in present day context. Such a rule can only be in the interest of all. The ruler and the ruled have an ethical relation. In fact the strength of the subjects only provide power to the king and the kingdom. This satisfies the public at large too. In the present day too, the strength does not lie in a particular group or class but in the nation as a whole. A united public gives force to the king in the faithful discharge of his duties of governance.

Sovereignty is exercised through autocratic welfare state or through democracy. In addition a third authority is that of the constitution and its correct application. Written constitution has a special place in the governance of the countries wherever it exists. India has a written constitution whereas Britain works on traditions. The constitution provides checks on the rights and duties of the government. The modern welfare state is the outcome of the provisions in the written constitution of today. So there are these sovereign ties in a country - an autocratic welfare state, democracy and constitution. In ancient period, the provisions of written constitution were available in vedas and Manu Samriti. Manu has written:

सर्वेषां तु स नामानि कर्माणि च पृथक-पृथक
वेद शब्देभ्य एवादौ पृथक संस्था च निर्ममे ।।

i.e. all commodities and creatures have been named as per functions performed and their uses have been illustrated accordingly. Further, Manu has in the context of division of mankind in four varnas stated :

चातुर्वर्ण्य त्र्यो लोका चत्वार चाश्रमाः पृथक,
भूतं भवद् भविष्यच्च सर्व वेदात् प्रसिद्धयति।

The four varnas and four ashramas, three lokas (earth, planets and patal) and everything that has taken place, that is taking place and that will take place, is known from vedas only. In Shankar Bhashya it has been indicated that:

महत मृगवेदादे शास्त्रस्य अनेक विद्या स्थानोप-
वृहिंतस्य प्रयोपवत् सर्वार्था द्योतिनः
सर्वज्ञ कल्पस्य योनिः कारणं ब्रह्म ।

Before we proceed further, it is necessary to explain vedas and shastras. Vedas and shastras being the book of knowledge blessed by the God for the well-being of the mankind, the knowledge gained and developed by the Aryans in the fields of philosophy, science and literature, has been detailed in four upvedas, six angas, and six upangas. These are all based on vedas and describe:

Upvedas

1. Ayurveda or life saving science, now known as surgery, hygiene, chemistry, physiology and anatomy etc.
2. Arth-ved or science of arts, mechanics and handicrafts
3. Gandharva ved or arts of music, poetry, drawing and dancing
4. Dhanurved or art of warfare, science of war and weapons

Angas

1. Education (Science of phonetics and orthoepy)
2. Dharma or Science of Laws (Principles of law and rules

of vedic ceremics, rules of domestic ceramics and principles of geometry)

3. Grammar (Vyakaran)
4. Philology (Nighantu)
5. Prosody (Science of poetic composition)
6. Astrology (Jyotish)

Upangas

1. Nyayashastra
2. Vaisheshik Shastra
3. Sankhya Shastra
4. Yoga Shastra
5. Memansa Shastra
6. Vedant Shastra

The philology in the above six upangas explains logic, metaphysics, psychology, ethics and physics. Since the basis of all the above shastras is considered to be vedas, one can conclude that all the sciences and technologies so far known to the universe, are contained in our vedas and shastras.

In Atharva ved, the stages of evolution of state leading to its full development is explained as under:

विराड़ वा द्रूदमग्र आसीत तस्या जाताया:
सर्वम विभेदियमेवेदं भविष्यतीति ।

There was no state in the beginning and so no ruler as such. Some human beings would have come up in the beginning of the universe. When all got frightened of such a situation, then families came into existence to protect oneself under one head of the family called Grihapatya. When the families further developed and many families came into being leading to their internal disputes, the families gathered together and constituted one panchayat, 'Ahavaniya' to protect all families under that panchayat. This also is similar to modern village panchayat, where the members of panchayat discuss the common causes of the people of the village. The increase in the number of panchayats led to the creation of one intelligent and brave leader (Dakshinagni). The leader was either elected by all the panchayats together or possibly one of the constituents of these Panchayats, who happened to be more intellegent and brave, became the leader of all of them-

सोदक्रामत सा दक्षिणाग्नौ न्यक्रामत।
यज्ञर्तो दक्षिणीयो वासतेयो भवति य एवं वेद।
सोदक्रामत् सा समायां न्यक्रामत।
यन्त्यस्य सभां सभ्यो भवति य एवं वेद।
सोदक्रामत सा समितौ न्यक्रामत।

After the leader came the stage of constitution of assembly. With the increase in leaders representing various clans, and the evolution of the people in trade, industry and other fields, the society came into being, which became rather complex and the panchayats and leaders were not considered sufficient to control the matters. This led to the need of creation of a 'State' also called the sabha as the state comprised of a body, under one leader, constituted by the people, who were experts in various fields. After the sabha, or further evolution of state, there came into being a bigger corporate body called samiti, comprising of the representatives of various sabhas.

यन्त्यस्य समिति सामित्यो भवति य एवंवेद ।

The final stage of the evolution of state is the creation of a body of representatives of various states in one Rajya Sabha or Virat Sabha. The above evolution of state has been given as propounded in shastras to satisfy the people knowing the evolution of the state or a country and its ruling body as per modern concept of polity.

Any developed state would be the creation of—

1. Land or country.
2. The representatives of various Panchayats etc.
3. The Chairman of the house of such representatives.

In vedas, land is known by the word Indra Gupta, protected

by the Samrat (Indra). From vedas, it is clear that Indra is not the mythological raja of swarga, but the emperor of the country, which has been protected by him. He, after defeating all his opponents, rules over the state. When land had come and people started living in it, they developed some sort of affinity with that piece of land or country called 'Nationalism'. All people fall in line in having developed the nationalism for their respective countries.

According to vedas, all the states or countries were independent of each other and the ruler did not grab the other's territory but only protected the same from external aggressions. Such a ruler being responsible for the protection of all the people, had to had the confidence of all such people and this could be possible when he was elected by the people as their leader.

त्वामग्ने वृणते ब्राह्मणा इमे शिवो अग्ने सवारणे भवानः।

Here Agni has been designated as the emperor and Agni has been elected by the brahmins (specialists) i.e. the representatives of the people in the sabha or samiti. Further too there is mention of the ruler being elected as:

अग्निं वृणाना वृणते कविक्रतुम,

and नाभा पृथिव्याः समिधाने अग्नौ रायस्पोषाय बृहते हवामहे।

(अथर्ववेद)

These mantras clearly state that the raja was the creation of the people only. Further Indra too has been mentioned in vedas as the emperor—

यो अद्य सेन्यो वधो जिंघासन्न उदीरते,
इन्द्रस्य तत्र बाहू समन्तं परि दद्मः ।

(अथ 6-99-2)

meaning that we are all with Indra in the protection of the country and the people from the aggression of the enemy. Further, the same Indra is invited to provide eatables, strength and intelligence i.e. education and to protect the people of the country to enable them to enjoy the worldly life.

शुनं हुवेम मधवानमिन्द्रस्मिन्भो नतमं वाजसातौ।
शृण्वन्तमुग्रमूतये समत्सु घ्नन्तं वृत्रणि संजितंधनानाम ।
(अथर्व)

Further the vedas indicate the raja as an elected body by the people and such a raja is all powerful, capable of governing and commanding the army and thereby providing all the people a comfortable living in the state. Such a raja is against the irreligious people and all enemies.

मरुत्वन्तं वषृभं वावृधानम कवारिं दिव्यं शासमिन्द्रम,
and विश्वासाहमवसे नूतनायोग्र सहोदामिहतं हुवेभ ।
(त्रृग 3-47-5 यजु 7-36)

words Agni, Indra, Varuna etc have been used in vedas at various places representing the raja/emperor/samrat such as—

(1) अग्ने राजन् (त्रृग 6-1-13)
(2) अग्निं सम्राजम (त्रृग 6-7-1)
(3) स सत्पतिः (त्रृग 6-13-3)

In these and other mantras, Agni has been mentioned representing raja, emperor, leader, ruler, saviour of people etc. Further the words "मानुषीणां कृष्टीमाम", "विशां मानषीणां विशाम" "जनस्य" etc represent the subjects. Agni has been requested to imbibe in the people the wealth, praise, intelligence and strength. So Agni in turn can grant these by dint of being the inchange of some well-organised society/state/country.

क्षत्रस्य त्वा परस्पाय ब्रह्मणस्तन्वं पाहि,
विशस्त्वा धर्मणा वयमनुक्रामाम सुविताय नव्यसे।
(यजु 38-16)

meaning that we accept Agni as our leader for protecting the brahmins, kshatriyas and vaishyas in the country so that they act according to the tenets of religion and have fair dealings with others. Even this aspect of Agni represents here being a raja only can bless and protect the people of all varnas. Here vedas also speak of existence of varnas at that time. Further Indra has also been indicated as samarat in the vedas—

1. पृथिव्या च सम्राट (ऋग 1-100-1)
2. चर्षणीधृतम (ऋग 3-51-17)
3. राजा यजातेवर आपृथिव्याः (ऋग 3-53-11)
4. पतिर्वभू थासमा जनानाम (ऋग 6-36-47)
5. कृष्टीनां विचर्षणि पतिर्जज्ञे वृषकेतुः (ऋग 6-45-16)
6. इन्द्र च सम्राट (यजु. 8-37)

The above mantras present Indra as raja, leader, ruler emperor etc. It may also be mentioned that on going through the vedas, we find that 'Indra' has more frequently been used as the raja, ruler of the people, rather than the head of gods or the raja of swarga. It can, therefore, safely be concluded that Indra as per vedas is the elected leader of the mankind to protect them; provide them a comfortable life and govern them. This is also clear from the jobs undertaken by Indra in the universe as distinct from those in the swarga—

1. इन्द्रेण दस्युं दरयन्त (ऋग 1-53-4)
2. वृहदेणुश्च्यवनो मानुषीणामेकः कृष्टीनामभवत सहावा। (ऋग 6-12-2)
3. वयम त एभिः पुरुहूत सख्यैशत्रे शत्रेरुत्तर इत् स्याम। (ऋग 6-19-13)
4. सनोबोधि पुरएता सुगेषुत दुर्गेषु पसिकृदृ द्ध विदानः। (ऋग 6-21-12)
5. अरन्धचः शर्धत इन्द्र दस्यून् (ऋग 6-23-2)

Meaning that—

(i) We kill the enemies with the help of Indra.

(ii) Indra is brave, killer of the enemies, expert in warfare, provider of comforts to all and humane to every one and by killing the enemies protects his people.

Revolt by public

Vedas also recognise the right of the people to rise against the ruler peacefully if the raja is not benevolent to the people.

But such a rising has to be suppressed by the ruler with force if such a rising arouses enmity amongst the people as also disturbs the peace of the people in larger interest. This shows the democracy or the voice of the people as also existence of a sort of institution of trade unions.

Requirements of a Raja

A raja, who is elected by the people should have the following qualifications as per vedas and Manu Samriti :

1. He has to get himself elected by the people with their consent only.
2. He should be knowledgeable in all aspects of religion, science, art etc.
3. He should be well-versed in usage of arms and ammunition.
4. He should speak sweetly and truth.
5. He should be able to drive the chariot.
6. He should be a matured young man.
7. He should be deep in thinking.
8. He should be overall intelligent.
9. He should be very brave as can protect the people from external aggressions.
10. He should be able to increase wealth of his kingdom.
11. He should be able to create new inventions and discoveries.
12. He should be very gentle.
13. He should be able to read the mind of the people.
14. He should always look for the well-being of his people.
15. He should be pious in all respects.
16. He should possess impressive personality and be very handsome.
17. He should be a grihastha (married) but rule without selfish interest.
18. He should be able to earn appreciation from all subjects.

19. He should be wearing all good clothes, ornaments etc to appear impressive.
20. He should always be vigilant about the affairs in his kingdom.
21. He should be able to speak well as to inspire confidence in his people.
22. He should be very religious.

These are some of the good characteristics to be found in the raja as indicated in the vedas. This list, however, is not exhaustive and as per vedas, the raja has to be one embodiment of all adjectives.

Ruling Period of a Raja

The raja, once elected continue for the entire life. It was not, however, necessary that his son should automatically succeed him. His capability had to be approved by the sabha. It was generally done during the reign of the previous raja itself so that there was no gap during the death of the raja, and the election of his successor. There is merit in selecting the raja for life. Since he was already considered capable at the time of election, his continuation was in the interest of the state as :

1. His experience of governance was of interest to the state.
2. His understanding of the people of his state.
3. He can make long time planning.
4. He has by then got used to the working according to the will of the sabha/samiti.
5. Still if not found up to the mark anytime, the sabha/samiti could dethrone him.
6. Frequent election, like in the present day, involve avoidable expenditure.
7. Vedas, therefore, provide for life-long raja :

त्वमिन्द्रा पुरुहूत विश्वमायुर्व्यश्नवत्
अहरहर्बल मिन्हे हरन्तोऽश्वायेव तिष्ठते घासमग्ने।

(अथ. 15-55-6)

Meaning that "sharp like Agni, thou have been elected for life. We shall continue paying you the part of our products like we feed the horse with grass every day". The whole life, however, meant only the period of grihastha ashram as per vedas. In banprastha, however, the raja has to hand over the rajya to the next successor and proceed to forest. So, life for the raja means about 25-30 years. The raja going to forest is proved by the fact that—

1. Poets mention of rajas proceeding for banprastha in old age.
2. Raja Dasratha intended handing over rajya to Ram and proceeding for banprastha.
3. Dhritrashtra had, after Mahabharat, proceeded for banprastha.
4. Raja Prithu, Bharat, Manu etc. had all gone for banprastha in old age.
5. After ruling for 36 years, Yudhisthra etc. Pandavas took up banprastha handing over rajya to Parikshit :

शैशवेभ्यस्त विद्यानां यौवने विषयैषिणाम,
वधिकै मुनिवृत्तीनां योगेनान्ते तनुत्यजाम्। (रघुवंश 1-8)

i.e. Raghuvanshi Rajas used to pass the childhood as brahmcharis, studying with the guru. In youth they passed the grihastha and in old age, they used to adopt banprastha and subsequently sanyas. It means that once the son was available to hold the throne, the rajas did not stay at their houses. This shows that even a raja had to pass through the cumbersome procedure of living in the four ashramas, as per tenets of vedas.

Nationality of Rajas

By and large, the raja had to be from the kingdom itself and, as already indicated, the successor raja had been selected during the reign of the previous raja itself. Raja Dasratha was worried as he did not have offspring for a long time and then had to perform some yagya to have the same. Such a raja would be understanding the kingdom; would have affinity with the country and the people of that place and the people would have also been familiar with his capability. A non-capable person was not allowed to succeed. There is, however, a provision according to which the person of another kingdom could also become the raja in a situation when—

1. A capable person is not available in the country ;
2. The raja of the other country has conquered the kingdom. In such a case, the ward of the conquering king becomes the raja.

Such a provision is available in vedas :

अर्वाचमिन्द्रममुतो हवामहे (अथ. 5-3-11)

i.e. we invite Indra from that place to this place.

इन्द्रं वो विश्वतस्परि हवामहे जनेभ्यः।
अस्माकमस्तु केवलः।।

We have selected a person from other country and pray that he shall be one amongst us to rule and protect us. In such a situation the person, so invited to rule from outside, shall care for our country only, otherwise a person from outside shall not be invited to become our raja.

"अस्माकमस्तु केवलः" supports this conviction in above mantra. So the rule of the Muslim rulers in India was covered by this vedic provision. Those rajas were sovereign rajas of India, distinct from the British rulers, who ruled from England as a colony and the rulers, here were not sovereign. We can, therefore, conclude that we had not lost our independence during Muslim rulers as they became one amongst us and cared for the well-being of the country, except for about 14 years, when Qutab-ud-din ruled as lieutenant of Mohammed Ghori, but subsequently he declared himself as a sovereign ruler after death of Mohammed Ghori.

Right of Franchise

Question now arises as to who shall elect the raja. Will everyone in the kingdom be eligible to express his wish or in modern term shall have a right to vote or only persons of a special category shall elect the raja or there shall be admixture of the two i.e. everyone shall have a right to vote but the persons with special capability shall have special right of voting. Vedas provide—

1. इन्द्र सुकृत – कर्तृभिर्भूत्। (ऋग 6-16-1)
2. त्वां ही भून्द्रावसे विवाचो हवन्ते चर्षणयं:। (ऋग 6-33-2)
3. विशस्त्वा सर्वा वाछंन्तु। (ऋग 10-173-1)
4. सर्वा विश: वांछन्तु। (ऋग 48-4)

These mantras prescribe that the raja shall be elected by all people, but there is also a mention that the brahmins shall have a special say in the election of the raja. This might be in view of the fact that the brahmins, having no interest in worldly ambitions, would give their consent with impartiality:

त्वामग्ने वृणते ब्राह्मणा इमे शिवो अग्ने सवरेण भवान:।

(अथ 2-6-3)

meaning that the raja had been elected by the brahmins and now we too elect him. He shall be well wisher of us all. This would indicate that at first the brahmins shall elect the raja after judging his capability as per yardstick laid down in this regard and then only the person, so elected, shall face the people for election and after such an election by the people only the person shall become the raja.

Ballot Paper

In Atharva Ved the word has been used in this context, which signifies the ballot paper, on which the voter expresses his consent.

ये राजानो राजकृत: सूता ग्रामण्यश्च ये,
उपस्तीन्पर्ण मह्यं त्वं सर्वान्कृण्वमितो जनाव्। (अथर्व)

We wish to use the ballot paper for electing the raja, who shall be having affinity with us. In vedas the educational institutions have also been given the right to express their intention (vote) for electing the raja. These educational institutions were 'Gurukuls', in which the students were absolved of pride, passion, rage, affection, greed etc. and they became pious persons bereft of telling lie, thefts etc. and persons of good moral and nationality, who could sacrifice their all for the sake of the nation.

Election Manifesto

There is a provision in vedas that the candidate to become raja shall proclaim his election manifesto :

1. त्वमग्ने राजा करूणो धृतव्रतः (ऋग 2-1-4)
2. धृतव्रतो धनदाः सोमवृद्ध (इन्द्र) (ऋग 6-19-5)
3. अग्ने धृत व्रताय ते (ऋग 8-44-25)

Here Agni and Indra have been shown as 'धृतव्रत'. Agni and Indra are synonyms of raja as has already been indicated. 'धृतव्रत' means the most intelligent and having been doing best deeds. Such person only shall succeed the throne. The qualities of the person, who is a candidate for kingship are put before electorate.

प्रेन्द्रस्य वोचं प्रथमा कृतानि प्र नूतना मघवा या चकार,

पदेद देवी रसहिष्ट माया अथामवत् केवलः सोमो अस्य।

"means that I explain the deeds of Indra - past and present-explaining how after killing all vices from his mind, he has come out as a pious person and with the pious thinking how he has reached this top position is also explained."

We have so far seen that according to vedic tenets .

1. The raja may not necessarily be in dynastic succession.
2. He should be an elected person.
3. His succession should have the support of the people.
4. A person, when elected, shall rule for the entire life.

5. Life in this context means the period of grihastha ashrama.
6. He cannot ordinarily be dethroned during his life period.
7. He shall devote himself completely for the well-being of his people.
8. A raja, who does not care for the peoples' well-being after having been enthroned, could be dethroned too during his life time itself.

   ध्रुवस्तिष्ठाविचाचलत्... मा त्वद्राष्ट्रमधि भ्रशत्। (अथ 6-87-1)

   The person can succeed the throne for life but he should not start doing foul deeds, which may entail his being dethroned.
9. There shall be an eligible voter, a ballot paper and the election manifesto of the candidate for becoming raja.

Institution of Federal System of Governance

We find in vedas a clear provision for the kingdom being 'federal state'. There should be federating units, which should be autonomous in their internal ruling and all these federating units may elect one person as their emperor. The emperor shall be responsible for solving all the inter-unit problems/disputes and keep all federating units in a very cordial understanding amongst themselves. He shall also be responsible for maintaining cordial relations with other countries. The smaller units shall elect their rajas and these rajas shall elect their emperor. The federating units and federal government shall have their own sabhas and samitis (lower and upper houses of legislature). The existence of federal system of government is supported by following mantras :

1. प्र सम्राजो असुरस्य प्रशंस्ति पुरूं (ऋग 7-6-1)
2. अग्निं कविं सम्राजमतिथिं जनानाम (ऋग 6-7-1)
3. अग्निः सम्राडेको विराजति (ऋग 12-11-7)

Here Agni has been proclaimed as the emperor and he has some smaller federating units under him, which he rules with equity. Like Agni, Indra too has been proclaimed as the emperor like:

प्र सम्राजं चर्षणीनामिन्द्रम (ऋग 8-16-1)

At other places the emperor is also stated to be having various departments to assist him in the governance of the country like:

वसवो रूद्रा आदित्या उपरिष्पृशं मोग्रं चेत्तारमघिराजमक्रन।
(ऋग 10-128-9)

Here the emperor seeks help from the authorities of various departments and the God to enable him to discharge his duties properly with their help. He also prays that he should not fall in any vice and always think of the well-being of his subjects:

ये राजानो राजकृत: (अथ 3-5-7)

Here there is a mention of the rajas, who elected the emperor. An emperor made with the mutual consent of the rajas shall always try for the maintenance of cordialily amongst these rajas of the federating units :

इममिन्द्र वर्धय क्षतियं म इमं विशामेकवृषं कृपुत्वम्।
निरमित्रनक्ष्णु ह्यस्य सर्वास्तान्रन्धयास्मा अहमुत्तरेसु।। (अथ)

This and other mantras of Atharva Ved confirm our thinking of the vedas prescribing for the federal system of government. Indra, Agni, Varuna etc. have been designated in vedas as raja/samarat/panchjanya, all indicative of being heads of the state. Also it confirms the rule by the panchayat, in which Indra being the emperor, the others like Agni, Varuna etc. are the members.

यत पांचजन्यया विशेन्द्रे घोष असृक्षत्,
अस्तृणाद्वर्हणाविपोभूर्ज्यो मानस्य स क्षय:। (ऋग 8-63-7)

Meaning that when the Panchjanya call for Indra, the emperor, Indra kills the enemies and becomes respectable to all elders. The mankind in Hindus had been divided into four-brahmin, kshatriya, vaish and shudra as per Yujur and Atharva Vedas. In vedas, the word 'varna' has been used for these four divisions. This is 'Varna' i.e. choosing, because the man used to choose any one of these according to his capacity/capability.

This also demolishes the idea of 'caste by birth' phenomenon, as varna means to chose only and anything got by birth is not chosen. Now since one himself choses a thing, even though it is the carrier in life, one starts loving that chosen thing and tries to abide by the tenets relevant to that chosen caste. There would have been some people, who did not come in any of the above four varnas. They were called 'unarya' or 'dasyu' or 'rakshas' etc. It was the duty of the emperor to eliminate such people if they caused any annoyance to the persons of the other four varnas:

हत्वी दुस्यून प्रार्य वर्णमावत।

The Aryans were only in varnas. This means the mankind were divided into two - Arya (in four varnas) and 'Unarya'. All the vedas confirm this classification. So the people of four varnas were Aryans. Infact the word 'Arya' means gentle, pious and non-Aryan means non-gentle/dasyu. Brahmin means, the person who cares for others by dint of his knowledge and tapsya. Kshatriya means a person, who by his bravery, protects the subjects in his kingdom from external invasion and internal criminals. Vaish means a person, who collects wealth and spends it on the well-being of others and shudra means, persons, who serve the people of the other three varnas.

For proper development of a nation, the division of mankind on the functional basis is quite essential. According to their taste and capability, some persons chose to be brahmins, others opted to become kshatriyas, if they were brave and those who were business-minded, they chose to become vaish and the remaining, who did not fit in any of the above three varnas, became shudras. The persons thus having chosen the varna as per their capability abided by the jobs assigned to that varna in vedas and serve the nation in that way. We, on looking back on history, find that whenever such following as per dharma, was in vogue, the country progressed and whenever there was breach in such affinity, there has been chaos and confusion in the country. Panchjanya, therefore, are the representatives of these four varnas and the fifth from the people not included in these four varnas but do not cause any annoyance to the people of the other four varnas, like Vibheesan, although from asuras, had joined the Aryan class. It also means that there was complete secularism in so far as the people did not rise in quarrel with the people of other varnas/ religions/castes; the person of non-varna, causing annoyance to other people was considered fit to be eliminated and not that one was ill-treated if he had not chosen to be one amongst the people of four varnas. The question of punishment arose only where such persons started causing annoyance to the people of four varnas. Otherwise people of all the five categories (four varnas and one non-varna) were entitled to attend the public functions/ceremonies etc.

ते न इन्द्रः पृथिवी क्षाम वर्धन् पूषाभगो अदितिः पंचजनाः।
सुशमणिः स्ववसः सुर्नाथा भवन्तु न सुत्रत्रसः सुगोपाः।।

The emperor and his other persons/staff and people of all the five categories should cause development of country; all should be of mutual help to each other; all should protect others and be of help, whatever is possible, to others. They should all live cordially."

Having discussed the formation of varnas and dasyus, we now have to see how far the institution of varnas was adhered to in the society in our ancient period itself. Although now the people of the world look down upon us as a society divided into thousands of castes, rigidly separate from each other, this actually was not the purpose when the institution of varnas was introduced. It was introduced by Manu, when he saw that there was complete chaos in the society. Each one, whosoever became mightier, started suppressing others and none had respect for the others. To do away with this anarchy and develop affinity amongst people of varied thinking, Manu introduced the institution of varnas, dividing the mankind in four varnas, chosen by each individual as already discussed and then adhering to the tenets relevant to that varna, as per Manu Samriti. Manu Samriti gives a detailed account how varna institution was introduced, the duties of people of each varna; the qualifications and duties of a brahmin, a raja, a vaish and the shudra. Brahmins used to learn and teach others; kshatriyas ruled over the people, protected them from external aggression and internal criminals; vaishas dealt with trade, agriculture, cattle grazing, industry and shudras served the people of the other three varnas. Vedas expect everyone to act as per assigned job, which was his dharma. This was also necessary to maintain social and political affinity. But although the division of mankind was made a religious necessity, it was not rigidly enforced on the people. As already indicated, each person, used to opt for the varna as per his capability and even after opting one, he could change over to the other as Viswamitra, although a kshatriya, had become Brahm-rishi by resorting to tapasya. Nishadraj, a shudra, had become Ram's friend and bhakta. After such change of varna, one was recognised by the changed varna only as Viswamitra was counted in rishis. Even Krishna has stated in Bhagwat that people were known and recognised not by birth but by their temperament and conduct.

वैराजात् पुरुषाज्जाता य आत्माचरलक्षणाः।

Accordingly people were classified as belonging to Group A (उत्तम), Group B (मध्यम), Group C (नीच), Group D (लघु). At the time of Sita svayamber, people were made to sit in above order and not as per varnas.

उत्तम, मध्यम, नीच लघु निज निज थल अनुहारि। (मानस)

Similarly in Yudhisthra's yagya also people sat as per their position. Temperamentally, brahmins were expected to have control on their senses, greed, pride, jealousy and be content and mercyful to others. A kshatriya was expected to be patient, liberal, strict in discipline, and cordial with mankind. A vaish was to be donor, god fearing, honest, without pride, good money lender and banker. Similarly a shudra was expected to serve the people of three varnas and remain contented with whatever he got by dint of that service. A brahmin could change over to kshatriya or vaish and an kshatriya to vaish if he was not able to follow the religious requirements of his varna. Bhagwat says-

सीदन विप्रो वणिग्वृत्त्या पण्येरेवापदभूतरेत।
and वैश्यवृत्त्या तु राजन्यो जीवेन्मृगयया आपदि। (भागवत)

Even if subsequently one could come back and do his job, he was free to have such come back -

कृच्छान्मुक्तो न गहर्येण वृत्तिं लिप्सेत कर्मणा। (भागवत)

In social and political functions, all people used to sit as per their capability. When Shukdeva narrated Bhagwat to Raja Parikshit and Yudhisthra held ashwamedha yagya, all public men and even gods had attended the function and their seating arrangement was as per their positions and not by caste. Such was the 'order of precedence' available in our ancient times, which is stated to be a western ethics. After Ram's coronation, he had once called a meeting of all people i.e. irrespective of caste, creed etc. and told them the way to attain salvation. So in India, there had always been equality of all people in social and political gatherings and everyone was eligible to resort to Ishwar bhakti, reading religious books and so on. The caste compartmentisation is something which came into being during Muslim rule and more during British rule because of their policy of 'divide and rule'. They made reservation on religion and caste basis in government service, legislative assemblies etc. Our present rulers have been causing a wider gulf in fighting elections on caste, religion basis and having arranged reservation in government jobs on the basis of castes. Ram had clearly told Sabri, who was a shudra, that he recognised only, bhakti, irrespective of his belonging to any caste, religion etc.

कह रघुपति सुनु भामिनी बाता, मानऊं एक भगति कर नाता।
and जाति पाति कुल धर्म बड़ाई, धन बल परिजन गुन चतुराई।
(मानस)

As we get the mention of four varnas in vedas, we also find in the Manu Samriti, Manu laid down the division of society in four varnas and their respective functions had also been written in the vedas. As per Manu Samriti the four varnas are:

लोकानां तु विवृद्धयर्थं मुख बाहूरूपादतः
ब्राह्मणं क्षत्र्यिं वैभूयं शुद्रं च निरवर्तयत। (मनु 21-5)

This division had been made by God himself on the basis of capability of different persons and not by birth. This would also indicate that the division of mankind in four varnas is from the very beginning of mankind. The job of brahmin was to learn and then teach, performing yagyas. The kshatriya was to protect the public from external aggression and internal crime, performing yagyas, doing welfare jobs for the public; the vaish was to do trade, agriculture, bringing up cattle, industry etc.; and that of shudra to serve the people of above three varnas. Now the varna was to be opted by each person as per his capability. One, who had interest in studies, he studied all vedas, shastras etc. and became brahmin to teach others. One who had inclination for warfare and was brave opted for kshatriya and was trained in that vocation. Out of the remaining, who considered himself fit for the jobs of a vaish, received such training and became vaish. Those, who could not find themselves capable of any of the above three varnas, were left over to become shudras. Since everyone opted for the varna of his volition, he had no grudge against the people of other varnas. Also there was provision for change of varna later on if one was able to improve upon his position such as Vishwamitra became brahmarishi from kshatriya and so on.

As per Manu Samriti, Bharat or Aryavrat or Brahmvrat was the abode of enlightened people with good character and it was spread from ocean in the west (Arabian sea) to ocean in the east (Indian Ocean/Bay of Bengal) and from Himalaya in the North to the area between Vindhyachal mountains. Vindhyachal mountains included present Vindhyachal with eastern and western ghats. In other words entire northern India and southern India were included in it present India, Pakistan, Bangladesh and Afghanistan. The jobs of each of the varnas have been given in detail in Manu Samriti and compliance of the canons pertaining to that job was called dharma. Therefore, the society or even governance was as per vedic tenets or dharma. Not only this, even the behaviour of the people in various ashramas has been given. Every one had to undergo the four ashramas—Brahmcharya, Grihastha, Banprastha and Sanyas. With banprasṭha and sanyas having in view no one indulged much in wordly affairs and hence everyone worked diligently, honestly as per his dharma leading to peaceful and contented life all around. It even gives the dharma of husband, wife, father, mother, son, servant etc., which if properly followed, makes every family a happy one. No where in any religion is so much written and observed by each person as in Hindu/ Arya dharma.

Manu Samriti particularly speaks of the jobs of a raja so that if a country is properly governed and protected from foreign invasions, the inhabitants would be happy and prosperous.

राजधर्मान् प्रवक्ष्यामि यथावृत्तो भवेन्नृपः,
संमवश्च यथा तस्य सिद्धिश्च परमा यथा । (मनु 1-7)

The raja had to be like Indra in providing happiness to his subjects; like Air in providing mobility; like Yama in providing justice; like Sun in eliminating ignorance amongst the people and making them enlightened; like Varuna in punishing the culprits; like Moon in providing peace and prosperity and like Kuber in providing richness amongst its people.

इन्द्रनिलयमार्काणामग्नेश्च वरुणस्य च,
चन्द्रवित्ते शयोश्चैव मात्र निर्ह्यत्य शाश्वतीः। (मनु 4-7)

The raja was an elected one. He could not act independently as per his whims but was guided by a samiti or sabha. The members of the sabha had to be consulted individually or collectively in arriving at important decisions. Also to enable the ministers/members of the sabha, there was skeleton of staff, who were intelligent, brave, with good conduct and well-versed in the art of governance. It is, perhaps, on this basis that the conduct of all government servants is got verified even today.

तेषामर्थे नियुंजीत शूरान्दक्षान् कुलोद्‌गतान्,
शुचीनाकरकर्मान्ते भीरूनन्तर्निवेशने। (मनुस्मृति)

The raja is also to have a net of spies and his representatives. The representatives or ambassadors in present term were well-versed with international protocol and laws to enable them to conduct with other rajas. The spies used to give all imformation about what had been happening in their kingdom and to see to the interest of their raja in foreign countries.

The government was run by the raja by raising revenues from land tax, cess on production, professional tax, octroi, customs duty. All these sources were known to our ancient rulers. The present arithmatic and decimal system of counting has also come from vedas. The check on measurements and weights was kept. It shows there was proper system of weights and measurements too.

There were laws of war, laws of peace, laws of international agreements, the concept of vassal states and suzerains. In certain conditions the force of one raja excused the other's force when they surrendered; who opened the hairs; who came with folded hands; who ran from battlefields etc. The booty captured as a result of the battle, was also distributed amongst raja, troops etc. in a fixed proportion. The territory captured was either returned to the defeated raja after taking some presents and after his having accepted the suzerainty of the winning raja or it was annexed with his kingdom but in that case full freedom was granted to the people of the defeated raja's territory as in the case of his own people unlike the present day system of colonisation.

There was full cordiality in the relations of the raja and his subjects. Whereas the raja considered his subjects as his children, the subjects also were always prepared to give up their lives for the sake and on command of the raja. This is how the raja, with the strength of all his subjects, was able to defeat the aggressor and it is the lacking of this cordiality, that led to our having been humiliated by the Muslim invaders/ rulers and then the English as the people thought that the job of their protection was that of raja only and that they did not mind, who their ruler was.

As already indicated, there was a structure of raja, sabha, ministers, employees of various ranks at the centre, and so in the villages too. There was one pradhan of a village, another pradhan over ten villages, then on twenty villages, hundred villages and on thousand villages. There was a panchayat in each village and a council in towns to manage their respective affairs. Also there was complete espionage system in the kingdom as well as in foreign countries to keep the raja apprised of all the information suiting his ears. Those government employees, who were found involved in bribery and other extractions, were punished severely.

The raja had diplomatic relations with the neighbouring rajas. These rajas are of two types—one who were friendly and the others, who were not friendly. Those who were not friendly were to be taken care of specially and were to be alert even in respect of the friendly rajas.

At the time of invasion by another raja, the raja worked as per policy of appeasement, through wealth and by division in the cadre of the enemy. This policy of Hindu vedas as enunciated in Manu Samriti, is followed even today in all matters of governance universally. English had applied these methods on Indian rulers and in fact it is because of these policies that they became overall lords of India.

Manu Samriti lays down various kinds of disputes for judicial award and how to deal with those and the punishment to be awarded in each case. In this way our shastras did provide the present day systems contained in Indian Penal Code, Indian Criminal Procedure Code and Civil Procedure Code etc. The British saying that India did not have a perfect judicial system is, therefore, farce. Infact what English had come across in India was the Islamic system of jurisprudence as applied during Mohammedans' rule. If we go through the contents of Evidence Act, Indian Penal Code, Criminal Procedure Code, and Civil Procedure Code minutely, we would find that these appear to have been taken from shastras only.

There was law governing the fixation of prices of essential commodities so that the traders could not over-charge. These rates were fixed by government persons and adhered to by all traders. If at harvesting time, the foodgrains etc. fetched less value, the government procured the same, kept in their godowns and released later on to public. The public distribution system was, therefore, comprehensive, keeping the interest of traders and public in view. There were also laws about the marriages, stridhan institution, rights of husband, wife and children on properties owned by various relations. All the present laws were, therefore, codified in our vedic time itself.

In vedas, the structure of the government prescribed is although monarchichal, yet there were checks on the raja/ emperor and government was run on limited democratic system. As already indicated, the raja was an elected person and he could be dethroned too if he did not behave. Further, for the purpose of governance, he was assisted by a sabha or a samiti.

Sabha and Samitis

As per vedas, the smaller rajas and the emperor, both established sabha and samiti for the proper governance of the state. Seventh chapter (12th sukta) of Atharva Ved provides—

सभा च या समिति चावतां प्रजा पतेर्दुहितरौ संविदाने,
येना संगच्छा उप मासं शिक्षाच्चारू वदानि पितरः संगतेषु। (अथर्व)

The emperor/raja wished that the duly constituted sabha/ samiti should assist him. These sabha/samiti are like his daughters and help him in the discharge of his royal jobs. The members guided him in respect of any problem pertaining to their respective departments. The emperor too by his address (similar to the Presidential address to the two houses these days) to the sabhas/samiti created interest in the jobs pertaining to well-being of the state with paternal affection. The above mantra, therefore, affirms that—

1. The sabha/samiti should assist/protect the king and the kingdom.
2. They both should discharge their respective duties for the governance of the kingdom and the king consulted them on any problem.
3. The members of these sabhas/samitis were quite capable and were able to guide the king in respect of any problem pertaining to their respective departments.
4. The king also gave 'due recognition to their position and the advice given by them. They, infact, were the actual protectors of the kingdom.
5. The king delivered useful address in the meetings of these sabhas/samitis, rather than enforcing his position on them.

स विशोऽन व्यचलत।

तं सभांच समितिश्च सेना च सुराचानुव्यचलन। (अथ 15-9-1)

The king, who cared for the wishes of the people, had his Sabha/Samiti, army and finances also cordially placed. The king too worked for the well-being of the people. The members of the sabha/samiti tried to be unanimous in all decisions taken. They also activated people to give their opinion on the affairs of the state. Such a country only could have alround progress. This also confirms that—

1. The samiti had its sittings in the conference hall.
2. The members of the samiti were unanimous in taking dicisions.
3. The king invited the members to meet and discuss the particular matters meant for such discussion.
4. The king acted according to the decision of the samiti.

The sabha and samiti might have been different but these have been referred without indicating difference between the two.

अहं राष्ट्री संगमनी वसूनां चिकितुषी प्रथमा यज्ञियानाम्।
तां मा देवा व्यदधुः पुरुत्र भूरि स्थात्रं भूर्यावेशयन्तीम। (अथर्व)

The word 'संगमनी' refers to both samiti and sabha. They are both raj sabhas-two houses of the national council like the present day system of lower and upper houses. Somewhere the word used is also 'Sansad' for these sabhas/samitis. These sabhas considered all matters pertaining to the state, including finance, law, defence, external relations etc. The sabha made rules/laws, which had to be abided by the people. These rules were drawn keeping the interest of all the people in view. The sabha also decided as to who shall be brahmin, who shall be kshatriya and who shall be vaish. Those, who did not find place in these, were shudras unless one did not agree to be shudra. In that case he was to be 'dasyu'. Therefore, brahmins etc. varnas were not as per birth but as per rules laid down by the sabha. Whereas sabhas and samitis were distinctly formed, the samiti was above the sabha. The persons in the samiti were more learned and specialists and the number of members in the samiti was less than that in the sabha. This would indicate that these are strictly as per Lok Sabha and Rajya Sabha of the present day. Like the raja, the duration of the elected members of the sabha/samiti was also life long subject, however, to the condition that this period was upto the extent one was in grihastha ashrama and ceased, when one went to banprastha and also till one worked without bias or annoyance to the public and worked in public interest only or one was taken seriously ill and was not able to discharge the duty as a member of the sabha/samiti or death. In such a situation another person was elected to fill up the vacancy. Such sabhas/samitis were both in the kingdoms of smaller rajas and the emperor in federal government and the constitution and other conditions were alike in both the cases.

World Government

In vedas there is also a mention of the World Government under the 'इन्द्रेन्द्र' (Indra of the Indras or emperor of emperors).

Under such a system—

1. The emperors were autonomous within their kingdoms and the rajas were further autonomous within their territories except for the subjects on which emperor only could take decisions.
2. Since both the raja and the emperor were elected representatives of the people, the Indra of Indras or emperor of emperors could not be elected as such but recognised as emperor of emperors by the emperors as a whole. Such a collective government is difficult to be thought of but if such a government comes into being, all disputes inter state, inter national etc. would get solved. All mankind shall live peacefully and cordially. In 3.4 mantra of Atharva Ved, there is mention of the election of raja, the emperor and the emperor of emperors, who is the emperor of the universe viz—

इन्द्रेन्द्र मनुष्याः परेहि सं ह्यज्ञास्था वरुणैः संविदानः।
स त्वायमह्यत्स्वे सघस्थे स देवान्यक्षत्स नु कल्पयाद्विशः।।(अथर्व)

This is an invitation to the emperor of emperors to come and make himself familiar with the culture of the people of various countries, through the respective emperors, who would recognise him as their overall Lord and in this way help the various empires to be all powerfull and self-sufficient. This implies:

3. Upsadya (उपसद्य) : All have free excess to the emperor of emperors.
4. Namasya (नमस्य): The governance of the emperor of emperors shall be such that all countries treated him with all respects.
5. ततो न उग्रो वि भजा वसूनि: All countries under the emperor of emperors shall receive wealth according to their respective capability. There shall be no bias in favour or against any country. This government should give equity and justice to all.

6. अधो मनो वसुदेवाय कृणुष्व: The main aim of the emperor of emperors shall be to grant peaceful and comfortable living to all.
7. जाया पुत्रे सुमनसो: भवन्तु: Each family comprising of husband, wife and children shall live comfortably in such a state of the emperor of emperors.
8. पथ्या: The emperor of emperors shall see whether people of all countries have been following or not the rules/laws made out by him/his government.
9. सर्वास्त्वा राजन्प्रदिशो ह्वयन्तु: All the constituents of the empire of emperor of emperors shall take part in the election of such emperor of emperors.
10. आ प्र द्रव परमस्या: परावत: The emperor of emperors can be from any constituent country.
11. बहुं बलिं प्रहि पथ्यासा उग्र: The government of the emperor of emperors shall collect some money from the emperors for running this government.

The Bhartiyata, as propounded through vedas, therefore, even provides for the kingdom of the whole universe under the emperor of emperors and the emperor of emperors was to keep all people in peace and comfort. He is also to constitute universal raj sabha to assist him as in the case of rajas and emperors. Such a sabha is to be called 'Amantran'. Such a sabha is to work for the peace, comfort and cordiality amongst all people. Such was the feeling of our ancient people. Even in the universal government, the constituent units are to remain autonomous. There is no concept of colonialism or extortion of a country by another like the system followed by europeans. Bhartiyata, therefore, teaches of equality of people of all countries, sovereignty of all countries and peaceful and comfortable living of all people.

Cabinet of the Emperor

As per tenets of Vedas, there shall be a Parliament (sabha) to apprise the raja of the feelings of people, to make laws for the governance of the empire and to assist the raja in the governance of the state. Such a raja cannot discharge all the duties of governance of the state. He shall, therefore, be assisted by a team of ministers, who shall look after the affairs of different departments under the overall control and shall act on behalf of the raja. This vedic principle is universally followed even today. In vedas, Indra, Varuna, Sun, Agni, etc. have been referred to as emperors as also to work as ministers. How this contorversy? There seems to have been a system of working 'for and on behalf of the emperor' in those days like the present day system of working by the authorities of the government to work and take decisions 'for and on behalf of the President of India'. So all such ministers, who were authorised to act on behalf of the emperor, were also called the emperors, although they were ministers under the overall emperor Indra. A mantra of Rig Ved recognises Indra as the only emperor:

एक राकस्य भुवनस्य राजीस शचीपत इन्द्र विश्वाभि सतिभि। (ऋग)

means that Indra is the only emperor of the subjects (praja) and he alone governs the entire empire. So Indra is the only emperor and all others are assistants to the emperor but sometimes called emperors as such by virtue of discharging the duties of the emperor in their respective departments.

Ambassadors

The vedas also provide for the posting of ambassadors by one emperor in the kingdom of the other emperors. These ambassadors are the people of complete confidence, well-versed with the culture and the religion of the country, where they are posted. Their main job is to take the messages of the emperor of his country to the emperors of the countries where they are posted and to take such messages from those countries to his country. These are, more are less the jobs even now done by the ambassadors. Also the ambassadors were immune from being killed by the emperor of the country to which they go with the message of the emperor of his country :

न यं रिपवो न रिषण्यवो गर्भे सन्तं रेषणा रेषयन्ति।

(ऋग 1-148-5)

This means that the representative of the country in the other country is not killed/harassed by the people of the country, where such representative has gone. This is even confirmed in Ramcharitmanas, when Hanuman had gone in search of Sita to Lanka and had killed Ravan's son and destroyed the vatika but could not be killed as the law did not permit doing so -

नीति विरोध न मारिये दूता। (मानस)

It means there were detailed rules on the subject and the same were invariably followed by the rulers, even by the rakshas kings like Ravan. Such ambassador/representative could speak freely and without any fear before the king of the country where he had gone with the message.

Ministers

As already indicated there is provision of ministers to assist the emperor, in our vedas. A few of such ministers' existence is discussed below as indicated in vedas—

Transport minister: Aswani is treated as the minister of transport of the emperor. He is also a colleague of Indra, the emperor. He would be discharging the duties of the emperor and can be addressed as emperor too by virtue of doing the jobs of emperor on his behalf. Aswani is minister of transport by dint of his name 'Aswa' meaning a horse or owner of horse. As chariot is driven by horse, he symbolises transport.

अथोह रथो रथ्या राथ्येभिः। (ऋग)

The transport minister was responsible for arranging the transport of honey, ghee, gold, silver, juices, chemicals, metals, animals, public and the army. These chariots could be carried throughout the kingdom without having to obtain any license etc. and were available to all irrespective of caste, varna etc. There is also mention of availability in those days of ships, for sailing in seas in international transactions. There is also mention of aeroplanes, chariots without horses, engines, rockets etc. in the vedas indicating that technology in vedic era must have been far advanced than even what it exists today. This is Bhartiyata which has been supreme in technology in the universe. Might be West have invented these after getting clues from vedas as lot of study of vedas had been resorted to in western countries in 19th and 20th centuries.

Minister for Police: Varuna is designated as minister of police, acting as such on behalf of the emperor Indra. There is mention of bond in reference to Varuna in vedas. Since 'bond' is issued by police only, varuna is designated as minister for police.

ये ते पाशा वरुण सप्त सप्त त्रेधा तिष्ठन्ति विषिता रुषन्तः।
and सिनन्तु सर्वे अनृतं वदन्तं यः सत्यवाद्यति तं सृजन्तु।

Meaning that the bonds required to tie up the criminals are lying and Varuna should use these to tie and present the criminals for punishment. Varuna has three types of bonds- number one for dangerous criminals, number two for middle class criminals and number three for criminals, who have committed small crimes. The punishment is granted by Indra, the emperor.

Varuna is also mentioned as incharge of spying in the vedas as Varuna keeps alert, as police minister, and keeps an eye on the activities of the people in the kingdom. Various spies under Varuna keep touring the territory and no one can escape the sharp eyes of these spies. Varuna, through these spies comes to know of what is happening in the kingdom and reports the same to the emperor for necessary action. Indra is the chief justice and incharge of jails, where criminals are kept under him.

निर्गता ऋृतिर्यस्या सा निकृतिः।

It shows how perfect the management had been in vedic era. Varuna is said to be having thousands of eyes so that none could escape his eyes. He at first warns the people for restraining from indulgence in undesirable activities and if the criminal still does not abide by his warning, he is caught and brought before the emperor for awarding suitable punishment. The spies have been mentioned in the vedas by the word 'स्पशः' as—

प्रति स्पशो वि सृज तूर्णितमो भवा पायुर्विशोअस्या अदब्धः।

asking Indra to depute his spies, who should not have any fear to detect the criminals in the country and to see that in foreign countries too there are no designs against our emperor.

Defence Minister: Rudra is the defence minister and commander-in-chief of army. Rudra means causing annoyance. He causes annoyance to the enemies for the defence of the territory and protection of people from external aggression.

Industries Minister: Twasta is the minister for industries, handicrafts, arts etc. The word came from 'त्वक्ष' ('twaksh'), which means mending, fabricating etc.

Minister for Religion: Brihaspati being the guru of Indra in god's parlance symbolises the minister for religion. Words 'Brihaspati' and 'Brahmin' have been used as synonyms in vedas; both representing the rajguru or purohit. Brihaspati is also considered as the creator of vedas and as such he would be knowing the vedas and in turn the religion through and through. Since the Purohit is without any greed, Indra, after conquering the enemies and taking lot of wealth as presents, entrusts the same to Brihaspati for being distributed amongst other gods for spending on the works of well-being of the people. Brihaspati by dint of his able guidance, leads the people on correct path to be followed and in this way he saves the people from falling into vices.

Finance Minister: Pusha, a god and collegue of Indra, is the finance minister—

ऐतु पूषा रयिर्भग स्वस्ति सर्वधातमः अरुरध्वा स्वस्तये।

Pusha as finance minister is incharge for bring up all people, think of their welfare and spend money on the welfare projects. He is the treasurer of wealth and has no dearth of money.

न कोषोऽव पद्यते **(ऋग 6-54-3)**

and **अन्ष्टवेदसम** **(ऋग 6-54-8)**

means that treasury of Pusha is never empty and the wealth is never wasted. Pusha is responsible for thinking of ways and means for the collection of wealth from production on land, cattle grazing, cess etc. He inspects standing crops and evaluates so that king's share is honestly set apart by the agriculturists.

Minister for Law : Savita is the minister of laws —

१. सवितुर्वः सवितुः सवे (अथ. 6-23-3)

२. सवितुः सवायं (ऋग 11-113-1)

३. सवितुः सवे सत्यसवस (यजु 9-10)

Here the relation of Savita is shown with 'Sav' i.e. the best way of tackling the matters. Law was made based on dharma as per vedas—

सविता सत्यमान्मा **(ऋग 1-73-2)**

means the law minister is a learned person, knowing all about the religious and human faculties to enable him to make laws, which may be as per tenets of vedas, and to the advantage of human beings.

Education Minister: As Sun is the custodian of all 'jyoti' (enlightenment), he is aptly selected as education minister of Indra as emperor :

1. **सूर्यस्येव ज्योतिरेषाम (ऋग. 7-33-8)**
2. **उत् सूर्यो ज्योतिषा देव एति (ऋग. 9-13-1)**

Sun has, therefore, been requested to imbibe enlightenment in all the people.

शनैश्चिद्य सूर्येणादित्येन सहीयसा,
अहं यशस्विनां यशो विद्या सूयमुपा ददे।

It is a request to the all powerful sun to enable the people to attain the knowledge i.e. education of all kinds.

Prime Minister: In vedas, Vishnu has been depicted as the colleague god of Indra although in mythology, Vishnu is above Indra and is his master :

इन्द्रस्य युज्यः सखा (ऋग. 1-22-19)

Vishnu is always closest to Indra and his friend . This has been mentioned as such in Atharva Ved and Yajur Ved too. Vishnu is indicated in mythology as 'Narsingh Avtar', 'Baman Avtar', 'Ram Avtar', 'Krishna Avtar' etc to help the gods and Indra in the mitigation of all their sorrows and on the earth to annihilate the rakshasas, who had been causing annoyance to rishies, sadhus, gods, and other people. As prime minister helps the emperor in the eradication of all his worries, so Vishnu, as prime minister of Indra, kills all undesirable people. Infact Baman avtar is not mentioned in vedas. Baman's three steps are indicative of the fact that Vishnu had access to all the three lokas. Vishnu puts his step on this universe to grant land to the people to live and to live praising Vishnu i.e. the right to own property is recognised by him. He also bestows the tilling of land to the people to produce and use the same for their living. Having access to the three lokas, he can bring all things for the comfort of the people of this universe.

Minister for Vigilance Department: Kutsa is god and colleague of Indra. Kutsa has been mentioned in Rig Ved and Atharva Ved at several places. Indra is able to annihilate the rakshasas with the assistance of Kutsa as a god and punishes the criminals as emperor on Kutsa finding out the criminals due to his vigilant eye on people. As per Panini, 'Kutsa' means to find out vices, deficiencies, crime, guilts in the people and specially the staff in discharge of their duties; to see that employees work with integrity and full devotion; employees work as per targetted plan; each employee puts desired time and labour in the discharge of his duties; does not work to meet selfish interest; does not take bribery; there is no misappropriation or embezzlement or encroachment on government property; to see that the people are honest, devout to emperor and do not suffer from any ailment or difficulty. vigilance department finds out the guilty persons and presents before Indra, the emperor, for punishment.

Friends of Emperor

There is mention in vedas of vassal states and the rajas of these vassal states, who act as friends of the emperor, the suzerain -

प्रियतमस्य नृणामं (ऋग 7-62-4)

Varuna/Agni etc. have been used as acting as the friends of the emperor also. This means that the friends circle of the emperor includes the rajas of vassal states as also his ministers and members of the Sabha/samiti.

Chief Justice and Minister for Judicial Affair: God Som is stated to be the chief justice of Indra as also his minister for judicial affairs. He has to be an intelligent person and expert in his job. He has the expertise of a poet, learned, alert, lawyer, understanding human culture and thinking; person of integrity; impartial minded; a patient listener to the grievances of the people; should not ordinarily resort to capital punishment; should be able to keep everyone above fear; should be well-versed with law, usages, practices, customs, ordinances, statute etc.; should abide by truth and help the gentlemen; should be friendly to all and give all the necessary requisites in the justice.

Courts of Justice

Indra, as emperor, is incharge of courts of justice, with Soma as minister for judiciary. Vedas mention that criminals should be tried in courts and punishment awarded. The courts investigate the matter and after having known the correct facts award punishment.

सुविज्ञानं चिकितुषे जनाय सच्चासच्च वचसी पस्पृधाते।
तयोर्यत् सत्यं यत रद्दजीयस्तदित् सोमोऽवहि हन्त्यासत्।।

The plaintiffs and defendants appear in the courts and advance their arguments and after hearing, finds the truth and false in the allegations, the court acquit the true persons (not criminal) and punishes the false (criminals). Here in the vedas, there is clear indication of the tracing of the criminals, referring the case to the courts, investigating the case after hearing the plaintiff and the defendents and after reaching a conclusion punishes the culprits. Punishment for each crime is also perscribed like the present day I.P.C., Cr.P.C. etc. The punishments are both pecuniary and corporal, including conviction and imprisonment.

We, therefore, find that in ancient times, as per vedas, we had all the systems of election, governance, succession to throne, institutions of sabha and Samiti, vassalage, control on finances, appointment of government employees, policing and vigilance, raja-praja relations, king's cabinet, three wings of government—legistative, executive and judiciary, penal code and procedure for awarding punishment, king as protector of public by help of army etc. This is the same as is prevalent in present time and considered to have been given by the West. Infact, it appears, in our ancient times, the countries were better governed and people were more in peace and comfort compared to what is available today. This is the bhartiyata, we should be proud of. Degradation in these values only resulted in degradation of Indian systems, ruling patterns leading to foreigners' rule, first by Muslims as sovereign rulers and then by British as a colony under England.

Economy in Vedic Era

There was capitalistic system. The main source of production was agriculture. Vedas also mention about the oxen, ploughs etc. There was a community indulged in trade. Trade was mostly inland through roads and rivers although there is also mention of existence of ships for international trade. The urban habitant was generally alongside the rivers only. The property was owned on hereditary basis. The succession of paternal property was equally amongst all sons. There was no community or society property.

Society: There is mention of Varna institution in Rig Ved. Brahmin was the mouth; hands symbolised kshatriya or the raja; vaish was the abdomen and lower part and the legs denoted shudras. According to Rig Ved, the society was a patriarchal one in which the family was known by father's name like Kanav, Atre, Viswamitra Rishi and their families etc. and not by mother. Vedic family was, however, a joint family inclusive of father, mother, brothers, sons, daughters etc.

Praja

Raja was considered god's representative and was worshipped. The praja was quite obedient to their raja.

यस्य विश्व उपासते प्रशिर्ष यस्य देवाः।

i.e. the orders of the raja were honoured and complied with by all. The rajya was generally a centralised organ and was very powerful. All powers were vested in the raja. The individual's liberties were checked but at the same time, there were Janpadas, who exercised their own control on the janas and to this extent the janas were independent of any oppression by the raja. The raja was, however, all powerful and sovereign. He had his army and police for internal security and protection from external invasion. The inter-state disputes were generally settled by negotiation, conciliation, understanding, mediation, consultation etc. but in case of their failure, battle was the only way for settling the issues. Therefore, ultimately might only prevailed. Ram had given several chances to Ravana through Hanuman, Angad and similarly before Mahabharat, efforts were made for reconciliation between Kauravas and Pandavas and even Krishna had gone for this purpose but on Kaurvas not agreeing to the reasonable demand of Pandavas, war had to be resorted to resulting in the killing of lakhs of people. Vedas speak of the rajas being sovereign and independent and the colonial system of ruling is not mentioned. Even after conquering a raja, generally the kingdom was restored to him after getting some presents and retaining it as a vassal state but autonomous in the governance.

Let us now see the extent of independence envisaged in vedas. As already indicated, there was no colonialism in vedic era. Each region was ruled by a raja, elected by the people of that region. Rig Ved amply mentions swarajya, like:

1. एह स्वराजो अश्विना वहन्तु।
2. इदम् कवेरादित्यस्य स्वराजो।
3.. युधमस्य ते वृषभस्य स्वराज उग्रस्य।
4. उतेशिरे अमृतस्य स्वराजः।
5. महो गोत्रस्य क्षयति स्वराजो।
6. इत्थादि सोम इन्मदे ब्रह्मा चकार वर्धनम,
   शविषं वज्रिन्नोजसा पृथिण्या निः शशाअहिमर्चन्ननु (ऋग)

"O king, you are all powerful. You have defeated the enemy by your force and protected the independence of the country".

प्रेह्मभीहि धृष्णुहि नते वज्रो नि चंसते,
इन्द्र नृम्णं हिते शवो वृत्र जया अपोऽचन्ननु स्वराज्यम्। (ऋग)

"Proceed further and face the enemy and win him. None can face you in view of your power, exercised by being a sovereign ruler".

इन्द्रो वृत्रस्य दोधतः सानु वज्रेण्हीड़ितः ।
अभिक्राम्याव जिघ्नतेऽपि समीय चोदयन्नर्चन्ननु स्वराज्यम ।। (ऋग)

"For the sake of maintaining the sovereignty of the kingdom, the raja faced the invaders and threw them out of the kingdom for the well-being of the people."

इन्द्र तुभ्यमिद द्रिवोऽनुत्तं वज्रिन्वीर्चम्,
यद्धत्यं मायिनं मृगं तमुत्वं माययावधीर चंन्ननु स्वराज्यम्।

"The raja is all powerful. He killed all his enemies for retaining sovereignty with surpassing power."

यामथर्वा मनुष्पिता दघ्यं धियमत्नत,
तस्मिन्ब्रह्मणि पूर्वथेद्रं उकथा समग्मतार्चन्ननु स्वराज्यम्। (ऋग)

"The yagyas performed by the fore-fathers were performed by the raja too so that the sovereignty could be protected."

The sovereignty propounded in these slokas of Rig Ved cannot be found anywhere else in such an ancient period and the same concept is prevailing even today throughout the universe. As per these, all powers are concentrated in the raja but still the praja had a lot of say in the governance directly and through the sabhas/samitis and the raja too had at his disposal the entire public. In Atharva Ved too, there is mention of swaraj as :

विराट स्वराजमभ्येति पश्चात। (अथर्व)

One who was born, he too desired to have swarajya initially. Swarajya, therefore, it is said, is the birth right of man. This is what Annie Besant had said in one of the Congress Sessions. Swarajya is, therefore, all important and there is nothing above that.

यदजः प्रथमं संबभूव सहतत् स्वराज्यमियाय,
यस्मान्नान्यत् परमस्ति भूतम। (अथर्व)

In these slokas of Atharva Ved, the public expects the all—powerful raja to annihilate all the enemies for the sake of protection of their sovereignty. This shows that as per vedas the public was interested in the nation being all-powerful, ideal, protected from external aggression, free from internal crime and for this the public honoured all orders of the monarch considering these orders for the well-being of the public only.

As already indicated, vedas have made independence a birth-right. The American declaration of independence also pronounces "All are born independent and equal". Indian freedom fighters had also said "Independence is our birth right". Let us now see what actually the independence is ?

Ordinarily, the removal of restrictions and controls is independence. Accordingly, a person is said to be independent, if he is not controlled by any restrictions and is allowed to do whatever he wanted to do. But such an independence would lead to barbarian age. In a cultured society, everyone is bound by some rules, morals, restrictions and laws. These have evolved as a result of the evolution of society. In modern concept, independence of a country is said to be when it is no more a colony. There are various kinds of liberties/ independence—

1. Natural Liberty: Some people think liberty is a natural gift. According to them man is independent by nature itself. According to Rousou, man is born independent but is tied with restrictions all around. So the government should put minimum restrictions on the human beings as unnecessary restrictions lead to harm the natural liberty bestowed on the man.

2. Civil and Personal Liberty: Although a man wants to be free from all restrictions, yet "Man is a social animal". Therefore, some restrictions have to be imposed on him - social or moral - to conduct well in the society, so that his conduct does not harm others. At the same time, government/ society too should not the impose unnecessary restrictions on the man. To safeguard personal liberty of a person, the constitution provides for fundamental rights—right of equality, right to speak, right to follow any religion, right to adopt any profession, right to live anywhere, etc.

3. Political Liberty: Taking part in the governance of one's country, is political independence. As per this liberty, everyone has a right to vote, to have government of his choice, to hold any office; to express oneself and to fight election to constitute government. Political independence is infact the synonym of democracy. There cannot be any civil liberty without political liberty. Political liberty/independence is the real understanding of independence in present context. Such an independence is available when one is free from colonial yoke and is not ruled by a person sitting in another country.

4. National Liberty: Political liberty and national liberty are almost same things. As an individual wants to be independent, so a country is sought to be independent as a nation or a nation can think of her development, which is tied down with so many consideration during colonial regime. Today almost all nations have attained independence. Colonialism, in fact, is a western concept of governance, not conceived during vedic era in India or elsewhere. But even national independence cannot be termed as complete liberty as this also involves imposition of many checks. Such checks have been prescribed by the country's constitution on its different organs as well as by UNO and International Court of Justice.

5. Economic Liberty: Along with political liberty, the economic liberty too comes to one's mind. By economic liberty we understand that one should enjoy the fruits of one's 'labour and not that ones' labour be exploited by others or is done for others. Such a liberty also bestows an independent work by an individual and should not be dependent on others. Such a liberty cannot be had when the capitalists enjoy the fruits of labour of the labourers working under them or from bonded labourers. English had been exploiting India economically by charging a lot of expenditure incurred on army and offices maintained by them in UK and taking away raw material from here on throw-away prices and bringing finished goods at exhorbitant cost. Accordingly as the political power passes on in the hands of the public at large, the financial power should not rest in the hands of a few capitalists but should go to all subjects. In other words, it is also called socialism.

6. Moral Liberty: Despite all liberties one cannot be considered to be independent without attaining moral liberty. Moral liberty means the mental condition of a man when he leaves apart the unnecessary greed, ambitions, passions, etc. and leads a comfortable social life. Infact greed only leads to the person doing all kinds of crimes - civil and criminal. In Manas also it is said—

"मोह सकल व्याधिन्ह कर मूला"

i.e. affection whether for money or persons or anything else is the root cause of all problems. Since in an independent democracy, the development of the nation depends on the alround development of each and every person, the moral liberty has more importance in this context.

Equality

1. Civil equality i.e. all citizens are equal before law.
2. Political equality means equality in taking part in the governance of the state.
3. Social equality is that there should be no distinction on the basis of caste, creed or religion.
4. Natural equality is when each person is considered equal individually.
5. Economic equality is where each person can adopt any profession and can have wealth as per his capacity and one should not be able to exploit other's labour to fill up his coffin. However, economic equality does not certainly mean each person to have equal wealth.

Nation and State

Nation is an abstract word, which unites the people of a state whereas the state is a geographical piece of land governed by one government. Nation can be outside state also but state is limited by its boundaries. India is a state but the people living in the state are a 'Nation'. Such people can go and settle abroad but still they continue to be Indian Nationals whereas the state cannot be thought of outside its boundaries. Inspite of diversities of language, religion, culture, customs etc. India is one nation. Sir Herbert Risley says in his book "The People of India" as under :

"Beneath the manifold diversity of physical and social life, language, customs, religion, which strikes the observer in India, there can still be discerned a certain underlying uniformity of life from Himalaya to Cape Comerin. There is infact, an Indian character and a general Indian personality which we cannot resolve into its component elements".

So one state should be one 'Nation'. Whereas we had many states in India till the 18th century, and these states were governed by various rajas, nawabs etc, they all constituted one 'India'.

The Origin of State

Following principles lead to the origin of a State :

1. Theory of divine origin
2. Force theory
3. Patriarchal theory
4. Matriarchal theory
5. Social contract theory

1. **Theory of Divine origin:** This is the oldest theory. According to this theory, every state is the creation of almighty. This is governed within by God himself or through his lieutenant. All that is available in the state, is also the creation of God. Jews are the foremost believers of this theory. They believe that God appoints the raja and he only can remove him from that position and that the service of the raja is the service of God. The raja also in turn considers the subjects as his creation. In Hindu granthas too some mention about the raja being part of God himself is seen. Such an instance is available in Mahabharat stating that there were no rulers or ruled in satyug. People had been acting as per dharma and had been helping each other live comfortably. Then there arose the need of owning the wealth and this led to disputes arising in the people. People went to God for their protection and introduction of some system under which people could live peacefully. At that time God created Manu, as their first protector/ruler. Manu during his regime felt the need of a permanent solution to the problem of who should govern the country. He wrote Manu Samriti, according to which mankind has been divided into four varnas - Brahmin, Kshatriya, Vaish and Shudra. The division was based on function as already discussed. It is with this institution that ultimately the dynasty of rulers came into being. The kshatriyas were to act as rulers and to protect the subjects. For this purpose raja was given sovereign powers of legislative, executive and judiciary. He was also the supreme commander of army. Then the evolution of the institution of governance started and to avoid any raja becoming tyrannical,

he could be checked and replaced by the people. Also the representatives of the public were there to constitute a sabha to assist the raja and to check him if he indulged in any action not connected with the well-being of the people. This checked the rajas from becoming absolute autocrats and whimsical. Manu Samriti, lays down the 'Donots' and 'Dos' of the raja. Ram rajya is an example of the rule according to dharma as per vedas and samriti. To make the public devote and obey the raja, it was propounded that—

1. Raja is the creation of God.
2. Office of the raja is hereditary, unless the successor is not fit to govern.
3. Raja is the ocean of knowledge and he is answerable to God only for his doings.
4. It is a sin to oppose the raja.

Such a concept has been seconded by Dr. Figs on the west. In 17th century, the divine origin of king was so much exploited by the Stuart King James I that the kings virtually became Gods as enunciated by James in his book "Law of Free Monarchy". This theory had been followed in Austria, Germany and Russia as well for a long time. In Muslims too Khalifa was considered as God's representative as a ruler. After the 17th century, people became vigilant and came out of this blind faith and made it that they themselves are the creators of governors. The reasons for the change were—

1. Social understanding according to which public opinion became supreme.
2. Religion was separated from the government.
3. Nationalism resulted in the abolition of suppression by the king.

The theory of king being God's representative was illogical; made the king very whimsical and tyrannical. Further combination of government and religion is wrong as it gave rise to immorality in the name of religion. This theory, however, was of use in ancient times, when the public was not vigilant and they could have faith in anyone in the name of God only. At the same time the kings too were to rule as per dharma according to which they—

1 Could be removed by the people if they continued to be tyrannical or the king was not able to protect the subjects from internal disturbances and lawlessness and external aggressions. Raja Bain is a mythological example.
2. Could not waste the money received in the exchequer from the public as part of the produce. Emperor Yudhisthra wanted to hold a yagya but when he found that there was no money in the exchequer other than the collection of part of produce, he was worried and in the situation, the Pandavas had to hold yagya by using some golden vessels etc. thrown as surplus by another king.
3. Could only think of the well-being of the people. Such a system had saved the society from chaos and anarchy.

The duties of the rajas were

1. To save the country from internal criminals and to catch and punish the criminals.
2. To protect the country from external aggressions and to himself fight with the enemies.
3. To work for the well-being of the people like construction of roads, sarais, plantation of trees, gardens, hospitals etc.
4. To see that the public get the necessary commodities at reasonable prices and of good quality and to correct measurement.
5. To hold yagyas so that rains took place in time resulting in good foodgrains production and no famines.
6. Raja was even held respossible for early death of the wards in Ram and Krishna periods.

To enable the raja to discharge the above duties properly, he was assisted by ministers, advisers and sabha and samiti. The raja generally accepted the advise of these bodies and in case he did not accept, then adequate reasons had to be given for the same. Like, at the time of Ram - Ravana battle, on Vibheesan coming to Ram for refuge, Ram asked all whether or not to grant him refuge. Then Sugreeva was against it as per canons of war but Ram granted him refuge and advanced reasons for his decision satisfying Sugreev. Sabhas had been in existence as per vedic pronouncements. In case the raja became tyrannical, the sabha could even remove the raja as had been done in the case of Raja Bain, who had been killed and Raja Prithu had been put in his place. These sabhas had been constituted by the people by election. There is provision in vedas for the election of raja also and wherever such elections were not held, the raja had to get the approval of the sabha for appointment of Yuvraj as Dasratha had taken the approval of guru first and then of his sabha for coronation of Ram.

वेगि विलम्ब न करिअ नृप साजिअ सबुइ समाजु। (मानस)

There were smaller rajas and the chakravarty samrat or emperor. The smaller rajas too were autonomous in their respective kingdoms but they used to be called vassal states, paying annual tributes to the emperor and to accept submission at the time of Aswamedha yagyas held by the emperor.

In royal functions, all people used to take part irrespective of caste, creed etc. This showed the equality of all as in Sita svayamber the entire public had attended and their seating arrangements had been made not according to their respective varnas but according to their position:

"उत्तम मध्यम नीच लघु निज निज थल अनुहारि।" (मानस)

The public was also quite devoted to the raja. At the time of Ram going to forest, all people followed him and with great difficulty Ram could proceed. Still for 14 years the people stopped all their rejoicings till Ram came back. The raja too cared for the well-being of the praja. Ram had said—

जासु राज प्रिय प्रजा दुखारी सो नृप अवसि नरक अधिकारी। (मानस)

Ram even had separated Sita on criticism by a washerman as to how he was keeping Sita with him after her having stayed in Lanka for a long time. This shows:

1. The freedom of speech, when public could criticise even the raja and,
2. Public's say in the matters of governance.

The duties of the people of all varnas had been specified in Manu Samriti and all the people had been living as per the dictates of dharma.

This shows, how the raja had been ruling over his subjects; how praja had been sincere and devoted to raja and how with the powers in the hands of the people and sabha, the raja was checked from becoming whimsical and tyrannical. This confirms the democracy at work in ancient Bharat and such a system, (Bhartiyata), even if followed today would lead the country to be prosperous, peaceful and give a very comfortable living to its people—an ideal way of living as per vedas. This had been partly observed by Shivaji as late as in 18th century and gave a peaceful rule to the people.

Force Theory: The raja became raja by dint of his force. He was incharge of army and the kingdom to rule over the people. The evolution of such a theory, which appears logical, started from the fact that "man was quarrelsome temperamentally". Due to this, some strong man became superior to others and then suppressed the quarrel. Subsequently with the passage of time and evolution of system, such a strong man became raja to rule over the subjects. In such a system, the public had no say in the governance and had to do as per wishes of the raja and is not apt to be existing in present day system. Even Hitler with such whimsical temperaments had to give up in the second world war. Such rajas were not satisfied with the creation of their kingdoms and started conquering other kingdoms and in this way, there had been constant aggression by one state on another and the kingdoms had always to be ready to face the invasion. At the time of the British advent too, the country was divided into various kingdoms, each fighting with the other to grab it.

English, taking advantage of this, further instigated them to fight amongst themselves and in this way finishing them, became the overall Lords of the country. It would be seen that such grabbing by the English was as a result of the fact that the country was not being ruled as per vedic tenets.

Patriarchal theory: Such a system was available in Greek, Rome and Jews. There, in the family, the father was supreme. The family expanded into community and then into kingdom.

Matriarchal theory: Such a system was rarely in existence, where mother was considered supreme.

Social contract: In this system also after the family, the people gathered in societies and then these societies developed contacts amongst themselves converting themselves into community and then into kingdoms. Socialistic pattern had been tried by many states but it did not work well. It can, with grace, work to the extent of small jobs executed and not for the governance of the country.

3 Pre Historic Period

India has been the cradle of civilisation in terms of antiquity and richness. Unearthing of India's rich heritage known as Indus valley or the Harappan civilisation began in 1921-22 at Mohenjo Daro, where, after digging, a highly developed urban civilisation was discovered. Indus civilisation remnants have been found in Gujarat and Mehargarh too.

Since the diggings in Harappa and Mohenjo Daro were done in 1921-22, when it was British rule in India, the approximation of the chronology has been given as about 3000 B.C. because the British did not want to place Indian civilisation an older one. In fact the remnants found there would be belonging to a period much earlier before Mahabharat or even Ramayan. Mahabharat itself is said to have taken places about 5000 years back and in this way the Mohenjo Daro-Harappan civilisation should be prior to 10000 years i.e. about 8000 to 10000 B.C. The diggings show that even at that time:

1. The weights discovered in Indus civilisation were very accurate, made from hard stone such as agate. The denominations of weights had decimal division like metric weights of today.

2. Copper objects recovered include antimony rods, pins, bangles, beads, arrow heads, hooks, rings, knives, fish hooks etc. Besides copper, other metals such as gold, silver, lead, arsenic, antimony and nickle were known to Harappan people.

3. Indus scripts comprise of solving cross-words puzzles, seals, pictures of animate and inanimate objects. There are 62 sign of Indus script.

4. Indus civilisation had urban life. City settlements are spread over an area of 5 to 7 kilometers in circumference.
5. Food consisted of beef, mutton, pork, poultry, turtles, fish, barley, palmdates etc.
6. Cotton fabrics were popularly used.
7. People knew art of toilets and cosmetics. Toilet jars were made of ivory, metal, pottery and stone. Face paints and other cosmetics were freely used.
8. Dancing, hunting, drums and game plays have been found indicating mark board and dice pieces.
9. Economy was based on irrigated agriculture, main cultivation being wheat, barley, peas, sesamum, mustard, cotton and rice.
10. A variety of crafts were developed like bangle making, beads, pottery work, seal cutting etc.
11. Peepal and other trees were grown. Bulls, tigers, elephants were worshipped.

The basic economy of Bhartiya people was agriculture. Peaceful, pleasant farmers carried on efficient farming operations in Iran, Baluchistan and Sind. The people exercised well regulated mixed farming. They lived in small village settlements in upland valleys and other plains alike. They also enjoyed commercial life with easy self-sufficiency. There was irrigated farming and riverine. Water was stored in big ponds. We find big granaries in the two Indus cities of Harappa and Mohenjo Daro.

This indicates that the agrarian system was so well organised that the peasants sufficiently produced and the surplus was stored in granaries. They cultivated cotton, wheat, barley, rice and other considerable varieties of farm produce. Fruits and vegitables were in plenty. International trade was centrally organised by the community. In Egypt, there was the whole-sale market. Foreign trade was royal monopoly. The economic life of the region, it appears, was organised on the basis of synthetic harmony of the individuals and society. Family was the social unit. As the family was based on a single individual, it was of necessity, small. Indus script has not satisfactorily been deciphered. Excavations at Mehargarh have been dated to the seventh millenium B.C. by potassium-argon method. Hence we have no access to the inscriptions obtaining in Bharat in 8000 B.C. or before. However, we witness a self sufficient, peaceful and homogeneous society throughout the vast Bhartiya region in that age. The prosperity of the villages and towns rested on agriculture, industry (mostly handicrafts) and trade.

Rig Veda is a Vincent-Smithonian interpretation of the pre-Aryan Bhartiya life by the invading semi-civilised nomadic Brahmanyans, still some truth may be gleaned from it, with the help of subtle discerning skill regarding the nature of the way of their adversaries, the Bhartiya people. The Brahmanyan adversaries were termed by them as asuras, dasas, dasyus, panis, rakshasas—all belonging to the non-aryan varnas. They were opposed to basic Aryan way of life of yajnas.

We have two important concepts of Rig Ved and later vedic literature, Panchajanab and Panchaksitanam. Both are co-related. One signifies the people and the other their territory. Panchaksitanam does not mean five classes of men or beings. Indra is said to be ruling over five dwellers on earth. Here significance of territory is indicated. Treasure of five territories in the hands of Indra refer to final Brahmanyan victory over Bharat.

The executive again of the Jana Republic was Parisada. Indra destroyed the Parisad of the asuras. The Parisads possessed great riches. Big granaries at Harappa and Mohenjo Daro justify the fact that Bhartiya peasants also produced for the community and the surplus belonged to the community. The supreme authority of the Jana Republic was known as Rajan. This word is from the word 'Jan' with prefix 'Ra'. 'Ra' is used in the sense of yield or surrender. The person, who surrendered or renounced his life in the service of Jana was, therefore, called Rajan. The epithet Raja had been given to the leaders of the ten republics' confederacy in Rig Ved. The best, the most illustrious, the greatest, the senior-most, the highest among leaders, supporter of people, shining and radiant Jana was the Rajan of the realm. The spiritual beliefs of the Egyptians are contained in the book "The Manifestation of Light", miscalled "Book of the Dead". The essential parts of the book originated in the most ancient times. The book claims to be a revelation from 'Thoth'. The oldest monumental evidence of the existence of 'Thoth' is available in the oldest existing Egyptian temple belonging to the reign of Chefran, the builder of the second Pyramid. He belonged to the fourth dynasty and lived in 2800 B.C. The first peaceful coloniser of Egypt under the leadership of Menes, came from Bharat. Hence it may safely be concluded that the Bhartiyan immigrants brought the truths contained in the book with them in the middle of the fourth millenium B.C. The most ancient original chapters of the book contained the fundamental conception of the continuance of soul after death—again a Bhartiya belief. The full and final purest attainment was achieved by the self-propelled individual effort. The Sumerians too believed in the soul and its life after death. Purer souls went to the Island of Blest after death. The Island of Blest may be compared to swarga of the Bhartiyas. The darker souls went to the northern world or hell. Bharat is the birth place of the ideology of spiritualism. We do not possess extant literature of the pre-historical Bharat. The Harappa script, even if rightly deciphered, only help a little. The neolithic cretans believed in the cult of Reshef and Mother Goddess. When Greek Aryans stabilised their authority in Greek and Aegeans, a Greek Dionysus, son of Jeus and Persephone developed a religion, which was savage and repulsive in original form. He was the God of primitive tribal Greek agriculturist following the ways of Ganapati and Indra, in tribal drinking of wine. The economic and social condition of the Aegeans and Greece is peculiarly similar to that of the rest of the Sramanic region. The election and republican political institutions are also of same pattern. The basic way conforms to the basic way of the region. But it has its own individuality. Minoanism stands by itself in history. Hence it may be rightly called an offshoot of an extensive Sramanic Society.

The Pre-Aryan Sramanic Society may be said to have economic condition as thriving and prosperous. An individual was the economic unit. He was free and independent. He wanted further happiness of his family/community. The individual enterprise of agriculture and industry gave rise to private property. The surplus agricultural and industrial produce belonged to the community. The international trade was the business of the community. Family was the social unit in which men and women enjoyed equal rights, social status and prestige. The succession of the private property of the family went to the family members. The descent was largely matrilineal as a rule. The political institutions were developed on the republican pattern. The region had numerous self-organised and self-sufficient local republics without any central force to keep their homogeneity and unity in tact. All the adult members formed the assembly, who chose their leader. The administration was carried on with the active consent of the people.

All these economic, political and social institutions had sprung from the living faith in the tenets of spiritualism. Further, spiritualism may be defined as the feeling of identity in freedom of the self with the other living beings and objects. People believed in the existence of spirit and final attainment. The ultimate goal of attainment or salvation had ever since the beginning of universe, been imbibed in Aryans and that is the Bhartiyata. Bharat was, therefore, the epicentre of this vast Sramanic Society. Panis of the Abi Race imbued with the driving force were the main founders in the regions of Greek, the Aegean, Egypt and West Asia. They carried Sramanic civilisation to the American continent also.

Sapta Sindhu Home Theory

Several early European and Indian scholars believed that Sapta Sindhu was the original Aryan Home. European scholars and majority of Indian scholars subsequently abondoned this theory but few Indian scholars still cling to it on the grounds—

1. Vedic Aryans do not have any memory of their foreign original home.

2. Vedic Sanskrit has the largest number of vocables found in Aryan languages.
3. Aryans did not leave any literary records in the intervening countries.
4. Sacrificial rituals developed in Punjab.
5. Archaic character of the Lithuanian language is due to the unprogressive character of the people speaking it.
6. Evidence of flora and fauna is not conclusive.
7. Geographical data of the Rig Ved clearly shows that the Punjab and the neighbouring regions constituted the home of the people, who composed these hymns.
8. Evidence of mythology in the shape of Ramayan, Mahabharat, Manu Samriti and other shastras show the existence of Aryans and vedic culture in Bharat since time immemorial, (may be lacs of years).
9. The ancient names of various provinces of Bharat are of Austric origin. Kosala-Tosala Taxila, Anga-vanga, Kalinga-Trilinga over the greatest part of Eastern Bharat. Pulinda along with Andhra, Pundra, Sahara, Mutibar, cover Dcecan. Kulindas are Himalyan people. Kamboj, Salva and Udanbaras were in Punjab and Sindh provinces. The process and formation of these names is foreign to Aryans; it is foreign to Dravidians, it is on the contrary, characteristic of the vast family of languages, which are called Austro-Asiatic and which cover in Bharat, the group of the Munda languages also after called the Kolarian. The Austric origin of these words reflect the culture and civilisation of the Proto Austroloid Pre-Aryan people of Bharat. These words suggest that the Pre Aryan Bhartiyans belonged to Abi and Ikswaku races. They were mainly urban people enjoying settled life. They had developed the art of agriculture, had weapons like bow and arrow. Their philosophy was based upon the conception of the existence as animates and inanimates.

10. The earliest literary evidence provided by vedic literature comes from Aitareya Brahamana. The lands of the Uttar—kurus are situated beyond the Himavanta. According to Pali tradition, the people originally coming from Uttarkuru colonised the land, which extended from Saraswati to Ganges, hence the name Kuru. Kuru kingdom comprised of three parts—Kurujingala, Kuruland proper and Kurukshetra. The Uttarkurus were the foreign intruders, who, as is common with the new colonisers, retained the memory of their original land in giving the name Kuruland to their newly won Bhartiya territories.
11. The brahmnical tradition as contrained in Manu Samriti also coroborates the event of Brahmanyan colonisation. The region between rivers Saraswati and Dusadavati was first colonised by the people coming from Uttarkuru. Aryan leaders were known as 'Devas'.
12. Vedic mythology also corroborates the above geographical location of Uttarkuru region in Pururava-Urvaslic legend.
13. Pururava was an ancestor of Purukutsa, the leader of the famous Puru republic, a confederating unit in Dasrajna war. He appears to have been very powerful and influential leader in the region. The Brahmanyan forces had, during his time, advanced from Iran upto Gandhara (Modern Afghanistan) under the military command of Indra and Divodasa. He chose the most beautiful and charming lady Urvasi of his tribal collective to ensnare the powerful hostile leader and win him to their side against his Bhartiya kinsmen. She stayed with him for four years and bore him sons. It was won by her to the side of Brahmanyan Devas to fight the great battle for victory against the Dasyus. He was converted to Brahmanism and Baptised by being given sacrificial Agni by the Gandharvas, the Brahmanyans of Gandharvas or Arachosias.
14. The remote ancestors of the Aryan nation passed through the states of savagery and barbarism. Their common basic society was "Gana", Gens, Genos and Gana in Latin,

Greek and Sanskrit signify one and the same 'Society'. Rig Ved is the oldest book of the Aryan society. The institution of 'Gana', occupies a significant place in it.

15. Ganapati was incharge of the Ganas. In Bharat, Ganpati is considered 'Adi-Dev'. Viswadevas, Brihaspati, Indra, Soma, Pusan, Agni and Marut were all Ganapatis and designated as Devas in Rig Ved and the later vedic literature. Rig Ved fortunately retains a happy memory of these Devas as real leaders of real human beings.

16. The main characteristics of Gana as per vedas are—

(a) Gana was a tribal collective.

(b) Gana was the supreme knower of the means of production in agriculture and industry.

(c) Wealth and property of the Gana was commonly owned, it was commonly distributed; basis standard being integrity, unity and strength of Gana. These are the basic instincts Bhartiyata has been carrying through all periods upto the advent of Muslim rulers when they got polluted with the company of the Muslim aliens, who adopted all kinds of unethical ways and means during war, and also during the governance.

(d) The military, economic and social activities of the Ganas were tribal known as Yajnas.

(e) The supreme political authority of the Gana was centered in Ganapati.

(f) There was no election or selection of Ganapati. The best hero in the tribal war amongst the Devas emerged as the next Ganapati.

(g) Ganapati assumed the name of his Gana. It was a continuing office.

(h) No religious rules had been developed in this ancient stage of society.

(i) Gana was continually in the process of growth. The strangers and foreigners, after the defeat, were assimilated in the victorious Gana. No distinction was further observed and all the members, old and new, became inseparable.

The origin of Aryans, has been under dispute. It is, however, a fact that Aryans had spread throughout the world. A section of this family, which ultimately occupied Persia and India called itself Aryans. There is, however, common borderland of Europe and Asia. The Steppes of South Persia is thought as the oldest habitation. Balgangadhar Tilak said their original house was Arctic Region but this conclusion has not been generally accepted.

The traditional Hindu view that the Aryans were not invaders has been received and supported in recent years by some scholars in India and in Europe although not considered on convincing ground. But in view of the fact that any proof is not available, everyone ponders and concludes in his own way. So far, India had been under the rule of Muslims for about 600 years, during which period, they destroyed all libraries and the collection of books existing in Nalanda, Taxila, Kashi, Kanauj etc., where even in about one thousand years B.C. a very prosperous civilisation existed. Although mythologically, Indian civilisation is dated crores of years back and Aryans (Dayanand Saraswati) have placed the existence of Bhartiya civilisation since then, atleast Mahabharat may be considered to have taken place 5000 years back and Ramayan about 10000 years back. The history of India has been written by western historians, who did not want to take into account these occurrences as they did not want to accept Indian civilisation being so old and the origin of Aryans being India only. They, therefore, based the existence of Indian history from about 6000 B.C. only for which signs of its existence could be seen in west and other countries.

The history of India as we read it today, had been written by the experts of Oxford with an object of presenting English as the most advanced of all nations in the world and to put down any culture, civilisation, history lower in position to that of evolution of civilisation of Christianity. In respect of India, they had to show that Indians had been barbaric and uncivilised, as the people in other colonies of Africa, America etc had been and it is they, who have made them civilised to the extent they today are. English Viceroys like William Bentinck etc. had been owning to themselves the responsibility of making Indians civilised and educated. The education, he introduced, made 'Baboos' out of Indians and civilisation imbibed in them is the westerm civilisation, annihilating, from their minds the past and the spiritual, educational, social, and scientific' attainments of people e.g. in ancient time, the ladies were also educated, who were secretaries in Vijayanagar kingdom. Also there were very able women writers etc. in various times but because of the Hindu girls being kidnapped by Muslims during their rule, the ladies were not sent for education as there is no such provision in Islamic concept. So by the time English came (after 600 years of Muslim rule), the 50% population of ladies was illiterate. Also the Muslims had closed all Hindu educational institutes and they could have the knowledge of whatever was taught in Muslim madarsas. English having seen and known the attainments of Hindus in various fields in the past, they created bias in their minds against their past and in favour of the English civilisation. English education, putting on English clothes, living like English was considered as the sign of modernity and those who still lived in Indian style were considered backwards. Even for studying Sanskrit, Hindus had to go to Oxford and Cambridge universities, where they could learn only westernised Sanskrit books so much so that Indians had started thinking that they were capable of nothing compared to English. Even in early twentieth century, the Indian National Congress had been demanding the right of self rule within the British empire and considered the Government of English in India as a must as Indians were not capable of governing the country. English too had been busy in converting Hindus to Christianity so that British could rule India for a long time. Their job, therefore, was to berieve them of the knowledge of their past. That is why a majorty of Hindus would not even be knowing the names of their vedas, shastras etc., what to speak of the knowledge of their contents. The Indian, if any one wanted to study vedas, could do it outside India. Palmerston, Prime Minister of Britain has written: "It is not only our duty but in our interest too that entire India be converted into Christianity". Mangles, Chairman of Board of Directors of East India Company had written - "Providence has entrusted the extensive empire of India to England so that the banner of Christ should wave triumphant from one end of India to the other. Everyone must exert all his strength that there may be no dilatoriness on any account in continuing in the country of the grand work of making all Indians as Christians". Dr. Radhakrishnan has written: "The policy inaugurated by Macaulay, with all its cultural value, is loaded on one side. While it is so careful as not to make us forget the force and vitality of western culture, it has not helped us to love our own culture and refine it where necessary." In some cases Macaulay's wish is fulfilled and we have educated Indians, who are 'more English than the English themselves' to quote his well-known words. Naturally, some of these are not behind the hostile foreign critics in their estimate of history of Indian culture. They look upon India's cultural evolution as one dreary scene of discord, folly and superstition. They are eager to initate the material achievements of western states and tear up the roots of ancient civilisation so as to make room for the novalties imported from the west. One of their number recently declared that if India is to thrive and flourish, England must be her 'spiritual mother' and greece her 'spiritual grand mother'.

This is the exact analysis of Indians' mind at present. The English do not recognise Indian history prior to Buddha or exactly prior to the invasion of Alexander. They do not mention about the grandeur and spiritual attainments of India, as Alexander had seen and admitted but only speak that India, inspite of longer force compared to Alexander, could not win because of the superior manupulating power of Alexander.

But the discovery of Mohenjo Daro and Harappa comprising the development of Indian civilisation even prior to Mahabharat i.e. about 10,000 years before Christ, though not still accepted by europeans as they cannot think of any country having developed 3000 years before Christ as according to Bible, first mankind was created at that time. This is further confirmed by the recent findings of Dwarka from under the sea. The Mahabharat is considered to have taken place about 3200 years B.C. and Krishna ruled upto about 40 years thereafter or about 3100 years B.C.

The western historians have put vedas to have been written 1200 B.C. They cannot take it prior to that as according to them the mankind took place only 4000 B.C. and if there was no mankind prior to 4000 B.C., they cannot accept Indian history having taken place prior to that. But the recent discoveries have belied this thinking and after the invention of radium, the scientists have accepted the start of mankind about two hundred crore years back as carbon radium cannot be converted into radium in lesser time. This is what has been indicated in 'Satyarth Prakash' too and so vedas would have been written crores of years back. The western historians place the time as 1200 years B.C. by Maxmullar; to 4000 years B.C. by Jacobe; whereas Indian historians place it upto 50,000 years (Devendernath Mukhopadhyaya). Tilak has on the basis of the indication of stars, placed the writing of vedas about 8000 B.C. But this too is not so correct as such junction of stars is repeated after 26000 years. Even Tilak has subsequently placed it about 10,000 B.C.

According to Christians, the evolution of mankind started from 6000 B.C. but according to Indian belief it is two arabe years B.C. Aryans knew the movement of stars. They had invented hours, days, weeks, months and years as per calculation of the movements of stars. This is still prevalent in the universe.

After going through the ancient and present languages of the universe, it has been concluded that Italian, French, English,

German, Spanish, Greek, Latin, etc. European languages, Persian, Pashto, Baluchi, Kurd, Arminiian etc. Asian languages, and Hindi, Punjabi, Bangla, Oriya, Assamese, Marathi, Kannad, Telgu, Tamil, Malyalam, Sindhi, Dogri etc. Indian languages have born from one common language as per similarity in the dictionary and various words. It shows that in ancient time, people speaking that one language had spread over to various countries of the world. Bop has written that Greek, Latin and other European languages have risen from same language. His indication was from vedic language. This would indicate that Aryans were the originals with vedic language and all other languages have been introduced by the people, who succeeded Aryans and with the passage of time, different styles in languages have come up. Wilson has in his translation of Vishnu Puran written, "the affinities' of Sanskrit language prove a common origin of the now widely scattered nations amongst whose dialects they are traceable and render it unquestionable that they must have all spread abroad from some central spot in that part of the globe first inhabited by mankind". It is now undisputed that all languages have born out of one language i.e. Sanskrit and the original people too had been living in one place. Now which that particular place is, has to be determined. Allenfriend Trambetti has concluded after deep study of languages that it is India only wherefrom all religions, castes and languages have spread to various areas of the universe.

Till sometime back, no one knew about Sindhu civilisation. This has come to be known after the discovery of Mohenjo Daro, Harappa and Mehargarh. People came to know of Mohenjo Daro only after 1924, on an article published by "Illustrated London News". Subsequent studies revealed that even whatever had been found in Mohenjo Daro is not something the final. Such things would have been evolved after thousands and lacs of years of evolution and the inhabitants of Mohenjo Daro were Aryans as proved by various remnants found there and the story of Aryans having inhabited India 4000 B.C. is proved wrong.

In 1983, Hensen has written that in Nevada, a sole of shoe has been found, which has been reckoned to be fifty lakh years old and the needle with which it has been sewn must be still older or in other words it is proved that needles were available in India so many years before Christ. Harappa civilisation has, therefore, been reckoned to be from prior to vedic era and the mention of iron in vedas would place them at least 50 lac years old. Vedic and Harappa civilisations are one and the same has been proved from the discoveries of Dwarka under the sea.

These things go to prove that—

1. Mohenjo Daro civilisation is at least prior to 5000 B.C.
2. Vedic civilisation was at least 5000 years prior to Mohenjo Daro i.e. 10000 years B.C.
3. According to Babu Sampurnanand, vedas' origin is about 16000 B.C., Mahabharat was about 3000 B.C., and Mohenjo Daro 8000 B.C.
4. Aryans are the original inhabitants of India and then they went to different parts of the universe. This is also confirmed from Bhagwat, according to which Raja Puru had ruled the entire universe. It must be at that time that Aryans from India had gone to various parts of the universe otherwise how could they know of six oceans and seven continents of the universe.
5. Prof. Vishnu Sridhar Wakankar, former Head of the Archaeology Department of Vikram University, Ujjain claimed on 3 August 1985 that he had successfully made a break through in solving the mystery of the writing of the seals found in the Indus valley civilisation of Harappa and Mohenjo Daro. He claimed that the Indus valley script was originial to India and its roots are found in the Aryan civilisation. He challenged foreign claims that the Indus valley civilisation was non-Aryan by stating that recent results were based on computers."

"His survey, when completed, might even drastically change the popular conception among historians that Aryans invaded

India from Central Asia etc. Swami Dayanand Saraswati wrote in 1875 in 'Satyarth Prakash' that no where in Sanskrit literature or history it is written that Aryans had come from Iran and after fighting with the aboriginals of India, settled here. Mayur has agreed with what Dayanand had said. Famous historian Alphinston has also written in 'History of India', vol. I, that neither in the code of Manu, nor in the vedas, nor in any book, which is older than the code of Manu, is there any allusion to the Aryan's prior residence in any country outside India.

About the war of Aryans and Dasyus in vedas, it has been surmised that Dasyus were the originals of India and Aryans, when came from outside, fought with them. This is, however, only spiritual perception as Dasyus were never the original tribes of India. It is rather a term for the people, who were not Aryans. The Aryans were the people, who were literate, content, having control on their senses, and always spoke truth. Any one who was not upto this standard was un-Aryan or Dasyu. Even in Mahabharat, when Arjun refused to fight with his own close relations, Krishna had called him un-Arya. Similarly Dasyu has also been defined as persons, who do not act as per their religion and after proper thinking, who is not truth loving, not mercyful, not non-killer and are very rude.

अकर्मा दस्युरभि नो अमन्तुरन्यव्रतो अमानुषः

(Gita 10-22-8)

Further in Manu Samriti it is written—

मुखबाहूरुपज्जानां या लोके जातयो बहिः
म्लेच्छनाचश्चार्यवाचः सर्वे ते दस्यव स्मृताः ।

i.e. those who do not behave are expelled from Brahmin etc. varnas and are called Dasyus. Therefore, it was the war between noble people and others. In vedas, there is also mention of the war between gods and asuras. Indra and other gods are on one side and asuras like Vritra, Shamber, Namuche, Dhuni, Shushna, etc. on the other side. But then all were not individuals but have been linked with rajas, on whom Indra had invaded, otherwise as per vedas, Indra had neither any enemy in the past nor at present. In fact the asuras mentioned above could check the water flowing on earth and Indra being the raja of rains put them aside and arranged rains. Therefore, the so called asuras were only the bottlenecks in the discharge of duties by gods and gods removed those obstacles which is symbolic of battle between Indra and asuras.

The origin of Aryans had been very much a talking point in the second half of 19th century and early 20th century. The following places have been indicated as the original places of Aryans—

1. Some people say Aryans originally lived in Europe between the Ural mountain and Atlantic ocean and from there, they went to different parts of universe. But it was not generally accepted by people, other than Europeans.
2. Aryans are from central asia (above Iran and in the east of Caspian sea). This was first indicated by J.B. Rhode in 1820. From there they went to other parts. This was accepted by many historians later on. This was based on the fact that there is similarity between vedas and Avesta. Maxmullar and Keith too believe Aryans having come to India from central asia via Hindukush. But this is not confirmed from vedas. Criticising this opinion, Prof. Vadel has indicated that Aryans generally lived on grazing animals and agriculture but the land of central asia is neither fertile nor having sufficient water. Moreover there are no Aryan signs in the modern habitants of that place. Further, there is no mention of this place in vedas, whereas there is praise of Saptsindhu at many places. This place is between Sindh river and Saraswati.
3. North Pole: Balgangadhar Tilak has indicated, based on movement of stars that Aryans originally lived in North Pole and later came to India and other places. They prospered more in India because of the better living conditions of that place. But Tilak had himself later on accepted that he had studied vedas with west's eye and so could not know the reality in vedas. Before death he

accepted his wrong calculation and had written a book dismantling his own concept but that book was never published. He had also accepted in this book that Aryans were originally from India itself.

Eversince we have discovered the Mehargarh, Harappa and Mohenjo Daro excavations, people have started believing this as the original place of Aryans and from here only they went to other parts of India and the universe. This is also evident from the similarity in Sanskrit and ancient Irani languages. This has also been confirmed on the basis of vedas :-

सुदेवो असि वरुण यस्य ते सप्तसिन्धवः
अनुरक्षन्ति काकुद सूर्म्य सुषिरामिवः । (ऋग - 8-69-12)

Sampurnanand has also accepted Saptsindhu as the original place of Aryans. They named it 'Arya-Niwas'. The theory of evolution of mankind also confirms that human beings could initially have been at one place and since in all religions this earth was submerged in water before mankind, the initial inhibitants must have been at an higher altitude but having all facilities of availability of eatables and other living conditions. They would have, therefore, been at a place:

1. Which is highest in the universe.
2. Where there are winter and summer weathers.
3. Where eatables and other necessities are available in plenty.
4. Where there is suitable environ for development.
5. Which is known to all the people.

Himalaya being at the top and fulfilling all the above requirements, must, therefore, have been the initial abode of mankind and subsequently as per theory of evolution of mankind, came to be known as Aryan race. North Pole, Central Asia or even Europe do not stand the test of this principle. The Aryans initially started living in Himalayas or on their foot and subsequently spread to other parts. That is why Haridwar, Rishikesh, Badrinath, Martund (Kashmir) are the places where initial education was imparted to Aryans. Famous archaeologist

Avinash Chandra Dass has written in Rigvedic India, "the original place of Aryans is Kashmir". Taylor has also written "the origin of mankind is Kashmir". Even the mention of northern stars in vedas refer to Kashmir and other himalayan mountain. From Kashmir, the Aryans came down to the valley of Sindh and Saraswati i.e. Saptsindhu and from there down to other places of India. Even 'Devlok', Kailash and other places mentioned in vedas also refer to himalayas. 'Bharat' has been named after Raja Bharat, who ruled entire India. In Manu Samriti Aryavrat has been told as-

आ समुद्रात्तु वै पूर्वादासमुद्रात्तु पश्चिमात्,
तयोरेवान्तरं गिर्योरार्यावर्त्तं विदुर्बुधाः । (मनुस्मृति)

It was from the ocean in the east to the ocean on the west, with Himalaya in north and Vindhyachal in south. In Satyarth Prakash, Dayanand has indicated Aryavrat as from Himalaya to Rameshwaram in south, as this entire area had been the abode of rishis of ancient Aryan civilisation and Vindhyachal has been taken as referring to the present Vindhyachal and east and west coasts combined. The himalayas must have been the present Tibet and from there the Aryans would have come down to Kashmir, and then to Saptsindhu Pradesh and then to other parts of India to have better and better living conditions and with further growth and discoveries, went to other parts of universe, so much so that Raja Prithu of Bhagwat, was the ruler of entire universe comprising of seven continents and six oceans. This kingdom, Raja Prithu subsequently distributed amongst his four sons to be ruled by them.

Even Maxmullar had later on written "We all come from the east - all that we value most has come to us from the east and by going to the east, everybody ought to feel that he is going to his old home, full of memories, if only we can read them—"India, what can it teach us"? French philosopher Cruisu has also written: "If there is a country, which can rightly claim the honour of being the cradle of human race or atleast the scene of primitive civilisation, the successive developments of which carried into all parts of the ancient world, and even beyond, the blessings of knowledge, which is the second life of man, that country assurely is India". William Durant has further stated : "India was the motherland of our race and Sanskrit the mother of European languages; She was the mother of our philosophy; Mother, through the Arabs of much of our mathematics; Mother, through the Buddha, of the ideals embodied in Christianity; Mother, through the village community, of self Government and democracy. Mother India is in many ways the mother of us all."

According to Swami Dayanand Saraswati, Aryans are the originals of Baharat (Aryavrat) descended from Tibet, which was then part of India. Its boundaries, as per 'Satyarth Prakash', were —

आसमुद्रात्तु वै पूर्वादासमुद्रात्तु पश्चिमात,
तयोरेवान्तरं गिर्योरायर्यावर्त्त विदुर्बुधाः।
सरस्वती दृषद्वत्योर्देवन द्योर्यदन्तरम्,
तं देवनिर्मित्तं देशमार्यावर्त्त प्रचक्षते। (मनु. 2-12, 2-17)

Himalaya in the north, Vindhyachal in south (indicating that north India was representative of Bharat at that time) ocean in west and east. Also in the north-west was Saraswati (since dried up) and Attack river and Drishduti (Brahmputra) in north-east, rising from eastern Nepal and joining sea after passing through east of Bengal and Assam and west of Burma. But entire north India and Deccan upto Rameshwaram was Aryarat as it was inhabited by Aryans, right from the beginning of the creation of the universe. As already indicated the people of all the four varnas were Aryan and those outside were Dasyus. All our mythological wars between Devas and Asuras were actually between the Aryans and the Dasyus as the Dasyus always interfered in the way of life of Aryans including the sacrificial yagyas etc.

Vedas: Like the dispute about the origin of Aryans, there is dispute about the origin of vedas. One fact is, however, admitted that vedas are the possessions of Indo Aryans. 'Vedas', primarily means 'knowledge' in general but in Aryans, they denoted their unwritten sacred 'Lore'. These are said to be the oldest scribes of Aryans and found in India only. That would mean that the Aryans had not come from anywhere else but are the originals from India as otherwise if they had brought vedas with them from elsewhere to India, they—

1. Would have been found in other countries - at least in Europe and Africa (Egyptian culture)—of their descendency;
2. Are only in Sanskrit, which is the language of Indus valley only;
3. Prescribe of varnas, ashramas, the gods to be worshipped, which are only in Hindus, who actually were pronounced Aryans earlier;
4. Mention of Ganga, Saraswati, Satlej, Vyas, Jhelum, Chanab, Narmada, Himalaya etc. These rivers and mountains are found in India only;
5. Do not anywhere mention of Aryans having come from somewhere else after invading India;
6. Contain praise of the gods, whose favours Hindus/Aryans tried to derive by prayers, yajnas and sacrifices. These rituals were performed by the Aryans in the times of Satya yug and Treta yug—also in Ramayan, Ram was born by performing yagya and the rajas, by yagyas and sacrifices, could bring rains in times of need; the ailments were kept at bay; no early deaths etc. were there, it is said that all this could happen only if the rajas performed proper yagyas, sacrifices etc. as prescribed in vedas. Also in Ram's time vedas had come to pay their respects to Ram, when he was coronated. Ram-rajya had taken place thousands or perhaps, lacs of years back, when vedas too were there and so the Aryans were there too many thousands of years B.C. Unfortunately, however, no documentation is available to affirm this conviction as also since the vedas had always passed by learning by heart and were not brought out in black and white, having been considered to have come

into existence by voice of God, which could not be narrated, we take the period of their existence only from a thousand years or so B.C., since when the written scripts are available but taking into account their existence in Ram period, they admittedly are from older period.

7. Indian culture had developed in ancient times, when the other countries still lacked such development. If Aryans had come to India from some other place, then Aryans in other countries too would have developed in similar way but there is no similarity rather no simultaneous development appears in other countries. This shows that Aryans were originally from India and they only spread their culture to other countries later.
8. Similarly, if Indian Aryans had written vedas and other samritis etc. then why the Aryans, who had gone to other countries or from where they had come did not write any such granthas.
9. It is, therefore, Indians, who had gone to other countries or to Central Asia and from there to other countries as is quite evident from Harappan civilisation now. The Harappan civilisation appears to be the oldest one now and no such development in ancient time is evidenced anywhere else.
10. Vedas mention of Brahma, varnas, ashramas institutions etc., which had happened in India only and no where else. The way of kingdom and the governance narrated in vedas was also in existence in India only. Therefore, vedas and Indian culture are many thousand years old and such a culture had started and evolved in India only.
11. Even in mythological granthas, the queen has been seen addressing their husbands as 'Aryaputra' indicating that they were from Aryan clan since the days of Ramayan and Mahabharat.
12. Fahien and Hiuen Tsang have written in third and sixth centuries A.D. that the people in Central Asia and to the West were all barbarians and only the monks knew the Indian languages and way of life.

From the fact that vedas in their present form being only collection of existing songs, prayers and spells, it follows that no particular veda could as a whole be regarded as of earlier date than the other. Portions of Rig Ved are, however, considered among the earliest. Sam Ved is practically a song book of the priests and contains for the most part hymns of Rig Ved subject to certain musical changes rendering them fit for chanting. The Yajur Ved contains for the most part, the verses to be recited at sacrifices, as well as a number of formulas and phrases explaining the nature and object of various rituals and ceremonies. It, therefore, evidently belong to a period when the priests had gained an ascendency over the other classes that is the varnas had come into existence. The Atharva Ved mainly consists of prayers and formulas and magics for the treatments of diseases etc. These formulas and magics are infact nothing but the treatment of all diseases by yogas and medicines, which hold good even today and are considered in some respects more effective than the allopathic or other sciences of medication.

Yajur Ved also prescribes Dev Pooja and donation. In their yagyas, the gods are pleased and the desired results are requested for. In other words by yagyas etc, some treatment was available or some commodities could be obtained by yagyas or by the mechanical process etc. Sacrifice was performed and the gods being happy gave the desired results. This too could be the attainment of some desired things by sacrifice or might be some surgical operation of transplant of organs from one being to an other or by processing certain treatment through fire etc. Similarly, there is mention of Aswamedha yagya to establish the suzerainty of the emperor over his vassal kingdoms. This would indicate emperors in ancient periods had large tracts of kingdom, which included many vassal states. The vassal states were autonomous within themselves but paid some annual tribute to the king emperors. Concept of such vassal states is in existence even in modern times. Further, by performing various yagyas, the kings could have rains, resulting in increased agricultural products, and cleansing the environ as a result of which many ailments could be avoided. By purification of soul, many heart diseases could be cured. Since the king was responsible to provide a carefree and peaceful life to the public, the public was free from all tensions and allied ailments etc. Yajur Ved also provides for the protection of the subjects. The people pray to God or king that one, who is protector should not allow his being annihilated.

Likewise Atharva Ved also provides for—

1. Redress of ailments ;
2. Prevention from early death;
3. Duties of the wife and the husband;
4. Duties of the king;
5 Duties of the public;
6. Conduct of the people etc.

As per vedas, the unit of the state was the family at the head of which stood the father as lord of the house. Descent was reckoned in the male line. The theory of primogenitor existed in succession as the head of the family or the kingdom. Women were having an honourable place in the household and some of the prettiest songs in Rig Ved are those welcoming the newly wedded bride into the family. The government of the vedic era was an imitation of the Aryan household. The king was the leader in the war and his position was hereditory. Sometimes he was elected too when there was none capable in the hereditary system followed by the principle of primogenitor.

By evolution of the society in primitive days, there arose three classes—the warriors (kshatriya), the priests (brahmin) and the body of herdsmen and traders and agriculturists (vaishas). The rest, who could not be accomplished in any of the above vocations, remained shudras and those who did not adopt shudras, were categorised as dasyus. As already indicated, the kings were made by the samitis or sabhas from out of the lineage of the royalty. When no such person was available in the dynasty, then another person from the royal family was made king. When no family member too was found fit, one from amongst the nobles was elevated as king. The kings were not autocrats in Hindu regime. There were many checks on the authority of the king—

1. Hindu kings were not despots and there were checks on their authority. The Samiti acted as a check on the powers of the king. The king could not go against the advice of the Samiti and if he chose not to agree to the same, he had to give reasons for the same.
2. There was another check by Ratnins, the ministers in charge of various departments in the kingdom. The king was expected to go to their places and make offerings to them, obviously to win over their loyalty and devotion.
3. Religious and spiritual sanctions did not allow the king to act as a tyrant; there was a threat of punishment by god if the king did not behave/act properly.
4. At the time of coronation, the king was required to take an oath to act according to laws and customs of the country and was expected to work as per the vow and in case of failure, there was opposition to his governance.
5. People could threaten to migrate from his territory if the king insisted on ruling arbitrarily.
6. If the threat of migration did not work, the people had the right to kill their king. For instance Raja Bain claimed divinity for himself. He was killed by the sages. Same was the case with Nimi, Sudersa, Nahusa, Sumukhe, and others.
7. People had a right to dethrone a wicked and a tyrannical king. There are examples of this type. This was possible as the military strength of the king was not greater than that of the people.
8. There was decentralisation of administration to a great extent, even though there was unitary form of government. In the sense that the major portion of the people lived in the villages and for their governance, the king had to act

through village panchayats and town councils and district councils. Even if the king issued arbitrary orders, the people did not suffer as the local authorities could refuse to enforce them.

9. Hermits and recluses exercised influence on the king in ancient times. They were famous for thier nobility of character and impartial thinking. Even the kings respected them. Narada advised Ram and Krishna in case of difficulties. Ajatshatru was advised by Buddha. Viswamitra was another such sadhu.
10. Another check was by learned brahmins, who were famous for simple living and high thinking. They were also called Raj-Gurus like Vashista, Vamdeva etc.
11. Public opinion also put a check on the powers of the king and he could not afford to go against the same. Ram left Sita because of the adverse public opinion for having retained her inspite of her having lived in Lanka for a long period.

The constitution of the government in those days comprised of—

1. The raja, or the king or emperor
2. The samiti and the sabha
3. Janpadas
4. Ministers (about ten)
5. Purohit/Raj Guru
6. Pratitnidhi (upraja) who acted in place of raja when he was ill or absent etc.
7. Pradhan/Prime Minister for superintendence of administration
8. Sachiv - War Minister or Senapati.
9. Mantri (Foreign Minister)
10. Pradvivaka - Incharge of judicial department.
11. Pandita - An authority on dharma shastras.

12. Sumantra - Treasurer incharge of total collection of revenue and expenditure. Also known as Samaharta or Bhandagrika.
13. Amatya - Revenue Minister, responsible for collection of tax on products.
14. Duta - He was used for inter-course between various rajas.

Republics in Ancient India: There were also republican form of governments, particularly during Buddhist regime. They were called sangha or gana. The authority was elected by the people. Even at the time of Alexander, large number of republics existed.

Condition of India from 6th to 4th century B.C.: Such information can be found scattered in Buddhist and Jain literature otherwise no separate historical record is available probably having been destroyed by various Muslim rulers.

Political Condition: When Buddha appeared, there was no paramount power in India. India was a congeries of states, whose rulers and heads had been fighting amongst themselves for supremacy. There were not only monarchies but also republics. These were Kasi, Kosala, Anga, Magadha, Vajji, Malla, Chedi, Vamsa, Kuru, Panchala, Machchha (Matsya), Saursena, Assaka, Avanti, Gandhara, and Kamboja.

Kashi: It was around Benaras. There had been fighting between Kashi and Kosala and ultimately it had been merged with Kosala.

Kosala: Modern Avadh in Uttar Pradesh with capital Saraswasti. There were quarrels between Kosala and Magadha rulers and ultimately Kosala was merged with Magadha.

Anga: Present district of Bhagalpur with capital at Champa. It was annexed with Magadha at the time of Bimbsara.

Magadha: Correspond to the present Patna and Gaya, with capital at Rajgriha. It came into prominence during the reign of Bimbsara and Ajat Shatru. It became so powerful that one by one all neighbouring states had been merged into it.

Vajji: With capital Mithila, it was on the ruins of Janak's kingdom. It came up as Republic of Lachchhavi.

Malla: It had two divisions with capital at Pawa and Kusinara, presently near Gorakhpur. Mallas were great admirers of Buddha.

Chedi: It correspondes to modern Bundelkhand.

Vamsa (Vatsa): It had a monarchichal form of government, with capital at Kausambi near Allahabad. Udayan was the ruler in 6th century B.C. He was a very powerful king.

Kuru: Correspondes to modern Delhi and Meerut divisions. It was the ruling place of Pandavas.

Panchala: It was Rohilkhand division with important cities of Kampilla, Kamany etc.

Machchha (Matsya): Corresponding to the modern Jaipur.

Saurasena: With capital Mathura, it was in the south of Matsya Desh.

Assaka: It was in the neighbourhood of Avanti on the bank of river Gomati.

Avanti: Roughly corresponds to Malwa with capital at Ujjain. Avanti became a very important centre of Buddhism.

Gandhara: Roughly corresponds to modern Kashmir and Taxila with capital at Taxila and was famous for learning.

Kamboja: It was in extreme west with Dwarka as capital.

Annexations: Vedic tenets provide for autonomous/ independent states. A king used to attack on another to take wealth and presents and then return the kingdom to the defeated king to rule as a vassal state. So far as such a vassal state continued to accept suzerainty of the king/emperor, he was not disturbed and rather had the protection of the suzerain king. After vedic period, however, during the ancient Indian time, when there were many small states, there was a continuous aggression by mightier kingdom, particularly the rise of powerful kingdoms created the problem for the smaller states—might be it was the effect of Alexander's invasion which gave rise to a powerful kingdom of Chandra Gupta Maurya. Till then small vassal states were in existence and were not generally annexed but left to be ruled after parting with some wealth.

Governance: It was not possible for the king to govern single handed. A large number of officers and mahamatras were, therefore, engaged like senanayak, vyvaharikas, etc.

Justice: King was considered as the fountain of justice and it was his duty to administer the same. There were different grades of courts and the king himself held the highest court.

Army: It was the duty of the king to protect the people from internal criminals and external aggressions. He, therefore, maintained strong army comprising of elephants, cavalery, chariots, and on foot. Weapons used were bows and arrows, spears, swords etc.

Source of Revenue: A lot of revenue was required to meet the expenses of royal household, civil administration and army. Most important source of income was land revenue called 'Rajbhag'. Money also came in the form of tax on trade and from vassal states as tribute.

Economic Condition: Most of the people lived in villages and agriculture was the main occupation. Number of people in a village was 30 to 1000 families. Share of king as land revenue was 1/6th to 1/12th of the produce. Village was a sole administrative unit, with panchayat chaired by Gram Bhojaka. The panchayat consisted of Gramvaridshas.

Social Condition: Society was divided into castes—brahmin, kshatriya, vaish and shudra as per Manu Samriti and people of each varna acted as per their respective dharma. The varna/caste was not by birth but by option as per one's capability in the vedic era but subsequently in ancient post vedic period, people adopted the caste of the birth only. Precise rules in regard to their marriage, food, mutual relationship between castes etc. were laid down.

Education: The art of writing was known but there was preference for oral instruction of teaching rather than through books as many books could not be made out. Taxila, Kashi,

Nalanda etc. were the seats of learning, where people from other countries used to come for education and admission was through tough competition. For local people, local gurukuls existed either by state or the village communities, where initial education was imparted. For higher learning, one had to go to Taxila, Kanshi etc.

Religion: In this period, Brahmnical way of life of Hinduism got a set back with the advent of Buddhism and Jainism and after Buddhism had become the religion of the king too. Still brahmnical religion was practised by many people.

Geographical Environ: India, encircled as it is by seas and mountains, is indisputably a geographical unit and as such, is rightly designated by one name 'Bharat'.Its type of civilisation too has many features, which differentiates it from that of all other regions of the world. While they are common to the whole country or rather such continent in a degree sufficient to justify its being treated as a unit in the country of the social, religion and intellectual development of mankind.

Twice in the long series of centuries of Hindu rule dealt with in the history, the political unity of entire India was nearly complete—first in the 3rd century B.C. when Ashoka's empire extended almost to the latitude of Madurai and again in 4th century A.D. when Samudragupta carried his victorious arm from Ganges to the border of Tamil country; others only could be paramount powers when there have been distinctly separate nations of north and south. The ancient kingdoms of the far south, although rich and populous, inhabited by Dravidian nations, not inferior in culture to the Aryan rivals in the north, were ordinarly so secluded from the rest of the civilised world, including north India, that their kingdoms remained hidden from the eyes of the other nations and analysts; their history previous to the year 800 A.D. has almost wholly perished. In a way India, south of Vindhyas, the Peninsula India, still continue distinctly to retain their pre-Aryan features, pre-Aryan languages, and pre-Aryan social institutions.

Dynasties Before Alexander: The political history of India begins from an orthodox Hindu more than about 6000 years before Christian era the reign of Ram and subsequently the war on the banks of Yamuna between the sons of Kuru and sons of Pandu as related in the vast epic known as Mahabharat in about 3000 years B.C. But in order to be available for the purpose of history, events must be susceptible of arrangement in definite chronological order and capable of being dated approximately, if not exactly. Facts to which dates cannot be assigned, although they may be invaluable for the purpose of ethology, philology and other sciences are of no use to the historians.

Modern research has brought to light innumerable facts of the highest scientific value concerning pre-historic India, but the impossibility of assigning dates to the phenomena discovered, excludes them from the domain of historians, whose vision cannot pass the line, which separates the dated from the undated. That line in the case of India can be drawn at the earliest through the middle of 7th century B.C. Upto about that time the inhabitants of India were the most intellectual races, but had been generally against bringing things to writing and to have been obliged to trust to simply trained memory for the transmission of knowledge. That is why the vedas, which are lacs of years old, but passed by memory from one person to another, could be brought to writing only about 1000 years before Christ because the people believed more in remembering by heart rather than bringing the same to writing and still a lot had been put to writing too, which had been destroyed by Mohammedan invaders in 11th and 12th centuries A.D. One slender stock of knowledge is limited to the fortunes of the vigorous races speaking an Aryan tongue, who are said to have poured down from the mountains of Hindukush and Pamirs, filling the plains of Punjab and the upper basin of Ganga, with a sturdy and quick witted population, unquestionably superior to the aboriginal races of those regions. The settled country between Himalayas and Narbada river was divided into a multitude of independent states, monarchis, some tribal republics owing no allegiance to any paramount power, secluded from the outer world and free to fight amongst themselves. Such a thinking of the western historians does not stand any test of time if seen from Indian point of view according to which although there were small independent states in India in ancient time as per the tenets of the vedas, yet they were the originals of Indian sub-continent. The difference between northern and southern Indian tribes has been because of the non-accessibility from Northern part to Southern part and vice versa because of Vindhyachal and other large rivers.

But the works of ancient Indian writers from which the present historical data are extracted do not ordinarily progress to be histories and are mostly religious treatises of various kinds. In such composition, the religious elements necessarily take the foremost places, and the secular attire of the world occupy a very subordinate position. In the pauranic list of earliest dynasties, which can claim historical reality is that known as Sai Sunga from the name of its founder Siyunaga or Sisunaka. He was apparently the king of a petty state corresponding roughly to the present Patna and Gaya districts, his capital being Rajgriha amongst the hills near Gaya. Nothing is known about his history too except the statement that he placed his son in Benaras (642B.C.) and himself took up his abode at Girivraj near Rajagriha. The second, third and fourth kings are like-wise mere names. The first monarch about whom anything is known is Bimbsara (582 B.C.) the fifth of his line credited with having built new Rajagriha. He may, therefore, be regarded as the founder of the Magadh imperial period. He strengthened his position by matrimonial alliances with the more powerful kings of neighbouring states taking one consort from the royal family of Kosala and another from the influential Lachchhavi clan at Vaishali. The later lady was the mother of Ajat Shatru, also called Kunika or Kuniya, whose son was selected as heir apparent and crown prince.

Mahavir and Gautam, the founders of Jainisim and Buddhism were preaching in Magadh during the region of Bimbsar although it is difficult to reconcile the traditional dates. Buddha died in the reign of Ajat Shatru. Ajat Shatru died in 527 B.C. He was succeeded by Darsaka, who in turn was succeeded by Udaya. The reign of Udaya may be assumed to have begun about 503 B.C. The tradition that he built Patliputra or more accurately the adjoining town of Kusumapura is all that is known about him. Udaya may be regarded as contemporary of Darius, the son of Hystaspes, autocrat of Persian empire - 521-485 B.C. Darius had put his officers in exploration of a greater part of Asia by means of expeditions. The conquered provinces in India were formed into a separate Satraps, which was considered to be the richest and most populous province of the empire. This would be around Indus valley.

4 Ancient Period

MAURYAS (325-232 B.C.)

Chandra Gupta Maurya (325-298 B.C.)

By putting the available limits together, we may conclude with tolerable certainty that the Nanda family of Magadh was the real base origin as legitimate king and retained possession of throne for two generations only. The accession to the throne of Magadh may be dated between 325-320 B.C. The kingdom comprised of Kosala, Tirhut, north Bihar and Benaras as well as Anga and Magadha proper or south Bihar. The departure of Alexander from India gave young Chandra Gupta an opportunity. He destroyed most of the Macedonian garrisons after the destruction of Nand royal family of Magadh.

Alexander proceeded to reach India, not through Khyber Pass but alongside Kabul river in 327 B.C. Most of the tribal chiefs on way preferred submission. One, Hasti, did not accept submission. So he was destroyed. The king of Taxila (Raja Ambi) too submitted against Porus. Unfortunately for India, the Indian rulers did not unite on foreign aggression. Rather they took advantage of such invasion and enjoyed subjugation of other Indian rival rulers. Similarly Raja Ambi helped Alexander in attack on Raja Porus. Alexander spent two days in careful personal reconnaisance of the position with the aid of small force assisted by local guides, whose services he had secured by subjugation. Spring had begun and the time being favourable, the refreshed army began the passage of the river at day break, on omans being favourable, with the help of the king of Taxila, effected entrance on the soil of India, which no european traveller or invader had ever before trodden. Raja Ambi recognised Alexander as his lord and provided the Macedonian army with liberal supplies and presented Alexander heavily. This is un-Aryan action. While Alexander was at Taxila, the hill chieftain of Abhisara, who really intended to join Porus to expel the invader, professed surrender to Alexander. On this, Alexander expected Porus to surrender too but he received a proud answer that he would come to meet the invader at the head of army for battle. Inspite of most elaborate preparations, the problem of passage of Jhelum river in the face of superier force of Porus could not be solved without minute local knowledge and unless Alexander had acquired the necessary acquaintance with all local conditions, he deferred decision. The cavalry could not be induced to clamber up the bank of flooded river in face of host of elephants and he sought some device to evade this difficulty. He left a division there, so that the enemy could think of army being there, and with balance army went upstream ten miles and crossing Jhelum from there, took the Porus army by surprise. It was lack of spying on the part of Porus, which failed him. In order to escape observation, Alexander marched by night and this movement was further concealed by a violent storm of rain and thunder, which broke during march. Then the chief reliance of Porus was on the 20,000 monster elephants, who would, it was calculated, terrify the foreign soldiers and render the dreaded cavalry unmanageable. Behind the elephants stood 30,000 infantry. But, contrary to calculation, the elephants having been injured by arrows, became amock and crushed Porus's army. Further, Indian horsemen were far inferior to Alexander's men. Porus was defeated and arrested. Alexander had the magnanimity to respect his gallant adversary and willingly responded to his proud request to be 'treated as a king'. The victor not only returned his territory but also added to it other lands of still greater extent and thus secured for the brief period of his stay in the country, a grateful and faithful friend. Porus, however, had shown the real Bhartiyata to Alexander and the world.

Alexander proceeded further and 37 towns and a multitude of villages readily submitted and were added to the territory of Porus. Alexander crossed Ravi river and all chiefs on way submitted. He came to Beas and proposed to subdue the nation beyond but Koinos, his general, remarked thus :

"Moderation in the midst of success, O'king ! is the noblest of virtues, for although, being at the head of so brave an army, you have naught to dread from mortal foes, yet the visitation of the deity cannot be foreseen or grudged against by the man."

Alexander was convinced that further advancement was impracticable and gave orders to retreat in 326 BC.

On his return back, he fought gallantly with many chieftains, including Satrap, and entrusted to the king of Abhisara. He managed reconciliation between Taxila and Porus and was cemented by marriage alliance. On way he also subjugated the tribal chief called Siboi and Agalassoi (near Jhang). The rival nations cemented the alliance by wholesale intermarriage, each giving and taking ten thousand young women for wives.

On the way Alexander was injured by falling of a wall and barbed arrow infested in him. It involved a bold operation, which Alexander triumphed and wound was healed. Malloi also submitted but the powerful monarch called Mousikonos, abstained from sending envoy or presents meaning non-submission and revolted. Mousikonos was captured and executed. All others on way subjugated.

"So much were the minds of all Indians paralysed with abject terror by Alexander and success of his arms, "that each one surrendered without resistance. At lower Indus, Brahmins, who had instigated against Alexander were executed (80,000) and multitudes sold as slaves."

While the army was in Karmania, a report was received that Philipos, Satrap of Indian provinces, had been murdered by mercenary troops. Alexander was then not in a position to make permanent arrangements and directed Ambi raja, commandment of Thracian contingent on the upper Indus to assume administration of the province. The death of Alexander in Babylon in following year (June 323 B.C.) prevented any attempt being made to retain effective control on the conquered countries east of Indus. Porus and Ambi were recognised independent kings.

When Alexander quitted Punjab, he did not post any Mecadonian garrison in that province making over the care of his interests to king Porus, who was independent in practice. Ambi too was independent as already indicated. Subsequently at the time of second partition of Macedonian empire in 321 B.C., Greeks could not exercise any effective control over Indian kings, who became independent. It is at that time that Chandra Gupta Maurya, of 25 years, appeared at the scene. His mother's name was 'Mura' from which the Maurya dynasty came in. Mahapada Nanda, was a barber and had secured the affection of queen. The two had murdered the king and Nand became the king. Chandra Gupta had been put in exile. During that period, he met Chanakya and after raising some force, attacked Greek's Garrison in Panjab under the guidance of Chanakya, and became king of Punjab and Sindh. He had already become the king of Magadh. He raised a large army and conquered entire Macedonian territory. Seleucus too surrendered and married his daughter to Chandra Gupta. He added Herat, Kabul, Bactria etc. He was, thus, the first Indian emperor, more than 2000 years ago, who entered into possession of that scientific frontier, sighed for in vain even by English successors and never held even by the Moghal monarch of 17th century. Chandra Gupta died in 298 B.C. and his son Bindusar became the king emperor. He used to show his subjects at least once a day and received petitions and decided disputes in person. The king's life was so constantly threatened by plots that he did not incur the risk either of sleeping in the day time or occupy the same bedroom for two nights in succession. Chanakya wrote :

The bravemen who were concealed
In the subterrene avenue that bed
To Chandra Gupta's sleeping chamber- thence
To steal by night and kill him as he slept.

Army was in numerical strength. It was not a militia but a standing army, drawing liberal and regular pay and supplied by the government with horses, arms, equipment and store. Their number was 30,000 horses, 9,000 elephants, 6,00,000 infantry besides chariots, all permanently enrolled in a regularly paid establishment. The above four – elephants, horses, chariots and infantry – were traditional but Chandra Gupta added coordinate supply and admiral departments, besides the management of birth and deaths registration. So the new additions by Chandra Gupta were—

1. Admiral and Supplies Department
2. C.I.D. Department
3. Irrigation Department

There was general honesty in the people and there was efficient administration of the criminal law. In Chandra Gupta's camp of 4,00,000 persons, the total of thefts reported in any one day did not exceed 200 drachmai or about 8 pounds sterling. Crime was repressed with terrible severity, ordinary wounding by mutilation of the offender, in addition to the amputation of his hand. If he happened to be in the royal service, then death was the punishment.

The review of civil and military system of government during the reign of Chandra Gupta proves clearly that northern India in the time of Alexander the great, had attained a high degree of civilisation, which must have been the product of evolution continued through thousands of years but unfortunately no monuments have been discovered, which can be referred to with certainty to the pre-Chandra Gupta period. Permanent peace with neighbouring states was regarded as unattainable. We are instructed that—

1. Whoever was superior in power shall wage war.
2. Whoever was rising in power would break the agreement of peace.

3. The king who was situated anywhere on the circumference of the conqueror's territory, was termed the enemy.
4. When a king of equal power did not like peace, then the same amount of vexation as his opponent had received at his hands, should be given to him in return, for it was power that brought about peace between any two kings; no piece of iron that is not made red hot will combine with another piece of iron.
5. Might was right. Nò prince pretented to trust any other ruler for a moment to keap faith if he felt strong enough to break the pact.
6. No considerations of morality were allowed to influence statecraft, which avowedly preferred the use of insidious and treacherous means, including every form of secret assassination.
7. The maxim that the 'vices of ordinary people are virtues in kings' was plainly enunciated and was constantly acted upon.
8. Skill in intrigue was a better qualification for kingship than either power or enthusiasm.
9. The government relied on highly organised system of espionage, pervading every department of the administration and every class of the population.
10. The king lived in continual terror of the members of his family for on account of the kingdom, the father hated his sons and sons hated the father. Jahangir long afterwards expressed the same sentiment in the maxim that, "Kingship regards neither sons nor sons-in-law; no one is a relation to a king."
11. The princes like crabs have a notorious tendency towards eating up their begetters.
12. The king shall attend personally to the business of gods, of heretics, of brahmins learned in vedas, of cattle (cows), of sacred places, of minors and the aged, of the afflicted and the helpless and of woman according to urgency or

pressure of work. Also all urgent calls, he shall hear at once but never put off.

13. The king was assisted by a Privy Council (12 to 16 members).
14. There were 18 departments of administration with chief officials—pay ranged from 48,000 silver panas a year to 60 panas for a labourer (about 9.46 grams).
15. Land tax was main source of revenue but in fortified towns the royal revenue was derived from taxes on sales. Commodities were not sold at the place of growth or manufacture but in the toll houses near the town gate.
16. The penal code was ferociously severe. The theft by a government servant to the value of 8 to 10 panas was punishable with death and so for a non-official for 40 to 50 panas.
17. Judicial torture for the purpose of extorting a confession was recognised and freely used.
18. Large number of republics in Punjab, U.P., and Bihar continued to exist under provincial Governors of Mauryas.
19. Monarchy was prevailing form of government. Chanakya was the greatest exponent of a monarchical form of government. King was the central pivot of all matters. Theory of primogenitor was generally adopted in the succession to throne.
20. The king, who was trained in governance and administration showed untiring energy in the disposal of official business and that was the secret of success of Maurya administration.
21. Army and treasury were under the direct control of the king.
22. Although king was guided by the council of ministers, he could ignore such advice in public interest.
23. The king followed the advice of Arthshastra and regarded the welfare and interest of subjects more important than his own interest. He treated the subjects as his own children.

24. The kings could not become autocrats on account of existence of checks and balances. There was the mantri parishad and two popular assemblies to which the king was responsible.
25. The king generally followed the advice of the Raj Guru (Chanakya).
26. There were Janapadas, the assemblies of people of the towns and country for the governance of towns and villages.
27. The kingdom was distributed in provinces like Taxila, Ujjain, Tosali, Suvarnagri etc. The governors were mostly the sons of the emperor. The provincial government was required to maintain their own law and order; they were quite autonomous and independent to deal with local affairs; collected taxes for the central government and reported the situation to central government.
28. Below the provinces there were district administrations under Sthanikas and Gopas.
29. There were village administrators and town administrators.
30. Construction of roads and irrigation works was the responsibility of the state.
31. Public health and sanitation were under the care of state for human beings, animals and birds, free of cost.
32. Impartial justice was granted. King was the fountain head of justice but law was held superior to him even. There were civil courts for contracts, agreements, gifts, sales, marriages, inheritance and criminal courts decided cases of thefts, robbery, murders etc. In the capital there was Supreme Court.
33. Ashoka had created the post of Dharma Mahamatras too.
34. During Maurya period, the social structure crystalised and rigidity of caste system became a permanent feature. Buddhism, however, could not keep in check the superior position of brahmins and they continued to play a leading role in society and polity of that age.

Magasthanese states that Indian society was divided into seven classes viz. philosophers, farmers, soldiers, herdsmen, artisans, magistrates, and councillors, although this classification is more economic than social. But there was rigidity in this classification as the soldier could neither become a farmer nor a philosopher or an artisan and vice versa. Chanakya in Arthshastra has referred to 15 such divisions. Magasthanese says that all Indians were free and no one of them was slave.

The marriage of widow outside the family of her in-laws was not unheard of. Divorce was permitted by mutual consent in certain circumstances but the marriage performed in accordance with the established social custom was considered respectable and was not to be dissolved. The above is the concept of governance by vedic/Bhartiya system and worked well till it was applied and whenever there was failure in its adaptability, the country was loser. The tenets of Arthshastra, derived from vedas are the universal principles of governance even today and all through the ages, unbeaten by any philosopher of past and present times.

Ashoka (272-232 B.C.)

As already indicated, not much information is available for the period prior to Mauryas. It is during the period of Chandra Gupta that Magasthanese, a representative of Seleucus (Greek ruler left by Alexander) was left at Maurya court and who has written about that period besides Arthshastra of Chanakya. But the largest information is obtained from the inscriptions by Ashoka in India and abroad. In Maurya period, there was Brahmnical, Buddhism and Jainism. Then India was in a state of firment about the beginning of last quarter of 4th century B.C. In Magadh, Nanda dynasty was brahmanical. Initially Chandra Gupta as also Ashoka were Brahmanical. After Bindusar, Ashoka succeeded in 273 B.C. He is said to have slewn his 99 brothers before he could succeed. This, however, seems untrue as some of Ashoka's brothers had gone abroad for spreading Buddhism. For 13 years, he carried on the

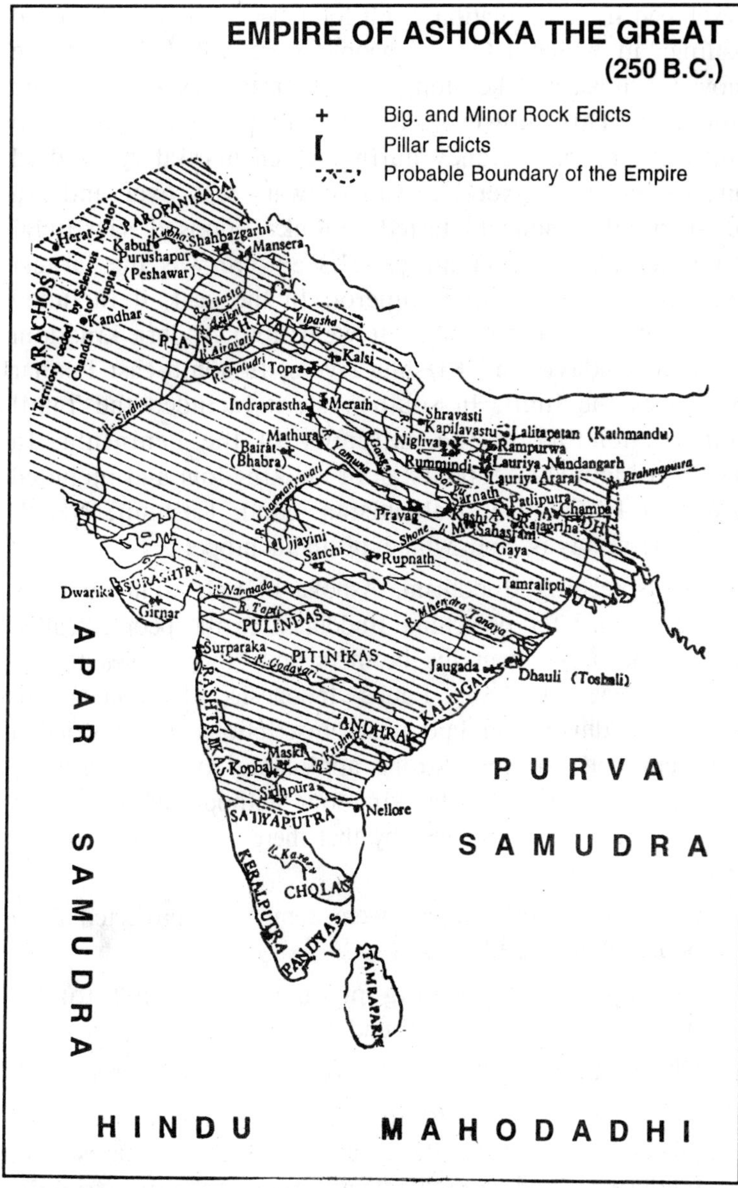
EMPIRE OF ASHOKA THE GREAT
(250 B.C.)
Big. and Minor Rock Edicts
Pillar Edicts
Probable Boundary of the Empire
PAROPANISADAI
ARACHOSIA
Territory ceded by Seleucus Nicator to Chandra Gupta
Herat
Kabul
Shahbazgarhi
Mansera
Purushapur
(Peshawar)
Kandhar
PANCHNAD
Vipasha
Topra
Kalsi
Indraprastha
Merath
Shravasti
Kapilavastu
Lalitapatan (Kathmandu)
Niglivan
Rampurwa
Mathura
Bairat
(Bhabra)
Rummindi
Lauriya Nandangarh
Lauriya Araraj
Brahmaputra
Sarnath
Patliputra
Champa
Prayag
Kashi
Rajagriha
Sahasram
Gaya
Ujjayini
Sanchi
Rupnath
Tamralipti
Dwarika
SURASHTRA
Girnar
PULINDAS
Surparaka
PITINIKAS
Jaugada
Dhauli (Toshali)
KALINGA
ANDHRA
RASHTRIKAS
Maski
Kopbal
Sidhpura
SATIYAPUTRA
Nellore
KERALPUTRA
CHOLAS
PANDYAS
TAMRAPARNI
APAR SAMUDRA
PURVA SAMUDRA
HINDU MAHODADHI

traditional policy of expansion of his territory in India and developed friendly relations with foreigners. Ashoka conquered Kalinga in which lakhs of people were killed. This battle moved Ashoka and he stopped further battles and became Buddhist. This, however, resulted in political stagnation and military inefficiency during which martial spirit died out for want of exercise. Era of wars was over and era of spiritual conquest started. Ashoka opposed sacrificial slaughter of living creatures. His empire was the largest ever had by any Indian emperor. In the east, it included whole of Bengal. In south, it went upto Andhra kingdom between Godavri and Krishna rivers. In south-east Pennar river was the limit. In south-west, it included the Tamil states extending to the extremity of the Peninsula. In north, it included Afghanistan in his kingdom and included south of Hindukush, Baluchistan, Sind, Kashmir, Nepal, lower Himalayas and whole of India proper.

For spreading Buddhism, Ashoka himself went on tours of the country for preaching Buddhism to the people, called dharmavijaya. He sent his brothers and other nobles too to different places in India, Lanka, Indonesia, Malaysia etc. to preach Buddhism and laid many inscriptions. He notified a stringent code of regulations applicable to all classes of population throughout the kingdom without distinction of caste or creed: meaning thereby that there was equality before law:

1. Many species of animals were completely protected from being slaughtered.
2. Slaying for flesh-eating population was not totally prohibited but hedged round by severe restrictions.
3. On 56 specified days in the year, killing was prohibited.
4. He made obligatory the reverence to parents, elders and preceptors, servants, slaves and all living creatures with tenderness and consideration. Also brahmins, friends, acquaintances and teachers had to be respected.

5. There had to be complete truthfulness.
6. One was to be tolerant and sympathetic to the beliefs and practices of others. In this way there was complete secularism.
7. Remembering all forms of religions alike as were aimed at the attainment of self control and purity of mind.
8. Alms-giving was commended for the deserving ones.
9. All officers of the state like Lieutenant Governors, Commissioners and District Magistrates were commanded to make use of the opportunities during their periodical tours for convoking assemblies of the Lieges and instructing them the whole duty of man. Certain days in a year were particularly set aside for such duty.
10. The system must have led to much espionage and tyranny and the punishment inflicted for breach of the imperial regulations had been terribly severe.
11. When a king died, he was succeeded by his eldest son and the other sons leaving the family entered a religious life and no longer allowed to reside in their native kingdom. Ashoka's brothers and sons worked as monks—Mahendra had gone to Lanka.

No Indian kings have had such an exalted sense of duty as Ashoka had and he apparently was still not satisfied with his unselfish devotion to the cause of his people. He says in one of the edicts:

"I am never fully satisfied with my exertions and my dispatch of business. Work I must, for the public benefit and the root of the matter is in exertion and despatch of business than which nothing is more efficacious for the general welfare. And for what do I toil? For no other end than this, that I may discharge my debt to animate beings and that while I make some happy in this world, they may in the next, gain heaven".

Ashoka's work did not stop with good intentions. From his capital at Patliputra, he struck at oppression wherever found it necessary and saw that his commands were enforced in the remotest parts of his dominion. As the poorest of his subjects were not beneath the king's notice, so the highest officials in the state and even the members of the royal family were not safe from his censure and from punishment where they went wrong. He was able to keep peace with his extensive and diversified empire for nearly half a century. He safeguarded his frontiers from violation during his long reign without once drawing the sword to protect them. By liberal treatment of the backward races subject to his rule, he ensured their loyalty and restrained their turbalance. With unlimited powers at his disposal and placed when still young at the head of an immense military force, he entered with reluctance upon the only war of his reign and after victory had the wisdom and moderation to sheath his sword and devote his life to the victories of peace. Such work would be ample proof of greatness in any king in any age. He had along with Buddhism, brought about and displayed fully the Bhartiya way of life and rule.

But the empire curmbled after Ashoka's death in 232 B.C. Most of the provinces declared themselves independent and the successors to Ashoka were reduced to naught within about a century after Ashoka's death.

The unity of the empire did not survive Ashoka in as much as after Ashoka only six Maurya kings ruled India for a total of about 27 years. N.F. gave chance to foreigners' attack from Bacteria and Parthia. Eukratides of Bactria reduced India under his power (156 B.C.). In his family Menendu had his capital at Kabul. He attacked India and annexed a large chunk of Ashoka's empire in his kingdom.

Reasons for downfall of Maurya empire: As already indicated, after Ashoka, the Maurya empire started crumbling due to:

1. Ashoka had spread Buddhism in India. After his death, brahmins revolted against the Maurya empire on religious basis for the revival of Brahmanical religion.
2. Strict insistence of Ashoka's officers on the principles of Danda-Samata and Vyavahara Samata i.e. equality of

punishment and equality in law suits irrespective of caste, creed, or colour. This was against the belief of brahmins, who maintained their superiority.

3. Ashoka's idealism and religious fervor considerably dampened the morale of the army.
4. The Maurya empire was a monarchy or despotic and no monarch can ensure in his successors, the continuation of qualities on which alone personal rule can rest.
5. Pleading for equality for all his states, Ashoka himself left certain independent and disintegrated elements to operate within the empire. They became free and sovereign like Gangaras, Kambojas, Yadvas, Rastrikas, Bhojas, Pulenders, Andharas Pitullas etc. They became stronger after the death of Ashoka.
6. Successors to Ashoka had been rather weak as they had been put to do religions jobs. They could not, therefore, control the empire.
7. Greeks had been repulsed by Chandra Gupta but they had been waiting for an opportunity to attack back. Failure of the Maurya kings after Ashoka, to check the Greek invasions ruined their prestige in the eyes of the people of India and when that was gone, the empire could not survive.
8. Oppressive rule of Maurya officials in the outlying provinces.
9. Centralisation of administration, which enabled the governors to become independent after Ashoka's death,
10. The officers loyalty was to the emperor and not to the state.
11. After cessation of wars, large army became superfluous and its expenditure was a drain on national exchequer without production.
12. Due to no wars, the army had become lethargical and, therefore, were neither able to check foreign invasions nor internal disunity.

13. The administration too had become peace-minded and could not think of facing the troubles again.

The conclusion of the matter about Indo-Greek dynasties and subsequent Maurya empire is that the invasions of Alexander, Antiochos, Demetrios, Eukratides and Menander were in fact, whatever their authors may have intended, merely military incursions, which left no appreciable mark upon the institutions of India and whatever was left in India from the Greek side subsequently got assimilated in Hindus.

THE SUNGAS (185-73 B.C.)

Mauryas were succeeded by Sungas. General Pushyamitra, a shudra, crushed his master Brihadratha, the Maurya but he had to meet many challenges. Two Yavanas wars had to be fought. Pushyamitra held two Aswamedh yagyas. He was a great persecutor of Buddhism and on the advice of his brahmin Chaplain destroyed teachings of Buddha. He was succeeded by his son, who ruled for 8 years. In Sunga reign, the renewed incursions of Yavanas were checked and Greek dynasties reverted to the prudent policy of their Seleukidan precursors. There was an outburst of activity in the domain of religion (revival of Hinduism), literature, art, comparable to the period of Guptas.

During this period, Greeks had been rather again active in India after second Greek war in 206 B.C. This conquest of India was more important for India than that of Alexander. The cultural contacts between Greeks and Indians for nearly two centuries were considerable and both parties reacted upon each other. It was not merely a case of Greeks influencing the civilisation of India or vice versa but the religious ideals and ideology of Indians were adopted by some of the great men of the ruling Greek race. A large number of Greeks were converted to different Indian religions. They adopted the Indian way of life and in course of time became the sons of soil.

KUSHANAS (40-160 A.D.)

Kanishka (120-160 A.D.)

Kadphises I engaged in subjugating the provinces south of the mountains. He made himself master of Ki-pin (Gandhara) as well as Kabul territory and consolidated his power in Bacteria and attached Parthians (India). His empire extended from Persia to Indus or perhaps to Jhelum including Afghanistan and Kabul. He was succeeded by Kadphises II in 77 A.D. who completed the conquest of northern India, including Punjab, and a considerable part of Gangetic plain upto Benaras sweeping away all Parthians.

The study advance of the victorious Chinese evidently alarmed Kushan king (Kadphises II), who did not accept vassalage. He attacked China. The army passed by Tashkarghan Pass (14000 ft. high) and was so shattered by its sufferings enroute that when it emerged into plains below, it fell easy prey to Chinese. Kadphises' paid tribute to China. He lasted upto 110 A.D. and was then succeeded by Kaniskha.

Kanishka was closely related to Kadphises II. His empire was from north-western India to Vindhyas and the remote region beyond Pamir Passes, including Kashmir. His capital was Puruspura (modern Peshawar). He erected great relic tower, which is a wonder of the world. It was a superstructure of carved wood rose in 13 storeys to a height of 400 ft. surmounted by a mighty iron pinnacle. Its final demolition must have been done by Mohammedan invaders.

The most striking military exploit of Kanishka was his conquest of Kashgar, Yarkand, Khotan, provinces of Chinese Turkstan to the north of Tibet and east of Pamirs. He not only freed himself from the obligation of paying tribute to China but also exacted the surrender of hostages from a state tributary to Chinese empire. Reign of Kanishka ended in 160 A.D. after 45 years of rule. Kanishka was from Kushana dynasty, which had come to India from China. He was the founder of the saka era which started in 78 A.D. and also ascended the throne in 78 A.D. Initially, his empire comprised of Afghanistan, a large part of Sind, Parthia, Bactria and the Punjab. He fought many battles in his reign. He annexed Kashmir and founded a town Kanishkpura, now Kanispore. After the capture of Patliputra, Aswaghosh, the great Buddhist philosopher fell into the hands of Kanishka and he brought the sage with him to his court. Kanishka conquered, Ujjain, Malwa, Kasgar, Yarkand and Khotan. He ruled upper India from Kapisa, Gandhara and Kashmir to Benaras with capital at Peshawar or Purushapura.

Before his conversion to Buddhism, Kanishka had no religion but was tolerant to all religions. He did a lot for spreading Buddhism and called for fourth Buddhist council attended by 500 monks from various countries. This would indicate India's relations with many countries in those days, when India was at the top of civilisation.

Kanishka was a great builder. He founded Taxila with great halls and monasteries. His empire reached its climax in the time of Kanishka. Then the Kushans were down not only in India but in Central Asia as well. Its successors ruled only in Mathura. Not much literature is available on the successor of Kanishka and the Kushana rule was over by 230 A.D. The Kushans, like the Greeks, had completely intermingled with other tribes and ultimately merged in Indian religions.

During Kushana reign, kingship was the prevailing type of polity although there are references to republics too. They possessed unfettered powers, although there was an advisory body too to assist the king. There was brisk trade with foreign countries in this period. There was no foreign invasion and within India, there was complete law and order. People were economically well off. The social life under the Kushans was richer in content and comprehensive in outlook and range of activities. The four varnas (brahmin, kshatriya, vaish and shudra) existed. In this period, Mahayanism made an appearance and Buddhist religion was divided into Mahayan and Hinyan.

During this period Nagarjuna wrote the Prajnaparamita Sutra Shastra; Vasumitra wrote the Mahavibhasha Shastra, Charak wrote the famous treatise on medicines, which even today holds good and is recognised throughout the universe. Metal industry rose in this period. Coins of gold and many metal stupas were cast. Indian goods were exported to Central Asia and Rome. Kushana period is also famous for Gandhara art.

If may be worth while to mention here about the Indain contacts with western world and Central Asia so far. India maintained her contacts with western world much before the Christian era. Discoveries at Mohenjo Daro show that there was intercourse between the Indus valley and the western world and eastern countries in about 3000 B.C. as—

1. There was a sea voyage to the East.
2. **Babylon**: There is reference to a trading voyage to the kingdom of Bavern (Babylon).
3. **Western Asia**: There was close contact between India and western Asia before 14th century B.C. as the inscriptions found in west, contain names of Mitra, Varuna, Indra etc.
4. **Persia**: Cyrus of Persia, founded dynasty in 538 B.C, sent an expediton to India and Indus valley was annexed with Persian empire.
5. **Greece**: Invasion of Alexander in 526 B.C. and subsequent intercourse between India and Greek and with other western and middle-east countries.
6. **East and Southeast**: Inscriptions of Ashoka exists in Lanka, Indochina, Bali, Sumatra and Central Asia and China.
7. **Egypt**: Intimate relations between India and Egypt accessible by sea.
8. **Rome**: There are indications of direct trade with India in 2nd centruy A.D. - Ambassies were exchanged too.
9. India exported large quantities of spices, fine fabrics, precious gems and aromatic articles to the countries of the western world. Greek physicians had studied the Indian way of medicines.

10. Indian philosophers had a lot of influence on Greek philosophers. Greeks borrowed from India their belief in reincarnation and doctrine of 'karma'; the doctrine of 'yoga' or meditation and ideas of asceticism.
11. Buddhism had spread in Western countries in the time of Ashoka in Khosan, Persia, Iraq, Mosal, Syria. Also Brahmanical religion prevailed in western Asia.
12. Similarly, India was also influenced by Greek in the field of architecture, literature and trade.

GUPTAS (320-455 A.D.)

Chandra Gupta I (320-340 A.D.)

During the time between the fall of Kusans and rise of Guptas, history of northern India is blank for three centuries. In the fourth century, there were kingdoms of Vaisali, Kosala, Patliputra, Benaras. Chandragupta, the raja of Patliputra, was raised by his Lachchhavi connections from the rank of a local chief to the dignity of an emperor in 320 A.D. and ruled Bihar, Tirhut, Ganga valley, Jamuna valley, upto Punjab. He died in 335 A.D. He was succeeded by his son Samudra Gupta. He was an orthodox Hindu, learned in all the wisdom of the brahmins and an ambitious soldier. His campaign for extension of his kingdom fell in four heads - directed against eleven kings of south, nine of Aryavrat (Gangetic valley) besides many chiefs of wild forest tribes and rulers of frontier kingdom and republics. At first he thoroughly subjugated the rajas of Gangetic plain known as Hindustan. The second campaign was to remote south. The rajas enroute were forcibly rooted up and their territories annexed with his dominion. He marched to South through Chhota Nagpur against the kingdom of South Kosala in the valley of Mahanadi and dethroned King Mahendra. He subdued all chiefs of forest countries in Orissa and part of central provinces. The third campaign was in east-coast of South. He vanquished Pishtapura (capital of Kalinga), Pithupuram (Godavri district), Mahendergiri Kottula (Gajar),

Vengi between Krishna and Godavri rivers presumably Pallava, Vishnu gopa, the king of Kanchi or Conjeevaram to the south west of Madras; Ugrasena, king of Palakka near Nellor district. In fourth round he retreaded through western parts of Deccan, subduing the kingdom of Devarashtra (Maratha country) and Erandapalla (Khandesh). The kingdoms of south were not annexed but kept as vassal states but got all riches of south.

Samudra Gupta (340-375 A.D.)

Samudra Gupta was selected by his father for the throne as he was considered to be worthy and the decision was publicly declared in open assembly before the counsellors by asking the prince "Protect ye this Earth". He is famous for his conquests that is why he is called Indian Nepoleon. His kingdom comprised of entire north India from Brahmputra to Jamuna and Chambal and from foot of Himalaya in the north to Narmada on the south. Besides these, Assam as well as southern slopes of Himalayas, Rajputana, Malwa, were attached to the empire by bonds of subordinate alliance and all kingdoms of south India as vassal states. His conquests in brief were—

1. Forest Tribes
2. Nagas
3. Conquest in the South India
4. Pistapura - Modern Godavri District
5. Kurala - Sonepur District of Madhya Pradesh
6. Erandapalle - Khandesh
7. Exterminated kings of Aryavrat like Rudradev, Matila, Nagdata, Ganpati Naga, Nagsena, Achyuta, Nandin etc.
8. Chandravarman of Bengal
9. Atavika - Central India
10. Frontier states - Samatata (south of Assam), Kamrup (Assam) Dervaka (Middle Assam) and Nepal
11. Republican states of Malavas (Punjab) East Rajputana, Bharatpur, Abhiras (Western Rajputana), Prarjunas Madhya Pradesh, Saka Murindas (Central India).

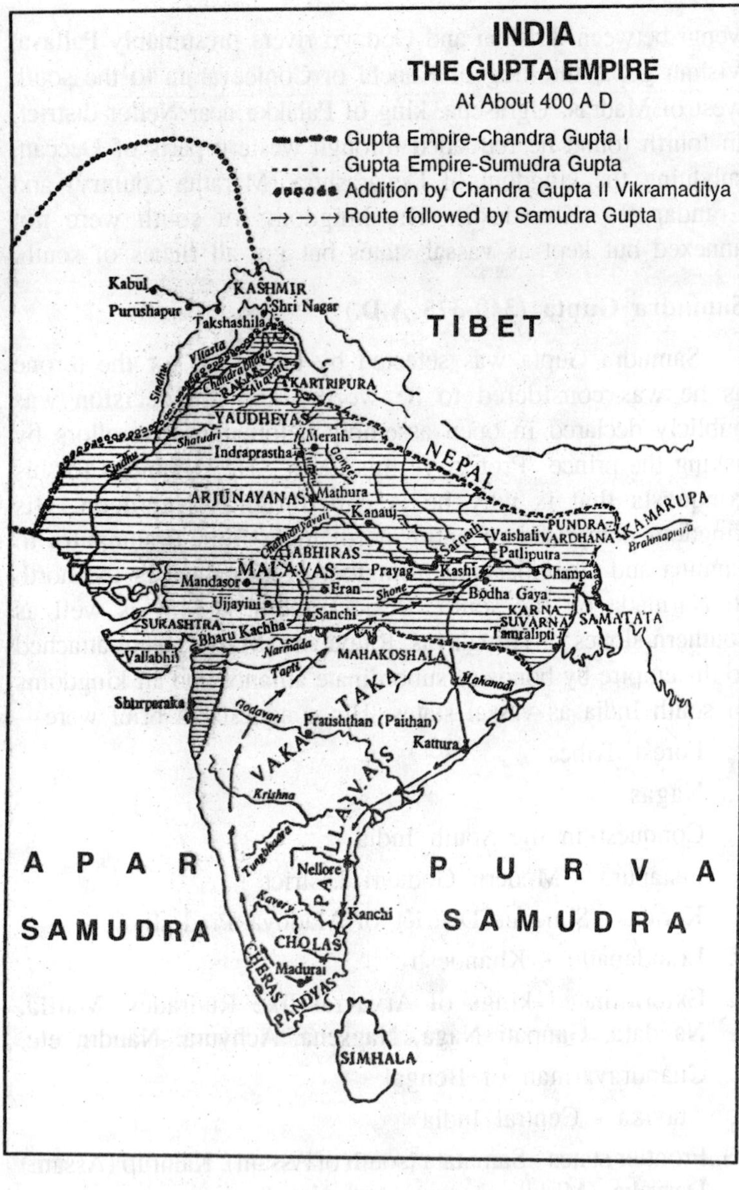
INDIA
THE GUPTA EMPIRE
At About 400 A D
Gupta Empire-Chandra Gupta I
Gupta Empire-Sumudra Gupta
Addition by Chandra Gupta II Vikramaditya
Route followed by Samudra Gupta
Kabul
Purushapur
KASHMIR
Shri Nagar
Takshashila
TIBET
KARTRIPURA
YAUDHEYAS
Merath
Indraprastha
NEPAL
ARJUNAYANAS
Mathura
Kanauj
KAMARUPA
PUNDRA-VARDHANA
Vaishali
Patliputra
Champa
MALAVAS
Mandasor
Prayag
Kashi
Eran
Bodha Gaya
Ujjayini
Sanchi
KARNA SUVARNA
SAMATATA
SURASHTRA
Bharu Kachha
Tamralipti
Vallabhi
MAHAKOSHALA
Shurparaka
VAKATAKAS
Pratishthan (Paithan)
Kattura
PALLAVAS
Nellore
Kanchi
CHOLAS
CHERAS
Madurai
PANDYAS
SIMHALA
APAR SAMUDRA
PURVA SAMUDRA

Samudra Gupta had good relations with Lanka, with whom monks were exchanged. Lankan Monks came for construction of Buddha monastries in India.

Samudra Gupta had also performed Aswamedha yagya. Aswamedha yagya was held as per vedic tenets by the Chakravarty raja to make his suzerainty felt by his vassal states, who used to give large presents to the emperor as also to establish his superiority over other rajas. By his conquests, Samudra Gupta, not only put an end to the domination of foreigners, who had been in India for long periods but also added neighbouring areas to the kingdom. Exact date of Samudra Gupta's death is not known but he peacefully transmitted crown by nominating his successor Chandra Gupta II, (Vikramaditya) in 375 A.D.

Chandra Gupta-II (Vikramaditya) (375-413 A.D.)

He conquerred Saurastra and Malwa and thus placed him in direct touch with sea borne trade with europe, through Egypt and his merchants went to middle east and europe. He occupied throne for 40 years upto 413 A.D. Fahien visited during his time. He calls it middle kingdom. He has said—

"The people were rich and prosperous and seemed to him to emulate each other in the practice of virtue. Charitable institutions were numerous. Rest houses for travellers were provided on highways and the capital possessed an excellent free hospital endowed by benevolent and educated citizens". "Here come, we are told, all poor and helpless patients suffering from all kinds of infirmities. They are well taken care of and a doctor attends them; food and medicines being supplied free according to their wants. Thus they are made quite comfortable and when they are well, they may go away". "It may be doubted if any equally efficient foundation was to be seen elsewhere in the world at that date; and its existence, anticipating the deeds of modern Christian charity; speaks well both for the character of the citizens, who endowed it and for the genius of the great Ashoka, whose teachings still bore such wholesome fruits many centuries after his death".

Fahien adds with a glance at Chinese institutions and congratulates Indians that they have not to register their households or attend to any magistrate and rule meaning thereby that there was no crime; they were not troubled with passport regulations and those who want to go away, may go; those, who want to stop, may stop. Most crimes were punished by fines according to the gravity of the offence and capital punishment was unknown. Person guilty of repeated rebellion suffered amputation of right hand but such a punishment was exceptional. Judicial torture was not practised. Throughout the country, no one killed any living being or drank wine, or ate onion or garlic, no killings of cattle, no butchers' shops, no distilleries".

Hieun Tsang in 7th century had said that India had never been governed better after oriental manner, than it was during the reign of Vikramaditya. The government was very popular. No religious torture or bias was seen. Although Brahmanical rule, Buddhism was exercised freely. Unlike Jainism or Buddhist despotism, Brahmanical Hindus had no tendency of harassing any one believing in other religions.

Kumar Gupta (413-453 A.D.)

Vikramaditya was succeeded by Kumar Gupta in 413 A.D. and reigned for 40 years. No events of his period are known. He, however, celebrated Aswamedha. Even during Buddhism and Jainism, orthodox Hindu way of worship was not annihilated. Even Kadphises II adopted Shaivism. During Guptas' period, there was alround development. Taking Gupta period in wider sense from 300 to 650 A.D., was a time of exceptionally intellectual activity in the fields—a time not unworthy of comparison with Elizebethan and Stuart periods in England. In literature apart from writings of Kalidas, Mudrarakshas, Vayu Puran etc. were the milestones. In science, (mathematics and astronomy), Gupta period is known by Arya Bhat (476 A.D.) and Varahamhira (died 587 A.D.). Music was encouraged too. There was the supremacy in architecture, sculpture, painting, die-cutting etc.

When Skanda Gupta ascended in 455 A.D., he had to face Huns. He inflicted defeat on them. In 489 A.D., Huns again attacked. Skanda Gupta was unable to resist successfully and was forced to succumb to repeated attacks and died. With his death the empire perished. The imperial line passing into a transition dynasty for eleven Gupta princes, who had only been local rulers in Magadh upto 500 AD. Nalanda, Pala, Benaras were the places of learning known in India and abroad, subsequently destroyed by Muslims.

Guptas period in Indian history is known as the golden period in view of the fact that full Bhartiyata was displayed in that reign and the rule was as per vedic tenets. It is, however, unfortunate that even with such past, India had been subdued by Mohammedans first and then by British for a total of about 750 years. Let us now have a glimpse of the all round development in Gupta reign as narrated by the Chinese/Greek travellers and inscriptions. with a view to see what Bhartiyata was as per historic evidence.

Literature: Great advance was made in literature in the classical age on every side and every branch. Some of the more important sciences such as grammar, mathematics, astronomy and astrology almost reached their fullest development. This period gave us Kalidas, who continues in himself, poetic and dramatic talents of an exceptionally high order. Besides Kalidas, other able writers of this period were Bana, Subandhu, Dandin etc. Kalidas's dramas 'Shakuntala', 'Malvikagnimitra', 'Vikramorvasiya', 'Raghuvansa', 'Kumarsambhav' and 'Meghdoot' are universally regarded as gems of Sanskrit poetry. Dandin had written 'Kavyadarsa' and 'Dasakumarcharita'. Subandhu wrote 'Vasavadatta' and Ban's 'Kadambri' are few of more popular books.

In field of grammar, Bhartrihari's comments of 'Mahabhashya' is known. In medicines Vagbhata is worth mentioning. He wrote 'Ashtanga-Sangraha' and 'Ashtanga Hridaya-Samhita'. In astronomy Varahmhira is known for his work 'Panchasidhantika'.

Religion: During Gupta period, Buddhism had gone down and Brahmanical religion had started coming up.

Administrative set up: The governance was as per vedic tenets. The samritis of Narad, Brihaspati and Katyayana based on vedas and shastras, belong to this period. These samritis expound the basics of governance, prevailing at that time when it was the best so far known in any country as explained by Fahien and Hiuen Tsang. The Guptas continued the traditional machinery of bureaucratic administration, mostly as per Arthshastra.

Art: It is an age of culmination and ultimate exhaustion of the earlier tendencies and movements in architectural types and forms. Among the works are—

1. **Caves** - Chaitya hall, Ajanta, Ellora, Vihar caves at Bagh in Madhya Pradesh.
2. **Temples** - At Ter in Sholapur district, Kapoteswara at Chezarla (Krishna district), Durga temple at Aihole, temples at Sanchi, Tigawa, and Eran.
3. **Monasteries and Stupas** - At Bharhut, Sarnath, and Mirpur Khas (Sindh).
4. **Sculpture** - At Mathura, Sravasti, Prayag and Sarnath.

Social conditions: Fahien has given an account of living conditions of that period. There was no crime, no corporal punishment. People divided in four varnas. No registration of birth and deaths. No slaves, all were independent. Marriages were held as per tenets of samritis. Females in higher families had sufficient opportunities for acquiring proficiency in general learning. Family life was quite cordial. There was high standard of living in this age with high standard of cleanliness and comfort. Approved foods were rice, wheat and barley, pulses, butter oils, raw and course sugar. Fish eating was also there in a limited way.

Education: There were advanced centres of learning at Nalanda, Taxila, Benaras, where people from various countries came for learning.

Economy : Agriculture continued to be the prime source of production. Also industry in textiles, jewellery, leather industry, metallic industry flourished making everyone prosperous.

Trade : There was inland trade by roads and rivers and foreign trade with eastern and southern Asia, China, Indonesia, Lanka, Persia, Adule (Ethopia) Central Asia, through land and sea routes.

HARSHA (606-647 A.D.)

The decline and fall of Gupta empire was, as usual, due to not so enterprising successors. This gave rise to new powers coming up, none of which, however, succeeded in building up a lasting empire. These powers in general, continued the old administrative traditions of Guptas. The Huna Toramana, who assumed the title of Maharajadhiraj had under him a viceroy called Dhanyavishnu ruling the Vishaya (modern Saugar district of Madhya Pradesh). Even the ferocious Hun conquerers sometimes left in tact not only the old system of provincial administration but also the ancient official families.

In first half of 7th century A.D., Harsha Vardhan of the ruling house of Thaneswar, made himself the strongest power in northern India by his successful wars and conquests. His administration was highly organised but we do not have much available except what is written by Hiuen Tsang, who has said that after the assassination of the Maharaja of Kanauj, Harsha succeeded him on the request of his ministers in 606 A.D., indicating how ministers were doing the job of governance in those days.

Harsh Charitam, also throws light on his life. Harsha had many officers like the Minister of Foreign Affairs, the Commander-in-Chief, Chief of Palace Goods, Head of Accounts etc. The kingdom was divided into Bhuktis and Vishyas. The

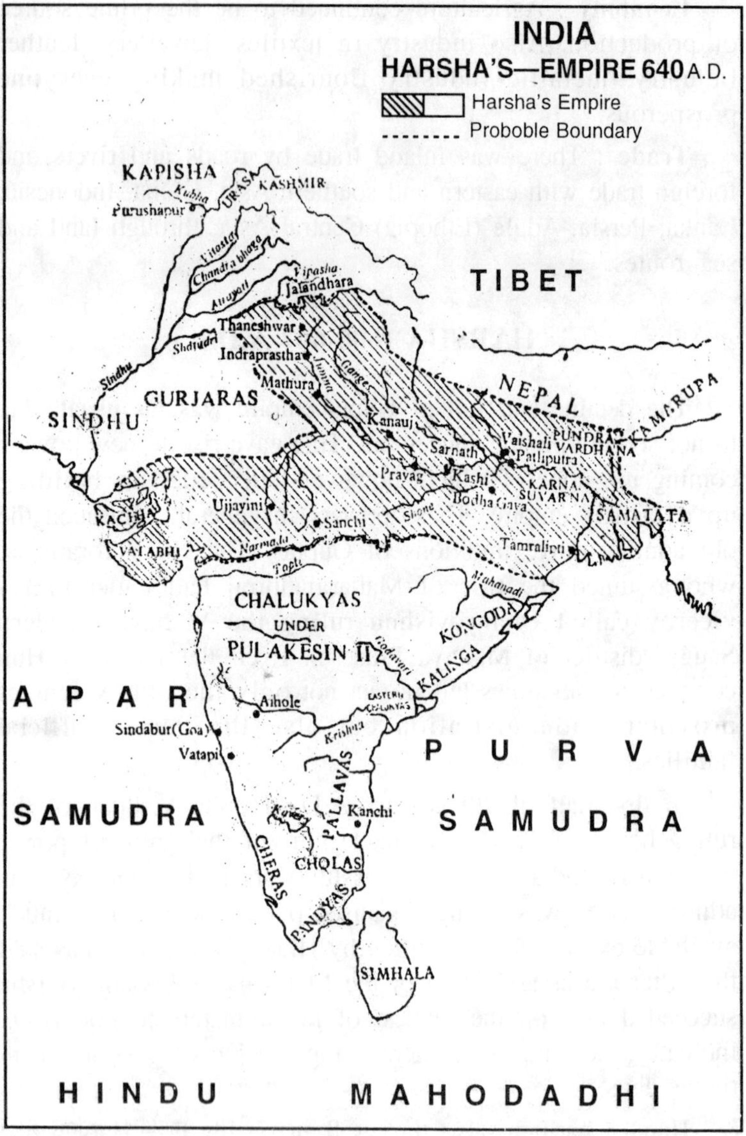
INDIA
HARSHA'S—EMPIRE 640 A.D.
Harsha's Empire
Probable Boundary
KAPISHA
Kubha
Purushapur
URASA
KASHMIR
Vitasta
Chandra bhaga
Vipasha
Jalandhara
Airavati
TIBET
Thaneshwar
Shdtudri
Indraprastha
Sindhu
Mathura
Jamuna
Ganges
NEPAL
KAMARUPA
GURJARAS
SINDHU
Kanauj
PUNDRA VARDHANA
Vaishali
Sarnath
Patliputra
Prayag
Kashi
KARNA SUVARNA
Bodha Gaya
Ujjayini
Shone
SAMATATA
KACHHA
Sanchi
Narmada
Tamralipti
VALABHI
Tapti
Mahanadi
CHALUKYAS
UNDER
PULAKESIN II
KONGODA
Godavari
KALINGA
APAR
Aihole
EASTERN CHALUKYAS
Sindabur(Goa)
Krishna
Vatapi
PURVA
PALLAVAS
SAMUDRA
Kaveri
Kanchi
SAMUDRA
CHERAS
CHOLAS
PANDYAS
SIMHALA
HINDU
MAHODADHI

officers were Bhogapatis. Harsha had a strong love for justice, unremitting industry and the benevolence of his rule have been strikingly brought out by Hiuen Tsang. He forgot sleep and food in his devotion of good work. He was virtuous and patriotic and all people celebrated his praise in songs. He made tours of inspection throughout his dominion; not residing for long period at any place and not going out during the three months of rainy season. He was, however, unable to ensure such complete peace and security as had been achieved in Gupta period. When going down the Ganges, with about 80 other fellow passengers on board a vessel to east of Ayodhya, Hiuen Tsang had the misfortune of having been captured by a gang of pirates from whose hands, he could save himself only by a miraculous rise of a storm. Harsha had built monasteries at Nalanda and Kanauj. Hiuen Tsang says the country was politically divided into about 70 kingdoms. The country was, however, far from being politically united. The kshatriyas were traditionally held to have exercised the ruling power for centuries. The few instances to the contrary being explicitly declared to have been caused by breach of the constitutional law.

In judicial administration, the standard of criminal law reforms set up by Guptas was maintained, if not in its fulness, atleast to a great extent. For violation of the statute law and plots against the king, the offender was imprisoned for life and by dint of suffering any corporal punishment, was not treated as a member of the community. The law of treason in the 7th century was evidently more severe than in Gupta times, when as per Fahien, the penalty for a second attempt at rebellion was only the loss of the right hand. For breach of social morality and filial duty, the penalty was mutilation or exile—a punishment which struck one as unduly severe. For the remaining offences, the penalty was only a money payment. In the branch of finance, there was moderation of the state demand and the absence of vexatious restrictions against the liberty of the subject, resulted in a complete security of property.

As the government was generous, official requirements were few. Families were not registered and individuals were not subject to forced labour contributions. Taxation being light and forced labour not being there, every man kept to his hereditary occupation and attended to his patrimony. This again confirms the hundred per cent liberty and independence of the people in those times in India which neither has ever been seen nor heard of in any other country ever. This actually is the Bhartiyata, which gave way after Harsha's period.

The great works of this period form a triumvirate in the realm of Hindu law and procedure. These are the samritis of Brihaspati, Narad, and Katyayana, as also the samritis of Vyas, Parasara, and others, which have been received as parts and compiled by the scholars piecing together. Law was in three heads:

1. Court of Justice
2. Judicial Procedure
3. Civil and Criminal Law.

Court of Justice: King's court was the highest on land called sabha, dharmasthan and dharmadhikarna. We have full account of its contribution in Katyayana, who requires the king in one place to decide suits in association with the learned brahmins, elders and ministers, well-versed with statecraft and in another place to do so in the company of the judges, the ministers, the purohit and the assessors, the scribes, the bailifs, the investigators etc. The king awarded the punishment, the assessors examined the disputes, the scribe wrote down the pleadings, dispositions and decisions and the bailif summoned the defendant, the witness, the assessors etc. The king was to abide by the decision of the judiciary, although he had over-riding powers, being fountain head of justice.

Judicial Procedure: This period marks the climax of Hindu jurisprudence. In the first place, the transaction of legal business has, according to Narad, four stages—receiving information from a person; finding out under what title of law the information fell; the consideration of the pleadings of the parties and the evidence and lastly the decision. As per Brihaspati, the four stages were the plaint, the reply, the evidence and the decision. The burden of proof was to lie on the plaintiff in a reply of denial and on the defendant in the reply of special plea or of former judgement. Proof was humane and divine. Former comprised witnesses, documents and possession and the later consisted of ordeals. The judgement was given in the form of a written document, called jayapatra. This indicated summary statements of parties, dispositions of witnesses, deliberation of the court and the decision.

Civil and Criminal Law: In the penal law of the late as of the early samritis, the punishment of crime occupied a more important place than compensation for wrongs. It is, in other words, a law of crime in the strict sense of the term, while the law of torts held the subordinate position. Under the head law, called abuse and defamation both Narad and Katyayana have idicated fines for these offences depending upon the distinctions as well as the castes of the parties. The idea of the compensation to the person injured was reflected in the clause that "he who kills an animal must provide another animal of the same type or pay its value to the owner". Thefts were of two kinds — patent and clandestine. Patent thieves were traders, employing false weights, measures and balances and clandestine were gamblers and quacks, those who counterfeited articles and those who lived by magic or palmistry by forfeiting good fortunes or portents. Punishment for thefts comprised mutilation, imprisonment, confiscation of property, exile and death.

As already indicated, Harsha was the last king of ancient Hindu India, who could consolidate an empire at least of whole of north India. After Harsha, his successors could not maintain the empire and it started dwindling. The history of India is, as would be seen, dependent on individual kings. Chandra Gupta Maurya by dint of his achievements created a large empire, which broke away after Ashoka. Similarly Samudra Gupta of Gupta dynasty created a big empire, which started dwindling after Chandra Gupta II (Vikramajit). After Harsha again small kingdoms came up and India was again distributed in many kingdoms.

Let us now have a look on the achievements of India in the ancient period in various fields. For this purpose, although India was fully developed in Vedic period, Ram period, Mahabharat period upto the reign of Parikshit, the Pandavas' successor, yet we are not taking that period and concentrate on Mauryas onwards.

Political Theory and Administrative Organisation: Narad and Brihaspati give us short accounts of the creation of the state and its institutions. At first human beings were created by Brahma. Manu divided the human beings into four according to their functions known as varnas. Such a varna was chosen by each according to his capability and, therefore, there was no grudge against the people of other varnas. Out of the four varnas, khastriya was to govern the kingdom; protect the people from internal crime and external aggressions; and to do the works of public well-being. There were many small kingdoms, each ruled by a raja and above many rajas was the Chakravarty raja (samrat). The smaller rajas were, however, autonomous within their territories and had to pay annual presents to the Chakravarty Raja, who in turn used to protect them against external aggression. Thus these kingdoms were a sort of vassal states of today. Generally, the aggression on other states was not with a view to annex it but to extract some presents from there and then return the same to be ruled as vassal states. As per vedic tenets, independence was fully enjoyed by all states.

The raja was an autocrat but his autocracy was also limited in view of the fact that he was guided by the samiti/sabha and also the raj guru. The sabha's approval had to be sought before anyone could be nominated as the successor to throne and in case the raja did not behave well, the sabha could also dethrone him. The raja also had several ministers-incharge of various departments such as Prime Minister, Finance Minister, Revenue Minister, Commander-in-Chief or Defence Minister, etc. Ashoka also had one Minister for Religion (Dharma Mahamatra), who used to see that the canons of religion were observed by the people. All important matters were decided by the raja in consultation with the respective ministers or the sabha.

Army: For the protection of the kingdom from external aggression, the raja used to keep adequate army. The expenses of the raja and the army were met out of the part of agricultural produce (generally about 1/6th). But the raja was prohibited from spending this collection on personal luxuries. It is understood that once a winner raja, after he had returned the kingdom to the defeated raja, had been called for a party. Next day the same raja had been called by a trader (vaish) for the party. The party arranged by the trader was more lavish. On enquiry by the raja, the vaish told that the raja had to spend out of the collection from them and so had to spend it conservatively whereas the Vaish could spend any amount as it was out of his own earnings. Such was the ethics observed by every one, including the raja.

Law: The law was also as per the samritis. These samritis gave details of various kinds of crimes, procedure to be adopted for final decision on the punishment to be awarded i.e. at first there is report, then the examination of defence and witnesses and then the decision. This is what is precisely being followed even now. There were two kinds of crimes—civil and criminal—and punishment for each offence had been duly prescribed. It means there were the codes like the present day Indian Penal Code, Criminal Procedure Code, Civil Procedure Code etc., which system is considered to be the best. So India too having the best systems in those days although English had condemned these systems as barbaric and rather appreciated the Islamic law. But none seems to have understood or gone into this system or the English did not want to appreciate this system. For civil cases, generally monetary punishment was awarded and for criminal cases too, monetary compensation was awarded in Gupta period, whereas coporal punishment was awarded during Maurya and Harsha's rule. On rebellion against the state, death was the penalty. In view of this detailed civil and criminal law management, English were wrong in saying that there was no proper administration of law in Hindu period and in fact it was better administered than through present Indian Penal Code, Criminal Procedure Code etc.

Society: As already indicated, the mankind had been divided into four varnas—brahmin, kshatriya, vaish and shudra. They were initially opted according to capability but in course of time had been adopted as per birth. But all people used to live and act as per their position in the society.

Raja-Praja Relation: According to samritis, king was the temporal ruler. The subjects were required to obey the king and the king too used to rule for the protection and well-being of the people. As per vedic tenets, the raja was an elected one by the people. He could be removed too although the election was for life; of course upto the time the raja proceeded for banprastha, handing over the kingdom to his son, who again was approved by the public and the sabha, represented by public men. The raja had to arrange for the welfare jobs like construction of roads, bapis, gardens, wells, hospitals and controlling the correctness of prices of various commodities and their weights and measurements. Strict punishments were provided for any cheating in weights and measurements. In Purans, the kings were responsible for timely rains, early deaths too. Chankaya's Arthshastra, which is the compilation from all vedas and shastras, was the guide for the king in the act of governance and held good during the Mauryas and later Hindu kings' reigns.

For the proper control of the vast kingdoms, the same had been divided into provinces called Bhuktis under the governors (uparikas), who were generally king's sons. The provinces were further divided into districts (vishyas) ruled by ayuktas and then there were villages, under the village pramukhs.

The towns had their own governing councils, (Nagarasreshthi).

Literature: Lot of work was done in the field of writing during Maurya, Gupta period and Harsha period but unfortunately it had almost entirely been destroyed by the Muslim invaders. It is said that the collection of books at Nalanda alone had been burning for a long time. And, therefore, we have to depend on the remnant inscriptions and the treatises of the Chinese travellers like Fahien and Hiuen Tsang and Greek writer Magasthanese, apart from a few Arabian writers. That is why having been ignorant based on any documentary evidence, India have been branded barbaric by the English, one to demoralise us and secondly to keep us down-trodden. Still some works are available even today which are testimony of intellect of that period like the Arthshastra of Chanakya, still recognised world over. More works are as under:

1. **Puranas**: The puranas give the history of the period. These are 18 in number like Brahma, Bhagwat, Padma, Siva, Vayu, Vishnu, Narad, Brihaspati, Varah, Skand, Vaman etc. Bhagwat Gita has no parelled even today in philosophy of 'Karma' propounded by Krishna.These puranas narrate about various dynasties, jobs in kingdom, society etc. Besides the Puranas, there are Upapuranas, Upanishadas, Brahamanas. Dr. Hazra has analysed the period when these puranas were written. Some of these puranas, according to him, have been written up to 6th century A.D.

2. **Dharmashastras and Arthshastra**: Dharmashastras are samritis written by Brihaspati, Indra and Kartikeya. These give in detail the duties of the raja, the principles of governance, revenues of the raja, distribution into departments, ministers, sabhas/samitics, districts judicial system etc.

Philosophy: Sankhya system is the earliest philosophy of Hindus. Nyayasutra by Vatsayan is a milestone in judicial system.

Dramas and Literature: Kalidas had been the most brilliant luminary of Gupta age. He was well-versed with all vedas and shastras. His best known works are 'Shakuntala', 'Meghdoot', 'Ritusanhar', 'Malvikagnimitra', 'Vikramorvasiya', 'Raghuvansha', 'Kumarsambhava' which are universally acclaimed as gems in Sanskrit poetry.

'Bhavbhuti' is also known for his dramas. His works are 'Mahavir-charita', 'Uttar-Ramacharita', 'Malati Madhava' etc.

Harshavardhan himself was a writer. He has written 'Ratnavali', 'Priyadarsika', and 'Nagananda'. Bana Bhatt has written 'Venisanhar', 'Ramabhyudaya', 'Kuttanimata'. Bhairvi has written 'Kiratarjuniya' and 'Sisupalavadha'. Panchtantra was also written in this period apart from 'Sahitya durpan', Kavyadarsa by Dandin, ' Avantisundri Katha', 'Das Kumar Charit', 'Vasavadatta' by Subandhu; 'Vakyapadya' by Bhartrihari.

Medicines: Charak is known for medical service of ayurveda, universally. Apart from him, Vaghbata and Susruta are also known in this field. Their works are Astanga-sangrah, and Astang Haridya-Samhita. There were also treatises on diseases of animals like Hastyayurveda.

Astronomy and Mathematics: Varahamihira, who flourished in 6th centruy A.D. has preserved in his 'Panchsidhantika' some account of five astronomical works, which were regarded authority in his times. They show more advanced stage of thought and spirit. These books also indicate the mixture of Greek and Indian knowledge in this science. Varahamihira also refers to several other astronomers such as Lata, Simha, Pradyuman, Viyayanandin, and the famous Arya Bhata. Aryabhat's works such as Aryabhatiya, Dasagitika-Sutra, and Aryashtasta have come down to us as great pieces of intellect in that science in ancient India. Aryabhat was the first to treat mathematics as a distinct subject and dealt with evolution and involution, area and volume, progression and algebraic identities and indeterminate equations of the first degree. Aryabhat was also the first to hold that the earth was a sphere and rotated on its axis and that the eclipse was not the work of Rahu but caused by shadow of earth falling on moon but those views were strongly criticised at that time and came true later on. One of the most important features of Aryabhat's mathematical system is his unique system of notation. It is based on decimal place value system, unknown to other ancient people, but now in use throughout the civilised world. There were also many works on horoscopy like Parasari, Jataka Sutra, Bhrigu Samhita, Nadigrantha, Minaraja-jataka, Laghu and Brihaj jatakas. These also have their influence on Greek writers.

Miscellaneous: In addition there were other works like Kamasutra of Vatsayan.

This shows that in ancient India, great advance was made in literature on every side and in every branch. Some of the important sciences such as grammar, mathematics, astronomy, and astrology, almost reached thier fullest development in this age, even recognised singularly in present day. Apart from Sanskrit, lot of works have been produced in Tamil (Nayanmars and Alvars, Saiva Saints, Sundaras, Manikkavachakkar, etc.), Prakrit (Jain and Buddhist writers) and Alvars.

Religion and Philosophy: The vedic tenets taught about the sacrificial form of worship, which was gradually going down with the advent of Jainism and Buddhism i.e. with the start of known history. Infact we know very little about the part except in Ramayan and Mahabharat as not much is available now ; all having been destroyed by Muslim invaders. Even the works on Buddhism are available in inscriptions and the treatises of Chinese and Greek philosophers. So from known history we come across to Buddhism and Jainism. Buddhism had spread in entire India, Lanka, Burma, Siam, Indo China, Cambodia, Japan, Korea, China, Tibet, Central Asia and middle east countries. It is found in these countries even today. The Hindus, it appears, were not very fond of spreading Hinduism in other countries and whatever it would have spread would have been diluted subsequently by the spread of Buddhism. In India, of course, Buddhism had almost gone with the re-advent of Hinduism.

Buddhism had started in about 6th century B.C. and spread throughout the country, particularly after it had been adopted by Ashoka. It was during the period of Ashoka only that Buddhism had spread outside India too. Ashoka held first convention of Buddhism. Subsequently it received great impetus during Kanishka's rule, who also held a convention. After that Hinduism became the religion of the rajas and continued as such up to the Rajputs via Harsha. But during Mauryas, although the kings were Buddhist, they equally acknowledged and respected the people of other religions. Similarly during Gupta and Harsha periods, the kings being Hindus, allowed others to follow the religion of their choice. Guptas even allowed the monks from Lanka to construct Buddhist monastries in India.

Hinduism as at present followed and was followed in ancient period, is as propounded in vedas, shastras, and samritis etc. Hinduism is technically vaishnavism or Bhartiyata. Guptas were devout followers of the Bhagwat religion. The important features of Bhagwat religion in Gupta age was the worship of incarnations of Vishnu like Vaman, Varah, Matsya, Kurma, Ram, Krishna, Narsingha, etc. God has three powers of creation imbibed in Brahma, maintenance in Vishnu and annihilation in Shiva. In Hindus, therefore, people were mostly followers of Vishnu and Shiva. Vishnu bhaktas were further distributed in Ram bhaktas and Krishna bhaktas in ancient time. In inscriptions of Gupta period, however, mention at most of the places is that of Bhagwat without reference to his name. Influence of Vishnu mythology can also be traced in archaeological remains in different parts of India like Udaygiri, Mamallapuram, Mahabalipuram, Mathura, Sarnath, Dasvtar and Kailashnath and in temples at Ellora.

Mention has also been made of the adoration of Vasudeva in Chinna (Krishna district) inscription and of a Narayan temple in Guntur. Similar inscriptions are available in Nepal, Bengal, Madurai, Alvars etc.

Coming into power of the Guptas in AD 320, gave a fillip to Hinduism. Though they were worshippers of Vishnu, they were not sectarians and under their rule Shivism flourished. Skand Gupta followed Shivism. During the period of later Guptas, Shivism spread in various parts of India, including Deccan. Tirumular's Tirumandiran is a highly obstruse work expounding the Shiva doctrine, very widely worshipped even today.

Apart from Shiva and Vishnu, people also worshipped Surya, Brahma (Prayag and Pushkar), Surya temple at Bhuvaneshwar, Shakti (Goddess) throughout the country and mostly in east and northern India.

Hinduism is a way of life easily adaptable by any person. That is why all the foreign invaders before the advent of Muslims, came, settled and got assimilated in Hinduism. One of the indirect results of India's intimate intercourse with the West is the migration of different religious communities from this region to India followed by Sungas and Huns from Central Asia and they all merged in Indian population without having any trace of their separate existence.

Islam, though preached by Prophet Mohammed as early as in 610 A.D. did not take a deep route in the soil of Arabia till 630 A.D. It is after the final conquest of Mecca in 630 A.D. that Prophet entered its great sanctuary and smashed its many idols said to have numbered 360 exclaiming "Truth hath come and falsehood hath vanished." The militant character of Islam and its extreme intolerance of other religions, specially those involved in worship of images, marked its subsequent history at every step and practically brought in its fold entire eastern europe, middle-east countries and partly India too. Indians being staunch followers of their faith, could not be converted to Islamism till about 13th century, when Muslim rule was established and many Hindus were converted into Islamism by force or by some consideration etc.

Art: Although the people of India had been arts-loving from ancient times, the period from 4th century to 8th century marks a parting of the ways in the history of Indian architecture. In one respect it is an age of culmination and ultimate exhaustion of the earlier tendencies and movements in architectural types and forms, few of which are discussed below:

Cave architecture: Rock cutting excavations represent an aspect in Indian architecture that had been characteristic of earlier period. The rock cuts are of two conventional types - the Chaitya-hall i.e. the shrine proper and the Sangharama or the 'Vihara' i.e. monastry. The most notable groups are found at Ajanta, Ellora, Aurangabad and Bagh in Madhya Pradesh. Ajanta caves can be of pre-Christian era and second are Chaitya caves and the rest are Viharas. The most significant innovation noticed in these caves is the wealth of figure sculptures which are made to cover every possible space, in place of plainer architectural patterns of the earlier caves.

The Viharas were planned in the form of row of cells round a central court, which in excavated examples took the shape of a central hall approached from one side and with cells leading out of it on the other three. There are numerous such Viharas in Ajanta dating from pre-Christian era to 6th century A.D. Indian architecture seems to have attained its perfection in Ajanta cave no. XXIV. The Bagh series consists of nine caves excavated so far dating about 500 to 600 A.D. The rock cuts near Aurangabad consist of twelve excavations in three groups. One is Chaitya and the others are Viharas.

At Ellora, the excavations extend for approximately a mile on the face of a low ridge of hills over-looking a vast plain and consists of three series of caves—Buddhist, Brahmanical and Jain. The most important are the two storeyed monasteries known as Don Thal and Tinthal, each rising upto three storeys. The Brahmanical caves at Ellora date from about 650 A.D. There are sixteen excavations belonging to this faith. There are a few Jain caves excavated at Ellora and it seems that with the Jain caves, the cave architecture of India ceased for all practical purposes.

Structural Buildings

Temples: In ancient India, the shrines and sanctuaries, being usually constructed of perishable materials like wood, bamboo etc. had but little scope for proper application of the principles of architecture as an art. In Gupta period, Indian builders began to erect their monuments with permanent materials, specially brick and dressed stone. The contemporary inscriptions not only give us a fair idea of the large number of temples erected during the period but also speak of great beauty and magnificance being adorned with lofty temples and other imposing edifices. Most of these buildings have, however, perished either with passage of time or having been destroyed by Muslim invaders. It is said, that in Kanauj alone, one thousand temples had been demolished. On account of their bearing upon future development, the ones that remained are invaluable for the study of Indian architecture. These temples are situated at Sanchi, Tigawa, Eran, the Parvati temple at Nachna Kaithara, Shiv temple at Bhumara and Lalkhan, Jain temples at Meguti at Aihole belong the rathas at Mamallapuram, the sea port city founded by Narsimha Varman. Brick temple at Bhitargaon consists of a square cell and a similar, but smaller, vestibule, connected with it by a passage, temple at Deogarh; Mahobodhi temple at Bodh Gaya was restored and renovated.

Monasteries and Stupas: Although temples form the most important class of monuments, a brief reference may be made to the stupas and monasteries, which were built in large number in ancient India. Of the numerous stupas built, two deserve special mention—the stupa at Mirpur Khas in Sindh and Dhamkesh stupa at Sarnath.

Sculpture: The pivot of Gupta sculptural art is the human figure. At Mathura and Amravati, there are figures of men and women away from and independent of the animal and vegital world that used to surround them at Bharhut and Sanchi. Now all animal and vegetal patterns are pushed together out of the narrative on to the borders or to panels where they keep themselves confined in their exclusiveness. In the art of this period, a deeper, qualitatively meaningful transformation of the human figure takes places and it is the vegetal life that causes this transformation. The sculptures of the ancient time are few but these few, particularly in Gupta period, help us to determine, howsoever roughly, the beginning and the early stages of the evolution of Gupta plastic conception. In Aryavrat, even other forces and traditions were at work. The Shiva-Parvati relief from Kosam and the Ramayan, parnells from Dasavtara; Deogarh (Jhansi) bring upto date an older tradition of narrative reliefs. These are more homely and more intimate due to a closer relation with day-to-day life.

It has already been pointed out that the human figure pushed all rich decorative patterns comprising the animal and vegetal world or purely abstract geometric devices out of the reliefs on to the borders or to sculptural and architectural bands and panels where they kept themselves confined in the exclusiveness. There they are vital, prolific and brimful in their richness and exuberance, but always chaste and elegant. A study of these rich vegetal and geometric decorative patterns of the period in a geographical context shows that they are most prolifically and profusely used in the plastic art and architecture of the Ganga-Yamuna valley and the Prachya country. The sculptures of Sarnath are the culmination of a spiritual quest that started its career in the early centuries of Christian era, when world was unaware of this art. The Mathura and Sarnath sculpture along with other Brahmnical sculptures of Aryavrat like Kartikeye and Benaras and Ekamukha Linga in Nagod state were inspired by this quest.

Paintings: The ancient India flourished in all arts then how paintings could remain unattended. Contemporary literature, including the epics, reveals that flat walls and ceilings of royal palaces and houses of the rich were elaborately decorated with mural paintings and furnished with separate picture galleries. A casual remark by Bana in respect of wall paintings seems to indicate that the themes of murals that used to decorate the walls and ceilings of palaces and houses were generally very broad and comprehensive and embraced the entire panorama of life and nature (darsita visvarupa). Not many paintings are available now but the ones at Ajanta caves, Bagh, Badami and Tirnmalaipuram are precious show-pieces of achievement in this art.

Terracotta and Pottery: Quite a different attitude of life and artistic vision are revealed by the deluge of terracota reliefs dug out from all over Mother India, particularly the Ganges valley and Bengal because of the inexhaustible supply of malleable earth and clay required for sculptural decorations. These are available in Harvan (Kashmir) Sahri Bahlol, Takht-i-Bahi, and Jawalgarhi in Punjab, Hanumangarh, and Bikaner (Rajputana) Brahmanabad and Mirpur Khas in Sindh, Kasia, Bhitargaon, Bhita, Basarh, Kosam etc. An examination of these finds would show that terracota plaques and reliefs were made and employed for various purposes. Made of soft, plastic and fragile material, these terracotas present the Indian modeller-artist relieved of iconographic injunctions and religious dictates and concerned more with things on the surface of vision. The artist in clay moves and works with an intensely playful and joyous freedom of imagination and action and uses his soft and pliable material with an easy sensitiveness of his fingers and palms. The high skill and efficiency of baking and burning and not-unoften of colouring also, the deluge of terracota seals, plagues and figurines and bricks and tiles testify also to a very high standard of the potter's art in ancient India. The pots were wheel-made but mould-made pots are also found in considerable number.

Coins and Seals: Gold and silver coins had been in existence in India since pauranic period. In Maurya times, metal coins were used. Kanishka introduced gold coins. Imperial Guptas' gold and silver coins are marked by refinement and elegance and represent the high water mark of early Indian coinage. These are marked by clarity and elegance of design and lettering, regularity of shapes and forms and precision and refinement of execution. The early Gupta gold and silver coinage was evolved from Hellenistic and Saka and Kusana coinage, not only in design but also in treatment and execution. This would indicate the advancement in metallurgy in ancient India.

Social Conditions: The start of documented history of India is from Buddhist and Jain era but even in these eras, the concept of varnas as propounded by the samritis continued. In Maurya period, the division of society was on the basis of varnas only. Chanakaya was a brahmin, who worked as raj guru of Chandra Gupta and khastriyas were the rulers, the vaishas did the trade, agriculture and industry and the shudras served the people of other varnas although Buddhisim did not recognise the concept of varnas. By the beginning of Gupta age, a strong Brahmnical reaction had set in against the ascendancy of the faiths of Buddhism and Jainism. This movement manifested itself in a tendency towards intensification of the social division into four fundamental varnas with its corollary of the pre-eminence of the brahmins.

The age old doctrine of division of society into four varnas is the key-note of the whole system of social life in samritis. The rules relating to the duties and mutual relationship of the four varnas in the vedic period were generally observed in Gupta age. Hiuen Tsang himself refers to four hereditary castes of Indian society together with their respective occupations, but adds that the members of the caste group married within the caste. Varahamihira in 'Brihat-Samhita' and Chanakya in Arthshastra have assigned the different quarters of a city to the brahmins, kshatriyas, vaisyas and shudras. The tenets of samritis, allowed the change of varana by individuals based on his capability and not determined by birth. Brahmans and kshatriyas had been adopting the occupations of the classes below them and vaisyas and shudras following those of classes above them. An inscription of 5th century A.D. refers to two kshatriya merchants, while another inscription mentions of a body of weavers from Gujarat having adopted various other occupations. Also there were authentic examples of inter-varana marriages, brahmans and kshatriyas were marrying the daughters and female slaves of courtesans. It follows from the above that samriti law upto Gupta age, though followed by people in general, was far from possessing the regidity of later times.

Removed further from other castes lying within the pale of Indo-Aryan society, were the aboriginal tribes, who lived in hills and forests.

The rules relating to marriage, formulated in samritis were not materially altered. Vatsayana contemplates marriage as normally being settled by the parents or guardians of the parties. There is detailed account of method of selection of the bride and the groom. A young man could, under special circumstances, apply himself to win the girl of his choice by courtship or even by trickery and violence. Girl was also allowed to select the groom by svayamber. There were, therefore, three types of marriages as per samritis viz Gandharva, Paisacha and Rakshara. Gandharva and Paisacha were more in vogue.

Female Education: Long before Gupta times, the Brahmnical sacred law had denied to women vedic study and even the utterance of vedic mantras. However, the girls of high families had sufficient opportunities for acquiring proficiency in general learning. In Vatsyayan's Kamasutra, princesses and daughters of nobles are mentioned among instances of women, whose intellect is sharpened by the knowledge of shastras. In particular, Vatsyayan gives a long list of 64 branches of knowledge, which should be learnt by women. These include solving riddles of words, chanting recitations from books, completing unfinished verses, knowledge of lexicon and metres and so forth. Vatsyayan drew a picture of good wife, as per samritis and may be taken as usual to be a faithful reflection of real life. There were the qualities of service, self-restraint and sound household management, which have remained the hallmark of Hindu wives down to the present day.

Life of the People: Hiuen Tsang recorded his opinion of the character of people in each region. While the people of Ganges and Brahmputra, basins were generally remarkable for their qualities of honesty, courage, love for learning, and so forth, those of north-western India and of Deccan Plateau as well as the people of extreme north, east, west and south were generally of a contrary disposition. In general, however, the character of the people was marked by an exceptionally high degree of honesty. The brahmins and kshatriyas in particular were distinguished for the purity and simplicity of their lives.

There was high standard of living attained in ancient India. Brihat Samhita proves that clubs, umbrella, elephant-goads, canes, bows, canopies, standards and chowries were in general use. The most costly of these articles were reserved for royal family. The gorgeous description of the splendours of Vasantsena place at Ujjain in the Marichhakatika conveys in general way the lavish magnificance of women of this class in real life. Kings and nobles adopted extraordinary rich dresses and modes of living which set the fashion for the rest. There were summer houses surrounded by water and fountains. The wearing of jewels was recommended not only for kings, queens and their nobles but also for those engaged in religious performance. Clothing was made of silk, muslin, calico, and fine wool.

There had been high standard of cleanliness and comfort in old times. The exclusive use of tooth-sticks is proved by Brihat Samhita. There were recipes for dyeing the hair and formulae for preparation of different kinds of incense, scented hair oils and hair lotions and other perfumes.

The approved foods were rice, wheat, and barley, pulses of three kinds,clarified butter, oils, molasses as well as raw and course sugar. People also took fish and meat and liquor although as per Fahien in 4th century B.C. killing animals, drinking wine, and eating onions and garlic were unknown throughtout Madhya Desha. In town, people lived more in fashion.

In Vatsyayan's Kamasutra, not only is the Nagrika's way of life described with considerable fitness but it is held as a model for others to follow. When a man had finished his education, he had to take up in large or small town, with the help of self acquired inherited property, the life of a nagrika. He first built a house and furnished it elegantly. It consisted of two parts, the outer one reserved for amorous enjoyment and the inner one for residence of his wife. Garden was attached to each house. Daily life was rising in the morning and attending to his physical needs, he arranged his toilet, used moderate perfumes in clothes, and wove a garland. After finishing business, he took his bath everyday, getting his limbs massaged and cleansed with soap leather, shaved/every fourth day and took two meals a day. Apart from daily chorus, he had periodical entertainment, such as samaj, worship of deities, gorthi (social gathering) udyanyatra (garden party) and samasya-krida (public sports). There were guilds and clubs. From Gupta age, we have glowing descriptions of the splendour and magnificance of many well-known cities at that time. The high level of Gupta urban culture evolved also a high and refined, delicate and elegant art of toilets and cosmetics. But whatever was done to beautify the body and the soul during this period, was raised to the standard of lalitkala or fine art in which simplicity, delicacy, refinement and elegance were the main watch-words.

Education: Four vedas were studied by the brahmins; the term of studies terminating at the 30th year. Hiuen Tsang spoke with high praise of learning and zeal of brahmin teachers. Among the Buddhist monasteries of the late Gupta period, none became so famous as the Nalanda, which was renowned alike for magnificance of its establishment and intellectual as well as moral pre-eminence of the inmates. It housed several thousands, who were maintained out of revenues of a hundred villages, separately endowed for its upkeep. The monks were looked up as models all over India. Nalanda attracted students from abroad but so strict was the admission test that two or three out of ten could succeed in getting admission. The ruins of Nalanda recently unearthed testify to its grandeur and vouch for substantial correctness of Chinese pilgrim's description. This had been destroyed by Muslim invaders.

There was long list of subjects of study extending from four vedas, and Itihas Purana down to snake charms and the arts of singing, dancing, and preparing unguents. The 'vidyas' included vedas, vedangas, puranas, nyaya, mimansa, dharmashastras, dharmavidya, gandharva veda and Arthshastra apart from sciences of sounds and grammar, arts and crafts, medicines, reasoning, Panini's sutras. Apart from Nalanda, Taxila, Magadha, Benaras, and Valabhi were the other centres of learning. For higher class the study was comprehensive.

Economic Condition: Agriculture had been the main stay of Indian economy. Long before the rise of Guptas, India had developed an advance system of agriculture, trade and industry. Guptas provided a government for the richest and most populous region of India i.e. Ganga valley, Malwa, Gujarat and Kathiawad. The age long dependence was on rainfall, inspite of richness of soil and abundance of natural supply of water, although some lakes were built and canals made out from rivers for adjoining areas. The main products were rice of several varieties, wheat, barley, peas and lentils, oilseeds of several kinds, ginger and other vegetables, pepper and other spices, medicinal and other herbs and sugarcane. There were seeds for sowing of various crops, trees indicating that agricultural science was quite developed in those days. Saffron was grown in Kashmir, sandalwood in Deccan, spices were native to Deccan, and foodgrains in Ganga valley.

Industry: Branches of industry were maintained at high level because of abundance of raw materials, and the skill and enterprise of artisans and craftsmen, variety of textiles of cotton, silk, wool and linen as well as barks of trees. There were fine and course types of clothes as well as bleached and unbleached silk, gold and silver brocades and dye work, and the spotted muslins. There was leather industry for leather shoes, leather bottles and boots. Copper, tin and lead had to be imported from abroad, but gold was taken in exchange of Indian products. Hiuen Tsang also indicates that gold and silver were the products of the country in abundance. Copper and iron were found between Beas and Satlej. Copper was also found in Nepal. The art of jewellers had been in advance condition. There were not less than 22 types of jewels including diamond, emerald, ruby, saphire, pearl, opal, etc.

There was inland trade through rivers and by roads. There were sea ports for exports and imports. There was inter-oceanic trade with China, Lanka, south east Asian countries, Korea, Japan, West Indian Coasts, Persia, Arabia, Adule and Ethopia. The trade was by large ships. Exports from India were spices, fragrances, sandal wood, saffron, textiles, jewellery etc. The imports included horses, copper, tin, lead, jewels.

The samrities prescribed detailed laws about dealing with labour, their wages, hours of employment, etc. There was no treachery. The master had to pay properly and the servant had to do his job sincerely. The breach of the master and servant relation was punished by the king severely.

The trade/industry was by guilds and partnerships. Samritis present details about the working of these organisations. The samritis also presented about—

1. Constitution of guilds;
2. Operation of their conventions; and
3. Rights and duties of individual members.

The general account of the living as detailed by Fahien indicates that the people were prosperous and happy. This is also proved by the pilgrims' reference to the luxurious dresses of the people and number of rich families in town. Above all the general prevalence of peace and prosperity is indicated in an unmistakable manner by the rich and varied specimens of architecture, sculpture and paintings mentioned earlier.

Inter-course with outside World

Central Asia continued to be a strong centre of Indian culture and influence and could justly be regarded as SER-INDIA. As in the earlier period, India have remains of ancient stupas, temples, monasteries, images and paintings as also a large number of Sanskrit, Buddhist texts and translations in different languages. Fahien and Hiuen Tsang throw light on these. Shen-Shen, the first kingdom visited by Fahien on leaving China, was situated at the eastern extreme of Central Asia. The king was Buddhist and there were more than 4000 monks in the country. The common people of this and other kingdoms as well as sramons (monks), all practised the rules of India only but the latter did so more exactly, and the former more loosely. So he found it in all the kingdoms through which he went on his way from there to the west, only that each had its own peculiar barbarous speech. The monks, however, were all students of Indian books and languages. The general picture is fully borne out by the details given by Fahien of the two kingdoms through which he passed before reaching India like Agni (Qara Shahr), Kuchi, Bharuka (Agsu), Kashgar, Khotan etc. In all these places, Buddhism was in a flourishing condition and Indian scripts and books were used. Buddhism was also flourishing in Turfan in the extreme eastern part of this region. There were several hundreds of monastries in Kashgar, Khotan, in the south of Kuchi. In the north there were two powerful centres of Indian culture in Tarim basin. The Khotan kings' new monasteries, the construction of which took 80 years and extended over three regions is about 250 cubits in height, it is much rich in elegant carving and inlaid work and covered above with gold and silver. The 'Hall of Buddha' is of the utmost significance and beauty; the beams, the pillars, venetianed doors and windows, being all overlaid with gold leaves. Six kings of eastern Turkistan gave all their valuables as offerings to this monastry keeping only a few things for their own use.

Like Khotan, Kuchi was also an important centre of Buddhism. The people of Kuchi spoke a language belonging to the Indo-European family. The intimate intercourse between India and Kuchi as early as 4th century A.D. is evident from the story of Kumarjiva. Kuchi had one hundred monastries, housing more than 5000 monks. They followed Indian doctrines and rules of discipline and studied the original Indian texts. The people played flute and pipe, which was Indian influence. Indian musicians actually went there and some even settled down in those countries.

We learn from Arab chronicles that Khalid, the Vizier of Caliph at Mansur was the son of a Barmak i.e. the chief priest in a Buddhist monastry in Bulkh, called Navbahar. The Arab conqueror of Bulkh captured Khalid's mother in 705A.D. The son was converted to Islam and founded the famous Barmak family. Khalid Ibn Barmak came to occupy the highest office under the Caliph. Among other localities, where Buddhism flourished are Ghazni, Kunduz, and various places between Badakshar and Kashgar. Rulers of two of these localities are said to have been descended from the Sakyas of Kapilvastu. Brahmanical religion also flourished in some of these places and specially Andarab.

Afghanistan: The testimonies of Fahien and Hiuen Tsang leave no doubt that a considerable portion of Afghanistan was still regarded as a part of India. It was indeed a part of north India. The people used language of central India. Foods and clothings too were like central kingdom. Kapisa (Faqiristan) was a large and powerful kingdom exercising supremacy over the neighbouring states extending as far as Sindhu. The king was kshatriya by caste and was a devout Buddhist. There were 100 monasteries with 6000 priests and many sacred relics and sites associated with the early history of Budhism. There were also some Brahmnical temples. Recent excavations have revealed the strong influence of Indian culture over the whole of Afghanistan as far as and beyond Hindukush. The remains unearthed show the existence of Indian art traditions, which had their full development in Khotan, Kuchi, Turfan, and other Indian colonies in Central Asia.

Tibet: The founder of Tibet, of a royal dynasty was the son of an Indian king. The kings of Ladakh and western Tibet also traced their descent from Sakya family of India.

Far-East Countries

Buddhism and along with it Indian culture spread from Central Asia, China and Tibet to other parts of northern and eastern Asia, Mongolia, Korea, and Japan. These were the most important countries to have been affected in this way. There is evidence of direct intercourse with these countries. Five Korean monks visited India in 7th century A.D. Two of them set out in 638 A.D. and lived and died in Nalanda. Two more had come and died on their way to India. The best known Indian monk Bodhisena, whose history has been preserved in Japanese chronicles was a brahmin of south India and his family name was Bhardwaj by gotra. Bodhisena went to China to meet Manjusri, who was generally believed in India to have lived there but Bodhisena had left for Japan. However, Bodhisena and Sanskrit were well known in Japan as Bodhisena carried on conversation with the Japanese priests, both in Sanskrit and Japanese.

Western Countries

Although Indian trade with Roman empire declined to a considerable extent after the third century A.D., there is no doubt that it continued for atleast two or three hundred years more. This is clearly demonstrated by the finds of Roman coins in southern India. At Madura, for example, were found a large quantity of copper coins of Arcadius, emperor of the east (395-408 A.D.) and Honorius, emperor of the west (395-423 A.D.); one gold coin of Constantius II (337-61), one of Theodosius II (408-50), one of Zeno (474-91) and one of Anastatius (491-518). Similarly more coins have been found in Travancore and in other places of south India. These coins as well as the Indian Embassies to Roman Emperors prove the continuity of trade between India and Rome down to the beginning of 6th century A.D. Trade relation with western Asia had also been flourishing throughout the period of 4th to 7th centuries. There was commercial intercourse between India and Arabia even in pre-Islamic days. The sword made of

Indian steel is proverbial in Arabic literature. Aden is mentioned as a centre of the perfumery industry, which had markets in Sindh and Hind and all other parts of the world. Indian spices were imported in large quantity into Arabia. An interesting evidence of close contact between India and Persia has been preserved by Tabiari (838-923 A.D.), the Persian historian. The Indian Navy is referred to even in historical times. Ubulla, near Basra, was known in those days as the gateway of India and its governor is said to have always had to fight against either the Arab Beduins on land or Indian Navy on sea. Many kings of west are said to have visited India and some of them conquered, or received tributes from different kingdoms in this country.

We have positive evidence that Indian literature and sciences exerted greater influence upon western countries during the period 4th to 7th centuries A.D. The Indian literature was highly valued in those countries and made a deep impression upon their people is proved by the history of a single book 'Panchtantra', which is a collection of fables containing wise maxims. It was translated in 6th century A.D. from Sanskrit into Pahelvi and then into Arabic and Sysian. Other Indian folk tales also found their way to Europe and can be traced in mediaeval collections such as the Gesta Romanorum and in the stories of Boccacio, Chaucer and La Fontaine.

Like Hindu literature, Hindu science viz medical science and arithmatic were highly prized in the west. Many scholars hold that the earlier Greek physicians were acquainted with medical works of the Hindus. Iran was also largely indebted to India for her knowledge of medicines and other sciences.

It is thus evident that Indian literature, arithmatic, medicines and religion made their influence felt and that, the cultural relation with the west was continued throughout the ancient period.

Colonial and cultural expansion in south-east Asia; Fahien has left us a thrilling account of the perilous sea-voyage to south-east Asia, which he made in 414 A.D. He embarked on a large merchant vessel at Tamralipti in Bengal and reached the island of Lanka in 14 days. Then sailed to China. He has stated that he had boarded a large merchantman, on board of which there were zoo men. The ship operated by wind and the directions were known by sun, moon and stars. There was, he has narrated, all risk of pirates, rocks, typhoons, tides etc. on way. But still Hindu kingdom continued to make rapid progress during that period. The Hindu kingdoms in Annam and Cambodia founded in Ist century A.D. continued to prosper and other new colonies sprang up into existence. Brief description of such colonies may be given below with a view to know the extent to which Bharat had progressed in her ancient times.

Indo-China

Cambodia: The kingdom of Funan passed through political troubles. There were several claimants to the throne. One of them was Hindu Chantan with title of the king of Fu-nan and sent an embassy to China in 357 A.D. The name of this Indian may be Chandana or Chandra. In 5th century, another Indian, named Kaundinya was elected king by the people of Funan. He was brahmin and had come from India. This would indicate that as per vedic tenets, Hindus believed in maintaining sanctity of independence. Hindus actually did not make colonies but ruled the other countries as their sovereign rulers, elected by the people of those countries as their kings. Another king mentioned is Jayavarman, a descendent of Kaundinya. He also sent embassies to China. He has left Sanskrit inscriptions. His son succeeded him. He has also left Sanskrit inscriptions. This kingdom was founded by Kambu Swayam Bhuva, the king of Aryadesh (India) and named after him. Bhava Varman, who occupied the throne of Kambuja in 6th century A.D. transferred the capital to Bhavapura. The dynasty and other Indian rulers continued to rule Kambuja for about 17 centuries, and during this time attained a height of splendour and renown, not acquired before or since by any other kingdom in Indo-China.

Champa: The king of Champa referred to in Sanskrit inscriptions of Champa as Bhadra Varman (349 A.D.). He was a great general and scored some successes against China. He had studied the four vedas and built a Shiva temple there. Subsequently many idols were installed in this temple and it is said that later on when China conquered this kingdom, they carried one lakh pounds of gold from these idols. Subsequently it came under the king of Kamboja, Rudra Varman. This dynasty ruled for several centuries. The last known king of this family was Rudrȧ Varman II who sent tribute to China in 749 A.D. and died about 757 A.D.

Burma and Shiam: We do not have much history of these kingdoms but Hiuen Tsang refers to several Hinduised kingdoms with its capital at Prome (lower Burma), Dvaravati, comprising a large part of Siam, Isanapur (Kambuja) and Maha-Champa (Champa). Hiuen Tsang heared these names while in Bengal, but did not visit these countries. But the fact that he refers to Kambuja as Isanapura, a name associated with his contemporary king Isana Varman, shows that there was a regular and intimate intercourse between India and these countries. Hindu dynasty called Sri Dharma-rajanuja vansa ruled Arakan from 600 A.D. to 1000 A.D.

Malaya Peninsula: The geographical position of Malaya Peninsula made it the centre of carrying trade between India and the Far East. Takkola (modern Taknapa) was the first landing stage of Indian traders and colonists. The Hindu colonists set up several kingdoms in Malaya Peninsula. Some details of these have been preserved in Chinese chronicles. We have record of Prince Lang Kia-Su having been called from India and made king of Malaya. He ruled for 20 years and was succeeded by his son Bhagadatta, who sent an envoy named Aditya to China in 515 A.D. Panpan (Bandon), another state was frequented by brahmanas from India. Some other kings' names are known from Chinese sources like Gautama,

Subhadra, Vijaya Varman etc. The archaeological discoveries in Malaya have thrown a flood of light on Hindu colonisation in this area. The most important of these colonies is Nakhon Sri Dhammarat (Ligor). It was a Buddhist colony which built the great Stupa of Nakhon Sri Dhammarat and part of fifty temples surrounding it. Also the persons of Indian cast of features are common on the west coast near Takna Pa, while colonies of brahmins of Indian descent survive at Nakhon Sri Dhammarat and Patalung and trace the arrival of their ancestors from Indian by an overland route across the Malaya Peninsula.

East Indies

Many Hindu colonial kingdoms were also established in various islands of the east India, which were collectively known as Suvarnadvipa. Some of these are discussed below—

Sumatra: The earliest Hindu kingdom known in Sumatra is Sri Vijaya (Palembang). It was founded before 4th century A.D. and rose to eminence in 7th century A.D. In 684 A.D. it was ruled by a Buddhist king Sri Jayanasa (or Jayanaga). Sri Vijaya was a centre of Buddhist learning in the islands of southern sea and king of Sri Vijaya possessed trading ships sailing between India and Sri Vijaya. The inscription of 775 A.D. refers to a mighty prowess of the king of Sri Vijaya. He was the overlord of all neighbouring states, whose kings made obeisance to him. Several embassies had come from Sri Vijaya to China during the period 670 A.D. and 741 A.D.

Java: There were several Hindu kingdoms in Java. Two of these, called Cho-Po and Ho-Lo-Tan by the Chinese sent regular embassies to China in 5th Century A.D. The names of kings in both these countries ended in 'Varman' like Purna Varman. His capital city was named Taruna and he reigned in 6th century A.D. There were ten kingdoms in Java, who acknowledged supremacy of the king of Java. The most important kingdom is Ho Ling recognised as Chinese form of Kalinga. So the colonist from Kalinga would have dominated Java. The predominance of Indian civilisation in Java is proved by the Sanskrit inscription of Purna Varman. Another inscription in central Java also shows that this region too was thoroughly influenced by Indian culture.

Borneo: The Hindu colonisation in eastern Borneo is proved by seven Sanskrit inscription found at Muarakaman on Mahakam river. They refer to king Mula Varman, son of Aswa Varman and grandson of King Kundunga. Mula Varman performed a sacrifice called Bahusuvarnaka and made gift of 20 crores to brahmins. These inscriptions were incised about 400 A.D. Grand father of Mula Varman, Kundunga is a form of Kaundinya, Indian brahmin. A number of Buddhist and Brahmanical images were found at Kombeng. Hindus had also colonised west Borneo and set up a number of settlements there.

Bali: Hindus had colonised the island of Bali and set up a kingdom there before 6th century A.D. Chinese history gives an interesting account of Bali—

"The king's family name is Kaundinya. When asked about his ancestors, he could not state this but said that the wife of Suddhodana was a daughter of his country." In A.D. 518 the king sent an envoy to China. The name Kaundinya shows the influence of that family in all Hindu colonies of Suvarnadvipa. There is hardly any doubt that in the 6th century A.D., the island of Bali was the seat of a rich and civilised kingdom ruled by Hindu colonists professing Buddhism.

Hindu Civilisation in South East Asia: We have so far discussed the history of Hindu colonial kingdoms set up in Indo-China and various islands of East Indies. The most important remains of Hindu colonists in this region are the Sanskrit inscriptions, written in Indian scripts. These have been found all over the region, in Burma, Siam, Malaya Peninsula, Annam, Cambodia, Sumatra, Java and Borneo. These inscriptions show that the language, literature, religion and political and social institutions of India made a thorough conquest of these far off lands and to a large extent absorbed the native elements in these respects. There are references to

Hindu philosophical ideas, vedic religion, puranic and epic myths and legends ; all the prominent Brahmanical and Buddhist divinities and ideas associated with them ; Indian months and astronomical system and Indian system of measurement. This reaches its climax in Burma, where we find a deliberate attempt to create a new India by locating there not only various places associated with Buddha and Ashoka but also scenes of subsequent episodes in history of Buddhism. The Chinese chronicles also testify to the dominance of Indian culture in this region. The story of Gunavarman shows the gradual spread of Buddhism in Java, and I-tsing has left interesting details of the influence of Buddhism in this region. We also have evidence of the colonists maintaining contact with India. Many kings came to India to spend their last days on the banks of Ganges. There can, therefore, be hardly any doubt that a 'New India' had taken shape beyond the sea.

5 Sultanate Period

After Harsha, no emperor of Hindu kingdom came on scene. India had been divided into small kingdoms. India had always been valuable to foreign invasions; the main reason being the plenty of richness. Foreign travellers and merchants had been coming to India during Gupta period and later on and had been talking to their master kings about the wealth of India. Every king, therefore, vied to conquer India. India had, however, been boldly facing all their invasions.

China is one such country, who had known about Indian riches through her travellers. But in the first half of the 6th century, the power of China in western countries, had vanished, although White Huns ruled a vast empire, which included Kashgaria, Kashmir and Gandhara, the region near Peshwar.

On the western side, the Ephth, a dominion, passed into the hands of western Turks and Persians, and their territory extended upto Indus. In 630 A.D., the Chinese under the guidance of emperor Taitsung, inflicted upon northern and eastern Turks a defeat so decisive that the vanquished became slaves to the Chinese for fifty years. Then Chinese turned their arms against western tribes, and in 640-48 succeeded in occupying Turfan, Karashahr and Kucha, thus securing the northern road of communication between the east and the west. At this time, Tibet was under Srong-tsan-Gampo, who founded Lhasa in 639, introduced Buddhisim in the country and with the help of Indian scholars devised the Tibetan alphabets. He married the princess of Nepal and China. The work of subduing Turks still continued and by 659A.D., China was nominally mistress of entire territory of western Turks and

China reached its height of glory. But a terrible defeat inflicted by the Tibetans in 670 deprived China of Kashgaria, which remained under Tibet till 692 when it was again conquered by China. Tibet, however, continued to be an independent country.

Nepal: History of Nepal is not available for earlier periods. The local tradition affirm that long before the time of Samudra Gupta, in 3rd century B.C., it was under Ashoka's control. Then it was under Samudra Gupta too. During the 7th century it occupied the position of a buffer state between Tibet and India. Subsequently the history of Nepal is again bleak till 1768 when Gorkhas are stated to have conquered the country and established the dynasty, which still rule. Buddhism had spread in Nepal but in course of time it turned to Hinduistic way of life, with the disappearance of Buddhism from India.

Kamrup or Assam: The ancient kingdom of Kamrup remained outside the kingdom of Hindustan. Even during Gupta period, it was outside its frontiers but paying tribute and was a vassal state of Guptas. It was a Brahmanical kingdom and was included in the dominions of some of the Pala kings of Bengal. In fact Assam is out of the few Indian provinces the inhabitants of which successfully beat back the flowing tide of Mohammedan conquest and maintained their independence. It was in 1204-05 that Mohammedan incursions had been successful.

Kashmir: It was in the terriotory of Ashoka and again under Kanishka and Harsha. After Harsha, it was an independent country under Durlabh Vardhan and subsequently remained under that dynasty for many years. A local Mohammedan dynasty obtained power in 1339 and religion of Islam gradually spread in the valley during 14th century. The great Sun temple at Martand, though partially broken by Muslims, stands in its ruined condition proclaiming the love of art of its builder.

Kanauj: After Harsha's death, the earliest known king of Kanauj was Yasovarman. He was slain in 740 A.D. He was author of 'Maltimadhav'. Next successor was Vajra Yudha. He was dethroned by Jayapada, who again was dethroned. Such struggle continued, when the king of Bengal and Bihar, Dharampal conquered Kanauj but after some tributes handed over to the defeated raja. In 816 A.D., Kanauj was conquered by Nagabhata, the king of Gujara Pratihara kingdom of Rajputana. Next king known as Raja Bhoj reigned for almost fifty years (840-90 A.D.), whose dominion may be called an empire and included CIS Satlej districts of Punjab, most of Rajputana, greater part of Uttar Pradesh, Oudh, and Gwalior territories. Next two kings ruled but now the ruler was under constant threat of invasion of Mohammedans. The waning power of Kanauj and the waxing strength of Jejakabhukti is shown by the incident that king Devpal of Kanauj was obliged to surrender a much prized image of Vishnu to Chandela King, Yasovarman, who enshrined it in Khajuraho. Devpal was succeeded by Vijaypal (960-90), but his terriotry got reduced.

At this period, the politics of Hindu Rajput states of northern India became complicated by the intrusion of Mohammedan invaders. The Arab conquest of Sindh in 712 A.D. did not seriously affect the kingdoms of the interior as they maintained good relations with other Indian kings.

Sabuktigin and Jaipal: In those days a large kingdom comprising the upper valley of Indus and most of the Punjab to the north of Sind, including westwards to the mountains and eastward to Hakra river was governed by Raja Jaipal, whose capital was Bathindah (Bhatinda), which was for many centuries on the military road connecting Multan with India proper. Sabuktigin, the Amir of Ghazni made his first raid into Indian territory in 986-87 A.D. Two years later Jaipal retaliated by an invasion of the Amir's territory, but having been defeated agreed to pay homage. Jaipal, however, broke the contract. Sabuktigin punished him, by devastation of frontier and annexature of Jalalabad. Soon afterwards, Jaipal made a Hindu Princes' conferderacy (of Kanauj, Rajyapala, Chandel king, Gonda) but the combined force was also defeated and Peshawar was occupied by Mohammedans in 991 A.D. Jaipal, who was again defeated in 1001, committed suicide and was succeeded by his son Anandpal, who again made a confederacy of Hindu powers and Chauhan Raja of Ajmer but Hindus again sustained heavy defeat.

At Kanauj, Vijaypal had been succeeded by his son Rajyapal. In 997 Sabuktigin descended and his son Sultan Mahmud made it a business to harry the idolaters of India and carry out their property to Gazni. He made 17 expeditions. Some of the rajas did not even offer any resistance and even from Kanauj, when the raja surrendered, Gazni took lot of booty, destroyed over 1000 temples and took many people as slaves. Kanauj had been conquered and occupied in 1090 A.D. by a raja of Gaharwar clan named Chandradeva, who also established his authority over Benaras, Ayodhya and Delhi. Delhi was founded in 993A.D. by Govindachandra, grandson of Chandradeva and enjoyed long reign upto 1155. The grandson of Govindchandra was Jay Chand, whose daughter Sanyogita was carried off by Prithvi Raj. His territory extended from border of China to province of Malwa and from sea to Lahore. Shihabuddin met him at Chandawar and carried huge booty after defeating him.

Chauhans: Chauhans ruled Ajmer for a long period. Its ruler Anangpal also was the ruler of Delhi. As a city in modern history, Delhi came on scene from Anangpal's time only, in middle of the 11th century. The iron pillar of 4th century was removed from Mathura and set up in 1052 A.D. as an adjunct to a group of temples from the materials of which, the Mohammedans afterwards constructed great mosques. Some years ago, during the repair of a mosque in Ajmer. six slabs of polished black marble were discovered bearing inscriptions in Sanskrit, which on examination proved to be large portions of two unknown dramas. One of these, the Lalit-vigraha-raja-nataka, was composed in honour of Vigreh raj, while the other, the Honakali-nataka, professes to be the composition of that prince himself.

His nephew was Prithvi Raj, Lord of Sambhar and Ajmer. He had abducted daughter of Jay Chand, the raja of Kanauj in 1175 A.D. He had captured Mahoba in 1182 and faced many invasions of Mohammedans. The dread inspired by the victorious Muslim army under Mohammed Ghori, who was now undisputed master of greater part of Punjab, constrained the jarring states of northern India to lay aside their quarrels, and combine against the foreign foe. In 1191 Prithvi Raj inflicted a severe defeat on invaders at Tarain, which forced them to retire beyond Indus but an year later in 1192, the Sultan again came with big force and faced Prithvi Raj, who had come with huge force of various rajas. Prithvi Raj was taken prisoner and executed, and inhabitants of Ajmer were either put to sword or sold into slavery, and with this, the kingdom of Mohammedans was established in India in 1194.

After defeat of Prithvi Raj, Ghori proceeded to Delhi and in 1193, Delhi fell. Kanauj does not seem to have been molested but must have come under the control of the invaders. In 1194, Benaras was conquerred. Mohammedans were now confident that the final triumph of arm of Islam over the land of the Brahmins was assured. Subsequently Gwalior surrendered in 1196 and Ahilwara, the capital of Gujarat was conquered in 1197. In 1203, Kalanjar was annexed, and when Mohammed Ghori died in 1206 he : "held, in different degress of subjection, the whole of Hindustan proper, except Malwa and some contiguous districts. Sind and Bengal were either entirely subdued or in rapid course of reduction. Much of Hindustan was immediately under his officers, and the rest were dependent or atleast tributory princes. The desert and some of the mountains were left independent from neglect."

Jejaka Bhukti and Chedi: The ancient name of the princes between Jamna and Narmada, now known as Bundelkhand and partly including Agra and Oudh in U.P., was Jejaka Bhukti and the present Central Province was the kingdom of Chedi. These kingdoms were ruled by Rajput rajas.

Chandelas: They came in notice in about 631 A.D. after overthrowing Parihar chieftain and became Lord of southern parts of Jejakabhuti. The Chandel princes were great builders and beautified their towns Mahoba, Kalanjar and Khajuraho, with magnificent temples, lakes and constructed many dams. The earlier rajas were subject to suzerainty of Raja Bhoja but in 10th century, Chandelas became independent. King Dhanga son of Vasu Verman (950-1025 A.D.) joined the new confederacy of Hindu princes, organised by Anang Pal but failed to stay the hands of invaders. In 1023 he had to surrender to Mahmud.

The account of the death of Paramal and the capture of Kalanjar was a good illustration of the process by which Hindu kingdoms passed under the rule of new Muslim invaders—

"The accursed Parmer, the Rai of Kalanjar, fled into the fort after a desperate resistance in the field, and afterwards surrendered himself and placed 'The collar of subjection', round his neck, and on his promise of all allegiance, was admitted to the same favours as his ancestors had experienced from Sabuktigin, and engaged to make a payment of tribute and elephants, but he died a natural death before he could execute any of his engagements. His Diwan or Mahtea, by name Ajdeo, was not disposed to surrender so easily as his master, and gave his enemies much trouble, until he was compelled to capitulate in consequence of severe drought having dried up all the reserviors of water in the forts. On Monday the 12th of Rajab, the garrison in an extreme state of weakness and destruction, came out of the fort and by compulsion left their native place empty and the fort of Kalinjar, which was celebrated throughout the world for being as strong as the wall of Alexander, was taken. The temples were converted into mosques and abodes of goodness, and the ejaculations of bead-counters and the voices of summoners to prayers ascended to the highest heaven, and the very name of idolatory annihilated. Fifty thousand men came under the collar of slavery and the plain became black as pitch with Hindus. Elephants and cattle, and countless arms also became the spoils of the victors. The reigns of victory were then directed towards Mahoba, and the government of Kalanjar was conferred on Hazabbar-Ud-din Hasan Arnal. When Qutab-ud-din was satisfied with all the arrangements made in that quarter, he went towards Badaun, which is one of the mothers of cities and of the chiefest of country of Hind."

Paramars of Malwa: The Parmar dynasty of Malwa, the region north of Narmada or the kingdom of Ujjain, was founded by a chief named Upender or Krishanraj in 9th century. Raja Bhoja is known from this dynasty (about 1018 A.D.) who reigned for more than 40 years. He cultivated with equal assiduity the arts of peace and war. He had fought with his neighbours and even with Mahmud of Ghazni, but his fame as an enlightened patron of learning and a skilled author remains undimmed and his name has become proverbial as a model king according to Hindu standards. Works of astronomy, architecture, poetry and other subjects are attributed to him. Mosque of Dhara is at the place of Bhoja's Sanskrit College and Saraswati temple.

Glory of this house faded in 1060 A.D. after the attack of king of Gujarat and Chedi.

Bengal : Harsha was a suzerain power of Bengal including Kamrup (Assam). After his death, the local rajas asserted their independence but no particulars are known about the history of Bengal for nearly a century. In 8th century, a chieftain named Gopala was elected king of Bengal. He extended his power over Magadha and reigned for forty five years. The second king Dharampal, is credited with a reign of 64 years. His rule extended from Bay of Bengal to Delhi and Jallundur in the north and to the valleys of Vindhyan range in the south. Devpal, the third sovereign of the dynasty, is regarded as having been the most powerful of the Palas. He is said to have conquered Assam and Kalinga. He was zealous in the cause of Buddhism and is reputed to have waged war with the unbelievers, destroying forty of their strongholds. He reigned for 48 years. Rampala is said as another powerful king in the dynasty. He conquered Mithila or north Bihar and his dominion also included Assam and Kalinga. He is last of the dynasty and was followed by several weak kings of his family. Pala dynasty was one of the most remarkable of Indian dynasties. No other royal line of important kingdoms lasted so long for four and a half centuries. Pala authority was shaken by Kamboj usurpation in latter part of 10th century. Two artists of that time Dhiman and his son Bitpalo acquired highest fame as painters, sculptors and bronze-founders. Some works of their school are believed to be extant.

The Palas were succeeded by Sena dynasty. Their chief Samantdeva had come from Deccan. They ruled in 11th and 12th centuries. In Bihar and Bengal—both Palas and Senas were swept away by torrènt Mohammedan invasions at the end of 12th Century, when Qutab-ud-din's general Mohammed, the Son of Bakhtyar, stormed Bihar in 1197 and Nadia, an year later. The fear of Mohammedan invaders was so much that the fort of Bihar was seized by a party of only 200 horsemen, who gained possession of the place. Great quantities of plunder were obtained and the slaughter of brahmins (Buddhist monks) was so thoroughly completed that when the victor sought for someone capable of explaining the contents of the books in the libraries of monasteries, not a living man could be found, who was able to read them. It was discovered that the whole of that fortress and city was a college, and in Hindi, a college is called 'Bihar'. There the library was destroyed too thus Buddhism was eleminated from Bihar, the last abode in India. Many ran away to Tibet and Deccan.

Similarly, the overthrow of Sena dynasty from Bengal was accomplished easily. Mohammed, after conquering Bihar, appeared at Nadia with a slender following of eighteen horsemen. The Rai of the city took him as a horse dealer but he surprised the Rai by an attack, and his whole treasure, wives, maid servants, attendants and women fell in the hands of the victor . The booty obtained is beyond all computation. Rai fled to Deccan.

Rajputs: The sudden introduction of Rajput states on the stage during 8th and 9th centuries is in part an illusion. Hardly anything is known about the caste or tribal position of the ancient ruling family. Rajputs, however, had considered themselves to be kshatriyas. From very remote days, ruling class of kshatriyas, similar to Rajputs of later days, existed and were forming new states even in mediaval period but their records have perished. Research has confirmed them to be of Scythian descent, who came from abroad about 250 B.C. It, however, appears that both Sakas and Kushans, when became Hinduised, were admitted in kshatriyas.

Deccan: The term Deccan (Dakshin) meaning the South is extended to cover the whole of India south to Narbada. The greater part is occupied by the territories of Nizam of Hyderabad. In this region, the reigning power for four centuries and a half was the Andhra in about 200 A.D. Between 200-550 A.D. the history is not known. The political history of Deccan, thus began in 6th century A.D. with the rise of Chalukya dynasty. They claim to be Rajputs from north, who imposed their rule on the Dravidians of Deccan, but had already been influenced by Aryans in 2nd.-3rd. centuries B.C. The dynasty was found by a chieftain named Pulakesin I (550 A.D.), who made himself master of Vatapi. His sons extended eastward and westward. In 615, Eastern Chalukya was founded, which lasted upto 1070 A.D.

All the southern kingdoms, Chola, Pandya, Kerala and Pallava came under the ruler of Vatapi. The fame of the king of Deccan spread beyond limits of India and reached the ears of king Khusru of Persia, who in 625-26 A.D. received a complimentary embassy from Pulkesin and reciprocated by Persia. The Ajanta caves are the hallmark of influence of Persia. But in 642 A.D., a long war started and Pallava King Narsinhavarman captured it and Pallavas dominated the south. In 655 again Kulakesin captured Pallavas. Then wars continued between Pallavas and Chalukyas. The end of Chalukya dynasty may be dated 1190 after which the rajas of this line remained chiefs only.

Mohammedan generals entered Deccan and destroyed the chieftainships in 13th century A.D., when Alla-ud-din, Sultan of Delhi, crossed the Narmada, the northern frontiers of Yadava kingdom in 1294. The reigning raja surrendered and paid great treasures, including 600 maunds of pearls, two maunds of diamonds, rubies, emeralds, and saphires and so forth.

In wide territories of south, the kingdom of Vijayanagar maintained the traditions of Hindu polity in unsurpassed splendour until 1565, when it was overwhelmed by a coalition of Mohammedan princes.

Afghanistan: Inspite of the ups and downs of fortune, the region, now known as Afghanistan, remained a part of India since the time of Chandra Gupta Maurya, who had conquered it from Seleukos Nikator in about 305 B.C. Hiuen Tsang found a kshatriya prince ruling over the Kabul valley. This dynasty ruled till about the end of 9th century A.D., when kshatriya ruling family was supplanted by a brahmin dynasty founded by Lalliya. Muslim historians called this Hindu kingdom of Afghanistan by the name of the kingdom of Kabul and Zabul. It was also called the Hindushahi kingdom. We, however, have no means of ascertaining the name of the ruler or the extent of this kingdom in the early years of 8th century, when Sind was invaded by the Arabs. Certain it is that the inhabitants of that region were Hindus or Buddhists or both and culturally, politically and economically, part and parcel of Indian people.

Sindh

Situated to the south-west of Hindushahi kingdoms of Kabul and west of Punjab, Sind had long been an independent kingdom, ruled by a shudra dynasty for about 140 years. Hiuen Tsang found a shudra ruler of Sindh. It was over-run by Prabhakarvardhan and was reduced to a vassalage by Harsha. It became independent after Harsha's death. After the death of the last shudra king, the throne was seized by his brahmin minister Chacha. Chacha was succeeded by his brother Chandra, on whose death, Chacha's son Dahir succeeded. After a few decades, it had to face Arab invasions under Mohammed Bin Qasim.

Kingship: The only form of government known to ancestors of 7th. and 8th. centuries A.D. was monarchy. Ancient republics of Buddhist time had disappeared. Kingship was generally hereditary. Usually the king nominated his successor, who was generally the eldest son. Election was, however, not altogether unknown. Gopala, the founder of famous Pala dynasty of Bengal was elected by the notable political elements of that province in the first half of 8th century A.D. and the Pallava king Nandi Varman, Pallava king of Kanchi in southern India was similarly elected at about the same time. At a time of crisis, the choice of a monarch was entrusted to a select body of nobles or brahmins or both. Many such cases of selection are on record; the most important being that of Harshvardhan of Thaneshwar and Kanauj, who was chosen by a council of nobles to fill the vacant throne of his late brother Rajyavardhan. Females were not debarred from succession to the royal throne and there had been women rulers specially in Kashmir, Orissa and some parts of southern India.

The monarchs of this period were absolute or despotic rulers. It was widely believed that the king was God's representative on earth and, therefore, superior and more intelligent compared to other people. The king's powers were, however, restricted by well-established laws and traditions and the council of nobles and also the fear of the public's rebellion to dethrone him. He was the chief executive, commander of the army and the fountain head of justice. Inspite of the combination of these wide powers and functions, he was not a tyrant, as he was governed by the 'Rajdharma', which was to be the father of the people and to always act for their welfare—physical, moral and material.

Every king had his ministers, who were his nominees. There were mantris and sachivas. The former were advisors and the latter were like minister of war and peace, minister of record, finance, foreign affairs. There was the Prime Minister, who was generally the Raj Guru and held the portfolio of religion also.

The kingdom was divided into provinces called as Bhuktis, Mandal etc. The province was incharge of governor called uparika. The province was divided into districts called vishayas, with a vishayapati at the head. Village was the lowest unit of administration, with a headman and a panchayat, consisting of village elders. The towns and cities were under an officer called Nagarpati.

Great attention was paid to finance. There were three main sources of income viz—

(1) Land revenue from the crown land i.e. those areas which were directly administered by the government.

(2) Tributes from vassal chiefs, and

(3) Taxes, other than land revenue such as excise, irrigation, duties on goods, roads, and frontiers of kingdom.

The items of expenditure were mainly on army and then the civil administration and king's household. The economic system must have been very sound as the country was extremely prosperous.

Buddhism was declining and most of the kings of this period were of the Hindu religion. These kings were, however, very tolerant towards all faiths. Infact they patronised Hinduism, Buddhism and Jainism at one and the same time. There was also no religious antipathy among the people and no religious persecution.

Caste system was gradually becoming rigid. The foreigners could, however, become Hindus and get absorbed in Indian society. During this period some of the brahmins took to the profession of arms while some kshatriyas lived as merchants. Even vaishas and shudras were powerful rulers. People married in their own castes but intercaste marriages were also not unknown. In central India, majority of the people were vegetarian. There was untouchability and chandals were required to make their presence felt by striking a piece of wood while entering the market. Girls of upper classes were given liberal education. Svayambers were not unknown. Sati was becoming a fashion in ruling class. The people were prosperous and happpy. Wealth was in hands of some, who were obliged to construct temples, hospitals, schools and eleviate the poverty and sufferings of the poor. There were many schools, colleges, universities and people were generally well-educated. The universities of Nalanda, Vaishali, Valabhi, Benaras and Taxila were most famous educational institutions in the universe. Science of astronomy, mathematics, medicines, vedas, puranas, dharamshastras were taught at the universities.

It would appear from the above narration, that execpt that the country had been divided into small kingdoms and each kingdom being independent and always trying to usurp the other, the condition of the people—economically, culturally and spiritually on the eve of Arab invasions, was, indeed good. The administration of the various states was on the whole efficient and it caused the welfare of the people. The main drawback known was the lack of unity and a sense of patriotism for the country as a whole.

The above position has been given, as it existed, at the time of the Mohammedan invasions with a view to know that :

1. The rule of religious law existed in all kingdoms in India.
2. India had been divided in many small kingdoms and each kingdom was independent.
3. There had, however, been frequent invasions by the raja of one kingdom on the raja of the other kingdom.
4. The people and the raja of each kingdom did not mind much for the national (Indian) interest but restricted their vision to their territory only.
5. The Rajput rajas were quite brave but were strategically very poor. Already having known the tactics of the Mohammedans in battle fields, they struck to their way of fighting only.
6. Although Prithvi Raj and other rajas like Jaipal/Anand pal tried to make confederacy of few princes but such confederacy was of rather smaller princes. They could not face the Mohammedans' attacks.

7. There was disunity amongst the rajas. Prithvi Raj and Jay Chand, two big rajas of north India, were enemies and rather Jay Chand is understood to have invited Ghori for an attack on Prithvi Raj.
8. The battle was considered to be the job of the warriors/ raja only and the other public was least concerned. They did not bother, who would be their ruler.
9. With so many invasions by Ghazni, the financial power had become bad.

It was at this juncture that power of Mohammendans had been rising. With Ghazni having taken huge booty from India, the Mohammedan rulers' eyes were on the wealth of India with the ultimate aim of ruling the country and spreading Islam as they had already done in most of europe and middle-east countries. Sindh was more or less already in the hands of the Mohammedans but Sindh being not very rich, the Muslims had eye on central India. The first expedition at Thana (Bombay) from sea route in 636 A.D. was repulsed. But their determination was strengthened when after giving up the sea-route, the Arabs adopted the land route and conquered Makran (Baluchistan) in early eighth century. They, then tried to have Sindh. For this purpose, Mohd-Bin-Qasim, an ambitious and able youth, came against Sindh at the head of a powerful force in 711 A.D. At that time, Sindh was practically isolated from rest of the country. The administration was weak and unpopular. It was not in a position to withstand the attack of such a mighty power as the Caliphate. Dahir's, king of Sindh, army was far inferior in number and equipment to that of the Arabs, under Mohammed-Bin-Qasim. After several days' skirmishes, a well contested engagement took place on 20 June, 712. Dahir himself mounted on an elephant led the army. But his elephant having been struck by a naphtha arrow fled into his army causing confusion. Dahir hit the army still but as ill luck would have it, he himself was struck by an arrow and fell from elephant. Although he immediately mounted a horse, the army fled in panick and Mohammed occupied the town. Following this success in Sindh, Mohammed proceeded to Multan. He met tough resistence but his army overcame. The town fell and Arabs got so much wealth that they named Multan as the 'city of gold'.

Causes of fall of Sindh

1. The province was internally disunited.
2. The population was sparce and heterogenous.
3. There were many Hindus and Buddhists, who did not want to fight.
4. Lower castes of society were badly treated. So they kept away. In fact there was little sympathy between the king and the people.
5. The spy system of the Arabs was good as also Indians supplied important information to them.
6. The Chiefs joined the Arabs against their king and country to gain favour.
7. Hindus for long accustomed to religious tolerance, had developed a cosmopolitan attitude towards other faiths and people and thought that in course of time, Muslims also would be assimilated in Hindus. They could not imagine the fanaticism in Muslims for their religion.
8. There was alround defection and treachery in the people.
9. Sindh was then an economically poor and deficit province and, therefore, with meagre resources could neither keep big army nor latest armaments.
10. The Arab army was large in number and better equipped.
11. They used arrows, whereas our people used barchhi and sword. Arrows could be used from distant place. Similar was the reason for the victory of Alexander over Porus but Indian rajas did not learn from history and manage to remove the deficiency in our ways of fighting..
12. Arabs had already been beaten several times as a result of which they were now better prepared and Sindh army, on the contrary was weakend because of previous battles.

13. Due to accidental injury to Dahir, he changed from elephant to horse and the army fled away not having known the change and taking the king as having been arrested or killed.
14. Dahir initially ignored the invasion due to lethargy. He also did not have proper spy system, who could alert him of the Mohammed coming for attack. Dahir also lacked leadership qualities and martial strategies. His silly mistakes, therefore, were also responsible for his defeat.
15. There was no cooperation from the neighbouring states, rather they helped the Arabs.

Mohammed appointed a military officer in charge and stationed 4000 troops to work under his orders. This was repeated in every town. To create panic in the minds of Indians, thousands were killed and many were made slaves and converted into Islam. Although Muslims did believe in absolute change of religion but due to the resistance of Buddhists and Hindus, Arabs had to find a way out and Islamic law opened up a new chapter in the history of Islam to grant partial religious tolerance to the Hindus in Sindh by payment of Jijiya. This subsequently became a common law for the entire country. Mohammed then laid down general principles of administration. He divided the territory into provinces headed by an Arab officer. Local administration remained in the hands of local people.

The Arab administration did not prove an improvement upon that of Dahir in so far as the lower classes were concerned. Rather in Dahir's rule, there were more restrictions and limitations. The provinces of Multan and Sindh remained parts of the Khalifa empire for a little over 150 years after which they severed connections with the Calphate and became independent governors. In 1871 Sind cut off relations with Caliph. Local Multan chief also declared himself independent.

Reasons for failure of Arabs in Sindh and Multan

1. Due to the weakness of Khalifa empire, revolution at Damascus in 750 A.D. led to the over-throwal of the Umayyaids by the Abbasids, which weakened the house of Caliphate. This quarrel effected Sindh too and Sindh severed connection with Caliphate.
2. Arabs had become fond of luxurious life and preferred speculative philosophy to the Quranian orthodoxy.
3. Primitive Muslim brotherhood tottered into fractions.
4. Religious schism also raised its head high, which had now subdued.
5. Unity in Arabs, which was on account of religious hegemony, had gone and all scattered.
6. The Turks had come up and Arabs got a shock on Turks coming up.
7. Arabs could not spare adequate force for the protection of their interest in Hindustan owing to internal convulsions.
8. Presence of powerful Rajput kingdoms in north and east had frightened Arabs from proceeding further to Sind and on the contrary these kingdoms started spreading their wings towards Sindh. They, it was felt, being very brave and devoted to motherland, were more than a match for the Arabs.
9. There was a powerful Hindu priesthood, which exercised influence over the people and were deadly opposed to foreign ways of life and thoughts.
10. Sindh was a desert land and its financial resources were inadequate to meet the expenditure of a top heavy administration and the army.
11. Sindh is situated at a wrong corner of India and it does not offer a geographical key to the rest of the country.

The Arabs conquest of Sindh, however, sowed the seeds of Islam in this land and a considerable number of Hindus and Buddhists had become converted to Islam. Also the wealth taken away by Arabs had watered the mouths of Turks too to subdue Hindustan and it led to the advancement of Turks to India.

Ghazni Invasion: Condition of India at the time of Ghazni's invasion:

1. At the time of the Mohammed-Bin-Qasim, all Hindus were there but when Ghazni invaded many converts to Islam were there in Sindh and Multan, who felt affinity with Muslims.
2. The Muslim invaders got support from Indian chiefs due to the informal discussions in expectation of favours from them.
3. Multan and Sindh had become independent in 871 A.D. but still professed allegiance to the Caliph for diplomatic reasons. Sindh was still ruled by Arabs and Multan too was ruled by Fateh Daud, a convert.
4. Neighbouring Hindu kingdoms had isolated the Sindh and Multan kingdoms and so favoured the Muslim invaders only.
5. Jaipal, the first Hindu ruler had already ceded a part of his kingdom, Afghanistan including Kabul. He had to face Ghazni but could not cooperate with him.
6. Reins of Kashmir were at the time in the hands of a woman and the condition of the kingdom was far from satisfactory.
7. Kanauj had passed on into the hands of a new dynasty known as Pratiharas in 836 A.D. Pratiharas had been defeated by Chandelas of Bundelkhand and so Rayjapal was a weak monarch, when Ghazni invaded. They succumbed before Turks from Ghazni.
8. While Mahmud of Ghazni was wasting north west India with fire and sword, Bengal was threatened by the powerful Tamil ruler Rajendra Chola. He was, however, not effected by Ghazni having been far away.
9. There were also small kingdoms like Chalukya of Gujarat, Chandela of Bundelkhand and Paramars of Malwa. They

had declared independence and individually were no match to Ghazni.

10. There was no powerful empire at the centre and the provinces, who had become independent, did not join hands to fight. The foreign invaders knew that individually they could not face the Turks.
11. The progress of people in south India was marred by constant warfare among the ruling families.
12. For nearly three centuries after the advent of Arabs, India enjoyed immunity from foreign invasions. This produced a feeling in the people and rulers that India could never be threatened by any foreign power forever.
13. External vigilance with Hindustani rulers, which is said to be the price of freedom, reached vanishing point.
14. Indian rulers neglected army. They failed to fortify North West Frontier and to make an effective arrangement for defence of the hilly passes through which foreigners could invade.
15. Indian rulers failed to keep in touch with new military tactics and with the newly invented armaments.
16. People, having become selfish, lost the sense of patriotism and national interest. They cared for their kingdoms only.
17. There was no territorial patriotism even, and whatever was there, it disappeared owing to false sense of security.
18. Narrow-mindedness became the characteristic of the people from 8th to 11th century. Infact in the absence of any all India empire after Harsha, people never cared for Indian interest having been coached to care for their mother country, which now was a small kingdom only and not India, as a whole.
19. The rulers did not associate the people at large with the army and protection of country rather they had learnt to obey the order of the raja that be—whether it was a Hindu or a Muslim raja, did not matter.

20. Al Baruni wrote "The Hindus believed that there is no country like theirs; no nation like theirs; no king like theirs; no religion like theirs and no science like theirs. Their ancestors were not so narrow-minded as they now were."
21. Indians ceased to come into touch with foreign lands and, therefore, became ignorant of happenings in the world—political, military and cultural.
22. Indian rulers cared to live lavishly, defended their own kingdom from attack and never thought of invading foreign lands. If they had done so, the foreigners would have learnt of their power and would not have dared invade India and at the same time they would have known the power of the rajas in their neighbourhood countries.
23. There was religious bigotory as many sects had come up, who did not see eye to eye. This caused disunity within the army also.
24. People had become luxurious. Even the great universities which had been great seats of learning, had become centres of luxury and idleness.
25. Economically country was rich and it tempted the wealth starved Turks to invade India and loot it.
26. India went on accumulating wealth, which attracted foreign invaders, rather than ultisting the same in securing effective defence of the country in owning improved armaments and better army personnel as had been done by Mauryas, Gupta etc.
27. Hindus had blind faith in God and thought that God would destroy the Muslims on idol-breaking and so did not care to protect the temples.

So the Turks, having known all above weaknesses through their spies and also from Indians, turned themselves towards this country. The Turks, who first came into contact with India belonged to an upstart ruling family of Ghazni. Their first attack was in 962 A.D. on the Raja of Punjab, who was of Hindushahi dynasty and ruled over the territory from Chenab to the Hindukush, including Kabul. Whole of Afghanistan was also under him. Sabuktigin was the king of Ghazni. Jaipal, the Raja of Punjab, invaded Ghazni in 986 A.D. to put him to his place. But due to a great storm, which disorganised Jaipals' army, the raja had to agree for peace by which he paid a large amount and a part of territory to Sabuktigin. Also he retaliated by an invasion and plundered Punjab. Jaipal called to his aid a number of rulers of Indian principalities and marched on Ghazni at the head of a forceful army but was defeated by Sabuktigin, who captured Lamghan and Peshawar. Sabuktigin died in 997 A.D. and was succeeded by Mahmud. He was an extermely ambitious youngman. He took a vow to undertake every year an expedition against the infidels of India, a holy war against Hind, or to serve the religion. He was also fond of wealth and he had heard availability of a lot of wealth in India. He invaded India 17 times, the earliest being in 1000 A.D. against Jaipal. A well contested battle was fought near Peshwar and Jaipal sufferred defeat. Jaipal, his sons and other relatives were taken prisoners and were left on payment of huge ransom. Jaipal could not stand the humiliation and burnt himself. He was succeeded by his son Anandpal in 1002 A.D. Mahmud again invaded and conquered Multan defeating Anandpal. Sukhpal, grandson of Jaipal converted into Islam and named Naushashah. Sukhpal again revolted against Mahmud and abjured his new religion. Hindushahi kingdom had shrunk due to frequent invasions and on each invasion ceding part of it. Yet Anandpal did not lose heart, but died soon. The decline and decay of the first Hindushahi kingodm enabled Mahmud to penetrate further. He beseized Bathinda in 1004 and captured. All men were put to death except those who embraced Islām. He went back with huge booty. In 1009, Mahmud captured Nagarkote; in 1014 plundered Thaneswar city and temple. Between 1015 and 1021, he made two unsuccessful attempts to conquer Kashmir. He gave up Kashmir and in 1018 started for Mathura, which was a very wealthy city and had many temples. He destroyed many temples, looted them and got huge wealth. Mahmud himself wrote thus—

"If any one should undertake to build a fabric like that he would expend there upon one lakh packets of a thousand Dinars and would not complete it in 200 years with the assistance of the most ingenious architects."

From Mathura, Mahmud proceeded to Kanauj. The Raja of Kanauj fled hearing of Mahmud's invasion. Again Kanauj was plundered from where he got booty beyond all calculations. Mahmud again invaded in 1022 and went with large booty from Chandela territory of Bundelkhand. His last invasion was of Somnath, where temple was looted and 50000 persons murdered on the Raja Bhimdev having fled leaving the town to be defended by God. One idol in the Somnath temple was in the middle of the temple hung without any support from below or to suspend it from above. It was held in highest honour in Hindus and they believed that the Loid would save them. Whosoever beheld it floating in the air was struck with amazement whether he was a Muslim or an infidel. Mahmud ordered the loadstones in the canopy to be removed as a result of which the idol fell. The idol was broken and the broken pieces were taken to Ghazni, Macca and Madina and cast in streets and staircases of chief mosques to be trodden by Muslims going there for their prayers. Mahmud died in 1030 A.D. He plundered huge wealth from India, murdered lakhs of persons, made lakhs as slaves, converted many to Islam, razed many temples to ground and destroyed art and literature available in India. There was no peaceful succession of Mahmud. All kingdoms in India gave up the rule of Ghazni and became independent.

After Mahmud Ghazni, there was no invasion as there was war of succession in Ghazni and no one thought of any attack on India for about 170 years. During this period, all Indian kingdoms had again declared themselves independent and made up some of the loss and build up their kingdoms again. It was only towards the end of 12th century that Mohammed Ghori came on scene. At that time, position of India was —

1. In last quarter of 12th century A.D., there were three foreign kingdoms in North West e.g. in Punjab, Multan

and Sindh. They had, however, declared themselves independent.

2. Peshwar and Sialkot were also ruled by Muslim rulers.
3. Jammu and Kashmir was Hindu kingdom.
4. Prithvi Raj Chauhan recovered Hansi from Ghazni Sultan of Punjab in 1167 A.D. and fortified it.
5. Prithvi Raj also wrested Bhatinda from Muslim ruler.
6. Turkish kingdom of Punjab suffered from decline and deterioration during the reign of Mahmud's successors, who became corrupt and inefficient.
7. Multan gained independence after Mahmud's death.
8. Sind became independent after Mahmud's death.
9. The rest of India was ruled by Rajputs, who were kshatriyas. They were very brave and execlled Turks but their qualities were marred by the presence of clannishness among them.
10. Chalukyas were the rulers of Malwa, Nadol, Girnar and Kathiawad. But by war with Chauhan, it was reduced to a second rate kingdom and he was left with the kingdom of Kathiawad and Gujarat only.
11. Prithvi Raj Chauhan ruled in Ajmer and Delhi.
12. Gahadwaras were the rulers of Kanauj.
13. During the time of Govindraj, the kingdom of Kanauj extended upto Patna. It included Kashi, Kosala, Kashmir (Allahabad) and Indraprastha. Jay Chand, the contemporary of the Mohammed of Ghor was its last ruler.
14. Other Rajput family worth mentioning is Chandelas of Bundelkhand. The last important king of this dynasty was Parmardi Deva, defeated by Prithvi Raj of Ajmer and compelled to cede a part to Ajmer.
15. The Parmars of Malwa, with their capital at Dhar, were very powerful at the time of Raja Bhoja. But at the time of Ghori's invasion, this was a vassal of Gujarat.

16. In eastern India, there were two Rajput kingdoms - Pala empire and Sena kingdom. Pala empire included whole of Bengal and Bihar. Rampala won Utkal, Kalinga and Kamrupa. After his death Pala dynasty relapsed in letharzy. Brahmputra valley, and southern Bengal declared independence and this kingdom could retain only Gaya and Hazaribagh districts.

With the fall of Pala empire, the Sena family profitted. They had come from south India and established in eastern India in 11th century. Their ruler Vijay Sena (1097-1159) ruled over Bengal, Kamrup and Kalinga and even north Bihar. His grand son lost the kingdom due to internal dissensions in 1206.

It would appear from the position indicated above that northern India was divided into many small kingdoms towards the close of 12th century. All the kingdoms were also on terms of hostility with one another. More than one dynasty claimed pre-eminence and paramountsy over others. The claim could be decided by sword only and hence Rajput rulers of north engaged themselves in constant warfare with their neighbours and paid little attention to the developments in north-west frontier provinces viz Punjab, Sindh and Multan, which were in foreign hands. Owing to this state of affairs, it was not possible for them, much less for the Indian people, to combine against foreign invaders. Rather these Rajput rajas, who were brave and egoistic, tried to harm the other Rajput rulers even by inviting the foreign invaders without caring for Indian interest. It is here that the Rajput rajas lacked the element of Bhartiyata, which led to the Muslim rulers establishing their kingdom in India and ruled for over 600 years in the face of so called brave Rajput rulers. History of India infact speaks that whenever there was no powerful king at the centre, the foreign invasions started and had been victorious. They were repulsed whenever a strong king came up and in this way the country heaved a sigh of relief for that period and after a few generations whenever there was weak link, the foreign invaders appeared. The difference in Muslim invaders and others had, however, been that whosoever came earlier to Muslims viz Sungas, Huns, Chinese etc, they became part of the Indians and adopted Hinduism but Muslims, being very fanatic, as they were, they kept their entity and rather converted many Hindus to Islam by force and monetary temptations leading to a huge population of Sind and Punjab having become Muslims.

It was in this disunited environ of the country that Mohammed Ghori became interested in invading India, not for the purpose of looting the country but for establishing his kingdom, so that the Indian wealth was ever available to him. Mohammed Ghori, was an ambitious and enterprizing prince. He looked upon himself as the heir to the punjab, which belonged to the kingdom of Ghazni. He wanted to establish a big empire and to bring the message of Mohammed to the Hindus of India and to put an end to idolatory. His first invasion was against Multan in 1175. He captured the city and appointed his governor. Then Sindh was conquered and annexed in 1182. Next was Gujarat but here he was defeated. He then turned to north-west and attacked and captured Peshwar from Ghazni ruler of Punjab, who had declared himself independent. In 1185 he invaded Punjab and plundered and captured Sialkot. He made alliance with Chandra Deva of Lahore and invaded further east Punjab in response to an invitation from a Hindu raja. Still he was not able to take the latter. Then by cheating Khusrav, the ruler was arrested and killed. Thus Multan, Sindh, Lahore and Punjab became the kingdom of Mohammed.

Now he was at the outskirts of Prithvi Raj's kingdom of Delhi and Ajmer. He had experience of Muslim Turk's invasions. Ghori made first attack on the fortress of Bhatinda in 1189. It was a surprise attack for which Prithvi Raj was not ready. This only indicates that there was lack of spying on the part of Rajput rulers. Mohammed, who was constantly knocking at Punjab and could reach Bhatinda and give a surprise to Prithvi Raj. The garrison at Bhatinda was defeated and had to surrender. Mohammed stationed his own men in the fortress under the command of Zia-ud-din and when the Sultan was about to return, Prithvi Raj appeared in the vicinity of the fortress. Battle was fought near Tarain (Teravadi) in 1191 and inflicted on Mohammed a terrible defeat. Mohammed himself was wounded seriously but was taken away. It is here that Prithvi Raj should have killed Mohammed and his men, who had been defeated to inflict fear of Indian force in their mind but he let him off and had to pay for it. On his next invasion it was the second defeat of Mohammed in Hindustan. On reaching Ghazni, he was never at peace and made furious preparations for avenging the defeat and when these were complete, he started again at the head of a select force of one lakh and twenty thousand cavalery. On reaching Lahore, he sent an envoy to Prithvi Raj for his submission. This was done in order to gain time for completing his preparations. Mohammed rushed to Bhatinda and appealed to Rajput rulers to assist him. With a combined force numbering five lakh of horses and three thousand elephants met Prithvi Raj again at Tarain. The Sultan, writes Minhaj-us-siraj "drew up in battle array leaving his main body in the rear. His plan of attack having been formed, he advanced quietly. The horsemen were made into four divisions and were directed to advance and harrass the enemy on all sides, on the right and on the left, in the front and in the rear, with their arrows. When the enemy collected his forces to attack, they were to support each other, and to charge at full speed. By these tactics, the infidels were worsted and Mohammed was victorious." The Rajputs fought with great gallantry but Ghori's tactics proved to be too great for them by an attack from all sides and when they were tired, Ghori sent his reserve. The Rajputs gave way. Prithvi Raj's chief Lieutenant Khandi Rai was killed. Prithvi Raj became dejected. He committed a mistake of alighting from elephant and mounting a horse. He was captured and murdered in 1191. There is another version of Chandra Bardai that Prithvi Raj had been taken to Ghazni where he killed Mohammed by voice target does not stand historically correct as Mohammed had died only in 1206 much after the defeat of Prithvi Raj.

The second battle of Tarain is a landmark in the history of India. Ghori achieved success and established his kingdom at Delhi. Immediately after Terain, Ghori captured Hansi, Kuhram, and Sarasuti, places of military importance. Mohammed planted his kingdom in the heart of Hindustan for the first time. He, however, realised that, for various reasons, it was not possible to take direct charge of the administration of Prithvi Raj's dominion. Therefore, he recognised Prithvi Raj's son on condition of his accepting the vassalage. Similarly another Tomar Prince was allowed to remain incharge of Delhi. A Turkish force had, however, been established at Indraprastha under Qutab-ud-din Aibak. In all conquered places, however, the temples had been destroyed and mosques created in their places. Islam was installed as religion of the state. At Ajmer, temples were demolished and famous college of Chauhan rulers was converted into a mosque. Having defeated Prithvi Raj, Mohammed in one stroke became the mighty ruler of northern India. He then easily conquered Meerut, Bulandshahar and other neighbouring areas. Ghori returned to Ghazni leaving Aibak as incharge of his conquests.

And thus India for the first time in history became a colony (non-independent) kingdom under Ghori in 1194. In Mohammed's absence Chauhans had raised their heads but were suppressed. Then Jay Chand had been defeated by Aibak. Jay Chand was about to win, when one arrow struck his eye and he was killed in 1194. Thus Ghori was victorious and Kanauj was added to his empire. Then he occupied Benares, looted the temples, destroyed and erected mosques in their places.

In 1195-96, Mohammed undertook another expedition against Bayana, capital of Bhatti Rajputs. The ruler surrendered. Then he beseized Gwalior fort but after a long seize Mohammed withdrew on the promise of its ruler Sulakshanpal to acknowledge his suzerainty. But Mohammed violated this treaty and again attacked. They cut off all communications to Gwalior, which had been isolated. The Rajput fought for a year and a half but in absence of army supplies, surrendered. Thus Mohammed had been victorious by cheating, martial tactics and other methods, which Hindu rulers could not even think of. They still had the vedic instinct of the laws of war in themselves, which failed them before the diplomatic ways of the Mohammedans. Mohammed then again went back to Ghazni. During his absence again several rebellions came up like in Aligarh and Ajmer, but were repelled. In 1197-98 Aibak captured Kalinjar, Badaun, Mahoba and Khajurabad. Then plundered and conquered Bihar. This place was also a university. The library was burnt and books destroyed. Vikramshila and Nalanda Universities had also been burnt. It is said that there were so many books that they kept burning for over a year. Then Bengal was plundered and conquered. Ghori was assassinated in 1206 by some Shia rebels and Hindu Khokhas in Indian expedition. Ghori suffered several defeats under Rajputs but he was a man of determination and was ultimately successful in establishing first Muslim kingdom in India.

Causes of defeat

1. Inferiority of Indian soldiers and superiority of Turks is given as one of the reasons but it is wrong as Indian soldiers had always been bravely fighting even after Aibak had been established ruler.
2. **Political disunity**: Jay Chand, Prithvi Raj and others had to fight single handed and they fought only for their kingdoms and not for the country. Infact for these rajas, their kingdom only was the country and there was no recognition of 'India' as a whole in their minds.
3. Lack of political unity and proper organisation and capable leadership.
4. Indian army organisation was on worn conception. They were ill-organised and ill-equipped.

5. Indian military leaders did not keep in touch with the development of tactics inspite of Sabuktigin and Ghazni's invasions, where they used their tactics.
6. Rajputs looked on battles as tournaments, whereas the Turks fought to win.
7. Rajputs believed in dharamyudh and so excused Ghori, when he had been defeated and left without being killed, whereas Turks believed in "every thing fair in war" motto. They not only killed the defeated enemy but also lakhs of other people to create terror in their minds. It is because of such a terror that later on the Muslim generals could conquer Bihar and Bengal (such vast and powerful kingdoms) only with a few hundred soldiers.
8. Masses of Hindu did not really cooperate with the leaders and soldiers. They laboured under a mistaken notion that it was none of their business to fight. They were rather prepared to be ruled by anyone. Rather because of incumbancy disadvantage, the Mohammedans were gainers.
9. The masses believed that their fate was same whether ruled by Hindu rajas or Muslim sultans. It was later when the tyranny of the invaders had to be faced that they realised the advantage of their own rulers.
10. Ghori made use of shock tactics to dishearten and demoralise country-men by devastation and killings.
11. Political and military demoralisation.
12. Turks were inspired by great religious and military enthusiasm, while Hindus had no such ideology. They rather thought that in course of time, as in the past, Muslims too would join the mainstream of Hindus.
13. Turkish invaders almost invariably acquired the correct knowledge of the topography, strength and alliance of the adversary and made full endeavour to exploit his weaknesses. Hindu rulers had practically no spying net and were mostly caught unawares by the invaders. They never cared to find out the loopholes in the organisation

of their enemy. Sultans had every time surveyed the prospective battlefield made and took the geography into consideration before engaging in the conflict whereas our people did not take advantage of Hindu's topography.

14. Hindu rulers divided the army into three traditional divisions—right, centre and left and they invariably made frontal attack on the enemy whereas the Turks divided the army into five divisions—right, left, centre and two in reserve to attack on the exhausted army of the enemy. This had two advantage—one the army of the enemy was already exhausted and so could face half-heartedly and second the enemy thought that there might be many more divisions in reserve and so got demoralised. This is how, Ghori captured Prithvi Raj in second battle of Terain.
15. Turks defiled tanks and rivers from where Hindu army got water. They also ravaged the territory in the vicinity so as to cut off the supplies of food grains and thus starve the army. These tactics even applied in Gwalior, Kalinjar and Bhatinda.
16. Hindu rulers committed many silly mistakes like those by Dahir and Prithvi Raj (who changed from elephant to horse); Jaipal (who burnt himself rather than prepare for fighting back); elephants were put in the front of the army and they crushed their own army—on being attacked by arrows as also necessitating change to horse by the rajas, which created confusion in the army not seeing the raja on the elephant.
17. The mobile Turkish cavalery was more than a match for the slow Indian mares and mountain like elephants.

SLAVES (1194-1290)

Qutab-ud-din Aibak

He laid the foundation of the slave dynasty as also became the first Sultan of Delhi kingdom from 1194-1210 when he declared himself a sovereign ruler. After the second battle of Tarain in 1192, Mohammed placed him incharge of Indian conquests. He crushed certain rebellions and conquered new areas during his period and included in his kingdom almost the entire northern India. He became defacto Sultan of Delhi in 1192 and declared himself sovereign ruler of Hindustan in 1206, when Ghori died. In this way except for the small period of 1192 to 1206 (14 years) when India was a colony under Ghori of Ghazni, India was again an independent and sovereign country although under Mohammedan ruler. Aibak did not make changes in administrative system which was allowed in local hands.

Iltutmish (1211-36)

He was Aibak's slave. Even Ghori was impressed with him and told Aibak to "Treat Iltutmish well for he will distinguish himself". He became king in 1211. He divided Hindustan in four principalities—Lahore, Badaun, Lakhnauti and Multan. When Iltutmish became Sultan, the Sultanate of Delhi was almost non-existant. He became master of Delhi and Badaun. Punjab was hostile; Multan became independent and Lahore too went out of hands. Ajmer, Doab and Gwalior also declared independence. Tajuddin Yulduz claimed sovereignty of entire Hindustan. Iltutmish settled with him to work as his vassal as he did not want to give a chance to Ghazni to come and rule over India again and in course of time rose against Yalduz and defeated him at Terain. Severence of Delhi's connections with Ghazni became complete and Sultan of Delhi became sovereign. He died in 1236. He was a brave, cautious and courageous soldier with modulation and foresight an able and successful administrator. He was the first Turk ruler to introduce purely Arabic coinage of silver. His achievements were:

1. Saving the infant Turkish kingdom from devastation;
2. Giving it for the first time legal status of sovereign kingdom; and

3. Perpetiating dynasty by ensuring the succession by his children.

Balban (1246-86)

He was defacto ruler from 1246-52 when he raised Nasiruddin to the throne and kept all powers in his hands. He dealt with several rebellions and in 1265 A.D. assumed the title of Ghayas-ud-din Balban. His immediate task was to restore prestige to the crown. He did it by his able experience. He believed in the theory of the 'Divine Right of Kings'. He reduced the authority of the Turkish aristocracy as they had reduced the crown to a mere figure-head and divided amongst its members all the great fields of the sultanate and all the highest offices in the state.

Balban's policy of despotism could be carried out successfully as he had realised that efficient spying system was necessary, which could inform him about the happenings in the state capital and in provinces and about the ambitious schemes of his nobles and officials correctly and promptly. In fact the efficient system of administration of Balban was because of his spy system on whose organisation he spent much time and money. The king placed secret reporters in every department and appointed secret news-writers in every province and infact, in every district. He took great pains in ascertaining the character and loyalty of the news-writers. He gave them good salary and made them independent of governors and commanders. They were required to transmit to him everyday the news of important occurrences. If a news-writer failed to do his duty, he was given exemplary punishment. The news-writer of Badaun, who had failed to report the conduct of Malik Baqbaq was hanged over the city gate. The well organised system of espionage then became one of the most important instruments of Balban's despotism.

Also the main prop of Balban's despotism was his powerful army. He concentrated his attention on its organisation. From the time of Qutab-ud-din Aibak, Turkish soldiers had been granted assignments of lands in lieu of their services. Some of them had been allotted fiefs before these were conquered and annexed to the sultanate of Delhi. Balban followed the old practice of granting land to many soldiers on condition of military service. The custom of sending proxies, and ill equipped hired men by the troops, however, was brought to an end due to Balban's strictness. The slave kings could not add new territories to the kingdom but had been busy in reorganising the house/army and reconquering again and again, with each king taking over, what Mohammed of Ghor had conquered but had been lost by his successors.

The areas around the capital city of Delhi was infested by robbers, who plundered the people of Delhi practically every day and the city gates had to be closed after the afternoon prayers. The condition in the distant provinces such as Bengal, Bihar and Rajasthan was much worse. Patriotic leaders in those days cleverly followed the policy of plunder and devastation, so as not to give sufficient time to the Turks to consolidate their hold in the country. There was, however, lack of first rate leadership, which prevented them from uniting together and mustering adequate force to fight and expel the Turks from the country. Balban was not deterred by the enormity of the task from carrying out his resolution of putting down rebellions and making the vicinity of Delhi safe from robbers and rulers. He punished them with a heavy hand and cleared the jungles and built four forts in the rural areas around Delhi and garrisoned them with ferocious Afghan troops. Similar action was taken in other provinces too. The kingdom was divided into areas and energetic officers were appointed to clear the forests and to conduct a ruthless drive against the local Hindu chieftains and their robbers through liberty loving hands. He also established military/police posts and garrisoned with semi-barbarous Afghan troops. By resorting to frequent slaying of men and enslaving the women, he created terror in the hearts of the people and depopulated the entire region which rose in revolt againt the government in Katihar. Historian

Barani has told that the Kateharias never after raised their heads and the entire region became safe for the travellers, the peasants and the government officers. Similar was the fate of other regions too.

Balban held the reins for forty years—first as Deputy of Sultan and then as Sultan. Throughout his aim was to consolidate the Turkish state in Hindustan and he attained success. He achieved his objective by ruthlessness and by striking terror all around. His most notable achievement was ensuring safety of the Turkish state and giving it a new base of life and the next lay in raising the prestige of crown.

Administration of the Slave Kings

1. Hindu rulers within the boundaries of sultanate of Delhi made repeated attempts to throw off Turkish yoke. Each sultan had to suppress such rebels almost every year.
2. The boundaries of sultanate of Delhi, therefore, fluctuated from reign to reign.
3. In general the boundary was Himalaya Tarai in the north and by a zigzag line in the south which included northern half of Bengal, north Bihar, part of Bundelkhand, Gwalior, Ranthambhore, Ajmer, Nagaur and Jaisalmer and Sindh in the west. In east half Bengal was the boundary line.
4. Turkish state in India was a theocracy like all Islamic states. Quranic law was the religion or common law and was known as Shariat.
5. The real king of a Muslim state was God and the kings were his agents.
6. The birth, ability and nomination by the dead king and the support given by the nobles often decided the selection of succeeding kings.
7. The sultanate was a military state and was based on force, not on consent of people. Entire territory was held by Turkish troops.

8. Dismantlement of temples, breakage of idols, conversion to Islam, making slaves and killing the people was the general rule with a view to terrorise the people.
9. Sultan was a full fledged sovereign ruler uncontrolled by any outside agency or authority. He was a tough despot and fourtain of law. There was always the fear of rebellion and, therefore, army and the Sultan were always on the alert.
10. Sultan hardly had time for planning. The central government was a haphazard growth. There were, however, four important ministers in the capital viz. the Wazir (Chief Minister), the Ariz-i-Mamalic (Army Minister), Diwan-i-Insha (to draft royal proclamations and despatch) and Dewan-i-Risalat (foreign and diplomatic correspondence).
11. The work of the other important dignitaries—Barid-i-Mamalic (chief news writer) of the kingdom under whom there were news-writers and the spies and the Qazi-i-Mamalik or the Chief Justice.
12. Goverment revenues were derived from five main sources:
    (a) Kharaj (Land Tax on land held by Hindus)
    (b) Tax on land held by Muslims and watered by national means.
    (c) Jiziya (Tax on Hindus)
    (d) Khams (1/5th of the booty captured in war from infidels)
    (e) Zakat (Tax on Muslims equal to 1/40th of their income), spent for the benefit of Muslims.

From an account of the administration by Balban, it is clear that whatever he had done to provide to the country a safe, secure and stable government, seems to be as per the dictates of Chanakya's Arthshastra adopted by Chandra Gupta Maurya. He would seem to either have read it or he would be having some Hindu politician in his darbar to guide him that way. The entire governance, therefore, had been Bhartiya and since the slave kings (Qutab-ud-din himself) had declared themselves as sovereign kings, thinking only of the security of the people, as enshrined in vedic tenets only confirms and lays the foundation of an independent Indian nation in Hindustan. This period, therefore, has to be conceded as of independent Hindustan except from 1194, when Qutab-ud-din had been placed as a lieutenant of Mohammed Ghori and upto the death of Mohammed Ghori in 1206, when Qutab-ud-din declared himself independent. Subsequent Sultans had fully devoted to the government of Hindustan only and had no connections whatsoever with the foreign authorities. In other words they had Indianised themselves.

KHALJIS (1290-1320)

Jalal-ud-din Khalji (1290-96)

He first took service under Sultanate of Delhi and rose when opportunity became available. For thirty years, Khaljis ruled Delhi. Jalal-ud-din's internal policy was one of conciliation. He tried to be peaceful, mercyful and humane and wanted to rule, if possible, without bloodshed. He did not undertake any notable expeditions against Hindu chiefs.

Ala-ud-din (1296-1316)

He was nephew and son-in-law of Jalalud-din. Very active and spirited soldier, who had already held important ports under Jalal-ud-din, he waded through blood to the throne of Delhi. He murdered his uncle to gain the throne. Then he had to tackle the nobles, who were pet of Jalal-ud-din. Mongols were hammering at the north west frontier. His first action after having been crowned in 1296 was to concilliate so that the people and the nobles forgot the heinous crime of which he was guilty. But as soon as he had established himself firmly, Ala-ud-din decided to revive Balban's theory of kingship of majesty or the monarch and his being God's representative on earth. His policy was in his own words:

"I do not know whether it is lawful or unlawful, whatever I think to be for the good of the state or suitable for the emergency, that I decrce; and as for what may happen to me on the day of judgement. That I know not".

Ala-ud-din did not invoke the sanction of the Khålifa's name for strengthening his claim to sovereignty. Yet he styled himself only as an assistant of the Khaleja i.e. to pay homage to the Khaleja not as to a political superior but only to keep the tradition of theoretical Khilafat, alive.

Domestic Policy

1. Suppression of rebellions: As usual there were rebellions from Hindu chiefs with each change in the Sultanate of Delhi, particularly during Jalal-ud-din's time as he was very benevolent. Even Muslim governors of provinces revolted against the centre.
2. He came to the conclusion that such a state of affairs was due to:
   (a) Inefficiency of spy system which kept the king ignorant of the doings of his officers and people.
   (b) General practice of use of wine promoted fellowship and provoked people to indulge in rebellions and conspiracies.
   (c) Social intercourse among the nobles and intermarriages between them gave the opportunity to combine against the king.
   (d) Excess of wealth in possession of certain notable people gave them the leisure for idle thoughts and for indulging in plots of rebellions.
3. Ala-ud-din accordingly issued important ordinances:
   (a) Confiscation of all religious endowments and free grants of land.
   (b) Reorganised spy system : An army of spies was created. News-writers and spies were placed in the houses of

nobles and officers and in all offices, towns and even in important villages. They were required to report all occurrences fit for the Sultan's ear and likely to be useful. The result of this ordinance was that gossip of nobles and officers and even of common people came to an end and they became filled with awe of the Sultan's wrath for he knew not only their doings but even their designs and thoughts.

(c) Third ordinance prohibited the use of liquor and drug. Sultan himself gave up wine and caused his wine vessels broken. Violators were cruelly punished.

(d) Nobles should not have social gatherings and that they should not inter-marry without his permission. This regulation was rigorously enforced.

4. Hindus, through out the kingdom, had been reduced to one dead level due to over taxation and conversion etc.; of poverty and misery; or if there was one class more to be pitied than the other, it was that which had formerly enjoyed the most esteem i.e. hereditary assessors and collectors of revenue.

5. Ala-ud-din had to maintain huge army to suppress the rebellion in India and Mongols from abroad as also to conquer more areas in Hindustan. To reduce the cost of army, he regulated the price of foodgrains, cloth and other necessities of life and cheapening them so much that a soldier could live comfortably on a mere pittance. He fixed the prices of foodgrains, cloth and other commodities far below the usual market rate. All merchants dealing in these commodities were required to register themselves.

6. Set up a department of checking prices, weights and measures and anyone, who sold a commodity under-weight, the same amount of flesh was cut from his body. All kinds of speculations and black marketting were rigorously put down. There was no hoarding. A department of Diwan-i-riyasat and Shaharia-i-mandi was created assisted by a judge called Sarai Adal and a host of subordinate officers.

7. With large army at his back, Sultan was able to suppress all lawlessness in his dominion and took steps for complete concentration of authority in his hands. Although ministers were there but he was his own prime minister. He did consult the ministers, whenever considered necessary but was not bound by their advice.

8. The governance of provinces or muqties too, unlike in the days of his predecessors, were brought under greater control of central government. His espionage developed to a frightful perfection, which over—awed the nobles and courtiers, who feared to exchange views within themselves or even to talk aloud. They could only take the means of signs.

9. Sultan put down the old nobility ruthlessly and raised the common people, who were possessed of merit and loyalty to position of importance. All chiefs were reduced to the position of his vassals, servants or subjects.

10. Conquests: As already indicated, Khalji had huge army to combat the rebellions, foreign aggressors and to conquer new areas. After subjugating the rebellious rajas in north India and repelling the invasions of Mongols in north west (14 times), Khalji set out for Rajputana, Gujarat and Deccan. He captured by force, treachery, seduction, alliance and cheating.

(a) **Gujarat**: The flourishing kingdom with capital at Anhilwara could not be subdued by Turks and was ruled by Baghela ruler Karan. Khalji beseized Anhilwara and captured it.

(b) **Ranthambore**: Ruled by Hamirdeva, a Chauhan King. Khalji invaded first because it was formely part of Delhi kingdom and secondly the king had given shelter to Muslim rebels of Ala-ud-din. Delhi besiezed Ranthambore but were beaten. Ala-ud-din himself proceeded and seize lasted for an year without any signs of surrender. Ala-udd-in seduced Hamirdeva's prime minister Ran Mal and with his collusion, the seize was brought to a successful conclusion. Hamirdeva and his family were killed. Ran Mal too was killed being treacherous to his master.

(c) **Chittor** : Ala-ud-din beseized its capital in 1303. His principal motive was to have Padmini, the beautiful queen. His efforts at seize failed. Despite stout defence by Rajputs, ultimately Rana Ratna Singh had to surrender. The women ended their lives in Jauhar. Ala-ud-din having frustrated, ordered killing of the army of the enemy. It is said that 30,000 rajputs had been killed in one day. Chittor, however, could not be kept for long owing to dedicated rajputs of the place. After Ala-ud-din's death, it was recovered by the Hindu successor.

Malwa: Raja Harnanda was defeated in 1305 and Ujjain, Mandu, Dhar and Chandrai were added to Delhi kingdom.

Jalor: Delhi army was once defeated but on further invasion conquered and killed the raja and his family. With this, conquest of north India was complete.

Deccan: Sultan then proceeded to Deccan. He was first Sultan of Delhi to cross Vindhyachal. At that time there were four powerful kingdoms:

1. Yadav kingdom of Devgiri.
2. Kakatiya kingdom of Telingana with capita' Warrangal.
3. Hoysala kingdom of modern Mysore.
4. Pandya kingdom of far south with capital at Madura.

Unlike in North, where the territories were annexed in Delhi kingdom, Sultan only wanted subjugation of Southern states and to send annual tributes as vassals. He reduced Devgiri and compelled its ruler to yield huge treasure and to become vassal. Another army attacked Warangal but was defeated and compelled to flee back. Devgiri too failed to send the agreed tribute money. The raja was defeated and he presented himself at Delhi with huge presents. He was allowed to continue as vassal.

Warangal was again surrounded. Its ruler Pratap Rudra II was taken by surprise. Warangal was beseized and heavy losses inflicted. Raja surrendered and paid large amount and accepted payment of annual tribute.

Hoysala: From Devgiri, royal forces proceeded to Dwarsamudra, capital of Hoysala kingdom and the ruler was taken by surprise. He was defeated. Rich temples were looted. Enormous indemnity was paid and accepted to become vassal state.

From Devsamudra, the Delhi army proceeded to Pandya kingdom in extreme south of Deccan. There was dispute amongst brothers to succeed to Pandya throne. One of the brothers had sought help from Delhi for recovery of throne. Delhi army reached Madura. The raja fled and the army plundered and destroyed the main temple and reached Rameshwaram, where the great temple was destroyed and a mosque erected. After these exploits, the army came back to Delhi in 1311 with enormous spoils, (312 elephants, 20000 horses, 2750 pounds of gold and chests of jewels. No such booty had ever been brought to Delhi).

The conquest of Deccan was now complete. Whole of Deccan had been subjugated as vassal and few garrisons were stationed at important points.

Ala-ud-din died in 1316. He had a non-disturbed time towards the end of his life. Mongols were repelled five times and afterwards they did not think of invading India for a long time till Babar ventured. Internally no rebellions could take place out of the fear of Ala-ud-din and his spy network. The people were at peace and treasury was with plenty of wealth. Except that he was cruel to Hindus, and a fanatic Muslim, he followed the rule of governance as adopted by Balban or in other words as adopted by Mauryas on Arthshastra or to say the view of Bhartiyata.

TUGHLAQS (1320-1414)

Ghayas-ud-din Tughlaq (1320-25)

He was a slave under Khaljis, where from he rose to position. He followed the policy of encouraging agriculture and protecting cultivators, concilliating with rules. The system of news-writers continued. The post was now carried by horses. He was faced with rebellions from Deccan and Bengal.

Mohammed Bin Tughlaq (1325-51)

After Gyas-ud-din's death in 1325, Mohammed Tughlaq sat on throne. He was very diligent ruler and issued numerous ordinances, such as:

1. Compilation of register of revenue and expenditure of the provinces of kingdom. He directed governors of provinces to send to the capital all relevant records and other material for compilation.
2. He increased taxation in Doab with a view to augment resources but the timing of this increase was wrong. It had been done when there was famine and people ran away to avoid tax.
3. He imposed house tax and grazing tax as a result all houses had been numbered and cattle branded.
4. He created a Department of Agriculture to bring uncultivable land under cultivation by giving direct financial support from treasury. But people ate away money so given as :
   (a) The land so chosen was not fertile
   (b) The scheme required monitoring by centre which was lacking
   (c) Period was short to give results and
   (d) Money was badly spent or misappropriated.
5. Transfer of capital from Delhi to Daulatabad, which was a failure.
6. Introduction of token currency : The idea was not bad but it was not backed by appropriate espionage as a result of

which base currency had been made out as there was no central control. It is said that every Hindu house became a mint. Then Sultan withdrew this currency and huge exchange money had to be paid for base currency.

7. He introduced secular consideration as against a biased (pro-Islamic) consideration, based on reason, expediency and appeal. Although a good and popular step, it brought Tughlaq in clash with the ulema.
8. He believed in divine right of king and said that behind the king there was shadow of God.
9. Most of the expeditions, though not unreasonable, failed due to lack of proper follow up/espionage.
10. Many Chiefs rebelled like in Malabar, Bengal, Daulatabad, Lahore, Kara, Bidar, Gulbarga, Awadh, Devgiril, Gujarat.
11. In South a Hindu kingdom of Vijaynagar was founded after ending the vassalage of Khalji, as an independent kingdom in 1336.
12. Tughlaq had good points in as much as his private life was of high standard of morality.
13. On the whole, Tughlaq was a failure despite having been very diligent and with new ideas.
14. Tughlaq also planned to conquer Khurasan and collected huge army for that purpose but had to disperse as project could not be taken up.

Feroze Tughlaq (1351-1388)

He succeeded when there were chaotic conditions and rebellions throughout. He abandoned many taxes to give relief to suffering people and improved quality of cultivation and superior crops. Provided water and 1200 fruit gardens as a result wealth abounded and people lived comfortable lives. The state did not suffer from financial bankruptcy during his reign. Feroze is popular for—

1. Constructed five canals—one from Yamuna to Hissar (150 miles); second from Satlej to Ghagra (90 miles); third from

Mandavi to Hansi; fourth from Ghagra to Ferozabad and fifth from Yamuna to Ferozabad (founded by Feroze Tughlaq).

2. Laid 1200 fruit gardens around Delhi.
3. Introduced many benevolent measures for the welfare of the people. He started employment bureau. Names of unemployed persons were registered and they were provided employment. He established Diwan-e-Khairat which gave pecuniary help for marriage of Muslim girls and aid to widows and orphans. He also established charitable hospitals (Darul safa), where patients were supplied freee medicines. He gave liberal assistance for education. Having born of a Hindu lady, he was tolerant to Hindu religion.

Feroz was fond of slaves and he ordered all his governors to send slaves. So slaves numbered about two lakhs. He died in 1374.

INVASION OF TIMUR (1398-99)

Amir Timur was born in 1336 and ascended to throne in 1369. Fabulous wealth of India attracted him in view of the Delhi Sultanate tottering and affording an opportunity to the Turkish conquerer to help himself at its expenses. India had been vulnerable to foreign invasions because of attraction of its wealth. These invasions had been repulsed whenever there was strong government and were victorious when there was weak government in India or when invited by another raja of Indian territory. Timur pretended that his object was to put down idolatory, which had been tolerated by Sultan of Delhi and had no desire of conquering or ruling India. He set in 1398 crossing Indus, Jhelum and Ravi. After plundering and massacring the people in all towns on the way, he reached Delhi in December 1398 and butchered one lakh Hindu captives in cold blood. Sultan of Delhi fled away. Timur occupied Delhi and ordered general plunder and massacre, which lasted for several days. Lakhs had been killed and imprisoned. It is said that—

'High towers were built with the heads of Hindus and their bodies became the food of revenous beasts and birds—such of the inhabitants, who escaped alive were imprisoned'. He conquered and acquired immense wealth. The conquerer quited Delhi on January 01, 1399. On way back also, he slaughtered many people in Kangra, Jammu, Multan, Lahore and Dipalpur.

There was all prostrate and bleeding and utter confusion and misery throughout North India. Lakhs had been butchered and another lakhs taken prisoners; all harvest destroyed and all wealth taken away. City of Delhi was ruined and devastated.

Causes of decline of Tughlaq Dynasty—

1. Mohammed Tughlaq's policies and character were mainly responsible for shrinkage of his dominion.
2. He inflicted excessively harsh punishments for disobeying him and made wild schemes of conquest.
3. Many governors rebelled and declared independence.
4. There was alround dissatisfaction and discontentment amongst the people.
5. After Mohammed Tughlaq, Feroze Tughlaq became extra lenient to heal the wounds of the people but this led to undermining the royal authority.
6. During Mohammed Tughlaq's regime, there had been complete central despotism, who would not listen to anyone.
7. Base coins caused drain on exchequer of capital.

It has been obseved that whenever the principles of Arthshastra had been followed as in the region of Bulban and Ala-ud-din Khalji, the government had been stable; no foreign invasions and there had been internal peace and when the same were not adhered to, there had been chaos and anarchy. Bhartiyata, therefore, had been the panacea for the governance in India. Tughlaqs lost because of non-adherence to the vedic tenets.

LODHIS (1451-1526)

Bahlol Lodhi (1451-85)

Lodhis were a clan of Afghanistan. They had served under Tughlaqs. Bahlol Lodhi became governor of Sirhind. His ambition was to occupy the throne of Delhi. He ascended in 1451 and added several Rajputana and other kingdoms to his dominion. He was a brave and intrepid soldier and a successful general. His objective was to establish Delhi control. He never truned away a beggar or a poor from his gate. When queen Malka-i-jahan of Sultan of Jaunpur fell into his hands, he sent her back to her husband with escort. He ruled from 1451 to 1488.

Sikander Lodhi (1485-1517)

He was succeeded by Sikander Lodhi. He insisted on proper audit of the accounts of revenue and expenditure of his governors and other officers and severely punished persons responsible for defalcations and embezzlements. He compelled his nobles to show formal respect to the king in the darbar and outside. He had kept a spies ring around all governors to inform him of what was happening there. Once nobles conspired to depose Sikander and place his younger brother Fateh Khan on throne. But the conspiracy was divulged and the Sultan banished twenty two of his nobles from the court. By this strict policy, Sikander succeeded in bringing the Afghan peers under proper discipline and the Sultan was given due respect. His farmans had to be received six miles in advance and with due ceremony. When the farman was read allowed, all had to listen to it standing. He borrowed the espionage system from Ala-ud-din Khalji. He had appointed trust-worthy spies and news-writers and posted them everywhere including even in the houses of nobles. This again is what has been indicated in Arthshastra. He was so much posted with up to date information that people credited him with super natural powers. It was widely believed that the Sultan was supplied with news by Genii. Sikander was not only a strict disciplinarian but he even tried to administer justice evenly according to the Islamic standard. That was another reason why he succeeded in restoring respect for law and order. Sikander's reign was marked by material prosperity for which the Sultan was responsible to some extent. He abolished duties on corn and removed the galling restrictions on trade. Food grains, cloth and other necessities of life became cheap. He was, however, a fanatic Muslim. He did not allow Hindus for taking bath in sacred tank at Thaneswar and in Yamuna. He destroyed temples and built mosques in their places. He broke sacred images of Jawalamukhi and gave its pieces to butchers to be used as weights. He destroyed temples at Meerut, Mandrail, Utagir, Narwar, Chandrai and other places. He was taken ill during an expedition against Malwa and died in 1517. Although born of a Hindu mother, he wanted to show to Muslims that he was a pucca Mohammedan and so was a relentless bigot.

Ibrahim Lodhi (1517-1526)

Soon after his ascendency to throne, a party of selfish nobles advocated partition of the kingdom and put his brother Jalalkhan to the throne of Jaunpur. There was continuous quarrel between him and Ibrahim and ultimately Ibrahim crushed him. He was defeated by Rana Sanga of Mewar in an expedition against him. He again sent a big force against Mewar but again the expedition was repelled resulting in a lot of killings. Punjab too rebelled and declared independence under Governor Daulat Khan Lodhi, who opened negotiations with Babar, the king of Kabul to invade India and over throw Ibrahim. He thought Babar would come, plunder the country and go back and thus enable him to establish his rule in Punjab. Another uncle of Ibrahim, Alam Khan too ambitious to become king of Delhi also opened negotiations with Babar. The result was famous battle of Panipat on 21 April 1526, in which Ibrahim was defeated and killed. This is how, the kings of India, right from Rajput era, had been inviting the foreign aggressors in rivaly against another king and lost the country and their own kingdoms too to the aggressors. So even having been brave, Ibrahim lost to the Mughals, who had been invading India for centuries.

Hindus in Sultanates

They formed 95 per cent of the population. Before Turks, they were the rulers. Even during sultanates, they were holding many posts, particularly in revenue and finance departments. Hindu Banjaras were attached to army for regular commissariat arrangements. The Turkish process of subjugation and conquest of the country continued for over 350 years during which period lakhs of Hindus were killed, lakhs massacred after battles, lakhs were made slaves and further crores were converted to Islam. Timur in one day killed over a lakh Hindu prisoners in addition to lakhs of Delhites killed after plundering the town and lakhs others killed on way back. Upper and middle class Hindus were denied employment in state service—civil and military—causing hardship to countless families. The big chiefs were compelled to part with their daughters, converted to Islam and married.

Hindu society was caste ridden. Turkish rule compelled Hindus to make the caste rules more rigid than they were in free India under Hindus so that there is complete division amongst them and they do not ever unite. Child marriage became common as Muslims married Hindu girls. Seclusion of women became a general practice in upper and middle class Hindu families. There was no female education at all. Hindus either converted or the remaning were devoted to their religion. However, the standard of individual honesty and purety of conduct was still fairly high. Muslim writers have said that Hindus were happier during Turkish rule than in Hindu rule. This belief has also been taken by europeans but thousands of instances indicate great tyranny on Hindus. So the opinion of the Muslim or european writers is not without bias. Hindus were employed only in revenue and finance departments.

One, who looks back on the history of conquests on India by the Turks, is struck by the fact that most parts of northern India were easily conquered by the foreign ingvaders. It is also amazing to read that Ghazni could repeat his annual raids, perpetrate into the heart of India, plunder prosperous towns and wealthy people and return to Ghazni without being effectively punished, much less checked. Political and military condition of India was so rotten that an invader could not be decisively beaten even once and prevented from making repeated raids. Even when the invaders were defeated like Ghori defeated by Prithvi Raj, he was spared to go back and again come with greater force to inflict defeat on Prithvi Raj. Had Prithvi Raj killed him, his commanders and soldiers, they would not have dared come for many years thereafter and history would have been different. Of course Ghazni was never defeated by any Hindu ruler although Indian soldiers were in no way inferior to the Turks. The only fact would be that the rulers did not combine and single-handed they could not face him. They, therefore, preferred to surrender rathar than face him and have consequent massacre. Even Rajput rulers were very brave and had all soldierly qualities.

India's bid for Freedom

Over-running the country was one thing and its effective conquest quite another. It did not mean that the Turks succeeded in capturing easily what they had over-run. The real and effective resistence from people began only when the Turks attempted to occupy the country and rule over it. Perhaps Hindus laboured under the mistaken notion that the invaders were not concerned with territorial sovereignty and would content themselves with mere plunder. But when they saw that their lieutenants were establishing military garrisons and occupying the country, they adopted concerted measurers to oppose them. The struggle between the Hindushahi kings of Punjab and their Arab and Turk neighbours is a story of a remarkable resistance, which was put up for centuries. The province of Punjab could be conquered by the invaders only after 350 years after having made efforts during the period 636-1026 A.D. The Chauhans of Sambhar and Ajmer revolted four times within a period of half a decade in order to drive away Mohammed Ghori's officers. The fort of Ranthambore could not remain in effective Muslim control even after 150 years of fighting. The entire Rajasthan could not really be conquered and occupied during this period. Tabquat-i-Nasiri indicates that annual expeditions had to be undertaken to the fertile regimes of Ganga and Yamuna Doab by the Sultans from Aibak down to Balban and yet it could not be thoroughly subdued. The process of annual conquest of this region or of several others, had to be repeated throughout the sultanate period and the revenue of the Doab could not be collected except at the point of the bayonet. In fact the Hindus continued their struggle against their Turko-Afghan rulers throughout the period of the Sultanate of Delhi. When we compare the fate of other Asian and Europeon countries, which so tamely submitted to the Arab and Turkish aggressions, one cannot but have admiration for Hindu ancestors, who fought for long and fought hard against the enemy, who had so quickly established his supremacy—political, military and religious—over many countries of the three continents of the world.

Why were foreign pocket allowed to exist on Indian soil

Another surprise that awaits the curious reader when he surveys the history of the age as to why ancestors did not make a concerted effort to drive the conquerors from the pocket, which they had conquered and occupied, or why had they suffered to establish their rule in Sindh, Multan and the Punjab. After their victory over Dahir of Sindh, the Arabs permanently occupied Sindh and Multan. Mahmud of Ghazni captured Punjab in early years of 11th century; the rest of India still being in powerful Hindu hands, should have made a united attempt to expel the Arabs from Multan and Sindh in the eighth century A.D. and the Turks from the Punjab in the eleventh century. The answer is that there was the same old problem as to how to bring about unity among the warring Hindu chiefs. Their bravery and local patriotism were out of question. It is only the Bhartiyata or the patriotism for India, which had been lacking and consequently no unity for defending India.

Infact they never thought in terms of India as their country and had always thought of their own kingdom only and saving the same from neighbouring kingdoms. Many dozens of contemporary inscriptions in Sanskrit have come down to us describing that the ruler of this state or that defeated the 'Malekshas' and occupied this town or that, which had been in their possession. The Chauhans, the Gurjar Pratiharas, the Guhilots, the Baghelas and several other rajput ruling families were credited with unusual valour and success in their wars against the Arabs in Multan and Sindh and the Ghazanavis of Punjab. Individually they could fight all right, but a collective and united attempt was never made. Secondly the spirit of aggression and offence seems to have been absent in Hindu rulers and people for ages in the past. Hardly did any king of India ever think of waging an aggressive war against any foreign country or foreign people. It was only Kanishka, who tried to invade China but failed and Jaipal invaded Ghazni twice but was defeated and had to cede a lot a territory to Turks. There is no other instance of Hindu rulers having invaded foreigners. They, on the contrary, had been on the defensive only against foreign aggression and there too did not inflict any terror on the enemy by man-killings to deter from fruther invasions. Thirdly the Arabs in Multan and Sindh and the Ghaznavis in the Punjab followed the cunning policy of treating the Hindus in their respective states as hostages. Whenever a neighbouring Hindu chief invaded any of these foreign states on Indian soil, the Arab or the Turkish ruler threatened the local Hindus with death and declared that he would demolish the principal temples and break their images to pieces. The contemporary Arab travellers and historians have described in detail this cunning device resorted to by the local Muslim rulers to save themselves from destruction. Al Idrise writes in his 'Nuzhatul Mushtaq': "The people make it (the image of Sun temple at Multan) the object of a pious pilgrimage, and to obey it is the law. So far is this carried that, when neighbouring princes make war against the country of

Multan, either for the purpose of plunder or for carrying off the idols. The princes have only to meet, threaten the aggressors with its anger and predict their destruction and the assailants at once renounce their designs. Without this fear the town of Multan would be destroyed" (*Elliot and Dowson* Vol. I : page 82). Another Arab historian, Al Masudi writes in his Murug-ul-Zabab, composed about 940 A.D."when the unbelievers march against Multan, and the faithfuls do not feel themselves strong enough to oppose them, they threatened to break their idols and their enemies immediately withdraw". (*Elliot and Dowson* Vol. I : page 23). Hindu superstitious ancestors, who were far stronger than the later Arabs and Ghaznavides, were thus duped and did not undertake the conquest of Multan or Sindh or the Punjab.

Causes of Frequent Dynastic Changes: When a comparison is made between the Sultanates of Delhi and the Mughal empire that succeeded it, one notices that while during the latter age, one single dynasty ruled over the country for more than 250 years, the former age was characterised by rise and fall of many ruling dynasties. There were many causes of frequent dynastic changes between 1206 and 1526. In the first place there was no fixed or universally recognised law of succession among the Turko-Afghan rulers. According to Islamic theory of sovereignty, any Muslim, irrespective of his birth and position in life, is qualified to be a king, provided he is fit and powerful. In view of this theory, ambitious men whether they were related to the ruling family or not, aspired for the throne. Powerful and ambitious provincial governors made a successful bid to reach the throne. Iltutmish, Jalal-ud-din Khalji, Ala-ud-din Khalji, Ghiyas-ud-din Tughlaq and Bahlol Lodhi, who became rulers of Delhi, were provincial governors and, with the exception of one namely Ala-ud-din, none of them was a member of the ruling family, which he supplanted. Many a rebellion was also due to above cause for the throne was not considered to be beyond the reach of one, who could wield the sword successfully. Secondly, the government was weak. It was based upon personal rule, as opposed to the "Rule of Law". The strength of the government, therefore, depended upon the personality and character of the ruling monarch. As a rule, powerful rulers had weak successors, as the latter were brought up in the luxury of the harem, which was full of vices. Since Turks had to continuously face opposition from local rulers, they could not afford to have a weak ruler on the throne. Hence the nobles generally preferred an able soldier, whether he belonged to the ruling family or not. Thirdly, the slave system, which had produced great leaders like Qutab-ud-din, Iltutmish and Balban, degenerated rapidly in India. The slaves being in thousands, could not be given proper education but since they led luxurious life, they became lethargical. Even the few slaves like Malik Kafoor and Malik Khusrav, who even though brave, were not loyal. They acted against the interest of their patron's family. Malik Kafoor inspired against the life of his master Ala-ud-din Khalji. He had even prisoned Ala-ud-din and blinded the prince and had he not been killed in time, he would not have left a single male member in Ala-ud-din's family. Malik Khusrav actually killed his master Qutab-ud-din Mubarak and seized the throne. Fourthly many of the Sultans of Delhi did not possess a powerful standing army. Ala-ud-din had wisely laid the foundation of this necessary institution but his successors allowed it to relapse and depended on the supplies by the governors. The powerful governors, thus acquired the position of king-makers. This is how many governors could reach the throne of Delhi. Fifthly Hindu chiefs, who had been deprived of their freedom and country, naturally entertained the ambition of getting back their kingdoms. The Rajputs of Ajmer and Sambhar and those of Gujarat, revolted again and again against Qutab-ud-din Aibak. In the time of Iltutmish too a powerful Hindu reaction occurred and lasted for many years. Bulban too faced the problem of saving the state from Rajput chiefs. Ala-ud-din tried to repulse them but after his death, our people again raised their heads. The Sultans were obliged to fight almost perpetually against the Hindu patriots. Weaklings in

Turk ruling families were, therefore, ruthlessly set aside. Sixthly, ever recurring Mangol raids, which began after 1240 A.D., had amassed themselves on north-western frontiers and made frequent attacks on Punjab and Multan. After Balban's death, they even seized Delhi more than once. These invasions diverted the attention of the so able a monarch like Balban from much needed conquest in the interior and suppression of rebellions. Further, the Mangol raids encouraged the force of discontent and whenever the Mangol raids took place, the local chiefs too raised their heads in rebellion. After Mohammed Bin Tughlaq, there was hardly any Sultan of Delhi, who was possessed of military ability of a high order. Disloyalty and corruption had become the rule in military commanders and officers. Seventhly, the government of the sultan was based on force and not on consent of the governed. The government cared for two duties only viz. the maintenance of peace and order and collection of revenues. No effort was made except by Feroz Tuglaq to advance even the material interest of people. As a result the sultans, rather than getting support of people, the people acted against them. The people were indifferent towards their foreign sovereigns and did not care as to who occupied the throne of Delhi.

Effect of Muslim-Hindu mixing up: Both Hindus and Muslims were fanatic to their respective religions. Whereas Hindus had absorbed the previous foreign aggressors, they could not do so in respect of Muslims. Of course as a result of mixing up with Hindus, Muslims produced sufis, who derived inspiration from Hindu vedanta. Muslim rulers converted Hindus to Islam by force or by monetary consideration and thus the Muslim population was raised enormously. Hindus, as a result, became more rigid in their castes and thinking and many became Monoists.

Why Hindus failed to absorb Muslims: The assimilative capacity of ancient Hinduism was so great that it completely absorbed within its fold the earlier invaders like the Greeks, the Sakas and the Huns. But on the contrary, the same absorbing

Hinduism failed to Hinduise the Turko-Afghan foreigners. It is sometimes believed that Hindu ancestors made no attempt to absorb new-comers and that the Muslims would have too readily agreed to become Indians in outlook, spirit and way of life, only if they had been given an opportunity by the Hindus to do so. But the latter kept them at arms' length and refused to inter-dine and inter-marry with them. This view is not altogether correct. We have evidence to show that during the early days of the advent of Arabs and the Turks in this country, Hindu rulers and people meted out a very generous treatment to them. In southern India, where the Arabs had settled in large number in as early as eighth century A.D., Hindu rulers not only gave the foreigners every facility in their commercial activities, but also definitely encouraged conversion to Islam. The Zamorian of Calicut "gave orders that in every family of fisherman in his dominion, one or more, of the male members should be brought up as Mohammedan". Like european traders in the later age, the Arabs were granted certain commercial privileges, which were not enjoyed by the indigenous business community. Hindu reformers and teachers emphasized that Hinduism and Islam were two different paths leading to the same goal. They preached that Ram and Rahim, Krishna and Karim and Ishwar and Allah were different names of the same God. An earnest attempt was made to bring about unity between the two communities by deprecating priestly ritualism and formalities and emphasizing religious devotion. Not only were the foreign Muslims honoured and respected but even Indian converts to Islam were shown regard and a treatment which was better than that meted out to lower castes among the Hindus themselves. In one respect, however, Hindus did not extend to the foreigners proper courtesy. That was the sphere of inter-dining and inter-marriage, and the reason was obvious. The Hindu has always believed in ceremonial purity that is the purity of body, dress, dwelling place and the mind, while not only the foreign Turk and Afghan but even the Indian Musalman insisted on leading the kind life led by the Arabs of the desert. Moreover, the Hindus in general were vegetarians, and even those of them, who were meat-eaters, abhored beef. Mohammedens, on the other hand, were almost cent-percent non-vegetarians and were not prepared to give up cow slaughter and beef-eating. They refused to accept the cult of bhakti. They believed in their superiority and branded the Hindus as an inferior people, effete and unprogressive 'dal ke khane wale'. They were proud of their religion, which is clear, definite and rigid in its dogmas and acted as militant missionaries of Islam. And they had little to gain by merging themselves in a society that was caste-ridden and torn by internal dissensions. Moreover, they had the conquerors' innate pride and were determined to retain their separate identity. If the Hindus looked down upon them as unclean, they returned the compliment by styling them as kafirs or infidels. It was not possible for Hindu missionaries and teachers to succeed with a people who punished apostacy from their faith with death and made it a capital crime for anyone to seduce a Musalman from his religion. If a Hindu, who was converted to Islam, showed any inclination to revert to the religion of his fore-fathers, he was, according to laws of the Sultan, to be put to death, and any Hindu, who preached that Hinduism and Islam were alike good religions, was liable to capital punishment. Moreover, the Muslim practice of converting a Hindu girl to Islam before marrying her and compelling a Hindu to become Muslim before he could be allowed to marry a Muslim women, stood in the way of a real matrimonial alliance between any two families and militated against the attempt at fusion of the two communities. The early Turks and Afghans did not resent their exclusion from inter-dining. In fact they tried to turn the Hindu prejudice to their advantage by declaring that so and so had partaken of the prohibited food and had, therefore, become defiled and unfit to remain a Hindu. Under these circumstances, all the efforts of Hindu rulers, peoples, reformers and teachers at bringing about unity between the Indian people and the foreigners met with inevitable failure.

Sultanates were sovereign Indian rulers: In theory the Muslim state was a theocracy. Although the sultan of Delhi professed formal allegiance to the Caliphate, the sultanate was always an independent state for all purposes. After Qutab-ud-din Aibak had been established as a ruler lieutenant by Mohammed Ghori in 1192 in Delhi; he was under his thumb but as soon as Ghori died in 1206, he declared cut off of his allegiance but as already indicated, allegiance to Caliphiate was only theocratical and had nothing to do with the governance of India, where the Sultan was independent. It was, therefore, only for a period of 14 years that sultan acknowledged political subordination to an extra authority. Otherwise sultan was an unlimited despot, bound by no laws, subject to no ministerial checks and guided by none except his own sweet will. People had no rights, only obligations to carryout the command. Sultan had a council but after taking their advice did whatever he felt like doing. Ala-ud-din ignored the racial and hereditary claims of the Turks and conferred high offices on nobles, whom he considered efficient and trust-worthy but he tried to break their solidarity by stern measures. Iltitmish was the first ruler of Delhi, who thought of organising army of the sultanate as king's army. Balban increased the numerical strength of the army and appointed able officers on attractive terms. Ala-ud-din further strengthened it.

It would appear that the strengthening of the army as king's army with commanders of confidence; institution of spying system and the king personally attending to their reports; putting spies on the nobles, governors, markets; non assembling of nobles, no liquor taking in meetings etc. were the steps as enunciated in Chanakya's Arthshastra. The kings, Balban and Ala-ud-din, therefore, either would appear to have gone through these treatises or there would be some Hindu advisor in their Majlis. It is also evident that the kings, who could enforce these tenets, had been able to have stable government. Otherwise the governance cracked. It is, therefore, the Bhartiyata and its tenets, which prevailed in a model governing system during the Sultanates.

With the downfall of sultanates, the Hindu rajas of Vijaynagar, Malwa, Mewar, Gujarat and governors of Madura, Bengal, Bihar, Punjab, Jaunpur and Orissa declared independence. Infact such was the situation with change of each sultan of Delhi and the first job of sultan was to suppress them.

VIJAYANAGAR

Foundation of Hindu kingdom of Vijayanagar deserves special mention here. This empire was founded as a result of political and cultural movement against the Tughlaq authority in Deccan by Harihare in 1336 and ruled upto the middle of 17th century as a Hindu kingdom amidst the Muslim sultanates of Delhi with all vedic tenets of governance with necessary changes, an example of Bhartiyata even in those days when although the Muslim kingdoms had frequent downfall, the kingdom of Vijayanagar stood like a rock for over 300 years. Krishna river was the dividing line. In Vijayanagar:

1. Kings championed the cause of protecting all castes; brahmins occupying most respectable; kshatriyas were absent from Vijayanagar. Brahmins were also merchants, traders, high officers, commanders and so on. In fact there were two castes—brahmins and non-brahmins.
2. Women occupied honourable position. They were wrestlers, astrologers and soothe-sayers, body-guards, accountants, writers, musicians and even went to battle fields.
3. It was centrally governed by monarch, who was the pivot of machinery of administration.
4. The succession to the throne was hereditary, subject to the incumbent being capable of holding the charge.
5. Primary duty of the king was to afford protection to all his subjects and redress their grievances. The other was to maintain an efficient Police and military organisation in the state to ensure preservation of law and order in the country.

6. There was efficient espionage system and the king was made aware of what had been happening in various provinces. There are instances in history of Vijayanagar, which show that the king interfered in the administration of provinces to put an end to the oppression of the people by their chiefs.
7. King was the highest court of appeal and when the lower courts failed to give justice, the sufferer could appeal to the king, who dispensed justice.
8. Though the king was most important organ in body politic, yet he was never an autocrat. His powers were limited by certain codes and institutions, one of these being the organised community itself.
9. There were communities, which made regulations and the king enforced them.
10. Royal council was another important check on the king's authority. King never ruled without this council and he consulted it on all state matters and policies.
11. There was also another council namely the Imperial Council consisting of a few influential ministers and others of less importance like Prime Minister, Dy. Ministers, Heads of Departments. Some of them were blood relations of the king.
12. Vijayanagar was divided into provinces, which were known as rajyas. The rajyas were divided into districts, sub districts and villages, which were self-sufficient.

From the above description of governance in Vijayanagar kingdom, it would seem that amidst the Mohammedan autocrat kings, there was still a Hindu kingdom governed according dharma and had always the interest of kingdom and welfare of people in view. A Telugu writer has written about the ideal kingship of Krishandeva Raya in his book 'Auktamalyada'.

"Though he was the supreme civil, military and judicial authority, he was not a tyrant or even an irresponsible despot. The king was like that of Frederick the Great of Prussia, 'A

Crowned King', who always ruled with an eye towards dharma. A king who should rule,' collecting round him, people skilled in statecraft, should investigate the mines yielding precious metals in his kingdom, and extract the same and levy taxes on his people moderately; should counter-act the acts of his enemies by crushing them with force; should be friendly; should protect one and all of his subjects; should put an end to the mixing up of the castes among them; should strengthen his fortress and lessen the growth of the undesirable things and should be ever mindful of purification of his cities."

There was complete religious tolerance, although it was a Hindu-ruled kingdom, unlike the states ruled by Muslims, where Hindus were specifically taxed, converted and killed. The society was well organised, where women occupied high position in political, social and literary life of the empire. Polygamy was only in wealthy people. The empire had high cultural and artistic achievements to its credit. The empire was richest state then known to the world. One Italian traveller Nicolo Conti wrote in 1420.

"The circumference of the city is sixty miles, its walls are carried up to the mountains and enclose the valley at their foot so that its extent is thereby increased. In this city, there are estimated to be ninety thousand men fit to bear arms.... the king is more powerful than all other kings of India".

The kingdom was very rich. In king's treasure, there were chambers with excavations in them filled with molten gold forming one mass. All inhabitants wore jewels and gold ornaments. This was said to be the best provided city in the world and there were ample stocks of food-grains, dals, and there was active commercial trade in diamonds, rubies, silk, cinnabar, camphor, musk, pepper and sandal. From testimony of foreign writers, it is evident that the empire of Vijayanagar was very rich and prosperous, ruled as per vedic tenets, tolerant in religion, even among the Mohammedan rulers all around, full of agriculture, and mineral wealth, having good relations with Malaya, Burma, China, Arabia, Persia, South Africa,

Abyssinia and Portugal. It had gold coins. The people were wealthy with high standard of living. In short, the empire "served a high historical purpose by acting as a champion of Hindu religion and culture against the aggressions of Muslims in southern India. This was the model of Bhartiya governance, where all people were healthy, wealthy and prosperous. We are proud of such a kingdom in those centuries when the governance of Ashoka, Kanishka, Guptas and Harsha seem to have been repeated and all as per Hindu dharma. The saying of British, and the subsequent historians that Indians were barbaric is absolutely false in view of the rule of this empire having been accepted as best in the world even by the Italian writers. The governance in other Hindu kingdoms too was more or less on the same pattern except that they had been victim of circumstances in having been conquered by Muslim invaders, time and again, affecting their economic, social and political life with secular ethics.

6 Mughal Period (1526-1857)

Babar (1526-30)

The sources of Mughal period are full and copious from chronicles, memoirs and letter books, archaeological sources, and accounts of foreign visitors. Born in 1483, Babur, the founder of Mughul empire in India, ascended the throne of Farghana a small kingdom in Khurasan and Transoxiana dominion of Central Asia in 1497, when he was only 14 years of age. He was from Timur on paternal side and Changiz Khan from mother's side. Having not been satisfied with what he got in succession, he waged a war for 26 years and gained the lost portions of the dominion. His eyes were then set on Hindustan. He bade farewell to the land of his birth and set out to try his luck beyond Hindukush. He captured Kabul in 1504 after winning the Mangols over to his side, without any opposition. After a few months of the conquest of Kabul, Babur made his first invasion on Hindustan in 1505. He reached upto Indus but then turned back to Kabul.

In India, at that time, situation was bad, Sayyads had failed and Lodhis took to rule. The kingdom of Lodhis was a loose confederacy of semi-independent governorships held by the Amirs, the leaders of Afghan tribes and the king was no more conspicuous than a royal oakling in a forest of oaks. The first two Lodhis—Bahlol Lodhi and Sikander Lodhi—managed the turbulant nobles. But Ibrahim, who ascended in 1517, was ambitious but tactless, arrogant and impatient. He tried to become monarch. He alienated the sympathy of Afghan nobles, who rebelled. Punjab and Jaunpur openly revolted and rajputs also defeated him. Outside Lodi kingdom, there were Muslim kingdoms of Multan, Sindh, Gujarat, Malwa, Khandesh and Bengal in northern India and Birar, Bidar, Ahmednagar, Bijapur and Goleconda in Deccan and Hindu states in Rajasthan and Orissa in north east and Vijayanagar in south.

Babar made five invasions on Hindustan, but failed. In India, Ibrahim's condition was, however, becoming precarious. His most serious enemy was Alam Khan, his uncle and Daulat Khan Lodhi of Punjab. They appealed Babar for help. Babar responded and made sixth invasion in 1524. He conquered Punjab but gave only Jullunder and Sultanpur, whereas Daulat Khan wanted entire Punjab. Babar had to again retrace and Daulat Khan again gained his lost territory. Alam Khan went to Kabul and requested for Babar's help. In 1525, he set on last and momentous Indian campaign with 12000 men army. Babar captured Lahore and proceeded to Delhi. Ibrahim also proceeded to meet him and the first battle of Panipat took place in 1526. For five days Babar invaded in the night. Ibrahim had a force of 100,000 men and 1000 elephants, while Babar had 24000 men. On the sixth day battle started in which because of Babar's espionage and strategy, Ibrahim was killed. Babar marched to Delhi and became emperor in 1526. He subsequently conquered Agra and Gwalior. Various Afghan leaders in India rose against him but Babur silenced them all. At first Afghan leaders thought that like Timur, Babar would go back with boot but after Babar established himself as a king, they realised that he would settle in India. Babar also defeated Rana Sanga, leader of rajput confederacy. The battle of Panipat broke unstable power of Afghan dynasty while that with Rajputs, shattered India's most splendid chivalery, the powerful rajput confederacy, which was making a bid for mastery of Hindustan. Babar captured Alwar, Malwa, Lakhnau, Kanauj, Bihar etc. He died at the age of 48 years in 1530. Babar did not have any links with Central Asia and was a sovereign Indian ruler.

Humayun (1530-38, 1555-56)

After Babar's death, Humayun ascended the throne in 1530. He divided his kingdom in three parts and gave one part each to his two brothers. The history of Humayun is a drama in four acts—first the hectic ten years from 1530 to 1540 during which he struggled for defending his dominion. Second is tragedy of exile from 1540 to 1545; the third tells the story of the period from 1545 to 1554, when from the base of Kandhar and Kabul, he made preparations for the recovery of his dominion and; the fourth deals with restoration in 1555-56, when he recovered the throne of Delhi and a part of his kingdom. He appointed viceroys for the provincial areas and to save from any of the viceroys revolting against him, he appointed and posted his men at strategic places, keeping them under his direct control and used to give him information about what had been happening in the region. He still had to face revolts from all his chiefs from Gujarat, Malwa, Bihar etc. In Punjab, there was Chaos. The nobles were discontent, the peasantry a prey to misrule and anarchy and the Afghans had been in pursuit to declare themselves as independent. He consequently had to run from India and again he came in 1554 and captured Punjab, Sirhind and proceeded towards Delhi and became emperor of Hindustan once again. With all his weaknesses and failings, Humayun has a significant place in Indian history which is not perhaps always duly appreciated. The well-timed restoration of the Mughal power was the real achievement which paved the way for the splendid imperialism of Akbar, while the Indo-Persian contact, which he enforced and stimulated, was a factor of far-reaching consequence in the history of Indian civilisation. Humayun died in 1556.

Shershah Suri (1538-45)

Most striking and redoubtable figure in medieval Indian history—Sher Shah ascended the Bengal throne in 1530 and Delhi throne in 1540. He had a tussel with Mughals throughout. He was very able strategist, known from the fact that as one plan he surprised the Mughal king Humayun. He gave out that he was proceeding against Maratha chief in Shahabad district as he had been defying him and after marching a few miles in that direction at night he crossed the Karmanasa about five miles below Humayun's position, unnoticed by the Mughals and in the early dawn of 26 June 1539, fell upon the Mughals from three sides. The surprise was complete; many were even killed in their beds asleep and many of those, who took to fighting, were drowned in Ganga. Humayun was wounded but was saved by a water carrier from drowning by his mask. Loss to Mughals in men and war material was heavy. He further won Bengal as vassal state and kingdom of Jaunpur in addition to Bengal and Bihar and then captured Delhi. A man of keen insight, as Sher Shah was, he remodelled the administration in such a way that rebellion would not occur in future.

The kingdom was divided into provinces and provinces into several sarkars and over each of them, he appointed a Chief Shiqdar (Shiqdar-i-Shiqdaran), a Chief Munsif and Qazi. Chief Shiqdar was primarily incharge of law and order within his jurisdiction except in big towns, where kotwals performed these duties. The former also tried criminal cases and had under him an army to be utilised, if necessary, for enforcement of law and order. Each Sarkar was subdivided into several parganas, over each of which there was a Shiqdar, one Amin, and a treasure. Over the whole province, he appointed Qazi Fazilat as Amin-i-Bangala to maintain the unity and smooth working of the provincial administration for settlement of disputes amongst the chief Shiqdars. He also established 'Thanas' of imperial troops changed yearly by him. He died in the midst of his carrier of triumph marches in 1545. At the time of his death, he left an empire comprising almost of whole of northern India, save Kashmir, Gujarat and Assam, bounded by Indus on the west, Gakhar on the north west, Himalaya on the north, Assam on the east and Vindhyachal on the south. Not only did he thus establish an empire by dint, of his great military skill, wounderful courage, ability and resourcefulness but also with his unusual skill and promptitude. He made necessary arrangements for its smooth and efficient administration. At the helm of the affairs was the sultan himself. He was despot and centralised all powers in his own hands. He was benevolent despot, whose primary aim was to do good to his subjects irrispective of caste and religion. He appointed several ministers to assist him but all policy matters were decided by sultan. He had created a full department of the intelligence under Barid-ı-Mumalik. So that the officers did not develop vested interest, he introduced the system of transferring the officers of the sarkars and parganas every two or three years. His land revenue system had earned undying fame. Sultan's instructions to his revenue officers were to show leniency at the time of assessment but to be strict at the time of realisation of rent. Due consideration was, however, given to damage to crops by movement of troops and paucity of yield, nature's vagaries etc. The charge was 1/4th of the average yield. He took special interest in the welfare of the cultivators and took steps against any oppression or harrassment to them, which could be known through his men.

The currency was then in a deplorable condition due to paucity of current coins, the debasement in regard to their metal and absence of any fixed ratio between the coins of gold and those of other metals. He took steps to remodel the currency. Coins of gold and mixed metal were abolished and separate coins of gold, silver and copper of fixed standard were issued. This removed the inconvenience and difficulties of general public and businessmen. Sher Shah's system of currency lasted in Mughal period, was also maintained by East India Company and was the basis of British currency upto 1947. Sher Shah had, however, put his men at all business centres, exchange places to see that no debased coins exchanged hands.

The police system of Sher Shah was simple and according to the Persian historians, worked well, achieving the objective aimed at. The Shiqdar-i-Shiqdaran and the Shiqdars had to maintain peace and order within their jurisdiction. In the villages, the system of local responsibility was followed and the village headmen had to bear the responsibility for crimes committed within their jurisdiction. If they could find out the culprits or produce them within the stipulated period, the latter were duly punished but if the headmen were unable to do so, they themselves had to face the punishment of such crimes. Abbas says that "the headmen used to protect the limits of their own villages lest any thief or robber or enemy of their enemies might injure a traveller and so be the means of their destruction and death". About the effect of the system, Farishta says "such was the public security during his reign that travellers and merchants, depositing their property on the roadside, lay down to sleep without any apprehension of robbery."

Sher Shah is known for construction of roads connecting important parts of his empire with his capital. This was necessary for imperial defence, quick and regular despatch of news to the emperor, improvement of trade and commerce and convenience of the travelling public. Longest road (1500 kosas-3000 km) ran from Sonargaon, near Dacca, via Agra and Delhi to the Indus; the second was from Agra to Jodhpur and Chittoor; the third from Agra to Burhanpur and fourth from Lahore to Multan, with shaded trees, sarais, for both Hindus and Muslims, every four miles and dak chowkies and rest houses.

Sher Shah had a well organised espionage system and his spies used to send him through the dak chowkies, prompt information of every important matter even from the remotest part of his empire. Such a system of conveyance of information by means of dak chowkies was not new to India and had been coming from vedic period, but had gone down during the periods. Sher Shah revived and improved it to a considerable extent and put it into practice. This department was under Daroga-i-Dak-Chowki and under him there were innumerable news-writers and news-carriers. The efficiency of this department contributed a lot to the successful administration of this emperor.

Sher Shah maintained a well organised army under him and not as a feudal levy. Army consisted of different nationalities including Hindus but the Afghans found most prominent part. His effort was to maintain as much direct touch with the soldiers as possible, hearing the grievances and removing them. In order to minimise the risk of any military rising, his reforms further aimed at establishing an official relation, in lack of any personal attachment, between ordinary soldiers and their officers. He had also put spies in the army to keep a watch on any untoward development. Contingents of imperial troops were maintained at strategic places of his empire, each of these divisions known as 'fauj' under 'Faujdar'. Sultan was stern disciplinarian and maintained strict discipline in the army and through them in the public. His rapidity of movement and the tact and foresight that he displayed in his campaigns were beyond the imagination of his adversaries, who had to face discomfiture. As far as possible he avoided open engagements and made sudden sallies on the enemies to take them by surprise. This required a very solid spy system even in the camp of enemies. He did not also hesitate to outwit them by cunning and craftiness. Despite the ignoble means, which he followed at times, his successes dazzled the eyes of his contemporaries and raised him to the pinnacle of glory.

Though he was an orthodox Sunny in his private life, his general policy towards Hindus was one of tolerance and goodwill. He allowed Hindus to follow their religion without interference from government and also appointed them in civil and military forces.

After Sher Shah, the Suri dynasty did not last long. Islam Shah ruled from 1545-1554 and Mohd Alid Shah from 1954-56 (a part of kingdom) when Humayun again appeared on the scene as the emperor of Delhi.

Himu (1556)

Inspite of Mughals menace, there was no cessation of hostilities among the Afghans. Himu, the wazir of Adil Shah defeated him twice. Taking advantage of death of Humayun and accession of young Akbar, Himu proceeded from Gwalior to Agra with a huge force and occupied it easily. He took possession of Delhi too. He assumed independence with title 'Raja Vikramaditya' and to gain support of Afghan chiefs, he distributed wealth lavishly amongst them. Then the battle of Panipat took place with Akbar in 1556. The fight was in his favour when an arrow pierced his eye making him unconscious. His army considering him dead, fled. He was taken to Akbar, who killed him. Himu was born in a Bania caste in Alwar as a grocer. He became superintendent of Delhi market and head of department of intelligence and chowkies. Emperor Adil Shah appointed him his Prime Minister. He fought many battles and wanted to form a Hindu empire. He fought 22 battles and won all. But had been unfortunate in losing the decisive battle, with Akbar which he had infact won, but for the arrow, which pierced in his eye and thus lost a chance to establish a Hindu kingdom in India and continuance of Mughal rule for another two centuries. The bravery of Himu has even been praised by Abul-i-fazal, who being pro-Turkish, did not want to paint a Hindu chief in fine colour; He writes:

"Battles took place between Himu and Ibrahim, who was a claimant for the sultanate, and the former was always victorious. Sultan Muhammad, who had assumed the kingly title in Bengal, was also defeated and was made to tread the land of annihilation. Himu also engaged in conflicts with Taj Kararani and Rukn Khan Nuhani and defeated them. He fought two and twenty battles with the opponent of Muharizkhan and was victorious in all of them".

When Humayun returned to India to recover his lost throne, Himu was sent to oppose him. Humayun succeeded in re-establishing himself for a few months when he met with his fatal accident in 1556. When Akbar was formally proclaimed at Kalanaur as padshah, Hemu advanced by way of Gwalior and Agra to old Delhi and inflicted a severe defeat on the Mughal forces. He thus gained possession of Delhi and Agra.

Himu looked for the sovereignty of Hindustan with the title Vikramaditya. The opportunities were really very good and the examples of Babar, Sher Shah and Humayun demonstrated the feasibility of a bold military adventure, seizing the throne of Delhi; Himu's chances of success were not less, than any one of them. Himu decided upon his course of action and made preparations accordingly. He won over the Afghans by distributing spoils of war and ascended to the throne of Delhi. Bairam Khan, the guardian of Akbar had been advised to retire from India but he decided to advance against Himu, whose army greatly outnumbered that of the Mughals. As already indicated but for an arrow piercing his eye, he had won the battle. It may, therefore, be held that Himu's future was in a great measure, due to that unknown and unknowable fact, called fate or destiny, which plays no inconsiderable part in the affairs of men. Himu was captured in unconscious state and killed by Akbar. His head was sent to Kabul and trunk was gibbeted at one of the gates of Delhi. The tragedy did not end here. The forces of Akbar proceeded to Alwar, where Himu's family lived. Abul Fazal says: "The place was strong and there was much fighting and the father of Himu was captured and brought alive before Nasir-ul-Mulk. The latter called upon him to change his religion. The old man answered "For eighty years I have worshipped my God, according to this religion. Why should I change it at this time and why should I, merely from fear of my life, and without understanding it come into your way of worship." Pir Muhammad, however, killed him. Such was the noble end of the family of Himu, a great Hindu, who made his way to the throne of Delhi and but for his accidental death, would have made a mark as the emperor of Delhi and would have led to the revival of Hindu kingship again. India have to feel proud of such Bhartiya nobles.

Akbar (1556-1605)

He ascended the throne in 1556 after second battle of Panipat under the guardianship of Bairamkhan. He was a self confessed annexationist. He conquered and annexed Ajmer, Gwalior, Jaunpur, Malwa etc. By 1595, Akbar's conquest of the northern portion of the Indian sub-continent excluding Assam was completed by annexation of Baluchistan. His north-west boundary was upto Kandhar, Kutch and Makram; In south, it was upto Narbada; in East upto Bengal and Khandesh, Berar and Ahmednagar in Deccan had been annexed. But the affairs of the kingdom were held in hand by Bairamkhan and Akbar with passage of time found that he was a mere puppet in the hands of Bairam Khan, who did not even consult him in gravest matters so much so that his personal expenses were sanctioned by Bairam with stringency. Akbar wanted to set himself free by dismissing Bairam. On the other hand Bairam Khan was harsh in temper, highly ambitious and jealous of power and would broke no rival. So the dismissal of such a powerful man by young emperor Akbar was not an easy task. The harem party, which was against Bairam; helped him. From Delhi, Akbar issued his dismissal orders. On receiving Akbar's message, Bairam was surprised and immediately sent envoys to Akbar begging to be excused and assuring him of loyal service in future. In 1560, Bairam presented himself before Akbar, who offered him the jagir of Kalpi and Chanderi but declining to serve where he had ruled, he left for Gujarat, where he was assassinated. Bairam was the real author of the Mughal restoration and without him Akbar would not have been able to retain the throne of Delhi.

Akbar had known that he would be a successful ruler of India only with the cooperation of rajputs, who had always been at daggers drawn with the Muslim rulers. In 1562 he made a pilgrimage to Ajmer. On the way Raja Biharimal of Amber paid homage and offered him the hand of his daughter. Akbar agreed and the marriage took place at Sambhar and Mansingh, the heir of Raja Bihari Lal was taken into royal service. The princess became the mother of Jahangir. The rajput alliance was not merely the stroke of a diplomat to win the support of militant Hinduism, it was the beginning of a

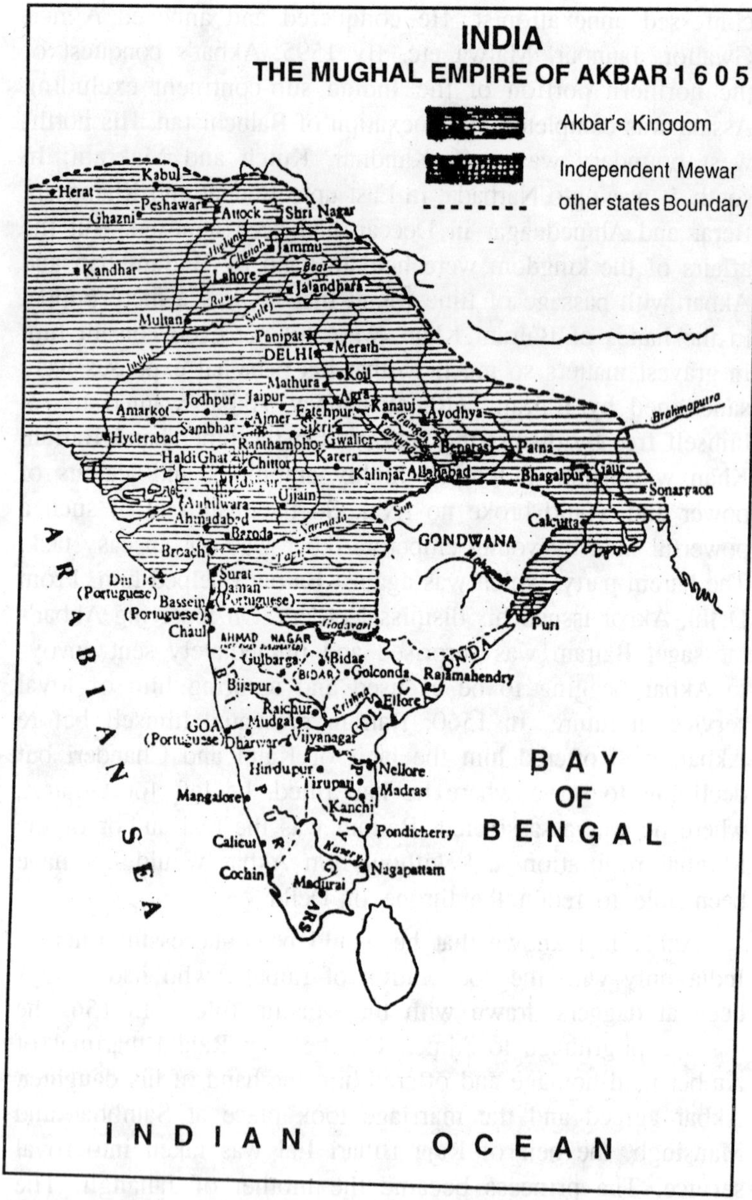
INDIA
THE MUGHAL EMPIRE OF AKBAR 1605
Akbar's Kingdom
Independent Mewar
other states Boundary
Kabul
Herat
Peshawar
Ghazni
Attock
Shri Nagar
Jammu
Kandhar
Lahore
Jalandhara
Multan
Panipat
DELHI
Merath
Koil
Mathura
Agra
Jodhpur
Jaipur
Kanauj
Ayodhya
Amarkot
Fatehpur
Ajmer
Sikri
Brahmaputra
Sambhar
Hyderabad
Ranthambhor
Gwalior
Benaras
Patna
Haldi Ghat
Chittor
Karera
Kalinjar
Allahabad
Bhagalpur
Gaur
Sonargaon
Ujjain
Ahmadabad
Calcutta
Baroda
GONDWANA
Broach
Surat
Daman
Diu Is.
(Portuguese)
(Portuguese)
Bassein
(Portuguese)
Chaul
Puri
AHMAD NAGAR
Bidar
Gulbarga
BIDAR
Golconda
Rajamahendry
Bijapur
Raichur
Ellore
GOA
Mudgal
(Portuguese)
Dharwar
Vijyanagar
Hindupur
Nellore
Tirupati
Madras
Mangalore
Kanchi
Pondicherry
Calicut
Cochin
Nagapattam
Madurai
ARABIAN SEA
BAY OF BENGAL
INDIAN OCEAN

new orientation of state-policy, the first doctrine of Sulh-i-kull (universal tolerance) as enunciated by vedic tenets. No Muslim ruler before, not even Sher Shah, with all his benevolence, held this exalted perception of state and kingship so definitely and vividly. In 1563 Akbar abolished the tax on Hindu pilgrims to holy places and next year he took the revolutionary step of abolishing jiziya or tax on non-Muslims. "It was an assertion of Akbar's will and conscience against a tradition of all the Muslim conquerers of India, sanctioned by centuries of custom, against all his advisers". Akbar had begun to enquire about the views of his subjects by nocturnal visits among them in disguise.

In 1567, Akbar undertook one of the most famous military operations of his life, the seize and capture of Chitor. To the ruler of northern India, the importance of Rajasthan was great and key to Rajasthan was Mewar, whose capital Chitor was the "Sanctuary of Rajput Freedom'. Akbar had made rajputs his allies but Mewar did not submit. In 1567 Akbar pitched his camp before Chitor. Rana Uday Singh abondoned the capital and took refuse in defiles of Arvalli hills but Jaimal bravely resisted the surrender. It was only after an year of all kinds of attacks that Chitor could be captured. Akbar ordered general massacre. Thirty thousand were slain, one thousand managed to escape. Akbar then made conquest in northern India, including Bengal and Bihar and Gujarat and other parts of Rajputana. The fight with Rana Pratap Singh is another landmark in the history of Akbar. Rana Pratap Singh did not surrender to Akbar and consequently a battle took place at Haldighati in which Akbar was victorious.

Religion: Akbar is also known for his reconciliatory religious policy. Having married rajput girl and providing high positions in administration, he had won most of the Hindu chiefs. He, being a religious minded man, honoured both Muslim faqirs and Hindu yogis. He visited Ajmer Chisti as also devi mandir at Kangra. He intorduced "Din Ilahi", a new belief taking common things from Hindu and Muslim religions. At

Fatehpur Sikri, he made Ibadat-Khana (home of worship), where all religions' discourses and discussions were held. Akbar even said "He was no longer a Muslim; he beleived in the transmigration of soul and idol worship, although Islam did not permit these. He was also tolerant to both Shias and Sunnis, although he himself was a Sunni.

Foreign Policy

(1) Akbar had diplomatic relations with the Portuguese, who had already established their authority on the Western coast of India with Goa as their capital. He also met many Portuguese merchants.

(2) He did not have proper diplomatic relations with England though some Englishmen visited his court and started trading in 1585.

(3) Kabul had been bone of contention between India and Iran. Akbar had by 1590 annexed Kabul to his empire.

(4) Had diplomatic relations with Isfahan.

(5) Diplomatic intercourse between India and Turkey could not be regular on account of geographical situation of the two countries. In fact Akbar considered the Sultan Caliph of Turkey as his great rival.

On October 3, 1605, Akbar fell ill and died.

Jahangir (1605-1628)

On Akbar's death, Jahangir ascended the throne. He succeeded a well administered and well organised kingdom from Akbar. His main job was the provision of a chain of justice, 30 yards long with 60 bells in the fort and complaints were listened to by Jahangir himself. He also issued 12 farmans with a view to make improvements in governance. He said: "I gave 12 orders to be observed as rules of conduct (dastur-ul-amal) in all my dominions:-

1. Forbidding the levy of cesses under the name of 'Tamgha' and 'Mirbahari' (river toll) and other burdens which the

jagirdars of every province and district had imposed for their own profit.

2. On roads, where thefts and robberies took place, which roads might be at a little distance from habitations, the jagirdars of the neighbourhood should build sarais (rest houses) mosques and dig wells, which might stimulate population and people might settle down in those sarais.
3. The bales of merchants should not be opened on the roads without informing them and obtaining their leave.
4. If any one dies, his property and effects should be left for his heirs. The police should see that they are not encroached upon.
5. No one should make wine or rice-spirit or any kind of intoxicating drug, or sell them.
6. No one should take possession of any person's houses.
7. No one should be blemished by the punishment of cutting off the nose or ears.
8. The officials of the 'crown lands and the jagirdar should not forcibly take the ryots' lands and cultivate them on their own account.
9. Government collectors or jagirdars should not without permission inter-marry with the people of the pargana in which they might be living.
10. Hospitals should be provided in great cities and the expenditure met from the Khalsa establishment.
11. No animal should be slaughtered from 18th of Rabi-ul-awal for the days corresponding to the years of king's life.
12. I release all criminals, who had been confined and imprisoned for a long time in the forts and prisons.

Through these orders, the emperor desired to ensure to his subjects freedom of person and security of life and property and his solitude for their material moral welfare. Like his father, Jahangir remained tolerant to religions inspite of considerable stir amongst Muslims of all shades of opinion.

New temples and Christian churches were freely built during his time.

Shahjahan (1628-1657)

Shahjahan ascended the throne in 1628, after Jahangir's death, after execution of his brothers and nephew. He had to face several rebellions, as usual with each accession to throne, but repelled all.

In his period, the Portuguese had secured the grant of the site of Hooghly in 1637 and soon raised a flourishing and well defended port at the entrance of the commercial high way of Bengal. They became a rich and affluent community, enjoying almost independent jurisdiction. Shahjahan, however, started a ruthless campaign against them, when the Portuguese started looting the neighbouring villages. Shahjahan also wished to conquer Tibet but when an army was sent against him, the ruler of Tibet submitted and paid an indemnity of one million rupees. Shahjahan also wanted to conquer central Asia and sent army there but it brought nothing but disaster, famine and death both to the Indians and Turanians. Mughal's prestige in central Asian affairs had vanished and the myth of its invincibility was shattered. We have seen that whenever India had tried to conquer the parts of China, or Central Asia or even Tibet we have failed. First by Kanishka, then by Jaipal and now by Shahjahan. Not only we could not win but also had to face irreparable loss of men, money and image.

Shahjahan's religious policy was more inclined toward Muslims. Although he did not reimpose jizia but reintroduced the pilgrimage tax which had been removed by Akbar. He also forbade the completion of the construction of some temples and prevented construction of new ones. He thus tried to hold the balance between the policy initiated by Akbar on the one hand and the demands of the fanatical and orthodox Muslim divines on the other.

Shahjahan's last days were embittered by the war of succession amongst his four sons. Dara the eldest son was most favoured to father. He was extremely liberal, stuped in Muslim mysticism and Hindu pantheism. Shahjahan fell ill in 1657. He made Dara as heir apparent. Aurangzeb was at that time in Deccan; Murad in Gujarat; Shuja in Bengal and Dara in Delhi. They faught àmongst themselves. Aurangzeb was successful after killing all brothers and ascended the throne after imprisoning Shahjahan, who had been taken ill. He passed his last days in very solitude in prison, where he later on died.

Shahjahan was harsh and vindictive to his enemies, but kind and generous to his friends. He punished the unruly and recalcitrant with severity amounting to cruelty but he was affable, kind and forgiving to those, who sought his friendship or forgiveness. His supreme endeavour was to eradicate lawlessness and rebellions; to guarantee security of life and property to his subjects and to promote their mateiral and moral welfare. Orthodox as a Musalman, he was never unfair or unmindful of the interest of non-Muslim subjects. Taj Mahal is highest contribution in his constructions apart from Red Fort, Jama Masjid and other palaces. The Mughal empire reached its greatest prosperity in the reign of Shahjahan. Lubbat Twarikh says: "To protect and nourish his people, his knowledge of what made for their welfare, his administration by honest and intelligent officers, the auditing of accounts, his care of the crown lands and their tenants and encouragement of agriculture and the collection of revenues together with his punishment and admonishment of evil-doers, oppressors and mal contents—all tended to the prosperity of the empire".

Aurangzeb (1658-1707)

As already indicated, he had ascended the throne of Delhi after killing his other three brothers and imprisoning his father in 1658. His reign is first 25 years in north and next 25 years in Deccan. Prolonged war of succession and consequent disorder and confusion in civil administration caused economic ruin of whole of north India and grains were selling at exorbitant price beyond the reach of ordinary persons. Aurangzeb abolished certain duties and reduced others to give relief to people. During 1661-1667, the emperor received embassies from many Muslim powers outside India, including from Sharif of Mecca; the Safavi of king of Persia, the king of Balkh, Bukhara, Kashgar, the chief of Urganj, Shahr-i-nau, the Turkish governors of Basra, Hadramaut or southern Arabia, to north-east of Aden, Yaman and Mocha, the ruler of Barbary and the Christian king of Abyssinia. His policy was to at first put all foreign princes in good humour by presenting to them costly gifts and then turned to internal administration. During the first decade, there were some rebellions, which had been put down. The territorial expansion of Mughal empire, continued by his predecessors, went on during his reign too. Aurangzeb's kingdom was the vastest ever in India after Ashoka. It was up to extreme south (except last south end). In the north west, it was upto Kabul; in east upto and including Assam and in west it included Sindh, Gujarat and Maharashtra.

Religious Bigotry and Orthodoxy: Akbar had started reconciliation between Hindus and Muslims. This had however, remained same during the reign of Jahangir but had started dwindling during Shahjahan's period and went on climax during Aurangzeb's period. He started with the aim of regeneration and rejuvenation of Islam in strict accord with the Shariyat and establishment of a true Islamic state conforming to Islamic ideas and practices. He issued a number of ordinances for restoring the Muslim law of conduct according to the teachings of Quran. In 1668, he forbade music in the court and the court musicians were pensioned off. He prohibited the construction of new temples and repair of old ones. He imposed Jizia. As a result, there were revolts. First from Jats of Mathura, which was repulsed; then in Mewat and Narnaul by Satnamase. These were repulsed after they had defeated the local chiefs of Mughals. Sikhs also took arms against him. In Kashmir, all Hindus were converted to Islam and Guru Teghbahadur was killed. Gobind Singh and Teghbahadur's sons created Khalsa

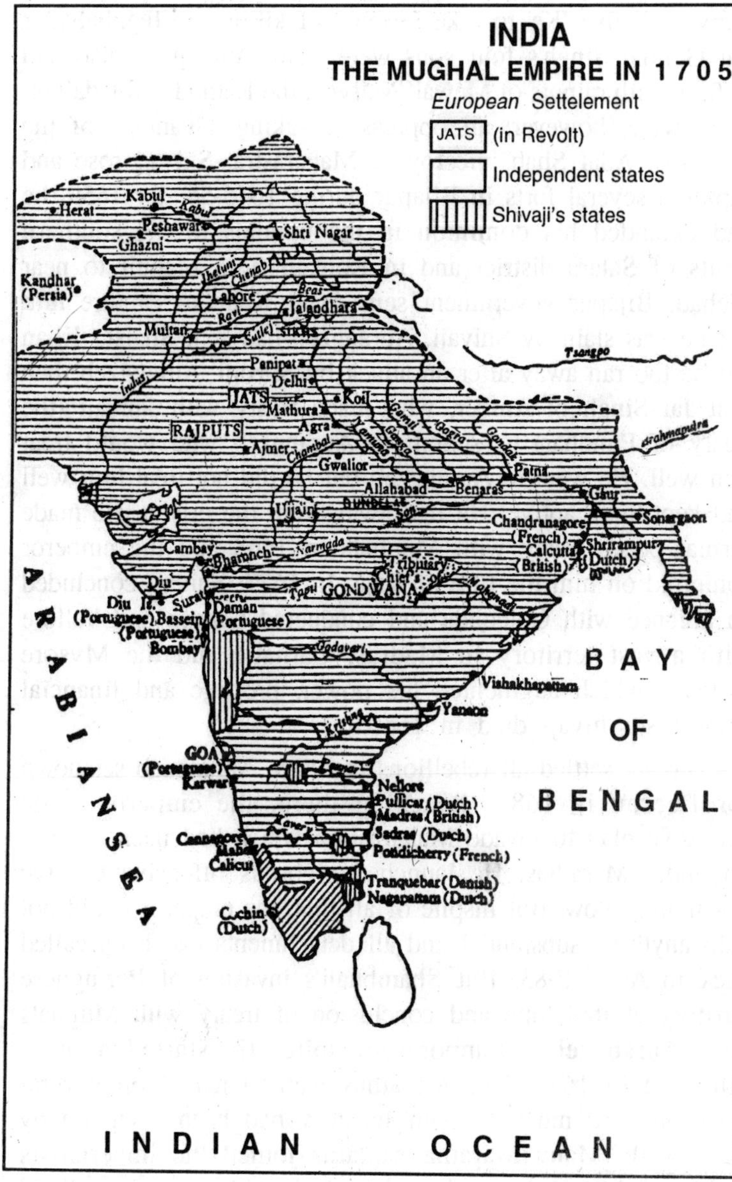
INDIA
THE MUGHAL EMPIRE IN 1705
European Settelement
JATS (in Revolt)
Independent states
Shivaji's states
Herat
Kabul
Kabul
Peshawar
Ghazni
Shri Nagar
Kandhar (Persia)
Jhelum
Chenab
Beas
Lahore
Ravi
Jalandhara
Multan
Sutlej
SIKHS
Tsangpo
Indus
Panipat
Delhi
JATS
Koil
Mathura
Jamuna
Gogra
Gandak
Brahmaputra
RAJPUTS
Agra
Ajmer
Chambal
Gwalior
Patna
Allahabad
Benaras
Son
Gaur
Ujjain
BUNDELAS
Sonargaon
Chandranagore (French)
Calcutta (British)
Shrirampur (Dutch)
Cambay
Narmada
Bharuch
Tributary Chief's
Mahanadi
Diu
Surat
Tapti
GONDWANA
Diu Is. (Portuguese)
Bassein (Portuguese)
Daman Portuguese
Bombay
Godavari
BAY OF BENGAL
Vishakhapattam
Yanaon
Krishna
GOA (Portuguese)
Karwar
Pennar
Nellore
Pullicat (Dutch)
Madras (British)
Sadras (Dutch)
Pondicherry (French)
Kaveri
Cannanore
Mahe
Calicut
Tranquebar (Danish)
Nagapattam (Dutch)
Cochin (Dutch)
ARABIAN SEA
INDIAN OCEAN

army with five 'Ks' to take revenge of killing of Teghbahadur but Gobind Singh's four sons were slain. Aurangzeb also had to fight with rajputs of Mewar, Marwar, the Rathod and Udaipur. They were, however, all oppressed. Taking advantage of the illness of Adal Shah, viceroy of Maharastra, Shivaji rose and captured several forts in Bijapur during 1646-56. By 1659, he had extended his dominion in the uplands to the southern limits of Satara district and in Konkan from Mahuli to near Mehad. Bijapur government sent Afzal Khan to capture him but he was slain by Shivaji. Aurangzeb had sent Shaista Khan but he too ran away after an attack by Shivaji. Aurangzeb then sent Jai Singh of Amber, who made treaty with Shivaji (the treaty of Pundhar) to suhmit to Aurangzeb who would treat him well. He went to Aurangzeb but he did not treat him well and kept him captive. He fled away from the prison. He made formal peace treaty with Mughals in 1668 and the emperor conferred on him the title of Raja. In 1677, Shivaji concluded an alliance with Golconda and conquered Gingee and Vellore with a vast territory in Madras, Carnatic and the Mysore plateaus which augmented his power, prestige and financial resources. Shivaji died in 1680.

Having settled all rebellions in north, Aurangzeb set down for Deccan in 1681. Reaching there, the emperor made extensive plan to invade Maharashtra which had been coming up under Marathas. He launched vigorous offensive to give a stunning blow. But inspite of all this, the emperor could not gain anything substantial and all detachments had been called back in April 1983. But Shambhaji's invasion of Portuguese territory at this time and conclusion of treaty with Mughals gave Aurangzeb a temporary respite. He started another offensive in 1683. The Marathas were defeated on several occasions and much of their territory had been occupied by Aurangzeb. Many Maratha captains joined the imperialists and two wives and one daughter of Shambhaji were confined in the fort of Bahadurgarh. Bijapur was annexed to Mughals' empire in 1686 after a prolonged fight.

Golconda was next attraction of Aurangzeb. The Nawab was defeated and a part ceded to imperial rule and heavy damages charged. The chief was defeated in further invasion and Golconda fully annexed. Aurangzeb then took steps to conquer the unoccupied territories of Bijapur and Golconda and brought in his possession Sagar, Adoni, Karnul, Raichur, Sera, Bangalore, Bankapur, Belgaun, Wandiwash and Conjeevaram in the course of an year.

According to historians like Elphinstone and Smith, the annihilation of sultanates of Bijapur and Golconda, without first crushing the Maratha power with their assistance, was impolitic on the part of emperor, as it freed the Maratha chiefs from any fear of local rivalry, which Aurangzeb could have used profitably against the Marathas. On the other hand, the busyness of Aurangzeb in Bijapur and Golconda gave a chance to Shambhaji to plan to overcome the Mughal menace that hung so heavily or Deccan and while he was busy in merry-making, he was surprised by a Mughal officer and captured. Shambhaji was brought before Aurangzeb who insulted and reduced him and put him to death. Thus by the end of 1689, Aurangzeb was the unrivalled lord paramount of northern India and Deccan alike. "All seemed to have been gained by Aurangzeb now, but in reality all was lost. It was the beginning of his end. The saddest and most hopeless chapter of his life now opened. The Mughal empire had become too large to be ruled by one man or from one centre. His enemies rose on all sides ; he could defeat but not crush them for ever. The administration grew slack and corrupt. The endless war in Deccan exhausted his treasury. Like Spanish ulcer, which destroyed Nepolean I, Deccan ulcer ruined Aurangzeb."

Shivaji (1674-80)

Taking a respite from the Mohammedan rule of India, let us see the rise of Marathas during the regime of Aurangzeb. Born in 1627 near Junnar, Shivaji was inspired by Hinduism by his mother Jija Bai. He possessed a pursuative tongue with which he at once won peoples' heart. He was alert and foremost in jumping into risks and facing conquences. He said:

"Why should we remain content with what Muslim rulers choose to give us? We are Hindus. This whole country is ours by right and is yet occupied and held by foreigners. They desecrate our temples, break holy idols, plunder our wealth, convert us forcibly to their religion, carry away our women folk and children, slay the cows and inflict a thousand wrongs upon us. We will suffer this treatment no more. We possess strength in our efforts. Are we not as brave and capable as our ancestors of yore? Let us undertake this holy mission and God will surely help us. All human efforts are so helped. There is no such thing as good luck and ill luck. We are the captains of our fortunes and the makers of our freedom".

Such an echo was sounded by Himu agaist the Muslim rulers in around 1556 and repeated by Maharana Pratap Singh against Mughal rule but unluckily Himu was defeated by Akbar in the battle of Panipat and because of pro-rajput policy of Akbar, which caused division in this martial race, Maharana Pratap Singh had been isolated and defeated by Akbar's forces. Now such a call was raised by Shivaji, again alone and he did achieve a lot in ultimately having established a Hindu kingdom in Maharashtra, if not in India. This was the call of Hindutava raised at that time against the common foe—the Muslim rulers. Such a call again was raised by Tilak and Subhash against the English in early twentieth century. Since by then Muslims had settled in India the clarion call was raised jointly by Hindus and Muslims and became a call of Bhartiyata against the colonialist British and it did work to push out the British from our motherland. The entire sufference because of Muslim rule as also that of British rule had been on account of non-availability of unity of purpose in whole of India. This had come up during the early years of 20th century but again culminated in the Muslims claiming their separate nationality resulting in the creation of Pakistan.

Shivaji had two main objectives in view—first to secure the utmost welfare of the people in his charge and secondly to have well guarded frontiers which he could easily hold. He was careful not to attempt any expansion at the cost of security. He accordingly established a small cohesive, independent state with ministers and officials charged with definite duties. The kingdom came into being some times before 1653 although the final shape took many years to be completed and was announced only at the time of his formal coronation.

He seized several forts. He also conquered Javli and captured Kalyan, its chief city, a wealthy mart of Adil Shah's west coast region. He also seized a large treasure on way from Kalyan to Bijapur. In the course of this affair, a young, fair Muslim lady, the daughter-in-law of the Governor, fell into the hands of Shivaji's officers and was presented by them for Shivaji's acceptance, as a trophy of the war. Shivaji disapproved this wicked action of his subordinates, reprimanded them severely and allowed the lady to return to her home, duly protected by his own escort. This was the basic fundamental of Hindutava and for Muslims this was an unprecedented generosity, which ran in the Muslim annals of India; and enhanced Shivaji's reputation far and wide as the great respector of the fair sex. Seeing the unfettered rise of Shivaji, Afzal Khan was deputed by the Mughal ruler to bring Shivaji—dead or alive. Leaving his headquarters, he came sweeping against Shivaji, putting down Hindu shrines on the way and plundering the prosperous regions of Shivaji's domain. Shivaji was alive to this development as his intelligence was quite alert. He obtained full details of Khan's atrocities through his spies and finding himself unable to encounter the Khan in open fighting, took his residence at his new fort of Pratapgarh in the midst of hills and planned to overcome his opponent by some subtle stratagem. Afzal Khan also knew the diffculty in facing Shivaji in the guerella tactics adopted by Marathas. He, therefore, proposed a personal meeting of the two in which Khan wished to kill Shivaji by an overgrip as he was quite tall and strong.

Shivaji too had come duly prepared and when gripped him tightly, he stabbed him with tiger claws and dagger.

Delhi then deputed Shayista Khan to subjugate Shivaji. He captured Kalyan and north Konkan from Shivaji. His strength was irresistible, being wholly backed by Mughal empire. Shivaji was rendered homeless. He employed secret agents to obtain minutest details about the arrangements and disposition of Shayista Khan's camp and hit upon a bold plan of a surprise attack at night. He entered his harem after midnight when the guards and the Khan's family were asleep and enveloped in darkness. Shivaji attacked the inmates in their beds, cutting and hacking indiscriminately when many were killed and wounded. Khan himself escaped losing his fore fingers. One of his sons, forty attendants and six women of harem were killed. Khan was transferred to Bengal.

For some time after the departure of Shayista Khan, Shivaji roamed freely as an invincible conquerer. His spies wandered far and wide, bringing news of treasures and wealth of cities and of the weak links in the Mughal government. His head spy Bahirji Naik, reported to Shivaji that all of the Mughal possessions, Surat was the most undefended and contained enormous wealth. It was also the richest port of western India and was highly prized by the emperor as an important port, which was used by pilgrims to Mecca. Shivaji established a secret camp near Nasik with specially selected five thousand stalwarts and without disclosing his destination, he left the base on 1 January 1664 and proceeded to north through the coastal region. He suddenly appeared at Surat and planted his flag at the eastern gate. On the previous day, he had issued a warning to the local governor and the richest merchants to pay a certain amount, which he demanded or stand the consequences of his wrath for non-compliance. The warning was not heeded to and in addition the governor contrived a foul attempt on Shivaji's life on the third day of his arrival. In retaliation, Shivaji attacked the town, burning and sacking in every posible way. Houses were dug up and set on fire.

chests were broken open and heaps of money carried away. He took care to inflict no wanton cruelty upon the innocent inhabitants. Possession of wealth was the only crime, which he punished. Hearing that the Mughal army was coming upon him from Burhanpur, Shivaji hurriedly returned with such booty as could be easily conveyed, which must be in crores of rupees and used in fortifying giant structure of his future capital in Raigarh.

Aurangzeb placed his new expedition under Raja Jai Singh with Dilir Khan to assist and probably to spy (being Hindu). A splendidly equipped force commanded by Jai Singh left the base in 1664 and arrived in Poona in three months, when Shivaji, entirely unaware of these moves of the emperor, was engaged in consolidating his southern possessions and conducting a war against Bijapur, where he had just overcome Khavas Khan, who had come against him on behalf of that state. Jai Singh secured implicit obedience and ungrudging help from all the chiefs and powers, whom Shivaji had over-awed and he actually supported those, who had suffered from Shivaji's aggression. Shivaji found himself paralysed from all directions, no longer able to oppose the formidable tactics now employed against him. Jai Singh held north Poona region and beseized Purandhar. Shivaji could no longer conduct any operation in open. He made approaches to Jai Singh and appealed to his religious sentiments but the latter turned deaf ear to all his entreaties and declined even to receive his visit, until all his possessions were conquered. Shivaji had to throw himself upon Jai Singh's mercy. Jai Singh advised Shivaji to win the emperor's favour by a personal visit to his capital and receive his pardon. Jai Singh thus hoped to bring about a permanent reconciliation between the two, although a vain hope, as it proved eventually.

Jai Singh made full report to his master on his transaction with Shivaji and explained how it was impossible to put down with their force and requested the emperor to receive Shivaji in a personal audience and employ his services in defending the Maratha country, which had never been fully conquered. Aurangzeb agreed and invited Shivaji to his presence on a solemn promise that no harm would befall him. Treaty of Purandar was executed. Though Shivaji had his doubts about emperor's favourable conduct, yet this enabled him to obtain a first hand impression about the inherent strength of the emperor to study men and matters on the spot and thus make it feasible for him to carry into effect his life's mission of a Hindu Padshahi. Shivaji and his son made their obeisance and offered the customary 'nazar' whereupon they were taken back and asked to stand in the third row of the nobles. Shivaji could not stand it and burst in open defiance complaining breach of trust. (A scene created unprecedented in Mughal Darbar). Shivaji and his son were imprisoned. Now alternatives before the emperor were—

1. To put Shivaji to death; or
2. Convert him to Islam and employ him in imperial service; or
3. To conciliate and send him back.

After consulting Jai Singh, alternative one was decided. For four months, Shivaji was in seclusion and ultimately succeeded in escaping. Search parties were sent but Shivaji, adopting detour reached his home uncaught. It was most thrilling exploit of all his wonderful deeds. Aurangzeb felt extremely mortified at Shivaji's escape and suspected Jai Singh and Raja Singh of being privy to Shivaji's plans and disgraced them both. Shivaji became an all India figure, divinely endowed with extraordinary powers. A formal peace was arranged, the emperor conferred the title of 'Raja' on Shivaji.

Shivaji spent two years in comparative quiet and would have possibly continued in offensive, had not a fresh impulse of fanaticism seized the emperor once more, when he issued general orders for demolishing all Hindu schools and temples and putting down all their religious teachings and practices. All Hindu fairs and ceremonies were forcibly banned. The famous temples of Kasi Visvesvar was pulled down in 1669 and that of Keshab Rai (Mathura) in 1670, the news of which flashed like lightening throughout India. New grand mosques arose on the sites of both the temples, which stand to this day visible from miles as one travels to Benaras and Mathura. Shivaji resorted to war against the emperor. After thirty years of hard struggle, Shivaji reached a stage in which it became possible to legalise his position as an independent sovereign ruler—a complete master of his home land, which he wished for a long time. Then Shivaji, to enable him to become a padshah, proved himself to be a kshatriya, as according to vedic tenets only kshatriya could become a raja. This could be traced form Udaipur records and then Shivaji also obtained sanction from the Benaras Pandits for his formal coronation. Grand preparations were made. A gorgeous throne of octagonal shape with profuse decoration was constructed and suitable edifice befitting a capital town had been completed. June 06, 1674 was fixed for coronation. The prescribed rites according to ancient tradition were gone through with vedic incantations befitting a kshatriya hero. Shivaji was weighed in gold and distributed amongst poors in charity. Cost of ceremony, inclusive of cost of throne, came to rupees five crores. The royal insignia adopted and the particular titles he devised as marks of the Maratha ruler (in fact as per vedic tenets) together with the cabinet of eight ministers nominated by him require some explaination to vindicate the Hindu rajya at work as per vedas and Manu Samriti—

1. Kshatriya-Kulavatamsa (Head of kshatriya dynasty)
2. Sinhasanadhiswara (Lord of the Throne)
3. Maharaja (Emperor)
4. Chhatrapati (Lord of Umbrella)

are the Sanskrit titles, which Shivaji assumed at the time of his coronation.

The eight Ministers were—

1. Peshwa (Prime Minister)
2. Muzmudar (Amatya) Revenue Minister.
3. Surnis (Sachiv) Finance Minister.

4. Waqenavis (Mantri) Home Minister.
5. Sarnaubat (Senapati) Commander-in-Chief.
6. Dabir (Sumant) Foreign Minister.
7. Nyayadhis (The Chief Judge).
8. Panditrao (Minister for Religion).

The Hindu character (Hindutava) of Shivaji's swarajya was clearly marked. He excluded all foreign elements. Instead of Urdu and Persian, which were the court languages for the centuries past, Shivaji introduced Marathi and coined Sanskrit technical words for administrative purposes and prepared famous Raja-Vyavahara-Kosa. This would indicate that if will is there, there is no difficulty in changing over the language. We are still hankering for English language inspite of the English having left fifty years back and inspite of the fact that Hindi has been adopted as the national language in the constitution and was to replace English within a specified period of 15 years. We have to give up the robe of English as language which is the first sign of a nation's identity. Even Pakistan in similar circumstances has adopted Urdu as the national language.

Karnatak expedition proved to be Shivaji's last great achievement. Shivaji's son Shambhaji, now aged 22, had been misbehaving for some time and was kept under close supervision. He succumbed to the temptations secretly offered to him by Dilirkhan of some splendid prospects under the Mughal government. Without sufficient forethought or regard for consequences, Shambhaji suddenly escaped from Panhala in 1678 along with his wife Yesubai and was welcomed by Dilir Khan. They together attacked Bhupalgarh, east of Stara, where Shambhaji knew, Shivaji had deposited valuable treasure and a number of Maratha families for safety. They captured the fort and committed a fearful slaughter of inmates. Then they proceeded to Bijapur, which was saved from falling into Mughal hands through timely help rendered by Shivaji. Meantime Shivaji had employed secret agents to induce

Shambhaji to return. At Tikota, Dilir Khan perpetrated severe atrocities by plundering and slaughtering innocent population. It was repeated at Athni. When suffering people appealed to Shambhaji for protection, Shambhaji protested and this caused rupture between them. Some of Shambhaji's friends told that Dilir Khan was playing foul game to hand him over to Mughal ruler. He was frightened and came back home. The year 1679 strained Shivaji's nerves in another direction also. Aurangzeb issued a farman, reimposing Jizia on all Hindu population. He was yet to react when Shivaji died in 1680.

What the earnest endeavour of a man can achieve in this wicked world is illustrated in Shivaji's life. The important events are sufficient to prove the divine gift of genius, which Shivaji possessed and which baffles analysis. A look at Shivaji's whole life closely, discloses his intense regard for religion. He infact is one, who stirred the feeling of Hindutva in Hindus as against the foreign Muslim rulers. He cared more for religious emancipation of his land than mere political dominions. At the same times Shivaji was never actuated by a hatred of the Muslims. He was no bigot and allowed equal freedom to all faiths. Here lies the difference in the thinking of Hindu and Muslim rulers. The Hindu rulers, though had passion for Hinduism, they allowed equal freedom to all faiths, whereas the Muslim rulers like Khalji, Aurangzeb etc. destroyed all Hindu places of worship, schools and imposed Jizia on non-Muslim population, besides forcibly converting crores of Hindus to Islam. Even in present day, whereas Pakistan has become a religious state, India continues to be a secular state. Of course the political parties have been labelling any party which may be pro Hindus but not against minority as non-secular only for political exploitation. The correct way is to give freedom of worship to all people as enshrined in constitution and not to award any favourable position to people of any religion as Hindus are used to tolerate the people of all religions right from the vedic era to date. Even amidst the Mughal rule and having seen the fanaticism and despotistic

Muslim behaviour, the Hindu rule in Shivaji gave freedom to people of all religions.

Shivaji's administrative measures, which were based on vedic tenets, were a marvel of his time and far in advance of his age. He strictly prohibited grant of land in lieu of military and other services thereby avoiding the patent evil of jagir system. This is strictly in accordance with Chanakya's—Arth shastra. His division of official work among eight ministers; his system of forts for the defence of his realm; his organisation of the navy; his army regulations, including those for discipline and plunder; his compilation of Raja-Vyavhar-kosh; his imposition of the system of Chauth; are all measures of his own creation, utterly unlike what was then in vogue. Each fort was made a self-sufficient unit; repaired old forts and constructed new. He gave the Maratha race a new life. He raised Marathas into an independent, self-reliant people, conscious of their oneness and high spirits. All historians have given Shivaji glowing tributes regarding him as unequalled by any hero of recent Indian history. He was not only the maker of the Maratha nation but the greatest constructive genius of medieval India. Jadunath had rightly said about him "the last great constructive genius and nation builder that the Hindu race has produced." He further observed:

"He has proved by his example that the Hindu race can build a nation; found a state; defeat enemies; they can conduct their own defence; promote and protect literature and art; commeree and industry; they can maintain navies and ocean trading fleets of their own and conduct naval battles on equal terms with foreigners. He taught the modern Hindus to rise to the full stature of their growth. Shivaji has shown that the tree of Hinduism is not really dead; that it can rise from beneath the seemingly crushing load of centuries of political bondage; that it can put forth new leaves and branches. It can again lift up its head to the skies".

Shivaji died at a young age in 1680. After Shivaji's death, his younger son Rajaram, a boy of ten years, was crowned with the help of a party. But another party in the state was in favour of Shambhaji, the eldest son. He succeeded in securing the throne in 1680. He continued his father's policy of raiding Mughal territories in Deccan and in winter of 1680-81, he plundered north Khandesh and the suburbs of Burhanpur. Aurangzeb had himself arrived in Deccan but even after an year of his arrival, he could not achieve anything decisive. The Mughals, however, achieved much better results in other quarters. The Marathas were defeated on several occasions and much of their territory had been occupied. Many Maratha chiefs joined imperialists and two wives and one daughter of Shambhaji were captured and confined in the fort of Bahadurgarh. Shambhaji himself, while he was plunged into drinking, and marry-making at Sangameshwar, 20 miles north-east of Ratnagiri city, without even due care for his own safety, was surprised and captured by a Mughal officer. His prime minister and 25 other chiefs following with their wives and daughters, were also taken prisoners. Shambhaji was publicly insulted and degraded and driven to despair. After severe torture for three weeks, both Shambhaji and his prime minister were put to a cruel and painful death in 1689. Shivaji's widows, son and other members of royal family were taken prisoners. By 1689, Aurangzeb was the unrivalled lord paramount of northern India and Deccan alike. Marathas, Qutab Shah and Adil Shah, had all fallen and their territories annexed.

Coming back to Aurangzeb, he stayed in Deccan for 25 years with best of his officers and his prolonged wars there with consequent drain of wealth and manpower; leaving the administration of provinces in northern India in charge of second rate officers with limited resources and insufficient troops, ushered in disastrous consequences for the empire. Centrifugal forces were let loose by the emperor's long absence from the capital and the lack of a strong administration at the centre. Besides the risings in the Jat territories, Rajasthan, Bundelkhand and Malwa, rebellions broke out in Gordwara, Bihar and Bengal resulting in utter lawlessness and anarchy which ultimately sapped the foundation of the Mughal empire. There were revolts from all sides—

1. Rajaram of Sinsani and Ram Chehra of Soghor, Jats trained their men in open warfare. They attacked and killed Mughal commander, plundered the tomb of Akbar at Sikandara; dug out the bones of the great emperor and burnt them. Jats founded a powerful kingdom of their own at Bharatpur.
2. Another outbreak of serious nature was led by Chhatarsal of Orchha in Bundelkhand. He was with Jai Singh in Mughal army. Inspired by Shivaji, Hindus received him cordially and elected him king of Bundelkhand. He also annexed Malwa.
3. Pahar Singh, a Gaur Rajput of western Bundelkhand raised rebellion and plundered the villages of Malwa.
4. In Bihar, a rebellion was led by Ganga Ram Nagar. He beseized Patna; went to Malwa and looted Sironj but died soon thereafter.
5. Deogarh and Chanda came into importance in Gondwana. They raised rebellion and in alliance with Marathas fought against the imperialists in 1701 and extended their kingdom after the death of Aurangzeb.
6. In Bengal, East India Company rose in arms against the Mughals. The grievance of English included the demand by Mughal authorities of an advalorem duty of 312 per cent on the actual merchandise imported in lieu of lumpsum of Rs. 3000 per annum. Unable to redress all the grievances, they resolved to protect themselves by force.
7. Despite the severe set back to Marathas caused by the capture and execution of Shambhaji, they ere long record for despondency and gained their first success in Stara in 1690. They subsequently, one after the other won forts from Mughals. The long and continuous endeavour of the emperor to crush Marthas proved fuile and Maratha nationalism flourished with all vitality as a truimphant force.

8. Mewar had not been invaded by Muslims and continued to be ruled by Rajputs but the annexation of Marwar enabled the Muslims to outflank the country and enabled them to enter Mewar. The Maharana closed the pass with huge walls.
9. Rathods of Jodhpur began their struggle to overthrow Muslim rule. There were frequent battles. Rathods established their rule. Aurangzeb's attention was also diverted towards south and he was forced to come to terms with Mewar and Marwar.
10. Muslims resistance to Mughal imperials: Mughals had to face resistance from Hindus (Rajputs and others) and the Turks. In Deccan, there was Bahmani kingdom. With their downfall, all the five declared independence—Ahmednagar, Bijapur, Birar, Golconda, and Bidar. Their respective position was that Ahmednagar was situated in south to Khandesh and north of Bijapur; Birar was on the north-eastern side of Ahmednagar; Bidar was on the eastern and south eastern sides of Bijapur and Ahmednagar and Golconda's western boundary was mostly identical with the eastern frontier of Bidar. Bidar was, therefore, surrounded by the powerful kingdoms of Bijapur, Ahmednagar and Golconda. Most of the rulers of these kingdoms were Hindus but during Bahmani regime, they were converted to Islam if they desired to retain the kingdom and so all these kingdoms became Muslim infested by further conversions.
11. Sikhs: Nearly seventy Muslim invasions had taken place during five hundred years preceding Guru Nanak. Lot of Hindus was a great misery and suffering. Forcible conversion, destruction of Hindu temples; imposition of Jizia and pilgrimage tax on Hindus; restriction on building of new temples and repairing the old ones, were the landmark of Muslim tyranny on Hindus. As a result, Hindus were not given generally any post of responsibility in civil and military administration. They could be employed only

in lower posts of revenue department because they were familiar with intricacies of local record keeping. Nanak was nine, when Sikander Lodhi ascended. Even as a prince, he wished to prohibit the Hindus from taking bath in sacred tank of Thaneswar. As a king, he broke idols of temples of Jawalamukhi and Kangra and gave them to butchers to be used as weights. He forbade Hindus from taking bath in Yamuna, Ganga and other holy rivers. Babar had ordered Hindus not to shave even. In Mughal darbar bribery and corruption were rampant. Guru Arjun was killed by Jahangir. Teghbahadur was killed by Aurangzeb. Four sons of Guru Gobind Singh had been killed during Mughal regime leading to rising of Khalsa army by Gobind Singh with five insignia with slogans Wah-e-Guruji-ka Khalsa and Wah-e-Guruji-ki-Fateh.

Mughal Empire

Let us now have a look in brief on the polity of Mughal empire. Before the death of Aurangzeb in 1707, Mughal empire consisted of 21 provinces of which one was Kabul; 14 were in north India and six in Deccan. Provinces in north India were Agra, Ajmer, Allahabad, Awadh, Bengal, Bihar, Delhi, Gujarat, Kashmir, Lahore, Multan, Tatta (Sindh), Malwa, Orissa, and in Deccan were Birar, Khandesh, Aurangabad, Bidar (Telengana), Bijapur and Hyderabad. The empire was from Kabul and Kashmir in north-west to Chittagong and Gauhati in north-east; on the west coast to the northern frontier of Goa and in south its boundaries streched to Coleroon river (north of Tanjore). The revenue was 33 crore and 45 lakhs of rupees. The entire empire was the result of continued expeditions from Babar onwards.

The volume of foreign trade of Mughal empire was inconsiderable. The principle exports were common cotton cloth, plain or printed muslin of very fine cotton fabrics, silks, indigo, saltpetre and pepper, while sugar, and slaves were sent out from Bengal and Madras. Main imports were silver, gold, cotton, lead, high class woollen clothing from Europe, particularly from France, glass-wares, cloves, nutmegs, cinnamon from Dutch Indies. Tobacco from America, horses from Persia and wine from Europe. Indian economy was basically self-sufficient and India had a favourable trade balance.

The Mughal emperors did not claim the right to decide the religious belief of the Muslims. Even in countries like Persia, Afghanistan or Egypt, where almost entire population had been converted to Islam, the Muslim rulers had felt it necessary to incorporate pre-Muslim customs in the organisation of the Government of India, where the prepondrant bulk of population refused to accept Islam, it was all the more difficult to organise government according to Muslim law. Akbar did not claim the authority to do what he liked, he simply asserted that his innovations should not be condemned unless they were contrary to Quran. Thus the Quran was recognised in theory atleast as the fundamental law of the state. Twice under the Mughal emperors, the theologians found themselves in opposition to the rulers. When Akbar changed the religious policy of the state and intended making the law of heresy and the discriminative code against the Hindus inoperative, it was opposed and incurred the displeasure of his Sadr, Abdun Nabi.

Emperor was the fountain of all honours, source of all administrative powers and the dispenser of supreme justice. He summoned a few of his highest officers inside his private apartments to discuss necessary business with them. Once a week or oftener held a court of justice and appearance in balcony in morning, where he received such complaints and demands for redress as his subjects chose to present. It was not a darbar as we understand the term today—a place for formal audience and amusement of the king. It did not provide any tamasha. It was the king-in-court, transacting state business in public or in an assembly of officials presided over by the king. In this meeting, the Dewan or the Bakshi read extracts from the official letters, they had received from provincial governors, district officers, commanders of garrison towns and collectors of customs. The emperor would listen and, when needed, issue orders promptly. When there were requests from public servants, the emperor would pause a little for deliberation and then announce his orders usually calling for a report from the Dewan, the Bakshi or Khan-e-Saman. The imperial news-writer would also read extracts from reports sent by subordinates from different parts of the country.

The appointments of all the mansubdars were also made here; question of their promotion, demotion and dismissal; grant of jagirs to them in lieu of salary; posting them to various jobs, all required emperor's sanction, which was granted in the darbar. Ambassadors, distinguished visitors, defeated rulers were also received in the darbar, bringing their presents with them.

There was another institution for doing important work and holding important consultations. This was called 'Ghusalkhana', which was retired place, where only the highly placed officials of the king were admitted. Admission was regulated by permits. A superintendent of Ghushalkhana secured the observance of its rule of etiquette. Another such arrangement was 'Khilawat Khana', where the emperor decided to hold confidential consultations in privacy. The Diwan and the Bakshi were almost always present; other officers concerned, could be summoned, if the emperor so desired. The Mughal emperors seldom missed attendance at one or another of these administrative conferences. As long as this continued, all went well with the empire and when it started fading due to corruption, the downfall of the empire started.

The Mughal ministry in Akbar's reorganisation came to consist of Diwan Mir Bakshi, the Khane-Saman and the Sadr, and the principle heads of the revenues, the military, the public works, industries, judiciary, ecclesiastical, and education departments respectively. Work of every department came under the Dewan. After the Dewan, came to the Mir Bakshi. The Mughal emperors never employed commanders-in-chief of their entire army. This was not found feasible because the Mughal army mainly consisted of independent contingents of the Mansabdars. Mir Bakshi was the chief military advisor. He worked as the inspector general of army and police of the contingents of the Mansabdars and their paymasters holding annual review of troops and troopers. The Khan-e-Saman was the third secular minister. He was an under-minister only being technically under the Diwan. In actual practice, however, he had independent access to the emperor and was usually allotted lumpsum grants, which he distributed as he thought fit. He presented his own requirements himself to the emperor-in-court. The Sadr was the chief justice, minister of eccelsiastical affairs, education and royal alms or all rolled into one. He was also the chief Qazi. The Sadr's main duty was patronage of learning, piety and scholorships. Akbar appointed provincial Sadrs besides the imperial Sadr.

The Muhtasib was both an eccelsiastical and secular officer. As a secular officer, he examined weights and measures and saw to it that fair prices prevailed in the market. He recovered debts and traced and handed over to the owner's fugitive slaves. He saw to it that the public streets or markets were not encroached upon. The public sale of intoxicants, wine, bhang and tadi were put down; sexual morality was protected by peventing prostitution openly in the cities, prevention of gambling was also within his functions. Besides all these, he had to secure the observance of the primitive law against the Hindus as promulgated by Aurangzeb. Thus putting down of public worship by the Hindus, closing down of some of their shrines, the enforcement of sartorial regulations, prevention of the celebration of Hindu festivals like those of Deepawali and Holi, and putting down of the newly erected temples, were some of his duties. He reported apostasy and blasphemy and secured punishment of the guilty. So far as the Muslims were concerned, he had to secure the observance of the Muslim way of life, as understood by Aurangzeb. He put down music, prevented the lighting of lamps on Muslim tombs and shrines on Thursdays; forbade the sale of toys representing animate beings ; hindered the growth of the beards of uncanonical length and shape and enforced sartorial regulations. He prevented the public's non-observance of the fast during the month of Ramzan.

The Daroga-i-Dak Chowkies ran the imperial post. His agents were everywhere. At every stage a horse was kept ready for use by his messages. They brought news from all ways on foot and on horse, by river or over the mountains. There were the sets of persons, who supplied news to the government—

(1) Waqahanavis

(2) Khufiyanavis,

(3) Harkarahas.

The first was a public reporter while the other two were secret reporters of government.

Every large town and province had a news writer. A Khufiyanavis was attached to every field unit and to the headquarters of provinces. The news writer stationed at provincial headquarters appointed his agents in different districts and officers of towns. Waqahnavises sent their reports every week. The Khufiyanavises sent their reports secretly to the imperial headquarters without the knowledge of the local authorities. The reports of the news-writers were received by the Daroga-i-Chowki, who submitted the same to the emperor. He used to read out to the emperor in Zenana, an arrangement to receive the spies by the emperor. The reports were sent in a hollow cylinder, the mouth of which was sealed. There were teams of men, stationed at a distance of every 2-3 miles, who ran to the next station and delivered the mail. The king's letters were transferred with incredible speed, because royal runners were posted in the villages, 4-5 miles apart, taking turns of duty throughout the day and night and they took over the letters immediately on their arrival, ran with these to the next village in one breath and handed it over to another messenger.

So the letters went steadily on and travelled about 120 miles between night and day. It is surprising to find the rapidity with which the imperial letters were carried from one end of the country to another. From the dates mentioned in these letters, collected in the Adab-i-Alamgiri in Aurangzeb's time, it took only six days for a letter to reach Hyderabad from Delhi. In Akbar's reign, a letter reached Ahmedabad from Agra in five days. Four thousand runners were on permanent pay roll, some of whom, on extraordinary occasions had performed a journey of 700 koses in six days; 1400 koses in 10 days with horses.

Aurangzeb kept himself well-informed. Some stray informers dropped in the privacy of the harem sometimes brought Aurangzeb's trenchant remarks reminding the princes of utmost care that they must observe in their words and deeds. The Mughal government confiscated the personal property of every noble after his treachery. The reason was that every officer was indebted to the state which took protection of his property until the accounts were cleared.

Revenues: Sources of revenue were direct taxes on income and persons, professions and property, commercial undertakings of various kinds and indirect taxes such as customs duties, transit dues, octroi, sales tax and the excise duty on manufacturers. Emperor received presents from the officers and subjects as also from the foreign rulers sending ambassadors to India; and Jizia on non-Muslims. Land revenue, however, figured most important. Several systems of assessment and collection of land revenue prevailed based on the principle that the land revenue demanded should not ordinarily exceed 1/3rd of the actual produce. Todarmal had organised the revenue system from land. Whenever crops failed, remissions were granted.

Army: The army was kept by Mansabadars. A roll of soldiers employed by the Mansabdars was kept. Akbar introduced the custom of taking detailed description of all the soldiers paid from treasury. The 'chahra', as it was called, secured that Mansabdars brought to imperial service soldiers of approved physique. Every horse carried a double brand—an imperial sign and the first word of the name of his commander. As it was, even the original organisation of the Mughal army was defective. It was a cumbersome, slow moving and leisurely. The Mansabdars were corrupt.

Law: Muslim law or the 'Shar', which is the basis of the Islamic government and society was considered divine by Muslims. Derived from Quran, it is supreme over all people. Muslim law, therefore, was primarily religious and the secular laws, if any, were all subservient to the canon law. Moreover the basis of Islamic legislation is not legal; it is ethical. All the schools of Muslim law were unanimous in holding that non-Muslims had no place in the Islamic state and that if for any reason they were supposed to exist, they could not be allowed to enjoy the same rights as Muslims, who alone were its citizens. The law for non-Muslims, particularly for Hindus, was Islam or death and failing that permission could be given to them, according to Hanafite school only to live as Zimmis i.e. people living under an agreement as second grade citizens with certain disabilities imposed on them. They were guaranteed safety of their lives and allowed to follow their religion but not to observe it in an offensive manner and not to carry on any religious propaganda and proselytism. They were also subjected to some legal and political disabilities such as not being allowed to wear fine clothes, ride on horse back or carry arms. They were discriminated against in the matter of testimony in law courts and in marriages and also in the matter of protection under the criminal law. They were not allowed to build new temples or repair the old ones. They had to pay jizia, which branded them as inferior people.

The Sultans of Delhi found it not possible to enforce the strict observance of the law as described in the books of Muslim priests. Some of them tried their ulmost to conform to the Islamic law and practise and enforce it in their administration but they did not succeed. Although they did not leave the Hindus undisturbed to follow their own laws and customs, yet circumstances obliged the Sultans to make a compromise with the law of the country. Nevertheless the administration of imperial justice, as far as Hindus were concerned, was unthinkable in that age. The system described above remained in force during the reign of Babar and Humayun and under Sher Shah but it was intolerable to Akbar, who was destined to be the first medieval Muslim ruler of Delhi to repeal the discriminatory laws against the non-Muslims so as to create one common citizenship and establish one uniform system of justice for all. He accorded recognition to Hinduism and other religions in the land with the rights of legitmate propaganda and proselytism. He issued an ordinance permitting non-Muslims to build churches, synagogues, idol temples and fire temples and there was no interference with any one on account of his religion and all were free to follow any religion, they liked. He also permitted converts to go back to their religions.

Akbar even amended Muslim personal law. Despite contrary view expressed by a modern writer, Akbar did make some vital amendments to the personal law of Muslims specially in those related to marriage and divorce. For example, he ordered that a man should marry only one wife and that if she were barren, he could marry another but normal rule was 'one man one wife'. He fixed the age of marriage of boys and girls. No one could marry a woman, who was 12 years older than himself and boys below 12 could not be circumcised. These laws were meant to be obeyed and the kotwals in the cities were charged with the duty of enforcing them.

Akbar also amended Hindu laws relating to age of marriage for boys and girls and monogamy. Widows were permitted to marry and 'Sati' was not allowed. He introduced the practice of marrying his sons with the daughters of Hindu rajas without converting these ladies to Islam and observed Hindu and Muslim ceremonies at marriages. He prohibited Hindus, Muslims, Christians and Parsies from slaughtering animals on certain fixed days aggregating about six months in a year and manufacturing and drinking wine. These rules were, however, allowed to lapse after Akbars's death. Jahangir favoured orthodox Islam. Aurangzeb was determined to make Mughal empire an Islamic state. He repealed all the legal reforms of Akbar and Muslim laws about marriage, circumcision, etc. were restored. Marriage with Hindu women were allowed after conversion to Islam.

Islamic jurisprudence recognised three kinds of crimes -

1. offences against God;
2. offences against state and
3. offences against private individuals.

The offences against God like apostasy, heresy and criticising or insulting the religion of Islam or Prophet Mohammed, were punishable with death. Akbar, however, repealed this law and permitted criticism of Islam and Mohammed. This is how he started the criticism of each religion by Pandits, Maulvis etc. Aurangzeb again introduced the same Islamic law. The offences against the state and private individuals were compoundable according to Islamic law like a man guilty of murder was not sentenced to death if the relatives of the killed man accepted monetary consideration, otherwise death was inflicted. The punishment for crime was prescribed under four categories-

1. **Hadd:** Punishment prescribed in Quran and could not be altered—a thief to lose left hand and a robber both hands.
2. **Tazir**: Punishment in order to refer the culprit not covered by HADD. It varied as per social status of the accused. Men of high ranks were let off with a warning; merchants were sent to prison and common people punished with the strokes of the whip.
3. **Qisas**: means retaliation. It was of two kinds—murder and cases which did not prove fatal. If there is murder then Qisa or retaliation was inflicted. The next of the kin of the murdered had the right to kill the offender, if so demanded. If compensation was accepted then it was agreed.

4. **Tashir**: Un-Islamic form of punishment inflicted in pre-Muslim period and was retained during medieval period as per Manu Samriti like riding on ass, shaving head etc.

Offences against the state such as misappropriation, default in payment of revenue and rebellions were punished according to emperor's pleasure. Islamic criminal law and punishment remained in force throughout Mughal period. Even Akbar did not make any change. Emperor was the Head of justice assisted by Head Qazi, other Qazis in states, districts etc. Akbar made a regular practice of listening to complaints and administering justice personally in open court every morning at 'Jharokha Darshan'. Jahangir followed and also hung a chain of gold from the balcony of his Jharokha Darshan to a pole fixed outside the Arga fort to which suitors for justice could tie their petitions, which were drawn up and placed before Jahangir. Such an arrangement was not discontinued even when the emperor happened to be on tour or military expedition. He also appointed enquiry commissions or held proper investigation through some agency indicating that there was some C.B.I. department in those days.

The duties of Qazi were—

1. To try and decide religious cases and those relating to Muslim Personal Law.
2. To execute judgements.
3. To visit jail and review the condition of prisoners and discharge those of them, that deserved freedom.
4. To recommend deserving candidates for appointment as provincial, district, pargana and other subordinate Qazis.

The panchayats had their role in administring justice. 3/4th of population lived in villages. Every village had its panchayat, which decided civil and criminal cases. There were as many caste panchayats in a village as there were castes inhabiting it. The members of the panchayats were elected by the people and the panches or judges were those, who had rendered some conspicuous service to their caste or the entire village community.

Mode of conducting investigations: Despite serious defects in the organisation, the system worked remarkably well. All the Mughal emperors, except Aurangzeb, who occasionally introduced religious bias in the working of the judicial administration, were inspired by high ideal of doing even-handed justice and the people felt that they were receiving justice. The judges had to find out the facts of the cases under dispute by every possible device and that "they should not be satisfied with witnesses and oaths, but pursue them by manifold enquiries by the study of the physiognomy and the exercise of foresight not laying the burden of it on others, live absolved from solicitude". The Mir-i-Adal and the Qazi were instructed to begin "with a thorough investigation and learn the circumstances of the case and should keep in view what is fitting in each particular case, and take the question in detail and in this manner set down separately the evidence of each witness". The judges were also required to give a gap between the hearings of a case so as to have time to deliberate over it and then take it up and reinvestigate and enquire into it anew, and without discrimination and singleness of view, search it to its core (in Aurangzeb's period, evidence of Hindus was not admissible in certain cases).

Akbar had even said in regard to giving justice that "I would rise in judgement against myself, what shall I say then of my sons, my kindersed and others". In order to see that justice was done impartially, he ordered that the trying magistrates should not tie themselves down to the letter of law but should be guided by its spirit. Expeditious justice was done and prolonged litigation was discouraged as far as possible.

Literature: All round development in literature in all languages—Oriya, Hindi, Gujarati, Malyalam, Sanskrit, technical and scientific literature, music, philosophy, Arablic, epigraphical literature, Persian, took place during Mughal period being a peaceful period.

Religion: The theory of Tengalais was introduced in northern India by Gopal Bhatt, the south Indian follower of

Chaitanya through his work "Hari-Bhakti-Vilasa". He quoted the authority of 'Skand Puran' to show that not only the brahmins, kshatriyas and vaishas but also shudras and women had got the right of worship. Same thing was also propounded by Tulsidas in 'Ram Charitmanas'. Tulsidas even tried to remove the differences between, Shaivites and Vaishnavites, Ram bhaktas and Krishna bhaktas and even in nirgun and sagun bhaktas to demar the influence of Islamic influence on Hindu religion. Akbar promulgated a new religion based on the four fold path or renunciation called the 'Din-e-Ilahi' in which emperor appeared as not only a prophet but an avtar of God himself.

Decline of Mughal Empire

The Mughal empire which inspired awe and administration in the whole world by its extensive territories, military might, economic resources, prosperous trade, commerce and agriculture and cultural achievements, showed signs of unmistakable decay towards the close of Aurangzeb's reign. Within half a century of his death, the disintegration of Mughal empire was nearly complete. The process has been described "As some imperial corpse, preserved for ages in its dread seclusion crowned and armed and still majestic, yet falls to dust at the mere breath of heaven, so fell the Mughal empire when the great name that guarded it was no more". The Mughals ruled for 181 years (1526 to 1707) Babar to Aurangzeb but their feeble successors numbering eleven were dismissed within one hundred years. Later Mughals were—

Bahadur Shah (1707-1712)

Jahandar Shah (1712-13)

Farukh Shiyar (1717-19)

Mohammed Shah (1719-1748): Never before had a more carefree, pleasure loving and indolent emperor addicted to loose habits sat on the throne of Delhi than Mohammed Shah.

Ahmed Shah (1748-54)

Alamgir II (1754-59)

Shah Alam II (1759-1806)

Causes of decline of Mughal empire

It was neither sudden nor surprising. Some of the crucial reasons were:

1. Mughal empire under Aurangzeb had expanded like an inflated baloon and its effective control was physically impossible under weak successors.
2. Aurangzeb by his religious fanaticism, had alienated Hindus, Sikhs and Jats, Rajputs and Marathas and they had all become rebellious to Mughals.
3. Deccan policy of Aurangzeb proved suicidal, with economically bad condition and loosening the control on North.
4. Suffered from defects of hereditary rule. From Babar to Aurangzeb, there was a line of competent rulers but the character of later Mughals was a sad contrast.
6. In the absence of an accepted law of peaceful succession, there was war of succession every time for the throne on death of the king.
7. Army had become a gorgeous heterogamous, pageant without morale, discipline and efficiency and with all vices.
8. National morale had gone low and patriotism was completely missing.
9. Mughal court politics futher degenerated the nobility, which divided the empire into different pressure groups—Central Asian and Persian.
10. Central despotism based on military strength could survive under capable rulers and efficient and dependable governors.
11. Economic and financial condition, which worsened during closing years of Aurangzeb, proved to be most crucial factor later on.
12. Rise of Marathas gave a blow to Mughal empire.
13. Nadirshah's invasions in 1739 made the empire pennyless and forceless and demoralised. It further deteriorated on Ahmedshah Abdali's attack.

14. Downfall of Mughal empire led to the rising of autonomous states. In Punjab, Ranjit Singh rose and ruled from 1792 to 1839. In Mysore, Haider Ali (1760-83) proved to be most formidable enemy of the English in India. He crushed them in first war and second war and then Haider Ali died and left to Tipu. Marathas and Nizam formed a coalition against Tipu. He defeated Marathas and Nizam but they then joined with English and in third war of Mysore, he was defeated and fourth war ended in complete collapse in 1799. Marathas had risen in west and had started marching towards north but were subdued by Ahmed Shah Abdali in third battle of Panipat. The Nizam had risen in Andhra Pradesh. In Bengal, Siraj-ud-daula rose and was defeated in Battle of Plassy by English in 1757 and again in battle of Buxur in 1764. This enabled English to come up and they became the overall lords of India leading India to a colonial status.

7 British Period

With Dutch and Portuguese having started trade with India and becoming rich with the imports from India, French and British also got into the fray in 16th and 17th centuries. British first came in Surat and then proceeded to Calcutta as Portuguese and Dutch had been having sway on the west coast. In 1711, the President of Fort William addressed the Nawab of Bengal "with the humblest submission, lay at his feet, that life wholly dedicated to your service." Two years later, the same suppliant ingratiatingly described himself as 'the smallest particle of sand', John Russel, Resident of the East India Company (with forehead at the command rubbed on the ground) approached emperor Farukhshiyar. In 1715 an Embassy was sent, which after two years of waiting procured at a total cost of over 6,00,000 rupees, a farman, which confirmed the company's privileges of free trade in Bengal and their old position at Surat, where they had been paying before Aurangzeb's enhancement to 20 per cent custom on condition of an yearly fee of Rs. 10000. They were now allowed to buy land at Surat instead of renting it; were granted two more villages near Calcutta and were confirmed in the old grant of 1708 of five villages near Calcutta.

Piracy had become almost the over-wasting fact of those years. As a pay product of the Europeans wars, where there was a wild archipelago, were swarms of desperados sallying out to pillage and hiding from reprisals.

In India, after Shambhaji's execution by Aurangzeb, his brother Raja Ram led the Marathas, who witnessed a period of disunion and persecution by the Mughal power. He too died in 1700 and his widow Tara Bai became regent. Aurangzeb died in 1707 and after his death there was confusion about the successor to Mughal throne. His successor Bahadur Shah released Shambhaji's son Sahu, who had been brought at the Mughal court. It is customary to say that the Marathas lost the empire of India by their wars with the British as the century closed. They, however, lost it no less in their internecine quarrels at its beginning. Further, whereas, Indians were still fighting with swords and spears, the Europeans had come with guns. Their gunners were greatly valued by the country chiefs. They were particularly welcome if skilled with artillery. When question arose about restoration of gunners held as captives or as employees, record shows that the Judge looked on them as clean artisans entitled to sell their abilities, when they worked to enable Marathas recover after Shambhaji's death, helped by follies of late Mughals. Aurangzeb destroyed the Muslim kingdom of central India, Bijapur and Golconda, which had acted as buffer between Delhi and Marathas. He and his successors by their bigotry and savage cruelty made Sikhs and Rajputs, their enemies. Bengal and Oudh had become independent. Hyderabad became sovereign. So was the Nawab of Carnatic. After Sahu's death, the descendents of Shivaji let the Peshwas rule the state for about a century.

In Maratha war and far-raiding expeditions, the great Maratha kingdoms surviving into India of today, we find Gaikwad's rise in 1724. In 1728, twelve districts were given to Holkar in north of Narbada. The Bhonsle family and Scindias also appeared in the same period. The Mughal emperor was destined broken as it was to endure repeated shocks as the century progressed. Nadir Shah invaded in 1739 from Persia and sacked Delhi. He revealed to the free-lancers of the north that the power of great Mughals had vanished. This led to Ahmed Shah Abdali in 1750 onwards looting India to its entirety. Marathas also progressed and became owners of central India and infact upto Delhi. Delhi was left with a few districts only, with Mughal emperor, of course, at the head.

In 1761, the third battle of Panipat took place in which Ahmed Shah Abdali defeated the combined forces of Marathas and Mughals and went back with huge treasure of Delhi, shattering Mughal and Maratha powers.

In 1755, Clive came to India as Lt. Col. in East India Company. Duplex of France had been dismissed in 1751 having cost his employers too much and having ruined the French interest in India. At that time Siraj-ud-daula became Nawab of Bengal in 1756. Company had sheltered a Hindu merchant, desired by Siraj, and turned his messenger out of the factory and off the show with derision and insolence. The Bengal governor had witnessed the frightening emergence in south India of alien powers, who possessed forts in his own territories. Both English and French factories in Bengal were being fortified and while the French to his pre-emptory command to desist, sent a conciliatory reply, the English answered:

"that in the late war between India and France, they had attacked and taken the town of Madras, contrary to the neutrality, we expected would have been preserved in Mughal's dominions and that there being at present apprehensions, they would act the same way in Bengal to prevent which only they were repairing their line of guns to the water side". Siraj wrote back furiously that he was marching on Calcutta immediately. He seized Kasim Bazar factory and swarmed across Hugli. The English fled into Fort William and the natives fled from vicinity. Aminchand was imprisoned and branded enemy. This followed the 146 prisoners having been thrust into a black hole, a room which barely contained the standing space. All, but some 20, died. Five ships of war under Admiral Watson and six transporters under Clive started from Madras in October, 1756. The spying of the governor was not upto the mark and he did not detain the ships on way to Calcutta. They reached Hugly in December. Clive and Watson took entire charge. Days had gone when the English were 'grains of sand' with 'forhead rubbed on the ground'. Watson suggested to Nawab an amicable settlement with a reasonable satisfaction for the losses and injuries. Nawab preferred war. In December 1756, Manick Chand, Nawab's Governor of Bengal, attacked the disembarked troops at Budge-Budge and lost 186 men. The fort which was to be stormed at dusk was prematurely captured by a drunken sailor, who was sent before the Admiral. However, the navy moving ahead recaptured Calcutta easily. English officially declared war on the Nawab and put their forces under Clive. He recruited warlike alien Indian races, which had come into the province with Muslim chiefs. This was beginning in Bengal to carry British dominion to the farthest boundary of India and beyond. The Nawab's intention to storm Calcutta was prevented and caused heavy loss. He offered Clive peace with jewels, elephants and role etc. Peace was signed. Clive now pressed the Nawab to attack the French. As the neutrality had been of the greatest value in recent fighting, Mill's opinion was that this was a shabby deal.

Another complication was Ahmed Shah, an Afghan chief, who had sacked Delhi and intended to conquer Bengal. To purchase English help, Nawab was inclined to throw French over. Watson wrote: "I will kindle such a flame in your country as all the waters in Ganges shall not be able to extinguish. Farewell remember that he promised you this, who never yet broke his word with you or with any men whatsoever."

Nawab wrote back that French were his tenants and desired his protection. Ahmed Shah turned his attention from Bengal and against Marathas. Nand Kumar collected bribes impartially from French and English and preserved a masterly neutrality. Clive became offended on what he did. Ethics disappeared from his conduct. Nawab loathed the English to insanity. He struck Jagat Seth, a Hindu millionair banker, in the face and threatened him with circumcision. Jagat Seth approached English and a plot was formed to make Mir Jafar, a noble, as Nawab. When the plot was ripe, Aminchand threatened to divulge it unless he was promised five per cent of the Nawab's treasure (estimated at 40 million sterling) and 30 lakh pounds.

Clive drew up double agreements—one on white paper (genuine) and another on red paper (fictitious). Both were signed by Clive, Watson ,and Select Committee and was shown to Aminchand. Watson's signature had, however, been forged by Clive. Watson learnt only on his death bed what had been done.

"The admiral said that he always thought the transaction dishonourable and as there was so much inequity among mankind, he did not wish to stay any longer among them. This was written just before his death."

Clive sent a letter to Nawab summarising the wrong to company and concluding with announcement of writer's throughtful intention. Clive crossed the river Bhagirathi and held his force in a large Mango grove at Plassy. The battle next day consisted of two parts—a morning cannonade, followed by a drenching monsoon downpour, which damaged the Nawab's ammunition, then an attack precipated by Major Kilpatrick's keenness and ending in complete victory at a cost of 65 casualties. As the battle of Plassy was ridiculous, Mir Jafar, who vacillated during the engagement, came timidly round with congratulations and was told that he was now the Nawab. Amin Chand was carried home, where he remained many hours in stupid melancholy, which paid into permanent imbecility. The more powerful conspirators did rather better than Aminchand. The company became Zamindar of the 24 Parganas, 880 sq. miles south of Calcutta with rents estimlated at £ 1,50,000. Clive received £ 2,34,000. Shiraj-ud-daula was betrayed to Mir Jafar by a man he had once tortured. Mir Jafar gave his English allies the soothing assurance that Mohammed Ali had given, when Chand Sahib was concerned. Siraj was waylaid to death with a sabre flung across an elephant and paraded through Murshedabad streets on the same day. The loot was received in Fort William. Clive desired to draw under his command if possible the then presidencies of Calcutta, Bombay and Madras. Walpole wrote about Clive:

"Though Lord Clive was so frank and high spirited as to confess a whole folio for his machiavellism, they were so ungenerous as to have to finish him for assassination, forgery, treachery and plunder and it makes him very indignant".

Mir Jafar's son-in-law Mir Qasim had proposed to Holwell to have his father-in-law cut off so that he became Nawab. He again offered the gentlemen of the council a longer gift, which was not necessary. He now, however, instructed Hastings to ask for it. The company received Zamindari rights and revenues of Bardwan, Midnapur and Chittagong as its public reward. Mir Qasim quickly retrenched expentiture and suppressed disorder. Hastings and Varsihart maintained that Farakhsiyar's farman and subsequent endorsements related only to trade at seaports. As to the company's earlier practice, when Nawab still had power, there was no manner of question. Everyone of company started free trade. The Nawab's revenues disappeared. The English under-sell the natives in their own market. The Nawab in desperation declared all trade duty free to everyone. This ended English monopoly. Mir Qasim was deposed and Mir Jafar again brought back with usual presents anew. Mir Qasim allied with Nawab of Oudh and the Shahzada (Titular emperor Shah Alam), raised a larger army. He had guns served by Europeans. The Company, however, routed him in Buxar in 1761 in the biggest battle they had yet fought; their loss was no less than 847 but of the enemy 2000 were killed. The company had finally ceased to be a mere trading organisation and had become in fact the most formidable commercial republic. In 1765, Hastings went home and found himself in bad repute of being dishonest. Clive was sent again in 1765. Jafar died. Clive made peace with the emperor, who possessed little beyond his title and was glad to grant the company the Diwani of Bengal, Bihar and Orissa in exchange of a regular payment of 26 lakh rupees. The administration of the Bengal was left in hands of Nawab's four Naibs of whom one was Nand Kumar afterwards hanged during Hasting's governor generalship. This was Clive's famous dual system. Clive made Nawab a toy in the hands of Englishmen. Clive re-arranged the territory of Oudh. Emperor was given the districts of Korah and Allahabad, a disposition territory which was to become important in the politics of less than ten years later. Hastings subsequently sold Korah and Allahabad to Nawab of Oudh for 50 lakh and cancelled the outgoing of 26 lakh tribute to Bengal. Hastings also established criminal and civil courts in Calcutta—The Sadr Diwani Adalat and Sadr Nizamat Adalat. Calcutta also had its own Mayor's court, whose powers were uncertain. He left Muslim criminal law in general force, which was more merciful than English law, which was in full tide of the century of activity, which crowded the penal code with capital offences. Muslim law, however, ran to the extremes of ferocity such as mutilation too common a sentence of the Muslim courts, which, though it may deter others, yet render the criminal burden on the public. Since the criminal courts remained in the native hands, impalement continued for some years. For dacoity, Hastings had no pity. He, of course, knew how oppressive hand itself made robbery widespread. But part of his work of bringing tolerable conditions back was to obtain security for the honest people. He decreed that dacoits should be hanged in their villages; their families made state slaves and the villagers fined. He was anxious to distinguish between the Ryot, who impelled by strong necessity in a single instance, invaded the property of his neighbour and professed and notorious robbers. The Quran, which was the law book of the native courts forbade sentence of death unless there had been murder as well as theft. Hastings was already (and naturally and rightly) indifferent to strict legality. For dacoity the punishment given by this government was to be super added by an act of the government.

The most mysterious episode of the government of Hastings is the depredation of sanyasis, whomsoever they saw. He called them gypsis of Hindustan. They moved stark naked in bands. They won successes against isolated bodies of sepoys and proved hard to hunt down from celerity with which they fled into dense jungles.

Oudh was a buffer state between Bihar and Marathas. In 1775, Nawab of Oudh died. Then English were their king.

They forced the new Nawab to cede the suzerainty of Benares zamindari and pay a subsidy of six more lakh annually so impoverishing him that he could not pay his troops and had to suppress a mutiny by a massacre.

Then there was Regulating Act. It had established Supreme Court in Calcutta with a Lord Chief Justice and three puisne judges under him. In 1785 Hastings went back and Cornwallis came.

Mughal courts had not encouraged litigation. Their methods were rough and ready and their officials were not over-zealous. Muslim law did not limit itself to much subtlety or chicanery and Hindus probably avoided the courts where possible. The first activities of English judges were terrifying and incomprehensible to any Indian but after a year or two the better educated Hindus saw that there were definite rules guiding the apparently capricious proceedings of the Supreme Court. A new field was opened to the higher caste Hindus, whose minds delighted in the tortuosities of eighteenth century law. Bengal was in much disorder for many of its inhabitants were affected by the system of civil law. On criminal side, every consideration was over-shadowed by the prevalence of dacoities and the close connection between dacoits and zamindars. This inter-dependence was abundantly proved in later days, when special departments were created to deal with the gang murders and dacoities. Hastings summed up the position in 1774.

"I am assured that the zamindars themselves too frequently afford their protection and that the ryots, who are the principle sufferers by these ravages dare not complain, it being an established maxim with the dacoits to punish with death every information giver against them".

Bengal, under Mughal administration, had no police system. The more important zamindars kept a few hired men, for the most part adventurers from upper India, Afghans and Rajputs. The villagers were accustomed to assign part of the crops to watchmen, who were usually members of some hereditary criminal tribes, a form of insurance well-known in the East or in any country, where organised crime is stronger than the forces of order. The larger cities had their organised watchmen and the courts had their runners but Hastings had no reliable force apart from the military with which to stamp out dacoity. Faced by this conspiracy between land-lords and robbers, he abondoned the use of purely Indian agencies for keeping the peace. The faujdars appointed in 1775 to deal with crime in each District had also proved ineffective. The difficulty was to get cases initiated and to find Indians in the Districts, who could investigate robberies and apprehend the criminals irrespective of their position. Hastings in 1781 dismissed the faujdars and appointed covenant civil servants as Magistrates with powers to commit to the nearest Indian criminal court. It paved the way for extended use of Europeans by Cornwallis and marked the beginning of criminal administration by District officers.

Cornwallis had much perplexity for two main centres of mischief left by Hastings. The Augean stables of Benaras and Lucknow. In Benaras, there was a scene of grossest corruption and mismanagement. The Resident, although not regularly listed with any power, enjoyed the almost absolute Government of the country without control. His salary was Rs. 100 a month but he received dishonestly at least four lakhs a year, as well as vast gains for the complete monopoly of commerce. The Raja was a fool, his servants rogues, every native of Hindustan corrupt. Cornwallis's first duty was to deal with the scandals. He established the world famed Indian Civil Service. Benaras Resident was told to be content with Rs. 600 a month. The Bengal Civil Service men were given enlarged salaries in addition to a percentage of revenue and the principle which had ruled Indian administration to our own day was explicitly laid down—its members were placed above the access for peculation and were expected to do within what they were paid. Cornwallis was resolute to keep the peace and told the Nizam and Marathas that it had been wrong to have promised to assist them in war against Tipu Sultan. So he won their confidence. By such method, he even wanted to deal with Tipu.

The efforts of Cornwallis were chiefly directed towards preventing further corruption and ridding India of the worst offenders. The process continued under his successors and a notable advance was made when Wellesly founded the Fort William College in which young gentlemen were to spend three years in remedying any defects that existed in their education by studying Indian languages, law and history. special mention is necessary of Cornwallis's permanent Settlement of Bengal, Bihar and Benaras with the help of Jonathan Duncan and John Shore. Revenues were annually assessed and unchangeable settlement and assessment was made to recognise zamindars, who were hereditary rent collectors, the government being the landlords, as the actual owners. This settlement upto thirty years ago was believed by most nationalist writers to be only good thing English had done, though not defendable now.

Apart from minor changes in general structure, criminal courts remained unaltered until 1831, when the system was revised by Bentinck. It had degenerated by that time but in these earlier years, it was probably an improvement on the older methods. The courts of circuit had their deliveries at regular intervals and there was no accumulation of arrears, which became such an unhappy feature of the civil courts. The weakness of the criminal administration lay in the detection of crime and Cornwallis entirely reformed the police system in 1792. Each district was divided into thanas under the charge of a Daroga and these were under the direct control of the district judge. Zamindars were deprived of all police authority. In 1808, superintendents of police were appointed in three districts and in 1827, this organisation was extended throughout the province. The so called thanedari system has survived till today and is probably the most efficient basis for police work. It had not been successful in Bengal partly because of physical

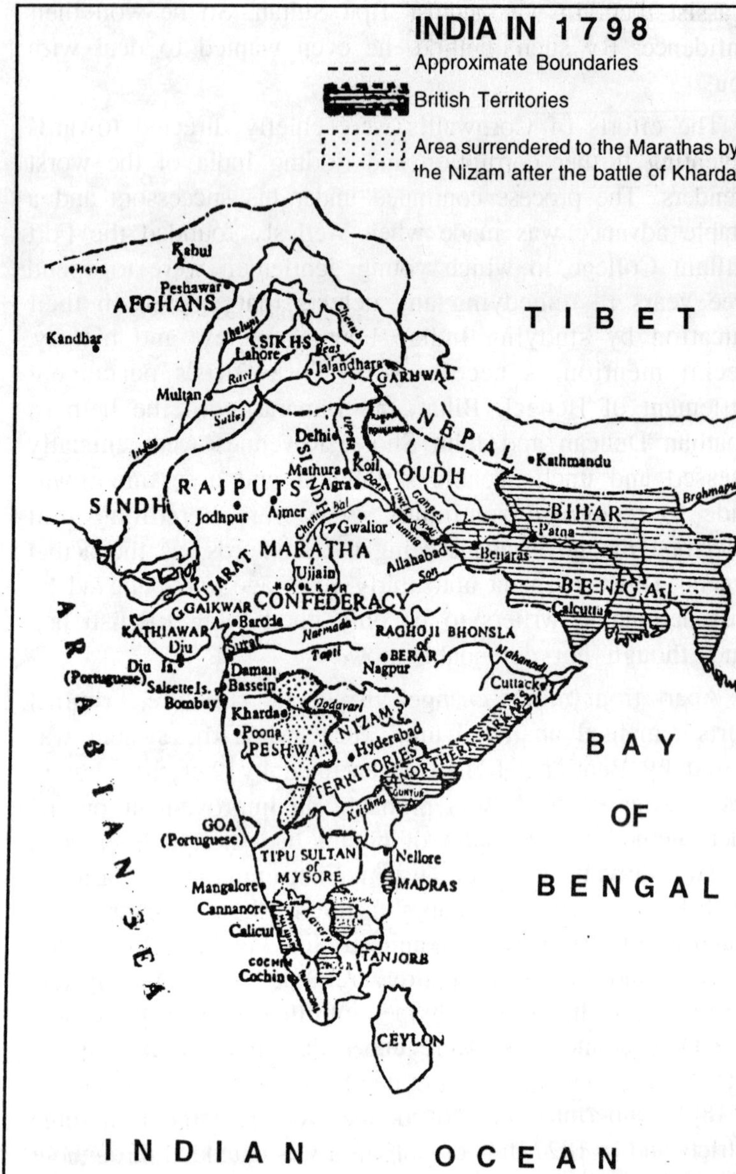
INDIA IN 1798
Approximate Boundaries
British Territories
Area surrendered to the Marathas by the Nizam after the battle of Kharda
TIBET
Kabul
Herat
Peshawar
AFGHANS
Kandhar
SIKHS
Lahore
Jalandhara
GARHWAL
Multan
Sutlej
Delhi
NEPAL
Kathmandu
Mathura
Agra
Koil
OUDH
RAJPUTS
SINDH
Jodhpur
Ajmer
Gwalior
Ganges
Jumna
BIHAR
Patna
Benaras
Allahabad
Son
MARATHA
Ujjain
CONFEDERACY
GUJARAT
GAIKWAR
Baroda
KATHIAWAR
Diu
Diu Is.
(Portuguese)
Narmada
Tapti
Surat
Daman
Bassein
Salsette Is.
Bombay
RAGHOJI BHONSLA of BERAR
Nagpur
Mahanadi
Cuttack
BENGAL
Calcutta
Brahmaputra
Kharda
Poona
PESHWA
NIZAMS TERRITORIES
Hyderabad
Godavari
NORTHERN SARKARS
GUNTUR
Krishna
BAY OF BENGAL
ARABIAN SEA
GOA (Portuguese)
TIPU SULTAN of MYSORE
Nellore
MADRAS
Mangalore
Cannanore
Calicut
Kaveri
COCHIN
Cochin
TANJORE
CEYLON
INDIAN OCEAN

conditions and partly for the lack of popular support in the eradication of dacoity. This has remained a characteristic of Bengal throughout English occupation. In 1845, Dalhousie complained that gang robberies were increasing and in 1918 Bhupinder Nath Basu observed "very respectable men, went the greater part of journey stark naked in India to show the dacoits that they had no money or valuables on them". Cornwallis insisted to make civil law cheap and accessible and have a well-defined law administered by disinterested judges. Accordingly in 1793, he issued a new set of regulations enacting all his criminal reforms of 1790 but entirely altering the system of civil jurisdiction. He appointed 28 judges in districts and further strengthened the four courts of circuit, which also now became civil courts of appeal. Below these were a number of Indian Sadar Amins and commissioners, the Munsifs of later dates, and these heard minor civil cases. The judges were European civil servants entirely divorced from all revenue work and every effort was made to give them a superior standing to the collectors. They took over the collectors' Magisterial work and committed minor cases to the courts of circuit. Cornwallis also codified the existing law and procedure into a form of regulations, a work in which that remarkable orientalist Sir William Jones was to take a leading part.

It was a period when the law's delays were a proverbial source of misery and oppression in nearly every civilised country but in Bengal these evils were intensified by the existence of professional informers and witnesses by the small regard felt for perjury and by the litigation of the zamindars, who found in the law a suitable outlet for their energies.

Subsidiary System: Lord Clive had started the subsidiary system according to which English company had to maintain army for the protection of the conquered territory and the territory had to pay for the maintenance of such army. Such subsidy was too much in many cases and the titular governor had to give up the governorship and transfer the territory to the company rather than continue paying this large amount of subsidy, which he was not able to pay.

Lord wellesley established finally what had existed before the subsidiary system. In exchange for the protection by the British force, states accepted a Resident and general control over external activities. This force was paid for by cession of territory, which theoretically had this value for the state protected that it became safe from vexatious interference on account of non-payment of tribute. The advantages to the British are set out by Arthur Wellesley as keeping "the evils of war at a distance from the source of our wealth and power. The system enabled the British to throw forward their military considerably in advance of their political frontier. Thus the native states became cat's paws. The military frontier to an uncomfortable degree they fomed, was the political frontier also. The statesmen were not aware of the virtues which the Governor General found in the system".

Nizam deserted by Shore, who refused to let him use his subsidiary force against the Marathas, had been defeated by them and their French helpers in 1795. Wellesley made it a law to have English/Indian force on subsidiary account.

When Nana Farnavis died in 1800, with him departed all the wisdom and moderation of the Maratha government. He had private virtues equal to his public abilities, a man of strict veracity, human frugal and charitable. He died with a mind filled with forbading from the ruin he saw coming on his people. It came swiftly. By treachery, Baji Rao obtained the person of Jeswant Rao, Holkar's brother and amused himself watching him being trampled to death by an elephant. This deed broke up what little chance there might have been of united Marathas front. Jeswant Rao swept up to Poona. The Peshwa fled to Bassein and applied to British for assistance. Company negotiated the Treaty of Bassein. Peshwa entered into a subsidiary alliance with the English Company. British troops were to be permanently established at Poona. Company was to control foreign relation of Peshwa and this marked the death knell of Marathas. Marathas were now the least dangerous enemies of the Company in India. The Governor General did not wish for a Maratha war but his considerable patience with Scindhia contrasts with his ruthlessness towards Tipu. British and Marathas had on the whole, two human foes and the Marathas had been sometimes casual but sufficient useful allies.

Company's army from Bombay and Bengal easily over-ran Gujarat and Orissa. In the north, the army defeated Perron at Aligarh. French officers came trembling in as fast as they could escape and surrendered. Scindia had to fight on without them and resulted in Aligarh capture by the company. Battle of Delhi cost more and was captured too in 1803. After his victory of Delhi, Lake had secured one of the main objectives of the Governor General, the person of emperor, who was regularly listed along with territories, an inanimate piece of tool. Agra too fell without difficulty.

Scindia's overwhelming defeat had been largely due to his war with Holkar, which had weakened him, due more to the western training, he had ĝiven to his troops, which had resulted in the strengthening by his infantry and the exposure of cavalry. In the wars of that period, cavalry was the determining arm.

In 1795, Nawab of Surat died. The company by arrangement since 1795, had defended Surat Fort. So Wellesley annexed the state under the justification anticipating Dalhousie's lapse doctrine. He ruled that when the company displaced the Mughal emperor in any district, it acquired the right to settle the fate and succession of principalities formerly under Delhi. Oudh was annexed under subsidiary system as the Nawab abdicated being unable to pay the subsidiary amount. In 1801 Carnatic passed to the company 1/5th of the revenue and the company settled the Nawab as a pensioner.

Mutiny in Bengal: In 1765, Clive had put down a mutiny of the officers of Bengal army since a decade had passed without an open struggle between military and the civil power. The mutineers were periodic and mutineers usually won, which justified their belief that representations made by mutineers and supported by clamour would not fail. In 1808, Bombay officers almost mutinied because it was found that a cavalry regiment might be more conveniently raised at Madras. In Madras next year, the government driven by the directors, who threatened to take the pruning knife into their own hands asked Quartermaster to draw up a report on a system, which gave the commanding officers of regiments tent allowance as for their men, whether they were in field or in cantonments. The system was regularly abused whereupon the officers called on the commander-in-chief to bring them to a court-martial for aspersion on their character as officers and gentlemen. The commander-in-chief complied. Governor of madaras countermanded his action. In Masilipatnam, officers put the commanding officers under arrest and seized the fort. Serirangapatnam followed suit. Hyderabad next rose. All concealment was thrown off and 30,000 men, it was threatened, would march on Madras. Public funds were seized; correspondence intercepted; in a word, civil war had commenced. But the sepoys loyally left the mutineers stranded.

Financial Problems: Until 1833, the Governor General had to serve financially two masters. He was responsible to the Directors of a large trading company carrying on business under different circumstances. He was also a colonial administrator in charge of mixed force, the king's and the company's, always liable to be involved in war with neighbouring princes or with representatives of some European powers. The latter character predominated from the time of Cornwallis. Each successive Governor General had financial disputes with the directors and in 1805, these were so acute that apart from questions of general policy, they must have led to wellesley's resignation.

The revenues were made up of four main items:

1. The land revenue was by far the most important, bringing in some £40,00,000 of which over three-fourth came from Bengal alone.
2. The salt monoploly produced about half a million.

3. The opium trade £80,000, and
4. Customs about £40,000

A police tax was collected and employed locally and the revenue of excise department were due to abkari regulations laid down by Cornwallis for taxing the sale of liquor.

William Bentinck

The arrival of Bentinck marked the beginning of a new era in numerous ways. His seven years' rule proved a peaceful interlude between two periods of severe and costly campaigning and thus made it possible to achieve reforms, which were long over due. He consolidated and reorganised the administration, which since the time of Cornwallis had been hastily adopted to the newly conquered countries. He believed in peace, retrenchment and reform in free competition, free trade and a strictly limited sphere of state action. These touched nearly every side of Indian life and formed the basis of the paternal government of Victorian era. Bentinck initiated new policies in sphere of finance, justice and education. He had problems of Suttee, Thugee, human sacrifice, Ghant murders and other excrescences of Hinduism and expressly enjoined by it.

One of Bentinck's first tasks was both dangerous and unpopular. Since the Charter Act of 1813, which separated the company's political and trading activities, there had been a rapid increase in the expenditure under the former head. By 1827, this had risen from about 16 million yearly to over 25 million, and the difference was only partially covered by receipts from newly added territory. Bentinck came with special instructions to cut down civil and military salaries and allowances and reduce expenditure generally. He cut down irregular military forces and part of civil administration. The provincial courts of appeal were showing signs of deterioration. The administrative side of the civil service had usually attracted ablest men and this tendency was specially marked when new areas were being brought under control. The courts had become "the resting places for those members of service, who were

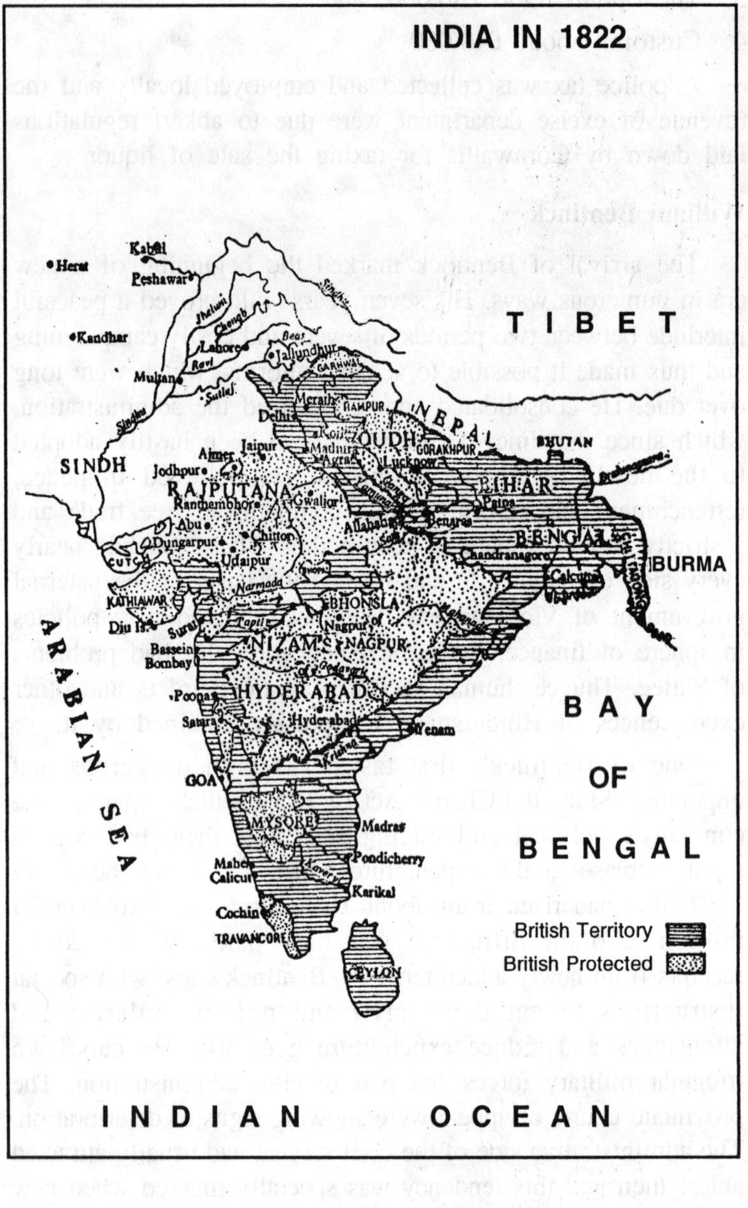
INDIA IN 1822
TIBET
NEPAL
BHUTAN
BIHAR
BENGAL
BURMA
SINDH
RAJPUTANA
OUDH
BHONSLA
NAGPUR
NIZAM'S
HYDERABAD
MYSORE
TRAVANCORE
CEYLON
CUTCH
KATHIAWAR
GARHWAL
GORAKHPUR
RAMPUR
Kabul
Herat
Kandhar
Peshawar
Multan
Lahore
Jallundhur
Delhi
Merath
Jaipur
Ajmer
Jodhpur
Agra
Lucknow
Patna
Benares
Allahabad
Gwalior
Ranthembhore
Abu
Dungarpur
Chittor
Udaipur
Chandranagore
Calcutta
Narmada
Tapti
Surat
Diu Is.
Bassein
Bombay
Poona
Satara
Nagpur
Godavari
Hyderabad
Yenam
Krishna
GOA
Madras
Pondicherry
Mahe
Calicut
Karikal
Cochin
Jhelum
Chenab
Ravi
Beas
Sutlej
Sindhu
ARABIAN SEA
BAY OF BENGAL
INDIAN OCEAN
British Territory
British Protected

deemed unfit for higher responsibility." The general standard of administration had improved but the courts remained hopelessly in arrears both with civil appeals and also their gaol deliveries. The courts were abolished and their criminal jurisdiction transferred to the commission of revenues. This experiment was a failure and the sessions duties were then allotted to civil judges, who were instructed to hold a monthly gaol delivery and thus become the fore-runner of the present district judges. The magisterial powers had to be transferred and were given to the district collectors, a 'blending of Somerset House and the old Baily'; which survives inspite of obvious theocratical objections. The main collector of revenues and head of the police, the sessions judge with criminal and civil jurisdiction were thus established. The concentration of powers in the hands of European district magistrates was originally justified by the difficulty of initial cases against gang robbers, many of whom were protected by zamindars and by the exercise of a single authority in times of disorder. This system received a new base of life in the mutiny and has continued since.

A weakness of Cornwallis's regulations had been the very limited use of Indian judges for civil cases. From time to time their jurisdiction had been slightly increased but the first real extension was made in 1827 when more subordinate judges were appointed as Sadar Amins and were empowered to try suits involving double the former amount. Bentinck established a superior type of Indian civil judiciary authorised to try cases involving property to any amount.

The tracking and apprehension of criminals, had always proved a more difficult task than the organisation of criminal justice. Cornwallis had taken up the management of police into government's hands and introduced thanedari system with Indian darogas incharge of each police district but the rank and file of the police force were the village watchmen, an enormous ragged army, who ate up the industry of their province. The idea of an organised and disciplined body of men had hardly been conceived in any part of the world.

It was considered a great innovation when Sir Robert Peel reorganised the London Metropolitan Police in 1829, the year after William Bentinck had become Governor General and England had first Peelers. In 1830, few governments thought it their duty to provide a patrolling police force with recognised stations anymore than they would have thought it incumbent upon them to provide universal juvenile education regular policemen, first found necessary in the larger cities. But in other countries as in India, the expenses were entirely defrayed by the residents. The extension of this system into country districts and the coordination of various forces, had proved a very slow process, which was far from complete even in countries like U.S., where a Sheriff may still have to summon a posse of fellow countrymen to pursue a criminal. Bentinck did not alter the thanedari system but he organised what might be described as a 'flying' squade' to deal with the specific crimes of thugee and dacoity. His successor Lord Auckland improved the pay and standing of the darogas but the village watchmen remained dependent upon the other villages for their support and shortly before it was recognised that while the special department was doing excellent work, the thanedari system was functioning very badly. The matter was under discussion in 1856 when a minute by the governor of Bengal sketched out a policy, which would have turned the watchmen into regular government servants.

The suppression of thugee was a notable achievement of the pre-mutiny era. The 'thug' or more accurately 'phansidar' was a member of one of those hereditary criminal castes, which have always been a feature of Indian life. Some of these still survive to worry the police officers. The phansidars or noose-holders were unusual because their invariable method of procedure was to murder before robbing. Working in gangs which were bound together by strict religious vows to the goddess Kali, the phansidars would ingratiate themselves with travellers and then strangle them and bury them. They formed a powerful confederacy operating over whole of north India and supported by many land-owners, whom they disposed off their booty. For some years after the British occupation, their activities were scramed by the Maratha and Pindari wars but the existence of the professed thugs had been established by Lord Hasting's administration and in 1829, a special department under Col. Sleeman was created to deal with them. The methods by which these gangs were finally dispersed and a description of their habits and curious mentality have been recounted in two classic works. Some idea of their depredations can be gathered from Sleeman's report of 1840, where the number of ascertained well known and bloody Bhils in Oudh alone was given as 274 and of the twenty approvers, one confessed to 931 murders in 40 years and another to 508 in 20 years. Over 1500 thugs were apprehended in the first six years. In 1837 Col. Sleeman was also entrusted with the suppression of dacoity but here the task was much more difficult. Many Indians of all classes must have known about the operation of thugs and in some cases assisted them and profitted by them, but a far longer and more influential section of the population was against the dacoities. There were parts of India, where dacoity was as much a national pastime as bull-fighting in Spain. It was considered by its participants as an honourable profession. They could not be hunted down with the ruthlessness employed against thugs and for some years, they were protected by the insistence of the law courts upon proof of specific offences, when all that could normally be proved was that a prisoner belonged to a gang of dacoits. This was partially corrected by an act of 1843 but the difficulty of obtaining evidence still remained great hindrance and the professional dacoits learnt to operate near the borders of Indian states, where their pursuit was made harder by question of jurisdiction. In western India, the most persistent robbers were Bhils, whose settlement and reclamation by Outram was a wholly admirable work. Whereas in the case of thugee and dacoity, it was the looting of the persons in the case of robbery, it was murder for the sake of robbery, even though the perpetrators claimed to be religious devotees. Other savage customs presented greater difficulties. The religious element was stronger, the element of gain was less. As Indian officials spread over the country, they were brought into touch with new side of Indian life, about which their predecessors had been ignorant or indifferent. Some of these offenders were strongly against all European ideas of civilisations. The way, these affected the Englishmen's idea of India, was the 'mariah', human sacrifices in Orissa, the prevalence of female infanticide and the custom of 'Sati' or widow burning, which was common throughout Bengal and Northern India. The first was confined to certain backward sects but the other two were practised by the highest castes and the last was enthusiastically approved by all classes.

The suppression of 'mariah' was a slow business 'not completed until the end of Dalhousie's time though the main work was done by Campbell. The sacrifices were to the spirit of natural fertility or 'Iti', a worship still existing in rural north India. Before being put to death, the children reared for such sacrifices were exchanged for similar children in another village, apparently because their own village had ties of affection with them. The sacrifices were always in public consisting of cutting of flesh off the living victim. Between 1837 and 1854, 1506 marihas were rescued.

The killing of girl babies was commonest amongst warlike castes in central and western India and was a natural development of a primitive civilisation in which an unmarried woman was considered as unchaste as a fair proportion of the men were killed in wars. Some castes carried the habit to extreme heights. The rajkumars kept very few of their female children and the custom was prevalent throughout Rajputana. It was extremely difficult for the early administration to deal with this problem. The systematic murder of children was an affair of the 'zenana'. The mother was usually the executioner. She either did not feed the child or rubbed a little opium on the nipples of the breasts. One economic reason for female infanticide was the high dowries demanded amongst certain castes such as in the Mairs.

"Suttee' presented a more difficult problem and the subject had far more publicity outside India. 'Sahmarna', dying in company with one's husband is a very ancient Indian rite. The anglo Indian word 'Suttee' is for 'Sati', the woman, who performs the rite usually by immolating herself, on the funeral pyre of her husband. It seems to have been confined to the higher castes of Hindus. Aurangzeb issued an order that in all lands under Mughal control, never again should the official allow a woman to be burnt. It was discouraged in the neighbourhood of Delhi but was common amongst Brahmins of Bengal. It was a religious spectacle, attended by large gathering. There was no opposition from Indians until about 1820, when a few educated and westernised Hindus led by Ram Mohan Roy started reformist movement. There were 438 cases in 1803. The government took the advice of leading Hindu pandits, who replied that the practice was recognised and encouraged by the doctrine of Hindu religion and for some years attempts were made to regulate the suttee and/to allow the practice in those cases in which it was permitted by their religion. As more European officers came out to undertake magisterial and police work in the districts, they began to investigate these cases and to discover the sordid-economic reasons as well as the sheer lore of cruelty, which found the background to so many cases of 'sahmarna'. By the twenties, there was a strong move for prohibition amongst the officials in the more settled areas. Bentinck's regulations prohibiting widow burning was not issued until 1829. Ram Mohan Roy himself considered that the order was premature.

In Punjab, Ranjit Singh had a sovereign kingdom comprising of Panjab, Sind, N.W.F.P, Baluchistan and part of Afghanistan. He did not allow English to march to Punjab. He had made a strong army duly trained by Europeans. After the death of Ranjit Singh in 1839, there was as usual, the war of succession enflamed by the treachery system adopted by English. Like the battle of Plassy, here too English played the role of bribing the commander and in this way aunihilating the Sikh rule and annexing Punjab to British territory.

Sikh War

1. The Sikh army was quite dreaded to English. English, therefore, resorted to treacherous activities. At Mudki, 20 miles from Ferozpur, Sikh detachment of about 2000 foot and 1000 cavalry supported by guns assailed two British divisions in 1845. They were repulsed but less decisively than Indian armies generally were. The Sikhs were practically deserted by their commanders Lal Singh and Tej Singh, who were both in correspondence with English and so English won.
2. The British troops attacked the Sikhs at Ferozepur first before sunset. The most terrible battle of British India history ensued. The resistance was wholly unexpected. Guns were dismounted and their ammunition was blown into air; squadrons were checked in mid-carrier, sent troops to the muzzles of the Sikh guns. A very little of the enemy line had been captured when darkness closed on what was called the 'night of terrors' and when day dawned, full extent of ruin was seen and so another victory for the English.
3. Another Sikh force appeared under Tej Singh from whose front the force had slipped away. The Sikhs cause was doomed having traitors in command.
4. In February 1846, British stormed strong entrenchments resting off the Satlej. The treacherous Sikh commander Tej Singh again fled and managed to break the bridge of boats. His troops were defeated.
5. The noblest of the Sardars 'Sham Singh' had hated the dreary course of wickedness, which led his nation to disaster. He was also killed.
6. A Treaty of Peace was concluded according to which the Sikhs lost all their Cis-Satlej land as well as Jullunder Doab.
7. Kashmir was sold to Gulab Singh for half a million as English treasury was empty. This was the selling of a Muslim people to a family of extravagantly Hindu family and resulted in rebellion but was suppressed by British.

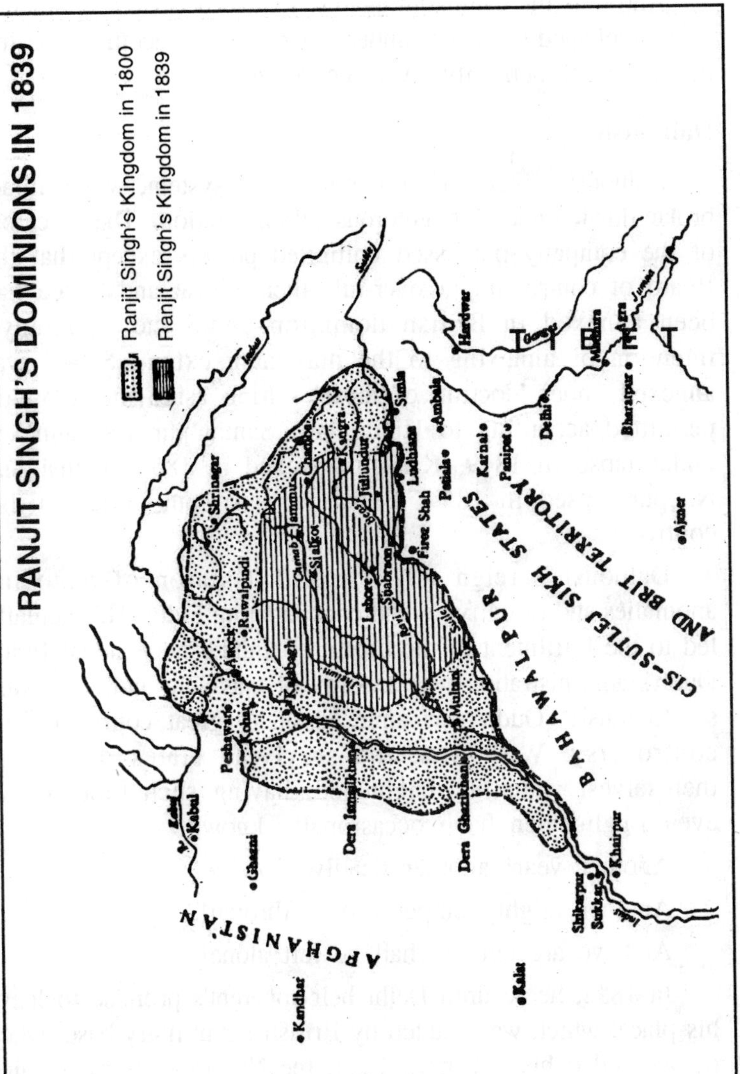
RANJIT SINGH'S DOMINIONS IN 1839
Ranjit Singh's Kingdom in 1800
Ranjit Singh's Kingdom in 1839
AFGHANISTAN
BAHAWALPUR
CIS-SUTLEJ SIKH STATES
AND BRIT TERRITORY
Kabul
Ghazni
Kandhar
Kalat
Peshawar
Kohat
Attock
Rawalpindi
Kalabagh
Shrinagar
Jammu
Sialkot
Lahore
Sobraon
Chamba
Kangra
Jullundur
Ludhiana
Firoz Shah
Simla
Patiala
Ambala
Karnal
Panipat
Delhi
Bharatpur
Agra
Hardwar
Ajmer
Multan
Dera Ismail Khan
Dera Ghazi Khan
Khairpur
Shikarpur
Sukkur
Indus
Sutlej
Jhelum
Ravi
Beas
Ganges
Jumna

And thus the campaign against Punjab was over. A regency was established in Lahore under Lawrence in peaceful possesion of vice-regal authority over the province.

Dalhousie

Dalhousie entered on our out-moded system, which infact broke down under his vigorous administration. The directors of the company possessed unlimited powers except that the Board of control might over-rule them. Surat and Satara had been annexed in British dominion under the Company's intention of annexing to the maximum extent. Satara was annexed under 'doctrue of lapse' setting aside the adoption permitted according to Hindu law. Sambalpur was annexed under lapse in 1849. Karauli annexed in 1852. Jhansi and Nagpur lapsed in 1854. Berar was also put under British control.

Dalhousie's reign was a crowded season of removing anomalies and of unifying and consolidating India. This actually led to the fulfilment of the dream of united independent India. Oudh's administration was an orgy of massacre and corruption set to music. Oudh was annexed under great confusion and controversy. With this, the surviving states drew into themselves, watchful, frightened, having such thoughts as even Englishmen have occasionally known.

Another year! another deadly blow!

Another mighty emperor over thrown!

And we are left or shall be left alone!

In 1852, he secured Delhi heir-apparent's promise to leave his place, which was wanted by British for military base, when he succeeded his father. In 1853, the Nawab of Carnatic died and the title was discontinued. Dalhousie suppressed the Santal arising. They had captured the area up to Calcutta but they had to be suppressed with great massacre. Dalhousie went back in January 1956. He is known as the Governor General of annexations.

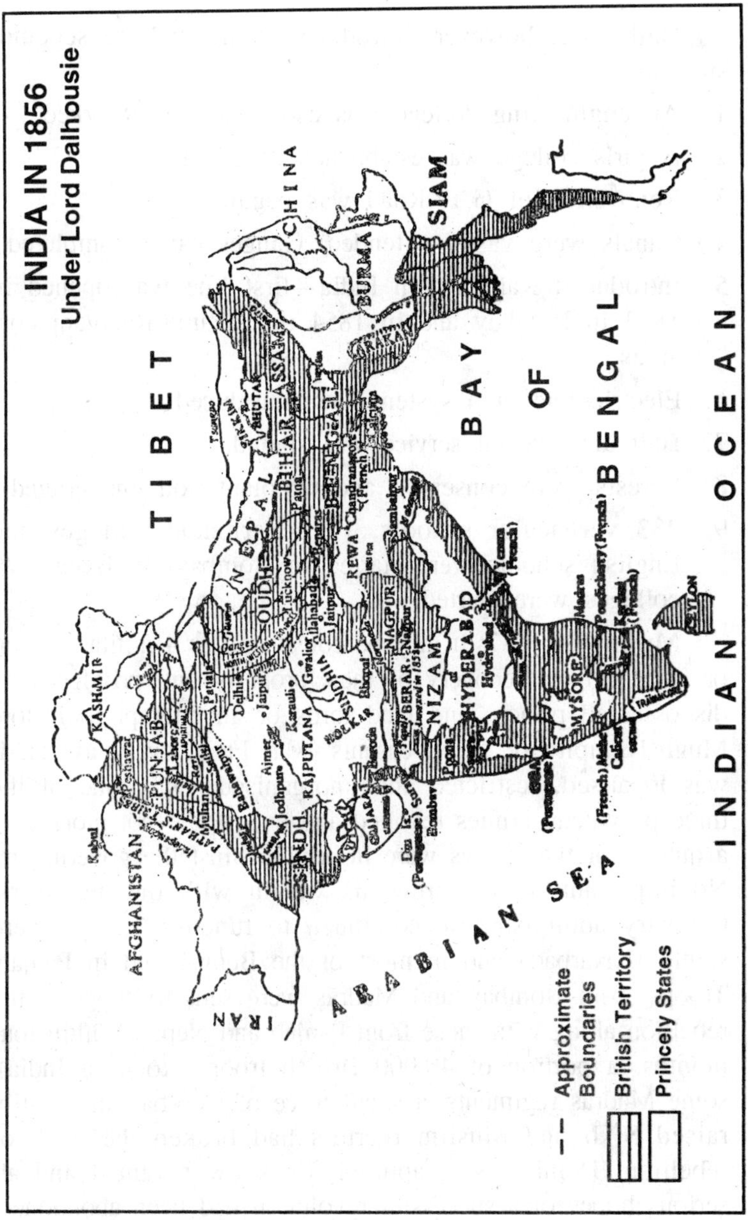
INDIA IN 1856
Under Lord Dalhousie
TIBET
CHINA
BURMA
SIAM
BAY OF BENGAL
INDIAN OCEAN
ARABIAN SEA
AFGHANISTAN
IRAN
KASHMIR
PUNJAB
SINDH
RAJPUTANA
NEPAL
SIKKIM
BHUTAN
ASSAM
BIHAR
BENGAL
OUDH
ARAKAN
REWA
SINDHIA
HOLKAR
NAGPUR
BERAR
NIZAM
HYDERABAD
MYSORE
TRAVANCORE
CEYLON
Kabul
Peshawar
Lahore
Multan
Patiala
Delhi
Lucknow
Allahabad
Benares
Patna
Jaipur
Ajmer
Jodhpur
Karauli
Gwalior
Bhopal
Nagpur
Baroda
Bombay
Poona
Hyderabad
Madras
Calicut
Sambalpur
Chandranagore (French)
Yenam (French)
Pondicherry (French)
Karikal (French)
Mahe (French)
Goa (Portuguese)
Diu (Portuguese)
Approximate Boundaries
British Territory
Princely States

Dalhousic, however, introduced some welfare schemes such as:

1. An engineering college was established at Roorkee.
2. A girls college was established at Calcutta.
3. Renovation of G.T. Road was begun.
4. Canals were vastly extended. Ganges canal completed.
5. Introduced Railways in India—first line was opened in 1853 in Bombay and in 1854 in Calcutta-Raniganj coal areas.
6. Electric telegraph system was introduced.
7. Half anna postal service was started.
8. Forests were conserved and tea-plantation encouraged.
9. 233 vernacular schools, 14 government colleges and English schools were started in Bombay. In Bengal 30 colleges were started.

Mutiny of 1857: It may be considered as a military revolt or as a bid for recovery of their property and privileges by dispossessed princes and land lords or an attempt to restore Mughal empire or as a peasants' war. From every aspect, it was localised, restricted and unorganised. Only one of the three provincial armies revolted and even there not more than a quarter of the sepoys were in arms against the government. No important prince threw his weight with the mutineers. Ordinary administration continued to function every where south of Narbada and in most of the Bengal and in Panjab. Troops from Bombay and Madras were sent to suppress the rebellion along with those from Panjab and Nepal. Within four months, a portion of 40,000 British troops (total in India), some Madras regiments, a small force of Gorkhas and hastily raised Sikh and Muslim recruits had broken the back of rebellion. Delhi was recaptured, Lucknow regained and all serious hopes of a successful revolution had been abondoned. Mutiny, however, had a powerful influence upon later generations of India and English. It was, however, like any other local rebellion, viz.

1. In 1766, a regiment of newly raised Bengal army rebelled.
2. Out-break of a rebellion in Vellore in 1806.
3. In 1809, company's European troops set an example of organised insubordination.
4. First Burmese war. led to a mutiny amongst high caste sepoys at Barrackpur.
5. Afghan war was followed by a marked deterioration in discipline.
6. From Bengal, regiments refused to march to south India.
7. In 1844 two regiments mutineed on Sikh Frontier.
8. A rebellion took place for payment of battle allowance in Madras.
9. After second Sikh war, four regiments refused to draw their pay in 1849.
10. In 1850, 66th infantry rebelled.
11. In 1852, 38th regiment refused to march to Burma.

Reason for 1857 rebellion

1. Threat of conversion of Indians into Christianity.
2. Destruction of Hindu caste and of the traditional Hindu life.
3. Secular education to both sexes.
4. Invention of railways, telegraph suggested the foreigners having decent knowledge and wanted to occupy India for good.
5. Sacred Ganga was tapped for irrigation.
6. Common messing system introduced in military and elsewhere.
7. Religions Disability Act of 1850 protected the civil rights of converts from Hinduism.
8. Passage of Hindu Remarriage Act.

9. Introduction of greased cartridges.
10. Discrimination against Indian troops in matter of promotion and salary.
11. Annexation of territories one after the other, particularly Delhi, Oudh by conquest.
12. Doctrine of lapse and annexation as a result of lapse of several kingdoms in British dominion.
13. Everyone of the rajas feared the English about annexation of their kingdoms on one pretext or the other.
14. Notice to Mughal emperor to vacate Red Fort.
15. Indians were not given any high positions in governance.
16. The English officers were aloof, exacting and unimaginative. They insulted the native gentry whenever they had the opportunity of doing so.
17. The administrative machinery was inefficient and insufficient.
18. Land lords were unhappy as their lands had been converted into the ownership of state.
19. There was principle of civil equity in law but the same principle was not applied to Europeans.
20. The Hindu law of property was changed with a view to facilitate the conversion of Hindus to Christianity.
21. The self respect of the Indian sepoys was trampled. There was an European officer over each 2-3 Indian troops.
22. On annexation of Oudh, 60,000 men were rendered idle or account of the disbanding of the state army.
23. The proportion of Indian troops to British troops was very high. In 1856 Indian army constituted of 2,33,000 natives and 45,322 British troops.
24. Use of mysterious chapaties or cakes which began to circulate from village to village from 1856. It created atmosphere of mystery.

25. The Indian troops were hard pressed to take revenge from the British officers controlling them and misbehaving with them.

26. The immediate cause of the mutiny was the greased cartridges. The sepoys were required to bite the end of the cartridge. There was a rumour that the cartridges were greased with fat of cows and pigs. This torched the sentiments of Hindu as well as Muslim troops. In April 1857, some troops refused to use the cartridges supplied to them. They were court martialled and sentenced to ten years imprisonment. On 9th May, they were publicly degraded and deprived of their uniforms and shut up in jails. This infuriated the troops, who had to openly revolt.

The Mutiny: On 10 May 1857, the day following the degradation and imprisonment of the Meerut troopers, the Indian regiments at that station shot their officers, broke open the jail, released their companions and set out with their arms along the road to Delhi. There was a general confusion as the crowd from Meerut bazaar came burning and plundering the cantonments. Next morning first mutineers reached Delhi. Some went to palace and proclaimed Bahadur Shah as emperor. Others approached the Indian regiments, which mutinied, murdered their officers and joined the killing of any European they could find. The opening of the rebellion was remarkably successful but it was soon apparent that no one opposed. The government was capable of pressing home their advantage though the British position in northern India was precarious. However, the telegraph lines linked all big cities and garrison towns. For some reasons, these were not cut off, which the sepoys afterwards admitted were the "strings that hanged us". Also if any able energetic leader had enjoyed the confidence of the sepoys, he could have established a rebel government over the land between Narbada and Satlej and destroyed or marred the British troops in that area. Three weeks elapsed and then only came fresh crops of military revolts and civil disorder in every garrison town throughout the north west provinces, Oudh and central India. But there was no sign of any leadership. The first weeks gave the evidence of "fatal weaknesses amongst those in arms against the government regional and religious disunity started showing up. The failure to establish a reputable authority on the rebel side was one powerful factor, which prevented the spread of rebellion.

The British rule in Punjab continued to be stable. They were rather able to have Sikh troops to fight out the militant rebels in the area upto Delhi and British were able to reconquer Delhi with their help; Oudh with the help of Gorkhas, Bengal was not rebellious; Bombay and Madras too were not rebellious, rather Bombay troops subdued Nana and Rani of Jhansi and Bengal troops helped maintain peace in Bengal and Bihar. Although by the end of June, rebellion had spread over a large area, yet the rebels had done little to consolidate their position. Large force had been collected at Delhi and Lucknow but no attempt was made to organise the population or to place the rebelling area in a state of defence. The British had begun to take the aggression with Nicholson and Chamberlain in north, and Havelock and Neil in south. Neil suppressed mutiny at Benaras, extended martial law in surrounding districts and killed thousands to panic the people. Similar events followed the capture of Allahabad. Cownpore was scene of massacre of women and children.

British were helped by—

1. Tantia Tope's force from Gwalior garrison.
2. Scindia's own state troops remained loyal to the English.
3. From Punjab, Sikhs helped.
4. From Nepal, Gorkhas helped.
5. Bombay and Madras regiments helped suppress the rebellion in central India.
6. Bengal was against other rebellions and were with British.
7. Rohilkhand and Oudh had been recaptured by British. Ahmed-ud-daula and Begam fought with great

determination but Ahmed-ud-daula was murdered treacherously by a brother of raja of Powani from whom he had sought help.

8. Nana Saheb, Begam of Oudh and Ferozshah escaped from India in 1858.
9. Tantia Tope was given up by Man Singh, a rebellion princelet, who hoped to recover his fief by this betrayal. He was tried and hanged for waging war against the king. Rao Sahib was arrested and hanged three years later.
10. Then ended an episode, lamentable in its origin, distinguised by great carnage but by few other virtues during its course and ending in a manner which left the seeds of much future trouble.

Trevelyan wrote

"After the capture of Delhi, every member of a class of religious enthusiasts, named Ghazees, was brief, as it were ex-officio and it is to be feared that vindictive and irresponsible judge, who plumed himself upon having a good eye for a Ghazee, sent to the gallows more than one individual, whose guilt consisted in looking as if he belonged to a sect, which possibly was hostile to our religion".

Reasons for the failure of Mutiny: Many causes were responsible for the failure of the mutiny—

1. In the first place, the mutiny was localised and there were certain parts of India, which were not affected by it at all. Particularly the territory south of the river Narbada remained undistrubed.
2. Sind was quiet, Rajputana was loyal, Dost Mohammed remained friendly, central and eastern Bengal remained undisturbed. Instead of joining the mutineers, the Gorkhas of Nepal rendered meritorious service to the British. Further, inspite of the fact that Punjab had been conquered from the Sikhs only eight years ago, after a lot of bloodshed, Sikhs helped the British in quelling the rebellion in Delhi.

As a matter of fact the rule of John Lawrence was not very popular and he himself was not certain of their loyalty. So much loyalty was there from Punjab that all the troops left Punjab and even then there was no trouble.

3. The personal character of the Bengal troops was also responsible for failure of the mutiny. They were arrogant and were hated in every part of India to which they were sent. At many places the mutineers were crushed by the people themselves.
4. The year 1857 was favourable to the British in many ways. The Crimean war and the Chinese war were just over. The British armies were free to throw their weight against the mutineers. Russia was defeated and there was no danger from that quarter. Internationally, the Indian rebels were isolated.
5. As the English had their control over the seas, they were in a position to pour men and materials into India.
6. The Indians fought with primitive weapons. They could not fight the Enfield rifle with their 'talwar'. The rebels had practically no war material at their disposal. They had with them what they had managed to capture.
7. The only hope of success for the mutineers was to have quick victories. Time factor was against them. It could be taken for granted that the English would be able to get reinforcements from outside.
8. While the mutineers made appeals to all other sections of society, no appeal was made to the peasants or tillers of the soil. While all other classes were promised a better deal and a fuller pail, the peasants were ignored altogether. The rebellion got its strength from the princes, ruined noblemen and other feudal interests, but these forces were incapable of over-throwing the British Government of India.
9. With the exception of the Rani of Jhansi, Taluqdars of Oudh and some other minor chiefs, none of the feudatory princes joined the rebels. Scindha and Holkar remained

loyal although their armies revolted. The chief of Sirhind rendered excellant help to the English.

10. The mutineers failed on account of lack of leadership among them. It is true that Rani of Jhansi was a capable woman but she was neither the head of all forces, nor a very experienced general.
11. The mutineers worked without any common plan. The result was that they were defeated separately.
12. There was no one common cause among the Indian leaders. Everyone had his own axe to grind. Infact no leader saw into the interest of India but restricted to his own kingdom only. For them their kingdom was the country and not India. It is here that there was complete loss of Bhartiyata.
13. The Mohammedans fought under the emperor and the Hindus under Nana Sahib and Rani of Jhansi. According to Holmes, while the mutineers lacked a head, many were half-hearted and fought reluctantly against the leaders, whom they had been accustomed to obey.
14. Fortunately for the English, the Lawrence, Outram, Havelock, Nicholson and Edward were great personalities. They controlled the situation from the begining to the end and the Indians were no match for them.

Effects of Mutiny

1. The mutiny of 1857 did not leave India unaffected. According to Griffin "Perhaps a more fortunate occurrence than the mutiny of 1857 never occurred in India". It swept the Indian sky clear of many clouds. It disbanded a lazy, pampered army which thought that in its 100 years of life, it had done splended service. It showed to the world that the English possessed courage and national spirit which made light of disaster and which did not care for the heavy odds."
2. The mutiny was a revolt against the aggressive European innovations. The conflict between the old ideas and the

new ones had to be fought out somehow. The fight was inevitable whether in 1857 on the issue of greased cartridges or otherwise. Such a conflict could not be avoided without suffering and shedding of blood.

3. The mutiny brought about changes in the policy of the Government of India towards the Indian states. The policy of subordinate isolation was given up and a new policy of subordinate union was inaugurated. Queen Victoria declared in her proclamation of 1858 that the British Government would not annex the Indian states. The Indian princess were assured the right of adoption and succession. The Indian government also began to rely on the Indian princes on account of the alienation of the feelings of the Indians.
4. The separate army of the East India Company was abolished and it was merged with that of the crown.
5. The Pitts India Act had established the system of dual control at home. The control was exercised by the Court of Directors and the Board of Control. In 1858, both of them were abolished and their place was taken by the Secretary of State and the Indian Council.
6. The mutiny was stamped out by 1860 but it left deep scars. It widened the gap between Europeans and Indians. The English soldiers despised Indians, even those who were fighting on thier side. They denied the Indians a common soil.
7. The collapse of the mutiny created a misunderstanding between the Muslims and Hindus. The Muslims had shown a keener and more widespread sympathy for the rebellion. Even in south India, where their number was small, many conspiracies were found among them between 1857 and 1859. When the rebellion began, both Hindus and Muslims took part in it in large numbers. But the Muslims were more violently anti British than the Hindus. The British feared the Muslims more than the Hindus. The result was that the hand of repression fell heavily on Muslims than

on Hindus. Many of their leaders were hanged or exiled e.g. Nawabs of Jhajjar, Ballabhgarh, Faruknagar and Farukhabad. Twenty-four Shehzadas were hanged at Delhi on 18 November, 1857 alone. Muslim property was widely confiscated. This was because of the fact that Hindus had already learnt to live under foreigner's rule and the rule of English was for them less tyrannysome than that of Muslims. Also Muslims had pinch of the loss of their nobledom at the hands of English.

8. The result of all this was that the Muslims came to have a sort of grievance against the Hindus. The differences between the two began to develop. The two began to drift away from each other and the problem of Hindu-Muslim unity became an unsoluble one.

9. Another effect of the mutiny was that the Muslim renaisance, which had been growing in Delhi before the mutiny, got an irreparable setback. According to C.F. Andrews: "It is not difficult to trace the fatal havoc to building spiritual life, which one year of mutiny wrought; decay immediately over took the revival of learning in Delhi from which it never recovered."

10. The lessons taught by the mutiny have led to the maintenance of two great principles of retaining in the country an irresistible force of British troops and keeping the artillery in the hands of Europeans. The native army was reduced by half, 77 regiments were disbanded. As the cost of a European soldier was 4 or 5 times that of a sepoy, the military budget of India swelled as a result of reorganisation. Sir Richard Temple wrote, "At every large military station in the Empire, there are now enough Europeans to hold their own, even in the event of a mutiny". Native artillery was abolished. In the new native army, men of higher castes were excluded.

11. The mutiny resulted in the lightening of the control of India from London. The Indian foreign policy was linked up with European politics.

12. As a result of the mutiny, the centre of interest in India shifted from external policy to internal development.
13. The lesson to English from mutiny was that they became axiomatic. Their duty now was to keep the peace, maintain law and order, bring to India some of Europe's material blessings but not to worry about the Indians' family life or private morale. The mutiny accordingly led to the following important changes in British policy—
    (i) Crown finally assumed control of Indian government.
    (ii) The army was completely reorganised.
    (iii) New attitude was adopted towards the Indian states.
    (iv) English took up not to interfere in private life and morale of Indians.
    (v) Recruitment to army was on the principle of balancing communities inside army.
    (vi) No annexations after 1860.
14. The mutiny did not cause any marked break in the administration. Most departments of the Government of India continued to function in normal manner. The mutiny, however, had more subtle effect upon district administration. The sudden outbreak suggested that British are out of touch with the people and Indian officials could not be trusted. From 1860; the general policy was to build up a cadre of British officials; encourage them to tour as much as possible and to appreciate the failure and effect of Mutiny, it was necessary to now post them in all districts. The district administration at the time of mutiny was of three types:

In non-regulation provinces like Sind, Punjab, Oudh, Nagpur, and Lower Burma, the commissions and by-commissions resembled the old British officials, and the Subedars and Tarafdars of Mughal times. They carried out all administrative orders; tried the criminals, after investigation, if necessary, collected revenues and decided all civil cases.

They had a rough criminal code but civil cases were settled by a mixture of customs, common sense and a reference to standing orders. The system was well-suited to rural districts. John Lawrence writes, "We have a procedure without any pretenion to exactitude but a procedure which provides for the litigants and their witnesses being confronted in open court, for a decision being arrived at immediately, and for judgement being delivered to the parties then and there".

In Old Regulation Provinces of Bengal, Madras, Bombay and Agra, the assistant officers had a very jealous rival in district courts. They administered an elaborate series of regulations to which had been given the authority of law. The collector there was far less of one autocrat than the Deputy Commissioner in Panjab, but in the ryotwari districts of Bombay and Madras, his duties took him to every village and his powers were various and comprehensive. In the zamindari areas, the collector magistrate was still more limited in his activities. In revenue matters, he dealt through the Zamindars and usually knew little of his district. The Bengal and the Punjab systems thus represented the extremes of rule of law and rule of men.

One result of introducing crown law into India was a wide spread thinking that the company's fromer actions had often been illegal and must be regularised. The Indian Council Act 1861, was followed by passing of land revenue, tenancy and forests act and by the great codes - the Penal Code, the Criminal Procedure Code and the Civil Procedure Code. All this legislative activity curtailed the executive authority of the district officers and his sphere of action was futher reduced by the development of technical departments.

The district administration instead of being centered in one man, was divided amongst a number of European heads of departments nearly all of whom looked to their provincial headquarters for orders. The Police Act 1861 laid the foundation of existing constabulary, traced originally on the Indian model, with each district force under the command of a British

Superintendent of Police. The crown government organised a number of new services. These were entirely under European control, partly because these were all technical and intended to be run on western lines but chiefly the mutiny had left an unwillingness to use Indians in key positions. India had now been flooded with European officers in the manner of French colonies and the whole of European staff in civil employ had never exceeded thirty per million of population but the heads of departments in each district remained predominently British until the war. P.W.D., Sanitary Boards, Public Health Departments, Agriculture, Forests, and Railway Departments were established as specialised services.

The climate and instinct of Indian clerical castes with inclination for offices were put to routine and such routine work did not attract very enterprising type of English men.

"On the first introduction of the constabulary police in 1861, the majority of the posts in the new department were given to officers of Indian army, and they continued to be filled from this source for some time. These were the men, who established the present police system in India. Side-by-side with them, entered another type of men, a type, which has been portrayed for us by Tollope and other lesser lights of victorian age - the amiable detrimental, the youngsons or the sporting public school boys, too lazy or too stupid for the army but prepared to go anywhere or do anything, which did not involve prolonged dredgery".

Maulana Azad wrote on mutiny in 1955 addressing Indian Historical Records Commission:

"You are aware that after 1857 the nature and scope of this struggle was for a long time the subject of controversy both within and outside India.

"Many books have been written from different angles and even if we consider the work of only recognised historians, the number of such studies can be counted in hundreds. It is, however, clear that they are all written from one point of view that of the British. They all seek to represent that this struggle was a rebellion of the Indian army against the constitutional government of the day. Some Indian states also joined in the revolt, but these were states which nursed a grievance because of their annexation by Lord Dalhousie. The British government as the constituted authority of the land, suppressed the revolt and restored law and order.

"Not one of the many books written on the subject has sought to interpret the events of 1857 in any other way. It may also be mentioned that while these authors describe in detail the many atrocities perpetrated by Indians on European men, women and children, not one has referred to the equal or worse crimes against Indians committed by the British".

"Discussing the causes that led to the Mutiny, Maulana Azad observed thus: "The question has often been asked as to who were responsible for the Mutiny. Suggestions have also sometimes been made that there was group of planners, who prepared a scheme according to which the movement was launched. I must confess that I have grave doubts on the point".

"During the Mutiny and in the years immediately thereafter, the British government carried out careful inquiries into the origin and causes of the Mutiny. Lord Salisbury said in the House of Commons that he, for one, was not prepared to admit that such a wide-spread and powerful movement could take place on an issue like the greased cartridge. He was convinced that there was more in the mutiny than appeared on the surface".

"The Government of India as well as the Government of Punjab appointed several commissions and boards to study this question, and all the legends and rumours current in those days were carefully examined. There was the story about the circulation of messages through 'Chapatis'. There was also the prophecy that British rule in India would last only 100 years and would come to an end in June 1857, 100 years after the battle of Plassy".

"Inspite of long and searching inquiry, there is so far no evidence that the Mutiny had been pre-planned or that the army and the Indian people had entered into a conspiracy to overthrow the government. I find it somewhat difficult to believe that the research we are now undertaking will throw new light on this issue".

"During the trial of Bahadur Shah, efforts were made to prove that he was a party to a pre-planned conspiracy. The evidence, which was adduced did not convince even the British officers, who conducted the trial and will be dismissed as frivolous by any man of common sense. In fact the course of trial made it clear that the Mutiny was as much a surprise to Bahadur Shah as to the British".

"Some Indians have written on the struggle in the early years of this century. If the truth is to be told, we have to admit it is are not history but mere political propaganda. These authors wanted to represent the Mutiny as a planned war of independence organised by the nobles of India against the British government. They have also tried to paint certain individuals as the organisers of the revolt. It has been said that Nana Rao, the successor of the last Peshwa Baji Rao, was the master-mind behind the Mutiny and established contacts with all Indian military establishments. As evidence of this, it is said that Nana Rao went to Lucknow and Ambala in March and April 1857 and the Mutiny started in May 1857. I think you will agree that this can hardly be regarded as conclusive evidence. The mere fact that Nana Rao toured Lucknow and Ambala sometimes before the Mutiny cannot be regarded as evidence that he planned it. How baseless some of these conjectures are is clear when we find that these historians regard Ali Naqi Khan, Wazir of Oudh, as one of the conspirators. Any one who has made a study of the history of Oudh will regard this suggestion as ridiculous. Ali Naqi Khan was completely the henchman of the East India Company. He was the man, whom the British used to try to persuade Wajid Ali Shah to give up his kingdom voluntarily.

"General Outram, the British Resident, had promised generous rewards to Ali Naqi Khan, if he succeeded in his mission. Ali Naqi Khan was so persistent in his efforts that Wazid Ali Shah's mother became apprehensive that he might secure his end by some subterfuge. She, therefore, took the State seal in her own possession, kept it in the zenana and issued orders that it should not go out without her orders. All these facts are well known in Lucknow and people there regard Ali Naqi Khan as a traitor. To suggest that such a man was one of the master-minds behind the Mutiny is on the face of it absurd.

"It has also been said of Munshi Azim Ullah Khan and Rangu Bapu that they had prepared the plans for the uprising. Azim Ullah Khan was the agent of Nana Rao and had been sent by him to London to plead his cause and secure for him the pension paid to Baji Rao. On his way back to India, he had visited Turkey where he met Omar Pasha on the battle field of Crimea. Similarly, Rangu Bapu had gone to appeal against another decision of Dalhousie regarding the incorporation of Satna into British India.

"The fact that they had both been in Lucknow on such missions is regarded as pointing to their participation in the conspiracy. It is, however, clear that such suppositions are not evidence. Besides, even if they had talked about these matters in London, this could not by itself justify us in describing them as architects of the revolt unless we can connect them with the events in India. There is no evidence of such connection and in absence of records or testimony, we cannot regard them as architects of the Mutiny. After the capture of Cawnpore, the British secured possession of all the papers of Nana Rao. The papers of Azim Ullah Khan also came into their possession. Among his papers there was a letter addressed to but never sent to Omar Pasha, informing him that Indian soldiers had revolted against the British. Neither this letter nor any other paper of Azim Ullah Khan gives any indication that he had at any time prepared plans for an uprising in India. In the light of the evidence, we are, therefore, forced to the conclusion that the Indian Mutiny was not the result of careful planning nor were there any mastermind behind it. What happened was that in the course of hundred years, the Indian people developed a distaste for the Company's rule and gradually realised that power had been captured by a foreign race. As this realisation became widespread, the conditions were created for an outburst which was due not to conspiracy of a few individuals or groups but growing discontent of the entire people.

"If it be asked why the revolt of the Indian people was delayed for almost 100 years, the explanation may be found in the following facts. The growth of British power in India has perhaps no parallel in history. It was not a case of outright conquest of one country by another, but a story of slow penetration in which the people of the land themselves helped the intruders. The fact that the incursion of British into India was not in the name of the crown helped to conceal the true nature of their activities. If the British crown had from the beginning taken any direct part in Indian affairs, the Indians would have realised that a foreign power was entering the country. Because it was a trading company, they did not think of it as a potential ruler. When the people of India realised the real nature of the authority of the Company, there was a lot of discontentment. It was this simmering discontentment which ultimately broke out in the outburst of 1857".

According to Azad, "The growing discontent was aggravated by two measures which may be regarded as immediately responsible for the outburst in 1857. One of these was the new policy which was initiated by Mr. Thompson, Lt. Governor of north west Province (afterwards Agra and Oudh). At first the Company had favoured a policy of maintaining or creating a class of Landlords, who would be natural allies of the government. Thompson was of a different view. He believed that the existence of big nobles and landlords could be a source of danger to the Company. He was, therefore, of the view that the landlords, as a class, should be eliminated and the Government should establish direct contact with the ryots. As a result of this new policy, the Company used every possible plea to dispossess nobles and landlords and bring their tenants directly under it.

The second and perhaps decisive factor was Dalhousie's policy by which he incorporated into British territory one Indian state after another. India was at that time passing through the last phase of feudalism. Under the feudal system, loyalty was to the immediate superior, who was a landlord or a noble. There was no sense of allegiance to the nation or country. When people saw that the Indian states were being liquidated as a class, it came as a great showing itself in its true colours and seeking to change the very structure of Indian social and political life.

The discontent reached its peak when Oudh was taken over by the Company. Oudh was a state which for 70 years had been a faithful ally of the Company. Never once during its connections had Oudh acted against its interests. When inspite of this, the king was forced to abdicate and the state taken over by the Company, the people received a rude shock. The effect of the dissolution of the kingdom of Oudh was the greater as a large proportion of the soldiers in the Bengal army was from this area.

They had served the company faithfully and been one of the major factors for extending its sway in different parts of the land. They suddenly realised that the power, which the Company had acquired through their service and sacrifice was utilised to liquidate their own king.

"I have little doubt in my mind that 1856, when Oudh was annexed, marked the begining of a rebellious mood in the army generally and in the Bengal army in particular. It was from this time that they began to think that the Company's rule must be brought to an end. During the Mutiny, Lawrence and others, who sought to find out the feelings of the ordinary sepoy have left ample evidence in support of this view. The affair of greased cartridge did not create a new cause of discontent in the army, but supplied the occasion, when the underground discontent came out in the open".

We may conclude with the following words of Ashok Mehta:

"The rebellion of 1857 was more than a sepoy mutiny, was an eruption of the social volcano, wherein many pent-up forces found vent. After the eruption, the whole social topography had changed. The scars of the rebellion remained deep and shining".

Lord Mayo (1869-72)

He was popular with Indian princes and the European community. He is responsible for:

1. The foundation of Mayo College at Ajmer.
2. Red Sea cable was laid in 1870 bringing out changes in the position of Governor General vis-a-vis the Home Government.
3. He started the process of decentralisation of finance in India. The provinces were given a certain amount of money and certain departments for management.
4. In words of Rushbrook Williams "with the governor - generalship of Lord Mayo, we may trace the beginning of that steady development of India along lines leading inevitably to the direction of responsible government within the British Common Wealth".

Lord Curzon

Lord Curzon was one of the greatest and most influential Governor General of India. He is responsible for following reforms—

1. **Tribal areas**: Ordered the gradual withdrawal of the British troops from tribal areas. The place of those British troops was taken over by the tribals, who were trained and commanded by British officers.

2. **Afghanistan**: The relations of Government of India with Afghanistan, were not very cordial from the time of Lord Elgin. Curzon asked for peace and policy of caution.
3. **Tibet**: The people of Tibet began to show a desire to become independent of China. New Dalai Lama proved himself to be a strong ruler. He was not prepared to tolerate the increase of Russian influence at the capital of Tibet. He entered into a treaty, The Treaty of Lhasa (1904), according to which Chamba valley was to be occupied by British troops till the whole of war indemnity was paid; amount being Rs. 75 lacs. The expedition to Lhasa was successful.
4. **Famine**: There was a famine in Elgin's time. Curzon toured the affected areas and asked for help from every quarter.
5. He increased Railway track. He abolished the railway branch of public works department in 1905 and the railway work was given to Railway Board. More than 28150 miles of railway line was completed and 3167 was under construction.
6. **Agricultural Reforms:** Curzon adopted many measures for the improvement of the lot of agriculturists. Punjab Land Alienation Act was passed in 1900 according to which land of agriculturists could not be had by non-agricultrurists.
7. **Police Reforms**: Police system introduced in 1861 was not upto the expectations of the people and there was a lot of dissatisfaction, when Curzon assumed office. In 1902, he appointed Fraser Commission to enquire into the working of the police administration in the country. After a thorough investigation of the matter, the commission submitted its report. It criticised in strongest terms the working of the police system. To quote:

"The Police Force is far from satisfactory; it is defective in training and organisation; it is inadequately supervised; it is generally regarded as corrupt and oppressive; and it has utterly failed to secure the confidence and cordial cooperation of the people".

The recommendations of the Fraser Commission aimed at the utilisation of indigenous local institutions, employment of a better class of people with improved position and prospectus; making arrangements for the better training of officers and rank and file, and close supervision of the lower classes in the police force. Some of the recommendations were:

(i) The commission recommended the substitution of direct recruitment in place of promotion to higher ranks from lower ranks.

(ii) The minimum pay of a constable was to be such as to give him a reasonable living wage and was not to be less than Rs. 8 per month in any case.

(iii) The Commission recommended increase in Provincial Police Force and the employment of existing village agencies available for police work. The system of beats of villages was to be abolished. The visits of the police constables to the villages were to be restricted for the purpose of obtaining specific information.

(iv) The establishment of training schools for the training of constables and officers was also recommended.

(v) The Commission recommended that the investigation of offences should be made on the spot. The detention of suspects without formal arrest was to be declared illegal. The practice of working for or relying on confession was to be discouraged. The police work was not to be judged by statistics but by local inspection and enquiries.

(vi) A Criminal Investigation Department was to be set up in every province and it was to work under the central department with its Director of Criminal Investigations/ Intelligence.

The Government of India accepted the recommendations of the Commission. The implementation of the recommendations increased the police expenditure considerably. It was £ 2691344 in 1901-02 and £ 46,02,977 in 1911. However, there was no proportionate improvement in the working of the police system.

8. **Military Reforms** : Moplahs, Gorkhas and Punjabis replaced local recruits in infantry and cavalry to a large extent. Native officers remained incharge of each company for internal administration but British officers commanded them in parade and in the field. In 1908, Indian Ocean defence was taken over by the Royal Navy and internal defence squadron was abolished.
9. **Financial Reforms** : For decentralisation of finance between centre and provinces, the quinquennial settlement made by Lord Ripon in 1882 was declared quasi permanent.
10. **Educational Reforms** : India Universities Act of 1904 was passed for raising standard of eduacation all around and particularly higher education. This Act completely officialised the Indian universities.
11. **Reform of Bureaucratic Machinery**: Curzon came across cases, which had taken years to reach him. One case was lingering on for 61 years. This was due to the amount of noting and report-writing that was going on in government departments and taking interminable time to wade through the file of a single case. Curzon induced the departments to settle their business by personal consultations; avoid protracted controversies, and reduce the practice of noting and prevent delay in arriving at conclusions.
12. **Policy of Officialisation**: Curzon believed that the Indians were lacking in all those qualities which made Englishmen good administrators. He decided to reserve all higher posts for Englishmen. He had no faith in policy of educating Indians for self-government. As a result the share of the people in administration of the country decreased and the development of self-governing institutions received a set-back. According to Henry Cotton:

"Lord Curzon had weakend and discouraged the schemes of self-government. He had officialised the universities and as far as possible the whole system of popular education; he had substituted a system of nomination to government service in place of competitive examination; and he had announced a practical declaration of race disqualification for the higher public offices. The end in view was to officialise the administration by every means in his power and this sinister aim was known to be underlying the partition of Bengal".

This is how the English had cut the wings of the Indians so that they are not able to climb up and they having left them ignorant about what was happening in the world and in India. The Indians were branded as inefficient and barbaric and it took decades in coming above this branding.

13. **Partition of Bengal**: This was another strategic move of Lord Curzon to enlame the Indians by dividing Bengal into two parts on the plea of its size being unwieldy but the fact was that it was a deliberate blow aimed at the growing solidarity and self-conscience of the Bengali speaking population. Originally intended to meet administrative requirement, it was fatal for any political progress and to that close union between Hindus and Muslims upon which the prospects of Indian advancement so largely depended. This led to strong agitation as the partition split the Hindus of Bengal into two parts. In Eastern Bengal, they were out-numbered by non-Hindus. Curzon refused to submit to the agitation started by the people. The agitation went on growing in proportion and became a great national movement which agitated the minds of all the Indians. The partition had to be cancelled in 1911.

Delhi Darbar of 1911

After his accession to throne in 1910, King George V paid a visit to India in 1911. A grand darbar was held at Delhi, now the present Radio Colony, on 12 December 1911. It was announced that capital of India would be transferred from Calcutta to Delhi. Provincial Governors were made more autonomous in their administration. On 23 December 1911, a bomb was thrown on Lord Hardinge, when he was to make his state entry into Delhi. He was wounded and the person sitting by his side on elephant was killed. Hardinge, however, maintained his attitude of sympathy towards the Indians.

In 1912, China was rumoured to be conquering Tibet but British Government gave a warning to the Chinese Government that the latter must desist from such a course and the proposal disappeared. In this way, British kept Tibet as a buffer state between India and China. This course was repeated by China in 1955 but India did not object and India was kept in good humour by China under the slogan 'Hindi-Chini bhai bhai'. The result was the 1962 war of China and India. British could visualise this but India after independence had been befooled by China and China occupied thousands of square miles of Indian territory and sat on its head causing everyday fear to India of any attack and further claiming that India still have 90,000 sq miles of their territory. They have declined to recognise the Mac Mohan line of partition between India and Tibet and India will continue to pay heavily for this folly.

After 1911, the Indian scene of governance has been more of the struggle for independence and this has been discussed in detail in following chapter.

Colonialism: The basic element of colonialism is economic exploitation but it does not mean that maintaining political hold is not essential to colonialism. However, the basic nature of colonialism is manifested through various means of economic exploitation. In India, the British colonialism passed through the different stages—commercial, industrial, and financial capitalism.

1. In the 18th century, the main objective of British colonialism was to trade with India and plunder its economic resources.

2. In early 19th century, India was used as a ready market for the sale of industrially produced goods of Britain.
3. In the later 19th and early 20th century, the process of capital investment by British industrialists started which resulted in colossal exploitation of Indian labour.
4. The battle of Plassy in 1757 laid the foundation of British colonialism in India.
5. The Indian agriculture broke down on account of the oppressive British revenue system. In order to maximise profit, the land revenue demand of Bengal alone was raised by four hundred percent in 30 years after 1765, after battle of Buxar.
6. The wealth of India helped England to become a great industrial power.
7. With the industrial outburst in England, second stage of dumping the industrial produce of England started.
8. From 1813, the Company was forbidden from doing trade in India and in 1833 complete ban was imposed on all commercial activities of the Company and India was left open for exploitation at the hands of British mercantile - industrial capitalists class.
9. The next stage of the British colonialism known as finance capitalism began after 1860 i.e. after 1857 mutiny, when British colonist rulers started catering to the commercial and social needs, roads and railways, post and telegraph, banking etc. were developed. These measures helped in augmenting the British capital, created out of Indian exploitation.
10. Investment in India and the burden of the British public debts on India kept on increasing enormously every year.
11. The effect of all this on Indian economy and social life was disastrous in as much as when there was famine in India, the goverment continued to export foodgrains to England for the use of their labour.

12. Raw material was taken from India at cheap rates and manufactured commodities dumped at very high prices.
13. Permanent zamindari settlements were made in Bengal, Bihar, Orissa, Varanasi and Karnatak, covering about 19 per cent of total area of British India. In 1793, it was made permanent. The zamindars were declared absolute owners and proprietors of the estate..
14. The expansion of British trade in India not only proved ruinous to Indian trade and industry but also radically changed the structure of India's trade.
15. India was forced to accept British imports while Indian products were subjected to high import duties in England.
16. Due to discriminatory duties, Indian traditional handicraft lost the world market. Even Mark had said, "The British intruders broke up the Indian handloom and destroyed the spinning loom, and inundated the very mother country of cotton with cotton growth of foreign capital."
17. The constant flow of wealth from India to England for which India did not get adequate economic return, constituted a special feature of British colonialism. India had to remit large amounts every year in the form of 'House Charges' i.e. the charges for paying the salary of secretary of state and his establishment; the payment of interest on 'Indian Public Debt'; expenses debited to India for military and naval establishments maintained in England; cost of British embassies maintained in Iran, China, and other countries, etc.
18. All high posts in India were monopolised by Europeans and after their retirement, huge sums had to be paid year-after-year (remitted to England) towards their pension, gratuity, etc. Because of these and the charges indicated in 17 above, India, the richest country of the world, became the poorest. This was the impact of colonialism under British and was not there during Muslim rule as at that time, the Muslim rulers were sovereign Indian kings not

under any foreign power and they cared for improving the Indian economy for India only.

19. Between 1854 and 1901, nearly 24 famines hit India, in which 29 million people perished. Matters did not improve in 20th century too. In Bengal famine of 1943, about 30 lac lives were lost, and the foodgrains were being sent to England and not to Bengal. This was again the effect of colonial rule as the British had no affinity with Indian people and cared for the English only like a daughter-in-law living in in-laws' house and caring for the people of her parent's side.

20. Loss of industry and trade caused unemployment and poverty in India. The Indians were totally at the mercy of English. Indian peasantry was bound hands and feet to the landed intermediaries, created as loyals of British, money lenders and tax collectors. Industry and trade were in foreign hands leading to drainage of country's wealth and its vast resources were monopolised and brutally exploited by the colonial masters.

21. Apart from wealth, Indian people had also been exploited in other ways. They had been sent as cheap labourers in England and other colonies of British. They were used and deployed in battles; English had to fight with European powers as also in first and second world wars. Many Indian soldiers were killed for which India could hardly get any compensation.

The above is the effect of colonialism under British rule. This is the actual period of non-independence. Such exploitation was not there under the Muslim rulers as they were sovereign Indian rulers and whatever was produced in India, was used in India for public welfare. The concept of colonialism is, therefore, of European rulers coined for Africa, America and Australia continents, which was applied on India too.

General Analysis of British Rule in India: Following the Dutch, Portuguese and French, English too came for trade to

India, as trade with India was very paying as per charter of 31 December 1600 granted by Queen Elizabeth to the Governor and company of merchants of London trading into-east India. In 1674 Shivaji enthroned himself as an independent king and an Englishman Henry Oxinder was officially present at the coronation. He returned with a peace treaty, which he believed would prove of no small benefit to the Company's affairs. Shivaji too realised that British Naval expertise might make the Company a valuable ally in his war against Mughals. Bombay had grown fast; its military strength and religious tolerance making it a heaven, not only for Hindus, escaping the Mughal terror but also for Christians fleeing from the inquisition in Portuguese Goa. In 1707, Aurangzeb died. The anarchy that followed was to give both, Britain and France, an opportunity and the incentive for an empire. The English were ready to keep afloat in the troubles to come. Their settlements had been fortified and a degree of friendship existed between them, and the men, who seized power in the provinces of the empire. The English had come as traders, then they became armed traders, soon they needed soldiers to defend their settlements and as the Mughal empire disintegrated, spheres of influence became necessary if the Company was to survive. Slowly, the rythem of empire-building had imposed itself on the traders. In 1751, one of Dupleix's intrigues had been mined by the military talents of a young English civilian turned soldier Robert Clive, who had captured Arcot and held it against a beseized force for a crucial 53 days.

In Bengal, English had become arrogant and lordly, because of company's success in south and acted as if they were independent and sovereign power. In 1756, Siraj-ud-daula became Nawab of Bengal. He was a weak youth with a violent temperament and an unsavoury reputation. Already prejudiced against the British, whom he suspected of intriguing in favour of one of his rivals to throne. Nawab was aware of what had happened in south and he ordered both English and French to cease fortifying their settlements immediately. The French were concilliatory but the English were offensive. The Nawab's answer was to march on Calcutta and take fort after it had been deserted. He put Holwell and 54 other prisoners for the night in the Black Hole. From Madras an expedition was fitted out under Clive. They captured Calcutta without great difficulty in January 1757. Nawab was surrounded by a web of deceit and treachery and at the heart of it were the English. They decided to replace Nawab with Mir Jafar. Fought the untidy but fateful skirmish at Plassey in June 1757. With treachery of Mir Jafar, English won. East India Company became landlords of 24 Parganas, 900 sq. miles of territory, south of Calcutta yielding substantial rent. Clive recieved gifts of £ 234000 and others lesser sums. Mir Jafar became a puppet—Nawab Siraj was murdered in his prison. Subsequently Mir Jafar, unable to meet the growing demands of English, was replaced by Mir Kasim (Jafar's son-in-law). He did not want to remain puppet and began to interfere in English trade. He protested on English doing free trade. English sent troops against him and Kasim and his ally Nawab of Oudh were defeated at Buxur in 1764. Now Company ceased to be a company of merchants and became a formidable political force. It took the office of Dewan i.e. collector and administrator of revenues of the province. This was granted by Mughal emperor, now practically a pensioner of the Company and so the entire civil administration of the province was the responsibility of English East India Company.

Warren Hastings became Governor General of Bengal with authority over Bombay and Madras. He was followed by Wellesley. By 1857, it was generally felt by British officials in India that Indians were a pretty evil lot and that it was Britain's duty to civilise and Christianise them. In the years before 1858, many military and civil officers contributed to a great deal to the rediscovery of India's past. Such men as Col. Tod, the Resident of Rajputana, not only compiled annals but collected antiquities and paintings. Similarly the British connections with India produced writers of prose and poetry.

Robert Orme wrote *'History of the Military transactions of the British Natives in Indostan'* of the period of Clive and Malcolini's *'Political History of India';* Cunningham's *'History of the* Sikhs'; Kaye's *'History of the War in Afghanistan'*. This, however, would only indicate that all historians of that time were English and they dubbed the Indians as uncivilised and English as most elite of the time. They did not present the good points of Indian civilization which was at the top of the world during Mughal period in resources, civilisation, administration etc. Now since English became the rulers of the country by treachery, creating disunity by helping one faction against the other, befooling the Indians and taking advantage of their mischievous tactics against the truth-loving Indians, the main thrust of Bhartiyata, they could write Indian history in any colour, particularly since during the Muslim rule of 600 years, Hindu civilisation, their literature etc, had all been destroyed by Muslim rulers. The Indians were only silent spectators of the doings of British and could not unite to force British out as Hindus could not force Muslim rulers out in previous 600 years by giving them a united front. It is how the English, a very small number could enslave the vast Indian population, a thing of apparent shame for the present readers of History.

When the British came to exercise power in Bengal, they were faced with a series of dilemmas. In fact they could never think of becoming rulers of such a vast country. The first was how to rule without revealing that the British had neither the capacity nor the man-power to operate an administration. Clive's notorious system of 'Dual Government' was the first solution to be tried. The native administration and its officials continued to function, while the British remained in the background. This was primarily a matter of expediency but what was in essence a puppet system also appealed to the British since their main interest was in profit. When dual government system was abondoned in 1772, the British were faced with second dilemma. To what extent should the government be anglicised? Were existing institutions to be preserved or swept aside? Warren Hastings felt that Indian institutions should be retained, wherever possible. During his administration, Hindu and Muslim personal laws received protection and Muslim Criminal Law was also maintained. In principle the duality was also continued except that now it was operated directly by the British, who were themselves subject to English laws as exercised by the new Supreme Court set up by the Regulating Act, 1973. With the intention of making individuals subject to English law. Cornwallis decided that English constitutional provisions should form the basis of the system of government. His purpose was to establish *'Rule of Law'* instead of the *'Law of the Rulers'*. Therefore, English political concepts were to be transplanted into the soil of India, and Indians were to be removed from the halls of the government. With Cornwallis's administration from English principles and institutions went a belief in the general superiority of Englishmen and the role they must play in preserving British rule in India. Indians were dismissed from all but the most minor offices. British concept of private property rights and their enforcement by legal process was a radical innovation and its effects were to alter the structure of Indian society profoundly. This was reinforced by a growing belief, not only that the British were racially superior to Indians and possessed of infinitely better political institutions but that their religion was superior too, although Hindu religion had so far been the best confessed religion of the universe. So the British in India, though conscious of their power, were equally conscious that it depended on the acceptance of the large mass of people who did not particularly care, who governed them as long as their customs and religion were not interfered with. They firmly believed that the industrial revolution, which was investing Britain with the commercial leadership of the world, resulted from a superior civilisation, and the passing of its benefits was not only good business but a heaven ordained duty. India lived in rural areas and every level of Indian society, outside the urban areas, depended in one way or the other upon the law.

Before, therefore, the fundamental rights of a rural community could be protected by law, these rights had to be determined and recorded in a procedure, which could be satisfactorily achieved only by means of Munro's 'Ryotwari' system, where the administration had a direct and unimpeded relationship with the cultivators of soil. Therefore, a movement towards individual ownership supported through the proper registration of title by precise and legally enforceable definition instead of unwritten and, therefore, legally unenforceable custom.

Law: Though the British India had its system of law and legal institutions, both Hindus and Muslims, generally speaking, had ceased to function or been distorted by the operation of irresponsible force during the collapse of Mughal empire. The village panchayat, the most widely surviving judicial institution had no precise code of law and its actions were governed by customs and precedents which were purely local in character and acceptance. Under the Mughals, Muslim criminal law applied to both Hindus and Muslims in urban areas. By and large in the 18th century, the Muslim penal code was far more enlightened than English law. Infact neither Muslim law nor English law could stand in comparison to Hindu law, which was since ages codified in Manu Samriti, Vedas, Arthshastra and other shastras but the same had ceased to be applied during the Muslim rule of 600 years and so British could not judge its application. Even English law of today is not as perfect. This was the Bhartiyata, which eclipsed in course of time of about 800 years of foreign rule. In Muslim law, death penalty was rarely imposed, whereas in England, it was the punishment on over one hundred and fifty offences. The foundation for administration of justice was laid by Warren Hastings in Bengal, and with modifications, the system then established, survived until the end of British rule. Hastings' first principle was that court should be open to all, whatever their religion. Such courts were set up in the administrative areas known as districts and two other courts—civil and criminal were created to act as courts of appeal. These were first established in Bengal and then spread to other areas of India. Until the new codes came into force after 1858, the British tried to retain and improve on the criminal law they had found when they began to exercise power in India. The foundation of criminal law was still Mohammedan but so altered and added to by English regulations that it was hardly to be recognised.

Revenue: The main source of revenue for government was from land. The Company's main agricultural innovations consisted of attempts to exploit and in some cases introduce exotic, commercial crops such as indigo, opium, cotton, jute and tea required in European market and as such the production of these crops was entirely an European monopoly. Indigenous indigo production was expanded, particularly in Bengal, and the export figures reached about 10,000,000 lbs. in 1848-49. The production of tea, whose large scale cultivation began with the importation of plants and seeds from China and the almost simultaneous discovery of wild plants in Assam, quickly expanded to reach approximately 22,000,000 lbs, in 1851. Opium contributed substantially to the total revenue of £ 3,309,637 in 1849-50. Its production was the monopoly of English till end.

Before the East India Company conquered Bengal, it had been obliged to send out from England large amounts of bullion between £ 4,00,000 and £ 5,00,000 a year to buy goods for export from India. After it gained control of Bengal, it stopped sending out bullion and used part of the revenues to buy goods and so derived in thirty years after acquisition of Bengal, profits of goods remitting 50 million sterling. Simultaneously, the industry in Britain flourished resulting in decay of Indian industry. Dacca, which was the Manchester of India, had fallen off from a very flourishing town to a very poor and small one in great distress. The real decline of indigenous Indian industry began with the increase of imports in cotton goods and continued through out the 19th century.

Handicraft industry had gone and muslin/silk production had gone leading to large scale unemployment and poverty.

Public Health: Government of India did not accept any major responsibility for public health until 1880. After that they started spreading English medicine system. The doctors were, however, not available. In the schools teaching indigenous Hindu medicines, there was no dissection of human bodies because of the Brahmanical injunction against touching the dead. Therefore, in Calcutta, when a medical college was established in 1835 where most of the students were Muslims, who had no prejudice against the practice of anatomy. Indians graduating from this and other medical colleges were permitted to become members of the Indian Medical Service, so far reserved for Europeans only.

Education: The story of educational progress under Company rule divides conveniently at the year 1835 when it was decided that English should be the language of instructions in higher education and the purpose of education should be to disseminate western knowledge. This decision was to have far-reaching effects on Indian cultural and political life as the type of education the British had found when they arrived in India was almost entirely religious and higher education for Hindus and Muslims was purely literary. In Hindus, higher education was a brahmin monopoly, who spent their time studying religious text in Sanskrit, a dead language. Vaish sent their children to accounts keeping schools only. Muslim higher education was conducted in Persian/Arabic, which was not spoken in India. So Hindus and Muslims, both studied languages not known to public. With English medium having been adopted for education, Government did not have sufficient funds for opening schools for higher education. Therefore, private individuals and organisations were called in to open such institutions. A number of Indians and British established the Calcutta School Books Society and the Hindu Colleges. This was followed by others and more schools teaching English were established by missionaries and Indian religious/

educational societies. These institutions were cordially disposed to promote the great object of improving India by spreading abroad the lights of European knowledge, morals and civilisation. Macaulay's Education Minute of 1835 gave the decision to make English the medium of higher education and all funds appropriated for the purpose of education were employed on English education alone. Though Macaulay and others looked forward to a future in which Indians, having acquired a taste for European civilisation might demand European institutions and even independence from Britain, it was a very distant future. This thinking, however, proved correct as English proved a binding force of unity amongst the elite class and through them to masses, who ultimately demanded independence having known through the knowledge of English what had been happening in European countries and how India was being exploited by British. Through English only Indians could know the latest developments in the field of science and technology in the universe and India produced many good scientists and technologists. Even today most of the technologists in U.S.A. and U.K. are of Indian origin. Any way the immediate thinking of English was to tackle the essential problem faced by an alien government viz. the avoidance of popular revolt. English education, it was believed, would play its part here too. Many thousands of Indians wanted to be enrolled in the new schools with English medium. English education at government institutions was available to all without religion or caste distinction, though among Hindus, it was the brahmin caste, who took most advantage of it. Muslims did not respond enthusiastically to the new education. In fact a vigorous protest was signed by 8000 Calcutta Muslims when English was made official language of the government. The attraction of English education was, infact, working amongst the Indian middle class, though it was not yet to produce an overt threat to British dominion. Among the English educated classes, a spirit of nationalism was slowly growing. It was the spirit of nationalism, which had enabled British to win over all the Indian rulers. In Indian rulers, there was no nationalism in terms of Bhartiyata but their nationalism was restricted to their own kingdom only. It is therefore—

1. The spirit of nationalism of British and
2. The medium of English education, which brought Indians on one comman platform.

There was symbolic significance in the fact that modern India's first three universities were founded in the year the Indian mutiny broke out. This was being surmised when decision to impart education in English was started but at that time Macaulay had said:

"I think it is clear that we are free to employ our friends in any one we chose; that we ought to employ them in teaching what is best and worth knowing; that English is better worth knowing than Sanskrit or Arabic; that the natives are desirous to be taught English and are not desirous to be taught Sanskrit or Arabic; that neither as the language of law, nor as the language of religion, have the Sanskrit or Arabic any peculiar claim to our encouragement; that it is possible to make natives of this country thoroughly good English scholars; and that to this end our efforts ought to be directed".

And this is what actually happened. In the mutiny of 1857, the imparting of education in English was also taken as a reason for spread of Christianity in Indian masses. As already indicated, there were many other reasons for the Mutiny to take place—political, administrative, religious, educational and martial. The Mutiny had, however, been suppressed and one of the principle factors in the suppression of the Mutiny was the fact that most of the leading rebels were united only on one simple issue, the ejection of the British. When this seemed impossible to achieve, everything else fell to pieces. Most of the civilian leaders either disappeared; were killed in battle, or executed.

After 1858, when India went under crown, the boundaries of British kingdom in India were fixed. This resulted in creation of over five hundred states, occupying nearly 2/5th of India. The reason for this new attitude by the British was that most of the princely states had stood firm or atleast neutral in Mutiny and the British hoped they would stand as firm in future against any internal rebellion. Furthermore, the British were unwilling to endanger their position by continuing a policy of political and social reform, which had contributed to the outbreak of Mutiny. After 1860 there was no annexation but the princely states had to accept the over-riding authority of the government in Calcutta. So the Government of India was now subject to the authority of the Secretary of State in London and the Act of 1858 set up a Council of India in London.

Fear of external aggression had always been there to India right from the invasion of Alexander; then Muslims and then English. During Hindu and Muslim rulers' time there had been invasions by Mongols, Turks etc. from north west. On the contrary India never tried to attack on foreign lands with a view to annex the same or to loot them. During English period too invasions from Russia, and Afghanistan had always been there. Russian expansion in Central Asia raised the possibility of an attack on India through Afghanistan. Similar fears had led in 1839 to the disaster of first Afghan war. History virtually repeated itself when in 1879, British troops once again entered Afghanistan.

From the Mutiny until 1890, was a period of civil peace in India but this was broken towards the end of the period because of outbursts of extremists and revivalists' nationalism. The history of India from the last decade of 19th century to the end of British rule is that of conflict between the Government of India and the nationalists movement by Indian National Congress. Its principal events are a series of constitutional concessions by the British government culminating in the Indian Independence Act of 1947. The evolution of these constitutional developments has been discussed in following chapter.

India, after first world war, began to take her place in international affairs and her representative appeared at the League of Nations and at many international conferences. At this time due to delay in operation of concessions granted, disturbances in Punjab came up leading to the imposition of martial law and culminating in Dyer's action at Jalianwala Bagh. Followed were also communal riots of 1923. Muslim League, which had virtually been dead upto 1916, was revived in 1917. One of the provisions of 1919 Act was that its results would be examined after ten years. In 1927, a Commission to go into it was appointed under John Simon. The Commission was boycotted by Nationalist leaders. The Congress in their session at Lahore in 1929 declared that its aim was complete independence, and civil dis-obedience was started from 6 April, 1930 with Gandhi's Dandi March. It continued till May 1934 when Congress decided to work within the frame work of the forthcoming Government of India Act of 1935, which was to come into force from 1937.

When second world war broke out, Congress refused to cooperate with the government and all Congress ministers in states as per Act of 1935 resigned in November 1939 but with German army's victory in Europe, Congress offered to cooperate with British government, if a provisional national government was formed at the centre. This was refused but an offer was made to set up, after the war, a body to prepare a new constitution. The Muslim League government had not resigned on the outbreak of second world war and it had become completely estranged from Congress. The struggle now was three sided—English as the rulers, Congress and Muslim League. The struggle continued till 20 February 1947, when British government announced its intention of leaving India by June 1948 and appointed Lord Mountbatten as Viceroy to carryout transfer of power. Independence was granted by dividing India on 15 August 1947 into India and Pakistan.

British had attained India on a platter by manoeuvring, treachery, bribery, creating disunity amongst the native rulers and gave independence on a platter, of course after a struggle of over fifty years. They started with Bengal in 1757 and ended further annexation after Delhi, Oudh and Punjab in first half of 19th century. They left India in 1947 practically after ruling India for about 137 years taking the annexation of Delhi in around 1810, as representative of Indian kingdom.

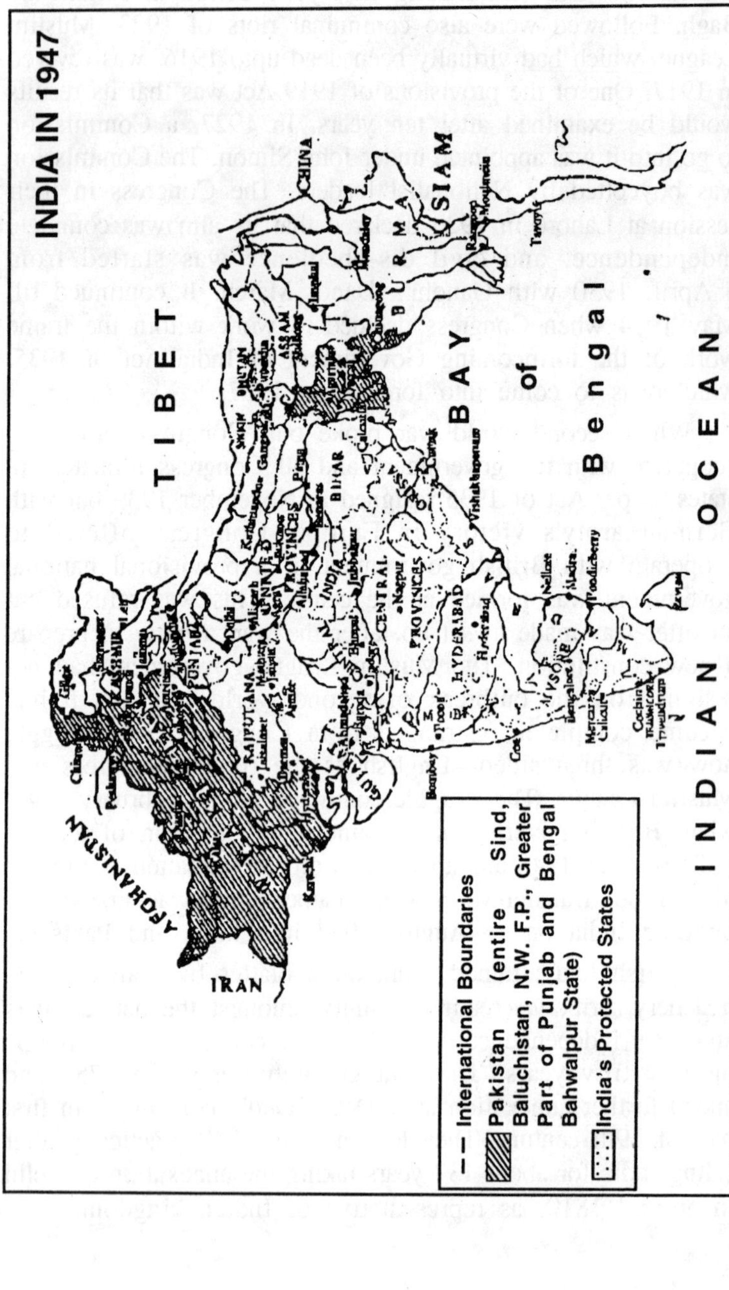
INDIA IN 1947
TIBET
CHINA
SIAM
BURMA
BAY of Bengal
INDIAN OCEAN
AFGHANISTAN
IRAN
KASHMIR
PUNJAB
RAJPUTANA
UNITED PROVINCES
CENTRAL PROVINCES
BIHAR
ASSAM
BHUTAN
SIKKIM
HYDERABAD
MYSORE
-- International Boundaries
Pakistan (entire Sind, Baluchistan, N.W. F.P., Greater Part of Punjab and Bengal Bahwalpur State)
India's Protected States

8 Constitutional Development

Let us now consider in brief the constitutional developments in India during the British regime.

Regulating Act 1773

After the battle of Buxar, East India Company actually started ruling their territory of Bengal and Bihar. In that direction, they first pronounced the Regulating Act in 1773. It was first land mark in constitutional development in India. Its main provisions were—

1. Setting up of the Governor General of Bengal in his council of four members; members to hold office for five years.
2. Governor-in-Council of Bombay and Madras to pay due obedience to the orders of Governor General-in-Council of Bengal.
3. Governor General-in-Council was given powers to make rules, ordinances and regulations for good order and civil government of Company's settlement at Fort William and other factories.
4. It provided for a supreme court with a Chief Justice and three Puisne Judges.
5. It prohibited receiving of presents and bribes by the servants of the company.
6. No British subject was to charge interest at a rate higher than two percent.

Amending Act 1781

It was passed to remove the short-comings of Regulating Act—

1. The public servants of the company were not to be subject to the jurisdiction of the supreme court for things done by them in official capacity.
2. The revenue collectors and judicial officers of the Company's courts were also exempted from the jurisdiction of the supreme court.
3. Supreme Court had jurisdiction over all inhabitants of Calcutta. It was to administer the personal law of the defendants.
4. Governor General-in-Council was given powers to make regulations for the provincial courts and councils.
5. It provided for appeals from provincial courts to the Governor General in Council.

Pits India Act 1784

1. Board of Control of six Privy Councillors was formed to supervise, control and direct the Indian administration.
2. Committee of Secrecy of three Directors to take place of the Court of Directors in political and military matters.
3. Directors to retain right of making appointments to different offices in India.
4. The Court of Proprietors was deprived of its right of over-riding the decisions of the Court of Directors.
5. Governor General-in-Council was given the power of superintending, controlling and directing the other Presidencies.
6. The official offenders were not to be pardoned if they were found guilty of having committed any offence.
7. The Act disapproved of the policy of intervention as followed by servants of the company in India.
8. Governor General was to be appointed by the Directors with the approval of the crown.

Charter Act of 1793

1. The Governor General and Governors were given power to over-ride their Councils.
2. Governor General was over the Presidencies of Madras and Bombay was emphasised.
3. Governor General was given power to appoint a Vice President of the Executive Council from the members of the Council.
4. The Commander-in-Chief was not to be member of the Council of Governor General.
5. No leave of absence out of India allowed to Governor General and Governors, the Commander-in-Chief and few other high officials.
6. Calcutta Supreme Court's jurisdiction extended to high seas.
7. Powers given to appoint members of civil service as Justice of the Peace ; to appoint scavengers for the Presidency towns ; to levy a sanitary rate and to prohibit sale of liquor without a license.
8. Payment of the members and the staff of the Board of Control was made out of the Indian revenues.
9. Two junior members of the Board of Control need not be Privy councillors.
10. Charter of the Company was renewed for 20 years.

Charter Act of 1833

1. Share-holders of the Company were guaranteed a dividend of 10.5% per annum out of the Indian revenues for next forty years.
2. Restricted patronage of the Directors.
3. President of the Board of Control became Minister for Indian Affairs.
4. Centralised the administration of the English Company in India. Governor General of Bengal became the Governor

General of India. Other Governors were under Governor General-in-Council.

5. Legislation was centralised by the Governor General-in-Council and not by Governors-in-Council.
6. Added a member to the Executive Council of Governor General and he was to be known as the Law Minister.
7. Number of members of the Councils of the Governors of Bombay and Madras was reduced to two.
8. Bombay and Madras were to keep their separate armies under the over all control of the central government.
9. Provided for the codification of laws in India for which a Law Commission was appointed.

Act of 1858

After the Mutiny of 1857, East India Company was disbanded and governance of India came under Crown. After this, the first act was passed in 1858, which provided—

1. India shall be governed by and in the name of Queen and Government of India to be carried on by a Viceroy on behalf of the Queen.
2. Board of Control and Court of Directors abolished and all powers given to Secretary of State for India and his Indian Council.
3. Council of Secretary of State to consist of 15 members, 7 elected by Court of Directors and the rest to be appointed by Crown.
4. Secretary of State to preside over the meeting of the Indian Council.
5. Secretary of State for India declared to be a corporate body which could sue and be sued in England and India.
6. Indian revenues not to be re-employed for military operating outside India except with consent of Parliament.
7. Divided the patronage between the Government of India and the Secretary of State in Council. All appointments and

promotions shall continue to be made in India. Appointments to civil service to be made by open competition as per rules made by the Secretary of State in Council.

Queen's Proclamation of 1858

Darbar held at Allahabad, on 1 November 1858 to declare the assumption of the Government of India by Crown—

1. No extension of present territorial possessions and shall respect the rights, dignity and honour of the native princes as their own.
2. All subjects of whatever race or creed be freely and impartially admitted to the offices in Indian service.
3. It assured the Indian princes that their territories will not be annexed by the British government and they shall be given the right of adoption.
4. Servants in India not to interfere in the religious affairs of Indians.

Indian Councils Act of 1892

For full 31 years, the British government did not consider it necessary to give a further instalment of reforms to the people of India. Ultimately Act of 1892 was adopted providing for—

1. The Act enlarged the functions of Legislative Councils. They were authorised to discuss annual financial statements.
2. The members of the Council were given the right of addressing questions to the government on matters of public interest.
3. The number of additional members in the council was increased.
4. Allowed election to be held in India under the rules.

Although the Act of 1892 fell far short of the demands made by the Indian National Congress, it was a great advance upon the existing state of things. By conceding the principle of election and giving the Legislative Councils some control over the executive, it paved the way for future progress on those lines, which were destined to place in the hands of Indians a large measure of control over the administration of the country.

Minto-Morley Reforms Act 1909

The essence of these reforms of 1909 lay in conceding what at once was evacuated of all meaning. Thus the elective principle of democracy was adopted. Yet at the same time the anti-democratic, communal representation was added. The official majority was done away with but the elected members remained in a minority. The membership was considerably enlarged but an emphatic disclaimer was issued simultaneously that the new Councils in no way meant the introduction of a Parliamentary system. The Council of India and even the Viceroys, Executive Council were opened to some very few selected Indians but the liberal aspect of admitting Indians to the arena of government could in no way disguise the fact that real power remained safely in British hands.

Act of 1919

1. The Secretary of State for India was paid out of Indian revenues. Now it was decided to be paid from British revenues.
2. It set up bicameral legislature at the centre in place of one house. The names of two houses were Central Legislative Assembly and the Council of State.
3. The life of Central Legislative Assembly was three years and Council of State five years.
4. It provided per direct election for both houses of Central Legislature.
5. In the case of Council of State, the voters were assessed either to income tax on an annual income of not less than

Rs 10000 to Rs 20000 or to land revenue of Rs 750 to Rs 5000. For Central Assembly the qualifications were either payment of municipal taxes amounting to not less than Rs 15 to Rs 20 per annum or occuption of ownership of a house of the rental value of Rs 180 or assessment to income tax on an annual income of not less than Rs 50 to Rs 150.

6. The Governor General was given the power to summon, prorogue and dissolve the chambers, and right to address the members of the two houses.
7. Central Legislation could make laws for whole of British India.
8. Central Budget was passed by Central Legislation. There were some non-votable items too.
9. The members of Executive Council of Governor General were nominated members.
10. It provided for two lists of subjects - Central List and Provincial List.
11. Size of Provincial Legislation was enlarged.
12. It introduced dyarchy in the provinces. Under this system, subjects to be dealt with by Provincial Government were 'Transfered' and 'Reserved'. The Reserved were administered by Governor with the help of Executive Council and the Transfered were dealt with by Governor with the help of ministers.

Government of India Act 1935

The reforms of 1919 Act were declared by Indian National Congress as inadequate, unsatisfactory and disappointing. Act of 1935 provided for—

1. Provided for an All India Federation. The Act provided for three lists - Federal Lists, Provincial List and Concurrent List.
2. Provided for dyarchy at the Centre, abolishing the dyarchy from provinces. Certain Federal subjects were reserved in

the hands of Governor General to be administered with the assistance of not more than three counsellors appointed by him. These subjects were Defence, External Affairs, Ecclesiastical Affairs and Administration of tribal areas. In the administration of other subjects, the Governor General was to be aided and advised by a Council of Ministers, whose number was not to exceed ten. They could administer all departments except those in reserved subjects.

3. Federal Legislature comprised of Federal Assembly and the Council of State. Assembly was to have life of five years and Council of State was a permanent body of which one-third members were to retire after every three years.
4. The Indian Legislature was debarred from making any law affecting sovereign or royal family or succession to throne or suzerainty of crown on any part of India, or Army Act, Air Force Act, Law of Prize Courts, amendent to act of 1935. There were many non-votable items of expenditure also.
5. Establishment of a Federal Court with jurisdiction over states and provinces, consisting of Chief Justice and two puisne judges.
6. It abolished the Indian Council of the Secretary of State.
7. The Governor, through the Governor General and the Governor General himself, were made strictly responsible to the Secretary of State.
8. The Legislature could not legislate on a large number of subjects. Also the Governor General or the Governors could over-ride their ministers and legislators in certain circumstances.
9. The Constitution of 1935 was rigid and only British Government had authority to amend the constitution.
10. The most important characteristic of the Act of 1935 was the provision of provincial autonomy.

Indian Independence Act 1947

The object of this Act was to legalise what had already been promised to the people of India i.e. the full independence. It provided:

1. The Act provided for the partition of India and the establishment of two dominions of India and Pakistan from the appointed day 15 August 1947. The Act also provided for the legislative supremacy of the two dominions.
2. The legislatures of the two dominions were given full powers to make laws having extra territorial jurisdiction.
3. The British government was to have no control over the affairs of the dominions, provinces or any part of the dominions after 15 August 1947.
4. Until a new constitution was framed for each dominion, the Act made the existing constituent Assemblies the dominion Legislatures for the time being. The Assemblies were to exercise all the powers which were formerly exercised by the Central Legislature, in addition to its power regarding the framing of a new constitution.
5. Pending framing of new constitutions, each dominion and all provinces were to be governed as per Act of 1935.
6. The Governor General could modify or adapt Government of India Act 1935 till 31 March 1948 after which Constituent Assembly could modify or adapt Act of 1935.
7. The right of the king to veto laws or to reserve laws for his pleasure was given up.
8. It provided for the termination of suzerainty of the crown over the Indian states, the existing arrangement between Government of India and Indian states to continue pending detailed negotiations between the Indian states and the new dominions.
9. Agreement with the tribes of N.W.F.P. of India were to be negotiated by the successor dominions. The office of the Secretary of State for India was to be abolished and his

work was to be taken over by the Secretary of State for Common Wealth Affairs.

10. The title of "Emperor of India" was to be dropped from the royal style and titles of the king of England.
11. The Act terminated British authority over India, set up two independent dominions, each with full authority to make any constitution it pleased. Both the dominions were given full powers and rights to leave the British Common Wealth of Nations, if they so pleased.

New Constitution of India

1. Established a sovereign, democratic republic. It declares that sovereignty vests in the people of the country. Also refers to justice, liberty, equality and fraternity.
2. There will be one Central Government and Governments of States and Union Territories.
3. Prescribes the conditions of Indian citizenship; there shall be single citizenship.
4. Provides for large number of fundamental rights, guaranteed to each citizen like right of equality before law; prohibition of discrimination on grounds of religion, race, caste, sex or place of birth; equality of opporunity in matters of public employment, right to freedom of speech and expression, right to assemble peacefully; right to form union, associations; right to move freely throughout the country; right to reside and settle in any part of India; right to secure, hold and dispose of property; right to practice any profession, trade or business; right to life and personal liberty; right to practice and propagate any religion, and right to constitutional remedies.
5. It also contains directive principles of state policy.
6. Provides for a President of Indian Republic.
7. Provides for a Vice President and ex-officio Chairman of Council of State.

8. Provides for a Council of Ministers to assist President.
9. Provides for Parliament consisting of two Houses viz Lok Sabha and Rajya Sabha.
10. Provides for the Supreme Court of India consisting of Chief Justice and other judges.
11. Provides for Union Public Service Commission and State Public Service Commissions.
12. Provides for a Comptroller and Auditor General.
13. Provides for distribution of powers between Union and the States with Union List, State List and Concurrent List.
14. Provides for freedom of trade, commerce and intercourse thoughout the territory of India.
15. Provides that Hindi in Devanagrai script shall be the official language of the union; English to continue for 15 years.
16. Provides for the procedure for amendment of constitution.

9 Freedom Movement

After the third battle of Panipat in 1761, the decline of Marathas started and there was no Indian power, who could hope to establish political supremacy. It was at that time that the advent of European traders started catching up. Simultaneously, the downfall of Mughal empire at Delhi encouraged the provincial Nawabs to declare themselves independent. So came in the Nawab of Bengal Siraj-ud-daula, defeated by English in battle of Plassy in 1757 by bribing his commander Mir Jafar. After that English started gaining power having been victorious in one battle after the other by treachery, bribery or causing division in Indian powers and by 1856, they were the masters of three-fifth of India. One reason of English victory was also the spirit of nationalism imbibed in them and the superiority of British army in training and armaments (guns), when the Indian princes still depended on swords. British were practically the masters of entire India. The two-fifth part outside British dominion too was under British suzerainty as they neither could deal with foreign powers nor have their own force except as necessary for maintenance of internal law and order. So far Indians thought that British would leave India but when they saw them permanently saddled in India, there was partial rebellion in 1857, when queen empress assured the Indian sovereignty with policy of no further annexations. It was this rebellion, which sowed the seeds of getting rid of British from India. It is, therefore, also called the first war of independence. Indians lost in this first war of independence due partly because—

1. Hindus, who were annoyed with Muslim tyranny, welcomed the British as they delivered from the yoke of Muslim tyrants.
2. Bengalis, like other people of India, did not look beyond the horizon of their own province. In those days, there was no concept of India as a country. There were Bengalis, Sikhs, Marathas, Hindustanis, (north Indians) but no Indians, as such.
3. To Bengalis, the Marathas were not only as much foreigners as English but were hated foreigners, which the English were not, having lived with them for over a century.
4. English from their pucca base in Bengal, fought against Marathas, and other Indian powers; Bengalis offered regular prayers to God for the success of British and openly came to help them with large proportion of their properties. It was only after the English decided partition of Bengal that Bengalis protested and sought help from other Indians in their cause, and came together to fight for independence of India. In other words, the partition of Bengal, stemmed the unity in Indians to fight against English unitedly.
5. Even Hindus of other areas helped British as the commerce and industry of the country were virtually in the hands of Hindus, which naturally brought them into close connection with the European merchants, who had settled in the country for the purpose of trade and formed tacit alliance based on material interests.
6. Traditional Hindu aversion to Muslim rule was voiced by Raja Ram Mohan Roy, who was great personality in Bengal at the beginning of 19th century and regarded as the representative of the most advanced political thinking of that time.

But still Indians, as a whole, were not in favour of continuance of the British regime due to—

1. Economic exploitation of the country by the British taking huge amounts to Britain right from the day they took over the Diwani of Bengal.

2. Slowly finishing Indian industry and encouraging flourishing industry in Britain by dumping their produce in India.
3. Bengal suffered heavely from the private inland trade of the servants of the Company.
4. The permanent settlement, ruined the old zamindari system although it ultimately secured peace and prosperity in Bengal.
5. The unsociable character of the English offended the sensibilities of Indians. English regarded Indians as barbarians and Christian missionaries held in open contempt the idolatrous practice of Hindus. The right of unrestricted entry of Christian missionaries to India was conceded by Charter of 1813. This poured forth venomous abuses against Hindus and this estranged the relations between the two communities.
6. Masses in Bengal and other parts of India did not revolt against English nor showed any disaffection to them when they first obtained political power. But shortly thereafter, there was general condemnation due to—
   (i) The English officials were not accessible and so people could not place their grievances before them.
   (ii) There was difference in language and customs between the English and Indians. The introduction of English as medium of imparting education in India, although brought Indians closer to English but then they also realised the importance of independence and the exploitation of India—by men and material—by the British rulers, who treated India as their colony unlike the Muslim rulers, who were sovereign Indian rulers and did not exploit India for filling the coffers of any foreign country.
   (iii) Lack of personal element in administration led to slowness in proceedings; delay in taking action and frequent changes in policies.

(iv) English deprived Indians of some privileges such as they were not listed in army to the same extent as before and whosoever was so listed was not paid equal to their British rankers.

(v) The British introduced strange character of their laws and judicial proceedings.

(vi) Non-admission of Indians into legislative and administrative branches of the Government of India.

(vii) Lack of cordiality shown by English towards Indians and in particular the officials treating Indians with contempt.

(viii) Discontent and disaffection against British in army because of—

(a) low scale of salary and poor prospectus of promotion in contrast to their British colleagues;

(b) being against religion for forbidding the men from wearing marks of caste on their heads; ordering them to shave off their beards; compelling them to exchange their old turbans for new ones with leather collars and spit on the cartridges with meat and defraying expenses;

(c) cutting the cartridges with meat by mouth.

(d) they had to board on ship, when religion did not permit crossing sea.

(e) tyranny in army by misbehaviour and crude treatment.

(f) non-payment of full bhatta—additional or special allowance for battle.

(ix) Resistance against the Britain—

(a) As they slowly and slowly annexed Indian kingdoms.

(b) Raja of Malabar openly defied on its passing in British hand by treaty with Tipu Sultan in 1792.

(c) Bundelkhand passed to British as a result of second Maratha war but new government was defied from the very beginning by numerous chiefs.

(d) Saharanpur passed in 1803 and Gujars rose in revolt in 1813 on account of resumption of enormous estate of Raja Ram Dayal after his death.

(e) Poligars of South India, who had maintained their independence from time immemorial, offered resistance to the imposition of British authority.

(f) General revolt in Kolhapur on its annexation in 1844.

(g) Rising in Bijapur district.

(h) Rising in revolt by Bir Bhadra Rauze (1830) and Jagannath Rauze in Palkonda.

(i) Rising on annexation of Gadkaris.

(j) Rising in Travancore state on intolerable misrule in protected state.

(k) General hostility against the British rule among Rajput chiefs of Kathiawad, Cutch, Baroda.

(l) Over-assessment of land, heavy extraction from cultivators, dispossession of Zamindari, and depriving large class of petty land-holders of their tenure.

(m) Sanyasis rebellion—Hindu sanyasis and Muslim faqirs with support of starving peasantry, dispossessed Zamindar's and disbanded soldiers.

(n) Faraizi movement of Shriat Ullala, who started a movement of social reforms in Muslim society on lines as done by Mohammed Ibn-Abdul Wahab as Wahabi. Wahabis movement created great trouble in Bengal under the leadership of Mir Nisar Ali known as Titu Mir. He preached Wahabi doctrine and gathered a large number of followers, mostly weavers and other lower classes against the British.

(o) Pagla Panthis of Mymen Singh led insurrection under one Tipu, who declared a no-rent campaign to any demand over a minimum rent.

(p) KOL rising against attempts to destroy the system of law and administration and independence particularly tribal ownership of land and peasant proprietorship.

(q) Rising in Jangal mahals of Man Bhum and Dhal Bhum in a family feud which culminated in murder of the Diwan of the Zamindars.

(r) Khasi, a hill tribe living in the region between Garo and Jaitia hills broke out in open rebellion in 1783.

(s) Khonds of Orissa broke out in open revolt in 1846 for suppressing the customary human sacrifice and female infanticide, which prevailed among them.

(t) Bhils of Khandesh revolted in 1818 at the instance of rebel Dewan of Peshwa Baji Rao II.

(u) Kolis in border of Cutch in the Western Ghats broke into rebellion in 1824 and committed various excesses.

(v) Santhals, a primitive but very industrious people were forced to migrate from their ancestoral lands on account of the excessive demands of the Zamindars after the permanent settlement.

The above uprisings, were all suppressed by the English but the fire had been smouldering in their minds and they were on the look out for an all round rising to take revenge. As a result, Mutiny of 1857 took place. This has been discussed in detail in previous chapter, how it arose and how it had failed. Whether it was a revolt or the war of independence, divergent views have been expressed. These views may be broadly divided into two classes. Some think the outbreak was really a rebellion of the people rather than merely a mutiny of the soldiers. Others told that it was primarity and essentially a mutiny of sepoys though in certain areas it drifted to a revolt of the people.

Present thinking is that the outbreak of 1857 was a general revolt of the people and the English had deliberately misrepresented the great popular rebellion as a Mutiny. The most of the Indians not only look upon the outbreak of 1857 as a great revolt of the people but go even further and claim it to be the first Indian war of independence. This view is by V.D. Savarkar, who played important part in fighting for freedom. Other national minded leaders and thinkers have also regarded it as planned and organised political and military rising aimed at destroying the British power in India. On the contrary, even within the limited zone, where the civil population revolted, there were considerable sections, who were friendly to the English. The ruling chiefs in east Punjab, Maharajas of Patiala, Nabha, Jind and Karnal, Scindia of Gawalior, Holkar of Indore, Nawabs of Bhopal and Jawra, Rajas of Jhabua, Dhar, and aristocracy of Bihar firmly and consistently stood by British. Even in Oudh and Rohilkhand, several chiefs, including Nawab of Rampur did the same. Even the greater number of sepoys were loyal till the end like Sikhs, Gorkhas, Madrasi, Bengali etc. The general attitude of the people towards the English, even in the worst affected areas was not uniformally hostile. Even restoration of Bahadur Shah as emperor of Delhi gave a signal of restoration of Muslim rule in India, which could not be digested by Sikhs and some other Hindu chiefs. Marathas and Rajputs too did not favour restoration of Muslim rule. But another thinking is that what began as a fight for religion (British converting Hindus and Muslims as Christians, which was opposed by sanyasis, wahabis and others) ended as a war of independence for there is not the slightest doubt that the rebels wanted to get rid of the alien government and restore the old order of which the king of Delhi was the rightful representative. Also this has been discussed by Maulana Abdul Kalam Azad in his speech extracted in previous chapter. Be as it may, apart from the small risings against the British enumerated above, which had been locally suppressed by British, the revolt of 1857, was comparatively on a larger scale covering more area and particularly the area around Delhi, although ultimately suppressed but there were chances of the British winding up their household if the rebels had a helping hand from some eminent leader and masses from areas, which remained loyal to British. Also this made the English have fear of any sudden rising anytime later on if they did not behave. It did change the mentality of the British thereafter in as much as further annexations were stopped and thinking of passing on more and more legislative and administrative powers to Indians in the time to come.

After the revolt of 1857, the Indians had been put to so much fear by the British by hanging many, killing many others, that they could not raise their voice against the British rule for several decades. One reason for such quietness can also be the fact that since further annexations had been stopped and all native princes given recognition as independent rulers under British supremacy with certain jobs being looked after by British only such as external affairs, defence etc; the fighting had stopped in the country and there was no uprising too. Also the Viceroys posted under crown after 1857 had also generally been going cautiously, not to offend the masses till about the time Lord Curzon had come as Viceroy in 1899. By that time Indian National Congress had also been established and they had started asking for self rule in a limited way to start with.

The reactionary regime of Lord Curzon is a great landmark in the history of the freedom movement in India. The crowning act of his folly was the partition of Bengal, which led to unanimous opposition. The protest took the form of 'Swadeshi' movement, which soon outstripped its original limitation of space and object and merged itself into an all India national struggle for achieving freedom from the British yoke. This was infact the first time, when Bengalis started any agitation and it having taken the form of a national struggle, Bengalis too started to have a feeling for the country as a whole. Gandhiji remarked—"The partition of Bengal led to the partition of the British empire". Lord Curzon undertook a tour of East Bengal with the object of ascertaining public opinion. He was convinced of the strength and solidarity of public opposition to any scheme for partitioning Bengal. This confirmed his views about the strength of Bengali nationalism and the danger it spelt to British rule in India. He, therefore, decided to remove the danger before it was too late by destroying the solidarity of the Bengalis. The motive behind partition of Bengal was that in East Bengal, the Muslims were politically less advanced and more loyal to the British than the Hindus. In Bengal, Hindus were in majority while Bengalis would form a minority by inclusion of Bihar and Orissa.

Accordingly, the Government of India communicated on 7 July 1905 their final scheme of partition sanctioned by the Secretary of State. The leaders of Bengal did not take it lying down and refused to accept the partition, as a settled fact. Public meetings were held; media was used for opposing the partition. The partition was even condemned by some papers in England. In a meeting under Maharaja of Dinajpur, it was resolved—

1. Resignation in a body of all Honorary Magistrates.
2. Resignation of all members of District Boards, Municipal Committees and Panchayats in a body,
3. National mourning for three months during which period the people should refuse to participate in any public rejoicing.

This was followed by many societies etc. However, with the approval of the Secretary of State, the proclamation was published on 1 September 1905. It was the final decision about partition of Bengal and gave a list of districts in Bengal, which, along with Assam, would form a separate province called the Province of East Bengal and Assam under Lt. Governor Fuller. New arrangement was to come in form from 16 October 1905. It was strongly protested by holding demonstrations/meetings, students agitation, picketing in markets etc. Even Muslims were not, abinitio, in favour of the partition. In a meeting on 25 September 1905, Muslims passed three resolutions—

1. Recording the protest of Mohammedan community against the current report to the effect that they had no sympathy with the measures adopted by Hindus for the amelioration of their country and offering their support to the Hindus.
2. Expressing their desire to join the Hindus, not merely regarding partition but also in other matters.
3. Expressing their strong support in favour of the use of swadeshi goods.

The agitation also spread outside Bengal although the main argument advanced by the government in favour of the partition was administrative consideration viz. lightening the burden upon Bengal. The real motive was to curb the growth of national feeling in politically advanced Bengal by driving wedge between the Bengali speaking Hindus and Muslims. The policy of dividing the politically advanced communities in separate provinces was already an accepted principle by the British. It was thus quite clear that the real motive behind the partition of Bengal was to weaken the influence of Bengalis, who had imposed an increasing burden on the government of Bengal by the spread of higher education and advanced political aspirations that accompained it, among others. But there was deeper apprehension among Bengalis that the partition was a measure of kindling rivalry and animosity between the Hindus and Muslims. As a result of the wide agitation, the Secretary of State pledged himself that the proposal of partition of Bengal would not be given effect to till all the papers, relating to it, had been laid before the Parliament, however, this pledge was broken.

The partition proposal led to the boycott of English in the form of not using the goods imported from U.K. and to use only swadeshi goods, particularly cloth and other luxury goods. Not restricting this policy to Bengal, it was adopted for the entire country, the idea of using boycott as a coercive weapon for securing political or economic objects was not altogether new to India. As early as in 1874, boycott was advocated as a means of reviving Indian industries, which had been ruined by the British commercial policy in India. Boycott of Manchestar cloth was preached in 1875, 1876 and 1878. In 1891, the boycott of British goods was preached to some extent by the opponents of Age of Consent Bill. However, the original concept of boycott was mainly an economic one. It had two distinct but allied purposes in view. The first was to bring pressure upon the British public by the pecuniary loss, they would suffer by the boycott of British goods, particularly the Manchester cotton goods for which Bengal provided the richest market in India. Secondly it was regarded as essential for the revival of indigenous industry (swadeshi industry), which being at infant stage, could never grow in the face of free competition with foreign countries which had a highly developed industry. Thus although the idea of boycott of foreign material was not new, it got a new meaning and a new impetus in 1905 because it was now instrumental in the fight for a common cause, inspired by national sentiments, whose origin had been traced above.

The swadeshi movement implied—

1. The swadeshi cloth would ultimately be sold cheaper than foreign cloth.
2. The clothes we wear were made of our cotton and jute.
3. The materials were carried in ships to England; many English coolies and skilled labourers were employed to make cloth out of the same and finished products were again brought back to this country in ships.
4. Indigenous cloth production would mean employment of our coolies and skilled labourers.
5. But we had to observe patience for some time till the production comes on steam.
6. There was no legal bar in the way of our purchasing indigenous goods instead of foreign products.

7. We must be very particular to keep the vow of swadeshi enflagging or the little glory we have already had would be extinguished for ever.
8. We must see to it that in making people take this vow, none may exercise force and violence nor in any other way may violate the existing law.
9. If there are men, who refuse to listen to the voice of reason and are determined to act against the wishes and sentiments of all their neighbours, there is nothing to prevent us from ex-communicating them.
10. To fulfil this and other objects and for the good of our motherland, there should be a people's association in each village. Even Brahmins and priests refused to perform puja and ceremonies in which offerings were made not of indegenous articles, thinking that sugar and salt had been refined with the blood and bones of cows and pigs. The ideas of swadeshi and boycott of foreign goods was kept alive and brought home to every one by articles in newspapers, processions, popular songs, enrolment of volunteers to keep vigilant watch and by occasional bonfires of foreign clothes, salt and sugar throughout the country. But after even these methods were not effective, shops selling foreign goods were picketed—this being the start of method of peaceful picketing. The students supplied bulk of volunteers and picketers. Government issued circulars to educational institutions asking them to control their boys and prevent them from participating in the Swadeshi movement in any way. Further four fold programme of boycott was resorted to—

    (i) Abjuring of English cloth, salt and sugar.

    (ii) Abjuring English speech.

    (iii) Resignation from honorary offices under government and seats in councils.

    (iv) Social boycott against persons purchasing foreign articles viz none shall eat and drink with them; none shall inter-marry with them; none shall buy from and sell to them; depriving them of service of barbers; boys and girls not to play with their children. Any violation was subjected to various degrees of humiliation.

So an undeclared war was started between the government and the people. This war was started in Bengal, cought the imagination of the rest of India and the question emerged not of boycott of English goods but of English rule and had emerged itself into the great national movement launching the struggle for freedom. The indirect effect of boycott on Indian politics and national movement was very great. It supplied the Indians a tremendous weapon which, if peoperly wielded, was capable of dealing a severe below to the British. Thus for the first time they could give up the policy fo mendicancy, which had been so long pursued by the Indian National Congress. As students were the main instruments in promoting boycott, the first step taken by the government was to send a secret letter to the Magistrates and Collectors on 10 October 1905, signed by Chief Secretary to Government of Bengal, called Carlyle circular, indicating—

(i) The use of school boys and students for political purposes is absolutely subversive of discipline and could not be tolerated in respect of institutes, which government either assists or countenances.

(ii) If any attempt is made by boys attending schools/colleges to take any public action in connection with the boycott, picketting or of the abuses associated with swadeshi movement, immediate cognisance and action be taken. The repression measures taken by government resulted in the expulsion of a large number of students from schools and colleges. The question of providing for this education naturally agitated the minds of leaders and so national schools were started in some localties. Thus came into prominence two educational societies—

Anti Circular Society and Dawn Society. National College was started under the best auspices possible. Arabinda Ghosh resigned from a post getting Rs. 750 per month to serve National College as Principal without any salary.

The national swadeshi movement had four fold ramifictions—industrial, educational, cultural and political. 'Bande Matram' was echoing everywhere but it was too forbidden by British government. The ideas of new nationalism preached by its high priests like Tilak, Arabindo, Lajpat Rai, assumed concrete shape which may be ragarded as the percursor of the civil disobedience movement of Mahatama Gandhi. It made the swadeshi movement an all India issue, which had its repercussions on Indian National Congress and alignment of Indian political parties.

Hindu-Muslim Riots: At early stages of anti-partition movement of Bengal, it was supported by the Muslims of West Bengal, even Nawabs were with the movement. But a section of Muslim supported the partition scheme from the very beginning. The government was very eager to enlist the support of these Muslims against Hindus. There were demonstrations and anti-demonstration in support of partition. But it was not the British government alone that was responsible for the change in Muslim attitude. Reference had been made to the anti-Hindu policy inaugurated by Sir Sayyed Ahmed at Aligarh culminating in formation of Muslim League, a rival organisation to Congress. The foundation of the League was laid in Dacca on 31 December 1906 and led to the beginning of an organised opposition on the part of Muslims to the Hindus; of course the government having a great share in fomenting the Muslim frenzy against the Hindus.

Boycott and Swadeshi: Twin ideas of swadeshi and boycott were largely complementary. It was the idea of boycott which first aroused the people and that of swadeshi came later in its train. In view of the attitude of moderate party, it is necessary to emphasize that it was boycott, which led to swadeshi. What we could not achieve in 500 meetings, executed over years could partly be secured by boycott in three months. Manchester Chamber of Commence requested leaders of Bengal to give up the boycott and exerted the Secretary of State to cancel the partition of Bengal. Swadeshi, though originally conceived as merely a boycott of foreign goods and meant only to be an urge to use indigenous in preference to foreign goods, it seems, attained a much more comprehensive character and became a concrete symbol of nationalism. Even Mahatma Gandhi, then unknown in name and fame wrote in 1908 that the real awakening of India took place after the partition of Bengal and also was shrewed enough to prophecy that, "the day may be considered to be day of the partition of British empire".

Swadeshi brought the classes and masses together on same platform and appealed to the sense of people in regard to all aspects of their national existence. It—

1. created new industries for producing swadeshi goods ;
2. placed struggle on a firm basis;
3. secured employment to labourers;
4. increased population and wealth;
5. stimulated the production powers of the nation;
6. raised the country to a scale in civilisation worthy of its past history and its present resources.

In Bengal, the swadeshi movement brought into vortex of politics the one class of people—the landed aristocracy—who had hitherto held studiously aloof from the Congress or any of the political organisations. Outside Bengal, it gave a rude shock of disallusionment to the whole of India and stimulated the political thought of the people. The different provinces were brought together in this hour of adversity—which the rest of India shared with Bengal. Gokhale said, "for the first time, since British rule began, all sections of the Indian community without distinction of caste or creed have been moved by a common impulse and without the stimulus of external pressure to act together in offering resistance to common wrong. The chief tracts of new cult of nationalism were—

1. The elevation of patriotism into a religion and transformation of religion into patriotism by conceiving motherland not only as a mother but as a supreme God, whose service is the only way of salvation.
2. Belief in God as the leader of the movement; complete freedom as its goal and passive resistance as its method.
3. Love has a place in politics but it is love of one's country, for one's countrymen, for the glory, greatness and happiness of the race, the divine 'ananda' of self-immolation for one's fellows. What Arabindo achieved in the realm of thought by his fearless writings, Rabinder Nath conveyed to the masses by his songs.
4. Swadeshi movement ushered in a new era in Bengali literature by Rabinder Nath, Rajnikant Sen and others, like-

"O my country's dust, on you I rest my head;
On you has she, the mother of all,
The universe mother spread wide her shirt".

Split between moderates and extremists:

The agitations following the partition of Bengal brought into prominence the rise of a new political party, which differed in essential points from the one so far dominated, the Indian National Congress. The new party is the product of a new spirit of nationalism e.g. the transformation of a moderate into extremists' party due to the agitation against partition. The moderates could not reconcile themselves with the boycott of foreign goods and the existing educational institutions. On the other hand, the emergence of extremists, party alarmed the British and made them turn towards the moderates as the only friend of British government. Hence unconsciously, grew the British policies of rallying the moderates, by coaxing them into belief that the liberal government in U.K. would grant a substantial instalment of reforms. So Minto (Viceory) and Morley (Secretary of State) wanted to win over the moderates with the help of Gokhale, who figured prominently in the correspondence between the two. But neither Gokhale nor the moderates knew that Minto and Marley did not look upon them as good friends but merely used them as tools to serve their purpose.

The extremists had formulated several secret societies throughout the country. The overt acts of these secret societies were the outward manifestations of a determined and violent resistance to the British with a deliberate view to overthrow their rule in India. They regarded the armed resistance as the only feasible way to destroy British power. As the immediate open organisation for this purpose was not possible, they had to prepare the ground for secret societies of militant nationalists. They were all inspired by common aim of driving away the British from India and establishing 'Swaraj' i.e. the government of the people, by the people and for the people. They wanted to free the country from British yoke by armed resistance—open or secret or both combined—as may be possible, but they had not the means to oppose the government openly by armed resistance. So they fell back upon secret societies as the only way to make preparations for it with their aim as "Attainment of Independence". The famous novel of Bankim Chander Chatterjee entitled 'Anandmath' formed the basis of the new spirit. It gives us the story of a band of sanyasins, who gathered together to rescue their motherland from the miseries of anarchy and oppression. The militant nationalism of Bengal was founded on twin rocks-- Swami Vivekanand based on philosophical teachings of Vedanta and Gita and the religious devotion to motherland preached by Bankim Chander through Anandmath and Arabindo's articles in newspapers. Rabinder Nath said:

"Are you so powerful that you will flout and break
All laws of providence ?
Are you so proud, you think you will
Break us and mould us ?

However firmly you may bind us,

The weak, they too have strength,

However big you be, remember There is God".

The swadeshi movement brought into existence, new types of samitis to popularise the boycott and swadeshi, but they gradually outgrew the original limits and became local associations for various types of social and economic, specially industrial improvement, through purely political work. Some of these samitis also served as breeding grounds and training centres as well as camouflage for terrorists movement. They hardly exercised any influence on freedom movement. Another feature of swadeshi movement was the tendency to invoke orthodox Hindu beliefs to the service for liberation of motherland. Even today almost every citizen regards himself as a Hindu or Muslim first and then only, if at all, an Indian.

As indicated above, two distinct parts in Indian National Congress, the moderates and extremists had come up. The real difference between the two lay primarily in the political goal to be achieved and the method to be adopted to achieve it. The aim of Congress, as defined in 1905 was 'Colonial form of Self Government', but the extremists' ideal was of absolute autonomy free from foreign control. Arabindo said:

"Political freedom is the life-breath of a nation to attempt social reform, educational reform, industrial expansion, the moral improvement of the race and for attainment of these goals the new party rejected 'petitioning' as mad and fantastic".

Therefore, the idea of passive resistance became the main plank in the policy and programme of the extremists. Shortly after the session of 1906, Tilak undertook a whirlwind tour to preach this new doctrine. He addressed numerous meetings, the main aim being:

"He ruled out armed revolt as a possible method for gaining independence, for we have no arms. But he tried to show that the boycott, if properly carried out on a comprehensive scale, would prove a more formidable weapon. We shall not give them assistance to collect revenue and keep peace. We shall not assist them in fighting beyond the frontiers or outside India with Indian blood and money. We shall not assist them in carrying on the administration of justice. We shall have our own courts, and when the time comes, we shall not pay taxes. If you can do that by your united efforts, you are free from tomorrow".

"There is great difference between asking and petitioning—you must be prepared to fight in the event of your demand having turned down. Protests are of no avail. Mere protests, not backed by self reliance will not help the people. Three Ps—Prayer, Please and Protests—will not do unless backed by a solid force the 4th P i.e. Passive Resistance. The essential difference between passive or defensive and active or aggressive resistance is that, while the method of aggressive resister is to do something by which he can bring about positive harm to the government and the method of passive resister is to abstain from doing something by which he would be helping the government. Arabindo added:

"We are dissatisfied with the fiscal and economical conditions of British rule in India into the foreign exploitation of the country, the continual bleeding of the resources, the chronic famines and rapid impoverishment which results in the refusal of the government to protect the people and their industries. Accordingly by an organised and relentless boycott of the British goods, we propose to render the further exploitation of the country impossible". The Moderate Party, on the other hand, criticised the ultimate goal set up by the extremists as well as the method suggested and persued by them. The moderates held that the further progress of the country was possible under the aegis of British rule alone and the reasons for this were the incapacity and disunion of the Indians. Gokhale even said: "Only mad men outside lunatic asylums could think or talk of independence". He said, "there is no alternative to British rule, not only now but for a long time to come, and any attempts made to disturb it, directly or indirectly, are bound to recoil on our own heads. But the attainment of democratic form of government is bound to be slow and weary affair and our average today is far below the English average to have independence and run it."

The arguments put forward by the moderates were also rational and logical, but on the face of it appeared quite unassailable. The real standpoint of the extremists was based on the new creed of nationalism, which was being preached by Arabinda, Tilak, Lajpat Rai, Bipin Chander and others.

Calcutta Session of 1906: Two events outside India in 1905-06 had some repercussions on the moderates and extremists. The victory of Japan over Russia gave a strong stimulus to the latter for it was now proved that Europeans were not invincible and the Asiatics could do their match in every field. In Bengal the moderates were losing ground. The two parties were gradually drifting apart from each other. A meeting was summoned by the moderates in Calcutta on 31 January 1906 to memorise the liberal Secretary of State for India, Mr. Morley with the prayer that Bengal be raised to the status of a Presidency Government as provided for in Parliamentary Statutes. This was resented to by students and other Extremists. Controversy continued through periodicals by the spokesmen of the two parties as both looked forward to a decisive trial of strength in December 1906. Although Morley had badly let down the moderates still the old veterans of Congress stood against the new fangled ideas of the extremists. A great deal of heat had generated in course of the discussion in the next resolution:

1. "This Congress is of the opinion that Boycott Movement inaugurated in Bengal by way of protest against the partition of Bengal was and is legitimate".
2. "That this Congress accord its most cordial support to the Swadeshi Movement and calls upon the people of the country to labour for its success.
3. "That in the opinion of the Congress we should take up the question of national education for both boys and girls,

and organise a system of education—literary, scientific and technical—suited to the requirements of the country.

4. "That this Congress is of the opinion that the system of government obtaining in the self-governing British colonies should be extended to India.

5. "This Congress in toto accepted the programme of Swadeshi Movement. The Extremists were happy too as—

    (i) Even the passing of the resolution as it stood, was a triumph of the Extremists Party.

    (ii) The reverance had been transferred from old leaders to the ideals of motherland.

    (iii) The ideal of Swaraj as self-Government, was termed by Naroji in an inspired movement and it became the watchword of the nation.

Muslim Politics: The scheme for partition of Bengal was at first opposed by the Muslims along with Hindus but Lord Curzon's visit to East Bengal brought about a change in the Muslim feelings. They found in the new province with a majority of Muslim population, a source of strength and a centre of their political activity. In the annual session of Muslim League held at Amritsar in December 1908, it expressed vehement opposition to all 'mischievous efforts' to unsettle the settled fact of partition of Bengal. The great nationalist leader Mohammed Ali, in his speach as Congress President in 1923 referred to the reversal of the partition of Bengal as an important cause for the aliention of the Muslims from the British government. Muslim leaders under Agha Khan met Viceroy Minto on 1 October, 1906 to represent:

"The Mohammedans of India, according to the latest census numbered over 62 million or between one-fifth and one-fourth of the total population of His Majesty's Indian Dominion. We, therefore, desire to lay jointly claim to adequate recognition as an important factor in the state. They outlined an elaborate scheme for Muslim representation from Municipal and District Boards to Imperial Legistature viz—

1. The Mohammedans, representation in Council should never be in an ineffective minorty.
2. As far as possible appointments by election should be given preference over nominations.
3. For pupose of checking Mohammedan members, Mohammedan land owners, lawyers, merchants and representatives of the important interests of status be taken into account. Mohammedan members of the Provincial Councils and fellows of universtities should be vested with electoral powers.
4. Employement of a due proportion of Muslims in government service.
5. Abolition of competitive examinations for recruitment to the services.
6. Appointment of Muslim judges in every high court and chief court.
7. Communal electorate for municipalities.
8. Muslim electoral colleges for election to Legislative Councils.

Lord Minto replied

"I am entirely in accord with you. Please do not misunderstand me. I make no attempt to indicate by what means the representation of communities can be obtained but I am as firmly convinced as I believe you to be, that any electoral representation in India would be doomed to mischievous failure, which aimed at granting a personal enfranchisement regardless of the belief and traditions of the communities composing the population of this continent". Minto called the Muslim deputation day as "an epoch in Indian history".

It is now definitely known that the whole of this deputation was engineered by the government or atleast by Englishmen under official inspiration—Even Ramsay Macdonald, the future Prime Minister of Britain later wrote: "The Mohammedan leaders are inspired by certain Anglo Indian officials and that these officials had pulled wires at Simla and in London and the afore thought sowed discord between Hindu and Muslim communities by showing the Muslims special favours". This one incident shows how eager the government was to wean away the Muslims from joining the political struggle, which the Hindus were raising against the British.

The Muslims were naturally elated with the fovourable reception that the government accorded to their deputation. As noted above, the partition of Bengal and the events that followed also filled them in to the new zeal and quickened their political consciousness. They now felt the need of a political association. Syed Ahmed Khan was not in favour of a political organisation and his European friends also supported this view as they were afraid that if Muslims were politically organised, they might follow in the footsteps of the Hindus in ultimately turning against the government. The first rift was caused by Hindi-Urdu controversy. In Uttar Pradesh the petitions were written in Urdu. The Hindus having protested against it, government passed an order on 8 April 1900 to the effect that government offices and law courts should also entertain petitions written in Hindi and Dev Nagari script. Muslims resented the order on the ground that it lowered the status of Urdu. This controversy continued for months worsening Hindu-Muslim relations to a considerable extent. The Muslims also now felt the need of forming an organisation to counteract the political organisation of Hindus. Nawab Salimullah of Dacca arranged a meeting indicating the aims—

1. To support British Government.
2. To look after the rights and interests of Muslims as a whole.
3. To check the growing influence of Congress.
4. To provide scope for the participation of Muslim youths in politics, thereby preventing them from joining Indian National Congress.

Scheme was accepted at the meeting held on 30 December 1906 and it was resolved to establish a political association named All India Muslim League. Aims and objects of the league were—

1. To promote amongst Muslims of India, feeling of loyalty towards British government.
2. To protect and advance political and other rights of Muslims of India.
3. To prevent the rise among the Muslims of India of any feeling of hostility towards other communities without prejudice to aforesaid objects of the league.

Regarding political importance it was pointed out by Muslims that they had ruled India for 600 years before British came. Apart from the fact that it is not quite accurate because just on the eve of British rule, the Hindu, Marathas and the Sikhs wielded far greater political authority than the Muslims ruled for 600 years before the British. The Hindus ruled for lacs of years before Muslims and there were many principalities ruled by the Hindus throughout the Muslim period. It was like Indias' celebrating 50th year of independence after having been under British rule for 140 years after having been independent for lacs of years.

The Act of 1909 and the regulations made thereunder embodied in substance the concessions virtually promised by Minto to Muslims. Under these regulations not only did they receive a separate electorate but their number of members in the council was much greater than would be warranted by the numerical strength of their population. This set the seal of government's approval on the "Theory of two Nations" or two races, or two separate countries with distinct interests and outlooks, which were preached by Syed Ahmed Khan and formed the basis of the Aligarh movement. Two years after the Minto-Morley reforms were enacted, Ramsay Macdonald, who later became Prime Minister of Britain said, "Some of the far-seeing members of the Mohammedan community are already beginning to feel that they had made a mistake". A Mohammedan gentleman wrote in the same strain that, "The attempt on the part of my coreligionists to create an irreconcilable Ulster in India, is not very laudable. This will veritably open pandora's box and India will then be confronted with a grave situation of the first magnitude". These words proved prophetic when the reforms of 1919 extended the principal of separate electorate to Sikhs and some scheduled castes besides Muslims.

Then happened serious communal riots in Bengal in the wake of the partition of the province—in particular to a series of dangerous disturbances in Mymensingh and Comilla districts since 1907—in the course of which the Muslims committed great outrages on the Hindus. But the communal riots were not confined to Bengal. In 1910, seven riots broke out at Peshawar. Two years later, there was a serious clash at Ayodhya and Faizabad on the occasion of Bakr-Id. Next year, there was a riot in Agra on the occasion of Moharram. Bakr-Id disturbances at Shahabad (Bihar) in 1917 were the most serious, which ever occured during British rule upto that time. More than 25000 Hindus attacked Ibrahmpur and neighbouring villages and with great difficulty peace could be restored.

British Politics (Policy of Repression)

As already indicated, a large number of secret societies were founded in Bengal, whose members prepared bombs and collected revolvers in order to kill officials, particularly those, who stood in their way. This new movement designated as 'Terrorism' was widely spread and was responsible for several members—both European and Indian—and a large number of political robbing as a part of political programme. The troubles were not confined to Bengal. The Nationalist movement made good progress in Punjab and in some other parts of India and the same causes were in operation everywhere. Punjab having the chief stronghold of Arya Samaj, with its strong nationalist tendency inherited from the founder Dayanand Saraswati. Riots took place in Lahore and Rawalpindi and Indian editors and printers were imprisoned in large number for national propaganda. The situation was further aggravated by unwise action of the local government in respect of canal colonies. The irrigation and land revenue rates were increased and according to Colonisation Bill, some privileges, which were promised to settlers in Chanab colony by the Act of 1803 were denied. Lala Lajpat Rai was the head and the centre of the entire movement and Ajit Singh, as his principal agent. Both of them had been deported. Repressive measures were in full swing in Eastern Bengal. But all this increased the spirit of resistance. In Maharashtra, the government prosecuted Tilak for seditious writing under Seditious Meetings Act of 1907 and was sentenced to six years tranportation and a fine of Rs. 1000.

This led to closing of shops and strike of students in entire India. Muslims, however, kept aloof from these demonstrations. Neither Morley nor Minto looked upon this ruthless repression as the sole means of restoring peace and order. Two principles of 'Repression' and 'Rally the Moderats' became henceforth the watchword of British politicians. To these two may be added the old policy of "Divide and Rule", which now meant in practice creating a split between the Hindus and Muslims by all possible means and showing special favour to the latter. Thereupon some reforms were introduced in Indian administration—

1. The appointment of an Indian member on the Viceroy's Executive Council, the first nominee being Sir S.P. Sinha, a renowened Bengali Barrister of Calcutta.
2. The appointment of Indian members in Provincial Executive Councils.
3. The enlargement of Legislative Councils both in the centre and the provinces by increasing both nominated and elected members.

As per Act of 1909, communal electoral was introduced, i.e. election of Muslim members by Muslims alone. This drove a permanent wedge between the two communities and made it impossible for them to regard themselves as members of a common nationality. Minto thus kept his pledge to Muslim deputation of 1906. Further, the regulations framed by the

Government of India under the Act also made sure that the nationalists or extremists might not take any share in the administration of their own country. The nationalists and extremists did not feel any enthusiasm for the reforms of 1909. The Moderates, first hailed the 'Reform Proposal' with jubilation and the Indian National Congress passed a resolution expressing it in their session of 1908 but the jubilation did not last long. The regulations under the act were issued five weeks before the next session held at Lahore in December, 1909 placing strong sense of disapproval of the creation of separate electorate on the basis of religion and regretted the regulations framed thereunder due to—

1. Excessive share of representation given to Muslims.
2. Humiliating distinction between Muslims and non-Muslim subjects of his majesty in the matter of electorals.
3. Wide, arbitrary and unreasonable disqualification and restrictions for candidates seeking election to the Council.
4. Distrust of educated class.
5. Unsatisfactory composition of the non-official majorities in Provincial Councils, rendering them ineffective and unreal for all practical purposes.

King George V announced new proposal in Delhi darbar on 12 December 1912.

So far as Bengal was concerned status quo was not restored. The capital of British India was moved from Calcutta to Delhi and the territories comprised in the two Bengals were redistributed as follows—

1. Bihar, Chhota Nagpur and Orissa were constituted into a Province under a Lt. Governer.
2. Assam reverted to a chief commissionership.
3. The rest constituted the province of Bengal under a Governor.

The annulment of the partition of Bengali speaking region was welcome in Bengal but this came too late to check the growth of nationalism as highlighted by the bomb thrown at Lord Hardinge on 23 December 1912 on the occasion of his state entry into Delhi, the new capital city of India. Hardinge was badly injured and the man holding umbrella on him was killed. New India was being heralded by the cry of 'Home rule' in public and conspiracy for armed revolt on a big scale in secret. They were in full swing even when Lord Hardinge was still on Indian soil, living in his fools' paradise. The revolutionists formed their centres at—

(i) Chandra Nagar in 1902.

(ii) Dacca Anusilan Samiti.

(iii) There was a network of Samitis throughout the length and breadth of Bengal. Whole Bengal was divided into—

(a) District Samitis.

(b) Mahakumar Samiti.

(c) Pargana Samiti.

(d) Certral Samiti.

(e) Small local Samitis.

Each of these was placed under an incharge. The most important activities of these Samitis were collection of arms; murder of abnoxious officials and political dacoities. For arms, riches were looted and then through the Kabulis, revolvers, pistols and cartridges were purchased. Another source of supply of arms was the body of sailors in foreign vessels and some Hindustani mechanics employed in Fort William and Manton and Company helped in repairing pistols, revolvers etc. Many murders had taken place. Dacoities were committed to take away money from government iron chests; the most sensational being that committed at village Barha in Dacca district, where 31 persons in a heat attacked the house of a rich man and substantial amount was collected. Hundreds of dacoities were caused in 1909, 1910, 1911, 1912, 1913, 1914, 1915, 1916, 1917 as a glimpse given below:

Year	Bank	Murders outrage	Dacoities
1908	6	9	8
1909	1	2	11
1910	-	1	7
1911	-	6	11
1912	1	3	10
1913	3	6	10
1914	1	3	13
1915	-	17	23
1916	-	9	11
1917	-	7	6

One of the preventive steps taken by the government was to institute conspiracy cases against a large number of young men on general charges of dacoity and murder. However, Anushilan Samitis were further formed in Assam, Bihar, Punjab, Uttar Pradesh, Central Province, Bombay and Madras. Towards the close of 19th century, the nationalists felt similar need of propaganda work in other countries of Europe and America in order to establish useful international contacts, interpret Indians aspirations and gain help and sympathy for Indians' cause. J.R. Shulays' writings in "Asia and Europe" show the views of even British, "If the 200 million Hindus did not submit to the British; if they did not enlist; paid no taxes; were not tempted by the rewards offered by the conquerors and did not submit to the English laws introduced among them, then all the Englishmen in the world could not enslave India".

Home Rule Movement: While the militant nationalism convulsed the whole country, the Indian National Congress, now representing only the moderates, appointed a committee, which met in Allahabad in 1908 and drew up a constitution for Indian National Congress and a set of rules for conduct of meetings. This was adopted in Congress session at Madras in 1908:

Article I: The objects of Indian National Congress are attainment by the people of India of a system of government similar to that enjoyed by the self-governing members of the British empire and a participation by them in the rights and responsibilities of the empire on equal terms with those members. The objects are to be achieved by constitutional means by bringing about a steady reform of the existing systems of administration and by promoting national unity fostering public spirit, and developing and organising the intellectual, moral, economic, and industrial resources of the country.

Article II: Every delegate to the Indian National Congress shall express in writing his acceptance of the objects of the congress as laid down in Article I of this Constitution and his willingness to abide by this constitution and by the rules of the congress hereto appended.

With this, Congressmen lost popularity. The Nationalist or Extremist Party, which was debarred from the Congress had no organised political activity after this split of 1907. Left to itself, it might have developed a separate rival organisation to the Congress, but that was not to be. Apart from the Indian National Congress, Muslim League was the only political party that showed new life and strength after the split of the Congress at Surat. It demanded of the Hindus, a frank recognition of the fact that communal and religious differences must be the basis of all political reforms in India. The first session of Muslim League was held at Karachi on 29 December 1907. They chose Karachi as Sindh is that pious place in India, where Mohammed Bin Qasim came first with the torch of religion and gift of *Hadis*. The oft repeated public declaration of the Hindu leaders that no political progess was possible in India without an understanding between the Hindu and Muslim led to inevitable tendency to raise the Muslim demands higher and higher.

The annulment of partition of Bengal in 1911 gave a rude shock to the Muslims, who were further alienated from the British on account of the latters hostility to Islam as evidenced by British occupation of Egypt; Anglo-French agreement with regard to Moracco; Anglo Russian agreement with regard to Persia and the invasion of Tripoli by Italy. The Muslim League in its annual session of 1913, adopted a new constitution, which accepted the Congress idea of self-government under British Crown and sought to achieve it by promoting national unity and cooperating with the other communities. Mohammed Ali reiterated that there were three parties in India—the Hindus, the Muslims and the government were there to cooperate with the one or the other according as it suited their interests—to protect and advance the political and other rights and interests of the Indian Muslims. This clearly foreshadowed what came to be known later as the 'Two Nation Theory' of Jinnah. The Muslims did not, however, hesitate to help the British in keeping India under subjugation but turned against them merely at the apprehension of similar danger to foreign Muslim states. In other words Muslims were less concerned with the British treatment of India than with the attitude of the British towards the Muslim states outside India. They refused to join the Hindus in a common political campaign against the British because they believed that their interests could be better served by following a pro-British policy.

The declaration of war by Great Britain against Germany automatically made India a belligerent and dragged her into the great holocaust. The Indians had of course no voice in the matter and the Government of India did not consult the people either in declaring war or in respect of the military assistance rendered to the British empire in the name and on behalf of the Indian people. Indians' contribution, great though it was, cannot, therefore, be regarded as voluntary. Nevertheless as Indian contribution persisted till the end, and played no small part in securing political reforms for India, it is necessary to describe briefly the part played by Indian troops. These comprised 80,000 British officers and men and about 2,30,000 Indian ranks, including non-combatants at the out-break of the war together with about 12,00,000 recruited during the war largely by press-gang method of terror and violence. This was the reckless manner in which Indian troops were sent abroad to fight the imperial war of Britain so much so that British garrison were left with 15,000 men only. Indian troops fought in France, Belgium, Egypt, Sudan, East Africa, Cameroons, North China, Persia, Mesopotamia, Kuradistan, Gallipoli, Salomika, Palistine and Aden. Indians' supply in men, money and material was so large that the Viceroy Lord Hardinge declared in the House of Commons and repeated in his autobiography that India had been 'bled white' by the war office. Prior to the war the normal recruitment of combatants for the Indian army was only about 15,000 a year; in 1917 this had been raised to 1,21,000 and in the following year 1918 to over 3,00,000 men. During war 11,61,789 Indians had been recruited and 12,15,338 were sent overseas of whom 1,01,439 were casualties. Apart from men, India had to bear the heavy expenses of maintaining this huge army and even the cost of their transport to the distant theatres of war mentioned above. Not satisfied with all this, India, represented by British master, made a free gift of one hundred million sterling to Britain for conduting her imperial war. The total war expenditure of the Government of India upto 03 March 1918 was about £ 12,78,00,000 besides contribution of £ 21,00,000 by Indian princes and £ 10,00,00,000 as free gift aggregating to £ 23,00,00,000 plus the death toll of over one lakh men.

In the session of 1916, Congress and Muslim League both adopted and specified in great details in their annual session at Lakhnau, the self same demand for reforms, which, if accepted would give the Indians an effective voice in all branches of the administration of their own country except military and foreign affairs. The important feature of the joint scheme was the provision of separate electorates for the Muslims and fixing the number of their seats, both in Provincial and Imperial Legislative Councils. Except this,there was no substantial difference between Muslim League and Congress. The Congress leaders gambled their whole fortune on one stake and sacrificed the future for the immediate gain. No one can doubt in the light of the subsequent events that the Congress action in 1916, well and truly laid the foundation of Pakistan 30 years later. A compromise fundamental issue of Indian nationality, once began, was bound to lead further compromises till the whole foundation gave way. However, the Hindu-Muslim pact was hailed with diligent then and the Government of India was more surprised than any body else for the fact seemed to deprive them of the one trump card, they held in their hand to stem the tide of Indian nationalism.

The reversal of the partition of Bengal and the Morley-Minto reforms had rallied the moderates to the cause of the government and as the Congress now was practically an organisation of that party, it had ceased to evoke popular enthusiasm or public support. This brought the question of re-admitting the extremists to the Congress so that it might again become what its name implies viz. Indian National Congress and not continue to be a mere party organisation. The Congress session of 1916 at Lakhnau, has justly been regarded as a landmark in modern Indian history. For the first time after 1907, the extremists or nationalists attended the session of Congress. About the middle of 1916, Tilak undertook an extensive lecture tour for instructing masses on Home Rule League. He explained Home Rule as a form of government within the British empire in which the rule of bureaucracy will be replaced by an administration responsible to the people. Tilak said, "The rule still remains, the emperor still remains". He posed the question, "Why do we ask for swarajya? Are we fit for it? "and answered, "we want only this one thing today, when this one is got, the remaining things come into our possession themselves". Tilak's homely speeches and direct appeals made him not only popular but a hero among the masses. He earned the epithet 'Lokmanya' and was almost worshipped as God. Although there were two Home Rule Leagues of Besant and Tilak, they acted in close cooperation. Besant's field was entire India except Bombay and Madhya Pradesh where Tilak would carry on the work. The Home Rule

Movement spread like wild fire due to participation of women and the religious colouring given to it as in the case of Swadeshi Movement in Bengal. More surprising is the fact that even prominent Muslim leaders like Jinah joined it. Indeed both the people were in politics and the real leaders of India. The Home Rule campaign had practically ousted the moderates from the political field, which they had dominated till the return of Tilak to active politics in 1914. The Congress session, held in Calcutta in 1917 with Besant as the President was a great triumph for Home Rule Movement. There was record gathering. It was decided in the session that:

"India demands Home Rule for two reasons—one substantial and vital, the other less important but weighty. First because freedom is the birth right of every nation; secondly, because her most important interests are now made subservient to the interests of the British empire without her consent and her resources are not utilised for her greatest needs". Hence rule for India league was also established in London with Headquarters at I-Robert Street, Adelphi. It worked in cooperation with British committee of the Indian National Congress, the Britain and India Assocaition and United India Society. The activities of the Home Rule League bore fruit. Eminent Americans and Englishmen wrote and spoke for self government in India. A committee of members of Parliament was formed in London for the purpose of pressing forward the claims of India to self government. The Labour Party conference at Nottingham early in 1918 unanimoulsy passed a resolution in favour of Home Rule for India.

The terrorists' activities in Bengal spread to other parts of the country through extremists, revolutionaries etc. The revolutionaries, both in Bengal and Punjab, were inspired by the idea of a general rising in India against the British. The situation was very favourable. India was denuded of troops, as they were sent to fight in various theatres of war in Europe, Asia and Africa. While England was in extreme difficulty owing to the overwhelming German successes at the beginning of the war, considerable help was expected from Germany, Turkey and Afganistan. Germany was to supply arms and ammunitions to India; Turkey's support would influence the Indian Muslims to array themselves against the English and Afganistan would create a diversion, either by an actual invasion of India or by assuming a hostile attitude which would compel the British to maintain a big army at North-West Frontier, leaving the rest of India, comparatively weak and defenceless. Rash Behari Bose took charge of organising the revolutionary activities in north India. The most remarkable of Bose's exploits was the throwing of a bomb at Lord Hardinge in December, 1912, when he was going in a ceremonial procession through the chowk of Delhi. Rash Behari was the brain behind the incident although bomb was actually thrown by Basant Kumar Biswas. Both managed to leave Delhi. Rash Bihari came to know of police doubt on them. He left Dehradun and hid himself. Such was his wonderful power of putting on disfigures that though the police made a most vigorous search for him and offered a reward of Rs. 2500 for his arrest, he always eluded their vigilance and continued his revolutionary work.

Rash Bihari made a revolutionaries' plan of rebellion. The general place of the rebellion had been outlined by Sachindra as under—

"On a particular night, fixed before hand, the sepoys in the contonments of all over north India would suddenly attack the English soldiers; those who surrendered would be imprisoned and the rest would be killed. During the same night, the telegraph lines would be cut, Englishmen imprisoned, treasuries looted and prisoners released from jails. This revolutionary plan was based on the fact that there was a very small number of English troops in India at that time, consisiting mostly of young new recruits of territorial force. These could be easily overpowered and the arms and ammunition stored in different cantonments were regarded as sufficient for carrying on fight for one year. There was a stir among youngmen of Bengal. Revolutionary groups gained new recruits; military training was imparted to them in jungles and theft of guns and revolvers increased to a considerable extent. After the arrangement had made some progress, Rash Bihari himself proceeded to Lahore via Delhi. 21 February 1915 was fixed as the date for simultaneous rising all over India. But a police informer Kirpal Singh, who had managed to enrol himself as a memeber of Rash Bihari's party, secretly communicated the date to the police. As soon as this was known, the date was changed to 19th February. But though Kirpal Singh was kept under strict surveillance, he managed to send word to the Police about the change of date. The government immediately removed the suspected regiments to other places and made a large number of arrests. Rash Bihari and Pingle evaded arrest and safely returned to Benaras but the whole plot was miscarried and the elaborate plan came to nought. However, the activities of the rzevolutionaries continued. Even some distinguished Englishmen also appreciated the patriotism of the Indian terrosists. When on 1 July 1909, Madan Lal Dhingra shot dead Sir Curzon Wyllie, Lloyd George expressed to Churchil his highest admiration of Dhingra's attitude as a patriot. Churchil shared the same views and quoted with admiration Dhingra's last words as the finest ever made in the name of patriotism. They compared Dhingra with Plutarch's immortal heroes. The Irish were more appreciative, "Huge placards from Irish papers paid glowing tributes of Dhingra".

Repressive Measures: Revolutionary measures continued throughout the war. In 1913, the government passed the Indian Criminal Law Amendment Act, which made 'conspiracy' as a criminal offence and laid down an elaborate definition of 'conspiracy'. Among the conspiracy cases, most famous was the Delhi conspiracy case in 1913, when a number of persons were put on trial for planning to murder Lord Hardinge by throwing a bomb on him in December 1912. Four of the accused—Aminchand, Avadh Bihari, Balmukand and Basant Kumar Biswas—received capital punishment, and two others were sentenced to rigorous imprisonment for seven years. The chief conspirator Rash Bihari Bose, however, managed to escape to Japan.

The Defence of India Act was passed in a single sitting of the Imperial Legislative Council on 18 March 1915. This was far more drastic than corresponding Defence of Realm Act (DORA) in Britain. The Defence of India Act, to which Gokhale and his Moderate Party gave their willing assent was not simply a war measure like the English DORA but it included clauses which authorised the government to supersede the provisions of criminal law and institute summary trial by special tribunals, appointed by local government to inflict sentence of death, transportaion for life and imprisonment upto ten years for violation of rules framed thereunder. With this the reign of law had ceased and India was henceforth to be governed by the fiat of the executive authority. A number of cases, were tried subsequently under this Act.

Lord Chelmsford, who succeeded Lord Hardinge as Viceroy in April 1916, followed the traditional policy of 'Repression-cum-Reforms'. The repression measures under Defence of India Act were pursued with full vigour. The authorities—both in India and Britain—could not, however, ignore the reality of the tense political situation in India. The game of playing Muslims against the Hindus and of rallying the moderates against the extremists had failed, and political India was united as never before. The Home Rule Movement had deeply stirred people. E.S. Montague, a liberal statesman of U.K. reply to a question of a private member is a historical one and is as under—

"The policy of his Majesty's Government with which the Government of India are in complete accord, is that of the increasing association of Indians in every branch of administration and the gradual development of self-governing institutions with a view to the progressive realisation of a responsible government in India as an integral part of the British empire. They have decided that substantial steps be taken in this direction as soon as possible".

There was, however, no change in the attitude of the official and ruling classes, who determined Great Britain's India policy. They appreciated heroic sacrifices of the Indian soldiers and the rich contribution in men, money and raw material received from that country but they tried to achieve their purpose in as indirect way of postponing reforms in India on the plea that no great and important changes should be introduced during the war. In other words, India must remain satisfied with vague promises, which were not considered sufficient by the Irish, British women and other interested parties. Inspite of the announcement of Montague promising responsible government to India, the traditional British policy of reforms-cum-repression was not forgotton by Lord Chelmsford in India. montague's, historical declaration was welcomed by Moderate Party as 'Magna Charta' of India, which the nationalists felt that it fell far short of the legitimate expectactions of India. In the session of Calcutta in 1917, the Congress strongly urged the necessity for immediate enactment of a parliamentary statute providing for the establishment of a responsible government in India, the full measure to be attained within a time limit to be fixed in the statute itself at an early date. On the whole, the historic declaration of 20 August 1917 created a stir in political circles almost unprecedented in the history of British India. Montague received a series of deputations from political parties or other groups. Montague, however, had to appease the Government of India and the British officials. A joint report of changes in the declaration was prepared and signed by Montague and Chelmsford at Simla in 1918. The most important point of the report is the enunciation of the goal of responsible government for India. None of the schemes for political reforms so far drafted by Indian leaders envisaged the idea of responsible governments. A scheme known particularly as the 'Dyarchy', was adopted as the basis in Montague-Chelmsford report. The main provisions of the report were—

1. Local Boards and Municipalities to have elected majorities and have full liberty to impose taxation within the limits laid down by law.

2. Central and provincial budgets should be completely separated; subjects being reserved for provinces and residuary powers to rest with centre.
3. The provincial executive would be of composite character—one element consisting of Governor and Executive Council of two members—one being from India and the other consisting of one or more ministers chosen by the Governor from Legislative Council.
4. Each province to have an enlarged Legislative Council with a substantial majority chosen by direct election, with separate electorates for Muslims.
5. Decision of ministers on transferred subjects shall be final.
6. The process of development will be one of adding to the transferred and/or taking from the reserved subjects.
7. In Government of India, there shall be a second Indian member in Executive Council and statutory restrictions on the appointment of members of this Council shall be abolished. Two-third members shall be elected and one-third nominated.
8. To secure affirmative power of legislation, the report records the institution of separate constitutional body known as Council of State upon which the government should cause a majority. Assent by both the Assembly and the Council of State should be normal condition of legislation.
9. Power of parliament through Secretary of State for India to be curtailed by rules.
10. If recommended, institution of Privy Council for India.
11. For native states, there should be Council of Princes presided over by Viceroy.
12. Recruitment to superior services in India upto a fixed percentage (33 per cent) being fixed for I.C.S. rising annually by 1.5 per cent.

The report was welcomed by moderates but the nationalists rejected it in toto. There was, however, counteraction in England against grant of responsible government to India. To counter this, Besant's Home Rule League had also developed to a great extent. Tilak made it clear that a deputation was going to England, not to appeal tò the generosity of the British people, as would have been the case ten years back, but was going to tell the British democracy to save the empire by trusting India instead of Japan, and granting her Home Rule, which would bring forth millions of people to die for the empire and the motherland. He appealed to the people to carry on the agitaion for swarajya with a persistence, the echo of which could be heard in England and would strengthen him in his mission. But passports of Tilak and others were cancelled. This evolved strong indignation and protests from all parts of India. British War Cabinet refused permission to Tilak to visit England on the ground that all political controversies should be hushed up while England was engaged in war of life and death. He, however, impressed upon people the necessity of helping Britain in her crisis. Tilak, however, spoke in a different tone.

Subsequently Tilak was granted permission on 8 June 1918 to visit England in connecion with his defamation case against Sir Valentine Chirol on condition that he would abstain from political agitation in England. While Tilak was still in England, momentous events occurred in India culminating in Jallianwala Bagh massacre and imposition of martial law in Punjab due to absence of Tilak from India and when leadership passed on to Gandhi. But at the end of 1918, Tilak held the unique position of the uncrowned king of the nationalist India. "The most powerful leader in India at the moment", as Montague truly declared.

Government of India Act 1919 (based on Montague-Chelmsford Report) was passed. It was a step forward in technique of responsible government but not in practice as the Governor General remained the real authority as he could rule by ordinances. India after first world war began to take her place in international affairs and her representative appeared at the League of Nations and at many international conferences.

At this time due to delay in operation, disturbances in Punjab came up leading to imposition of martial law and culminating in Jallianwala Bagh in 1919. Followed were also communal riots in 1923. Muslim League, which had been virtually moribund since 1916, was revived in 1917. One of the provisions of 1919 Act was that its results should be examined after ten years. In 1927, the Conservative Government in Britain appointed a Commission of investigations consisting entirely of British Members of Parliament under the chairmanship of John Simon. The Commission visited India in 1928 but was boycotted by Nationalist leaders. Its report was issued in 1930. The Congress in their session at Lahore in December 1929, declared that its aim was complete independence and decided to boycott the forthcoming conference in London and began a Civil Disobedience Movement from 6 April 1930 with Gandhi's famous march to Dandi in western India against the government salt monopoly followed by mass strikes, boycott of English goods and violence. In repression, many were killed, many injured and 60,000 imprisoned in less than one year but these repressive measures proved unsuccessful and conciliation was attempted. On 4 March 1931 the so called Gandhi-Irwin Pact between Congress leaders and Viceroy was concluded. Government abondoned its repressive measures and releassed political prisoners and Congress called off the Civil Disobedience Movement and agreed to join Round Table Conference, when held. But no action was taken. Gandhi was again arrested in 1932 and Congress was declared illegal organisation. More than 1,20,000 people had been arrested and there was wholesale violence, physical outrages, punitive expeditions, collective fines on villages and seizure of landed properties. Civil disobedience continued till May 1934, when Congress decided to work within the famework of the forthcoming Government of India Act of 1935 which was to come into force in 1937 with the following main provisions:-

1. Provinces, numbering 11, were to be given full responsible Governments subject to certain reserved powers in the

hands of the Governors used in case of complete breakdown of law and order.

2. At the Centre, a federal structure was to be set up. The central legislation was to consist of two houses of representatives and from princely states. Viceroy's Executive Council was to consist of Ministers responsible to Central Legislation with the exception of portfolios of foreign affairs and defence. It was laid down that India would by usages and conventions quickly acquire all the freedoms—external and internal—enjoyed by other dominions. But that part of the federal structure never came into force as the princes could not agree to any lessening of their sovereignty. The federal principle was also denounced by both congress and Muslim League. Thus Government of India remained what it always had been—an autocratic government with executive responsible only to the Secretary of State in London.

In elections held in 1937, Congress formed ministries in seven out of eleven provinces. In some provinces Muslim League wanted to form coalition ministries with Congress but Congress refused. Congress administrations were reasonably successful and the prestige of organisation had grown to such an extent that its membership reached five million by 1939.

When second world war broke out in 1939, Congress refused to cooperate with the government and all Congress ministers resigned in November 1939 but with German armies victorious in Europe, Congress offered to cooperate with the British Government if a provisional national government was formed at the centre. This was refused in August 1940 but an offer was made to set up after the war a body to prepare a new constitution; to enlarge Viceroy's Executive Council with more Indian members and to create a War Advisory Council of representatives from British India and provincely states. Congress rejected the offer and a new Civil Disobedience Campaign was begun. After the fall of Rangoon to Japanese in March 1942 and the possibility of an immediate attack on

India, the British Cabinet Minister Sir Stafford Crips was sent to India with what was virtually the same offer as that of August 1940. In the meantime Muslim League ministers had not resigned at outbreak of war and had become totally estranged from Congress. On 8 August 1942, Congress called for a widespread return to mass civil disobedience. Government acted immediately and declared Congress illegal and arrested its leaders. Riots and sabotages, throughout India, followed. Repression was again resorted to and over 60,000 people were arrested, 18,000 detained without trial, 940 killed and 1630 injured in clashes with police and troops. In 1944, Gandhi was released from jail on health ground. Shortly afterwards a Labour Government came to power in Britain and decided to hold fresh elections in India. These were held in 1946 and the result was overwhelming victory for Congress in general seats and Muslim League for reserved seats. On 19 February 1946, British Prime Minister sent a mission to India and its recommendations were—

1. Federal Government to include the princely states.
2. Division of India into three provincial groups consisting of (i) NFWP and Sindh, Baluchistan and Punjab (ii) Bengal, Assam and (iii) the rest.
3. Constitution to be framed by Constituent Assembly.
4. Provinces could, if they wished, become the new Federation after the election of Assemblies.
5. A provisional National Government should be established from leaders of different parties.

The proposals were accepted by Muslim League but Congress rejected them. On 20 February 1947, British government announced its intention of leaving India by June 1948 and appointed Lord Mountbatten as Viceroy to carryout transfer of power. Muslim League embarked on direct action violence; murder and arson convulsed the Punjab and NWFP. Congress reluctantly accepted the fact that if independence was to be achieved, India must be divided. On 3 June 1947, the Viceroy broadcast a declaration of British government policy. Its substance was—

1. If Muslim majority areas so desired, they should be permitted to form a separate dominion and a new constituent assembly would be set up for the purpose. In that case, however, Bengal and Punjab would have to be partitioned if the representatives of Hindu majority districts of those provinces, so demanded.
2. A refrendum to be carried out in NWFP to ascertain whether or not it wanted to join Pakistan.
3. The district of Sylhet would be joined to Muslim area of Bengal after the people's views had been discovered by a refrendum.
4. Boundary Commission would be set up to define boundaries of Hindu and Muslim provinces in Punjab and Bengal.
5. Legislation would be introduced in current session of Parliament at West Minister to confer immediate dominion status on India (or on the two countries if partition was decided upon) without any prejudice to the final decision of the constituent assembly or assemblies in this respect.

Both Congress and Muslim League accepted the plan and the Indian Independence Act passed through parliament on 1 February 1947. The date set for transfer of power to India and Pakistan had been advanced to 15 August 1947. On that day the Constituent Assembly in Delhi declared India, a dominion within the British Commonwealth and Mountbatten to be its first Governor General. In Karachi, Jinnah was chosen the first Governor General of Pakistan. British Indian empire came to an end.

The Indian Independence Act 1947

1. The Act provided for the partition of India and the establishment of two dominions of India and Pakistan from the appointed day 15 August 1947.
2. The legislatures of the two dominions were given full powers to make laws having extra territorial jurisdiction.

3. The British government was to have no control over the affairs of the dominions, provinces or any part of the dominions after 15 August 1947.
4. Until a new constitution was framed for each dominion, the Act made the existing constituent assemblies the dominion legislatures for the time being. The Assemblies were to exercise all the powers, which were formerly exercised by the central legislature, in addition to its power regarding the framing of a new constitution.
5. Pending the framing of a new constitution, each of the dominions and all provinces were to be governed in accordance with the Government of India Act 1935. Each dominion was authorised to make amendment to 1935 Act under Indian Independence Act.
6. The Governor General was given power to modify or adapt the Government of India Act 1935 upto 31 March 1948 after which the constituent assembly could modify only.
7. The right of king to veto was given up. This power was given to Governor General.
8. Provided for the termination of suzerainty of the Crown over Indian states. All treaties with them lapsed on 15 August 1947. Existing arrangement between princes and Government of India to continue till negotiation between the states and the new dominions.
9. Agreement with the tribes of NWFP to be negotiated by successor dominions.
10. Office of Secretary of State for India to be abolished.
11. Title of Emperor of India to be dropped from royal style and titles of the King of England.
12. Terminated British authority over India; set up two independent dominions, each with full authority to make any constitution it pleased.

On 15 August 1947, India became independent. Constituent Assembly prepared a new Constitution of India in February, 1948. It came into effect from 26 January 1950.

The New Constitution

1. Established Soverign' Democratic Republic. Sovereignty vesting in people with preamble to grant justice liberty, equity and fraternity.
2. There are States in the Republic.
3. Rules granting citizenship of India.
4. Fundamental Rights granted to each citizen.
5. Directive Principles of State Policy.
6. Provides for President of Indian Republic, elected indirectly and a Vice President and ex-officio Chairman of Council of States.
7. Council of Ministers to assist the President.
8. Provides for Lok Sabha and Rajya Sabha.
9. Provides for Supreme Court of India.
10. Provides for Union Public Service Commission.
11. Provides for Controller and Auditor General.
12. Freedom of trade throughout the country.
13. Hindi in Devanagari Script as Official Language of the Union after 15 years.
14. Procedure for amendment of the Constitution.

10 Conclusion

Having written entire history of India—The Vedic period, Ancient period, Hindu period, Mohammedan period and the British Period—we find that whenever a feeling of 'Bhartiyata' was there, the country flourished as a Hindu Kingdom and there had been decline of kingdom with the loss of Bhartiyata.

As per vedas, the actions of all beings are connected with 'Karma' and 'Dharma'. As per 'Dharma' the human beings were divided into four varnas—Brahmin, Kshatriya, Vaish and Shudra. The division was on functional basis and there was flexibility in owning the varna by an individual. One, who wanted to continue studies after preliminary studies, a must for all, he was included in Brahmins. His job became to impart education to all. Similarly, who was keen in fighting, including the Rajkumars, were given education of fighting and governance and became Kshatriyas. The Vaishas were trained in industry, trade, agriculture and the one who did not fit in any of the above three vocations, became Shudras, to serve the people of all the other three varnas. Now since all opted the varnas of their choices, they did not have any grudge about their being in a particular varna. Also since all were given elementary education, all could opt from one varna to another even at later stage and then he was recognised as the person of that varna. In vedic periods, Ram and Mahabharat period, there are ample examples of change of varna later on. Viswamitra, a Kshatriya became a Brahamrishi; Nishadraj became Ram bhakta; Krishna, a Yadav, had become a ruler and warrior, even though Yadavas were Vaishas; Karan born of Kshatriya but brought up in a low caste, became a ruler and warrior because of his interest in that vocation and having attained expertise in that direction. So, persons of all varnas did discharge the duties of their respective varnas as a matter of 'Dharma' and no one could affford to go against the tenets of 'Dharma'. In case of a war or aggression by a foreigner, all unitedly rose to face the same. Even Daronacharya took arms against the Pandvas. In Vedic and Pauranic periods, the rajas had their kingdoms. The duties of the rajas and the praja have been given in our shastras and compliance with the duties by the raja and praja was again considered a 'Dharma'. Whereas the raja did everything possible to remove the grievances of his subjects, the subjects too were always prepared to give their lives for the sake of the kingdom. It is said that in a state worked on 'dharma' there was no famine; the rains were in time; no chronic diseases, no premature deaths etc.

The concept of the kingdom in those days was generally, the portion of the region on which a raja ruled. These were small areas and there was one Chakravarty raja, who was paid annual tributes by the smaller rajas and in turn the Chakravarty raja provided protection from any aggression to the small rajas or vassals under him. To establish his suzerainty over the vassals, the Chakravarty raja used to hold Aswamedh Yagyas in which the vassal rajas paid their tributes in recognition of his overall Lordship over them. Otherwise these rajas were autonomous within their regions. The invasion of one raja over the other was generally not for the purpose of annexing the rajya but to take presents and return the rajya to him to be ruled as a vassal state under the suzerainty of the conqueror. In this way although there were small kingdoms yet were under the suzerainty of an overall Chakravarty raja. Raja Prithu had been the ruler of the entire universe and he distributed the rajya in his four sons. There is also the description of several oceans and continents, which come true even today confirming that our ancestors had fully surveyed the entire universe. Similarly Bharat (on whose name the country is called BHARAT) ruled over the entire universe. Sri Krishna too has named 'Bharat' in his Gita -

यदा यदा हि धर्मस्य ग्लानिर्भवति भारत,
अभ्युत्थानमधर्मस्य तदात्मानं सृजाम्यहम् ।

Meaning thereby that Bharat was the whole country, divided into various kingdoms and ruled by small rajas. Indraprastha and Hastinapur were such big kingdoms having many vassal states under them. Even Dwarka is stated to be a state under Hastinapur. It is only subsequently that the Chakravarty rajas lost their eminence and the small rajas became sovereign. In that case the small kingdom itself became their motherland and any other kingdom within India was treated as an alien state. Also with the passage of time the four varnas came into divided into various sub castes and there was no change from one caste to another. There were no inter-caste marriages; no eating together; no living together and no sitting together. It was in this situation that slowly and slowly the term Bhartiyata started vanishing and everyone cared for his kingdom only and there was no national spirit or Bhartiyata. Also in the case of an aggression by foreigner, it was for the state invaded upon to defend herself and no assistance was offered by other states so much so that in the case of Alexander's invasion on India, Raja Ambi of Taxila, helped Alexander against Raja Porus of Punjab. Jay Chand invited Ghori against Prithvi Raj. The Governor of Punjab invited Babar to attack India on Lodhis. British had been invited by one Raja/Nawab for assistance in fighting against another Raja/Nawab and so on. We, therefore, come to the conclusion that—

1. Shastras treated Bharat as the mother-land and everyone was imbibed with patriotism as Bhartiyata.
2. The varnas were chosen according to one's choice as per one's capability to perform certain job and so he had no grudge in having chosen that varna. He, therefore, performed his duties as per that varna treating this as his 'dharma'.

3. The varna could be changed at a later stage, depending on one's attainments.
4. Inter-varna marriages could be performed on the willingness of the bride and groom.
5. All the people, irrespective of the varna they belonged to, combined together to help the raja in case of foreign aggression.
6. The invasion by one raja on another was generally not for the purpose of annexation but to get presentations and then restore the raja, who could rule as an autonomous ruler but as a vassal under the overall suzerainty of the conqueror, restricted to annual presentations and recognition as such.
7. The raja and the praja cared for each other to the utmost extent possible—like father and sons.
8. As theory of primogenitor ruled and, as per dharma, the eldest son succeeded the throne, there was no war of succession amongst the children of any raja. The other brothers only assisted the raja in the matter of governance of the state as directed by the raja.
9. The people did know the importance of 'swarajya' and they never permitted the motherland to be enslaved by a foreigner.
10. The foreigner, if anyone was successful, was assimilated within the Hindus.

These, in other words, were the tenets of Bhartiyata and as far as the people observed these tenets, there was peace and prosperity amongst the people and India was considered as the most resourceful, advanced, richest and most educated country of those days.

India later on was divided into small kingdoms and each king having jealousy with the other one and the people too did not have nationalists feeling for India. Even upto the British arrival in India, Bengalis were not prepared to interact with other Indians and it is because of such feeling only that we lost in the Mutiny of 1857 as major provinces did not participate in the same. It was only Chandra Gupta Maurya, who established a vast kingdom and again brought the thinking of Bhartiyata in the people. The Mauryas ruled the vastest kingdom ever in India, inclusive of present India, Pakistan, Bangladesh and Afghanistan. There has, however, been some sort of tradition in India, that the country progressed, when it became one but disintegrated after a particular king died. So after Ashoka again the country disintegrated in view of the weak successor and loss of the feeling of Bhartiyata in the people and the rulers. Mauryas' rule was a landmark in the history of India as during that period India was the most resourceful and powerful country in the world. India being a land of riches, had always been the target of any foreign ruler. In Maurya time also foreign invasions did take place but they were all defeated. The rule at that time was as per the tenets of Arthshastra, which was again based on various shastras, adopted as per need of the time by Chanakya (Kautilya).

After Mauryas again disintegration took place and for a few centuries small rajas ruled. Then only Kanishka came as a strong ruler of India with again the feeling of uniting the land as a nation 'Bharat'. But after his death again the country was divided. Then came on the scene the Guptas. Here again Samudra Guptas and Chandra Guptas II (Bikramajit) were the most effective rulers, who again united the country and the feeling of Bhartiyata came in the people. The rule was as per Arthshastra and other tenets of Hindu dharma. This is treated as the golden period of Indian history as during this period there was alround development in the country in the field of agricultural production, mining, construction of roads, arts, literature etc. But again decline started and the country was divided into small rajyas. Then came, Harsha, who united India till he lived and again division took place.

After Harsha, the country was divided into small kingdoms under Rajput rajas, who again followed the tenets of dharma but they had been fighting within themselves and no forceful king came up. On the other hand Islam had been picking up in Middle East and in European countries. Entire Eastern Europe, Russia, Turkey, and Middle East and Central Asian countries had come under the influence of Islam. The Mohammedan rulers had an eye on India, first to convert this vast land into Islam and to loot the riches of this place. It is just irony of fate that India at that time was the richest country in the world and the people of Middle East were starving. After the discovery of petrol there, those countries became the richest. The Mohammedan rulers were fanatic Islamic and wanted to spread Islam throughout the universe. They came via sea route and settled in Sindh but they were not able to proceed further. Mahmud Ghazni invaded India seventeen times and each time took a lot of wealth from India. Indian rulers, as they were, were not able to face him individually and they did not unite to give a fight, each time of invasion thinking that it would be his last expedition. He was able to go deep upto Gujarat and looted Somnath temple without any fighting. It was :

1. Due to disunity of Hindu rulers and each of them not being able to give a fight individually.
2. There was neither unity nor any effort in that regard.
3. The rulers thought each time of the invasion that it would be his last invasion and in this way faced the country having been looted seventeen times.
4. The rulers cared for their kingdoms only and there was no feeling of Bhartiyata left.
5. One Jaipal dared to send his troops across the Hinduskush to demoralise the Afghan and Turk invaders but he was badly defeated and could not recover from the shock. It is of interest to mention here that time and again India had very powerful rulers and they could even conquer the entire universe during Mauryas or Guptas period but they never thought of going beyond India or maximum upto Afghanistan and nothing beyond that. Kanishka had tried

to send his troops to conquer Central Asia and China but they got consumed even while crossing Himalayas and thus suffered heavily. Again Jaipal, the ruler of Punjab dared sending troops across Hindukush but he too suffered a shocking defeat. Shahjahan also sent an army to conquer central Asia but here too the army met with disaster. There is no other instance in the history of India of any ruler having attempted an invasion outside the frontiers of India. Might be climatically they could not crors Himalayas, having lived in the plans of India or they were very leisurely persons who had never passed a tough life. Thus Indian rulers had always been only defending the country from foreign invaders. Sungas had come and then Huns had come but they had ruled for some time and then lost to powerful Hindu rulers and got assimilated in Hindu religion.

6. So Hindu rulers thought that Muslim invaders had been coming only to loot and go back. They did not evaluate this much worth giving a fighting.
7. But this led to Mohammed Ghori invading the country and having been defeated several times, he tried again and again and ultimately taking advantage of the enmity amongst Prithviraj, the ruler of Delhi and Ajmer and Jay Chand, the ruler of Kanauj, the two big kingdoms of north India, he invaded and defeated Prithviraj and established his kingdom in India.
8. The Rajput rajas did not work as per tenets of shastras of Bhartiyata. As per Arthshastra, they did not have spies' net. So much so that Prithviraj was caught napping and enjoying with his new bride Sanyogita, when Ghori suddenly appeared and he could not face him. Similarly Shivaji's son Sambha had been caught enjoying in harem, when caught and killed by Mughal chief.
9. Bhartiyata provides for unity of small rajas in cases of foreign invasion. This was not attempted or it had not been possible in view of the inter-rajya rivalries, jealousies and

enmity. Anangpal did try to join hands of a few rajas but still he lost as the union was not sufficient to face Muslim invaders.

10. The only display of 'Dharma Yudh' by Indian Rajput rulers was to forgive a defeated invader and so did Prithviraj and let Ghori go back when defeated. But this was not the time, when forgiveness had to be applied. The Muslim invaders, who were using all sorts of wickedness in battles, were not to be forgiven. Only mass killing would have been deterrent for them from again invading.

After the establishment of Qutab-ud-din Aibak as the ruler of Delhi by Ghori, he was able to go upto Bengal and even after having known the intentions of the Muslim rulers of establishing a kingdom in India and to spread Islam, the Hindu rulers did not wake up to unitedly face and put Aibak out. They, on the contrary, prostrated before him and willingly accepted his sovereignty over them. The Indian rulers, who were so much in for the autonomy and independence, yielded before Aibak, although he did not have much of force at his command. Main reason being the lack of unity and nationality, and demoralisation, particularly in the masses, who were not considered as part for governance and had been put to be governed only. They did not care whether they were ruled by Hindu rulers or Muslims. It is only very late, when they adopted tyrannical methods, in murdering Hindus, converting them to Islam, breaking their shrines and capturing their ladies that some-what of nationalism woke up amongst them. But by then it was too late. Even then many of the Hindu rulers kept their independence and dignity throughout the Mohammedan rule of over 600 years. But again such rulers only cared for their kingdoms as such and did not think of India, as a whole.

Whatever had happened, it is pucca that :

1. Entire India had never been under the Muslim rulers.
2. Though many Hindus had been killed, many converted to Islam and many were enslaved and packed to foreign

countries still majority of the people could retain themselves as Hindus and entire South, Rajputana and pockets in Saurastra ramained independent and in these states governance was as per Hindu tenets e.g, Shivaji's rule in Maharashtra.

3. Even the Muslim rulers were sovereign Indian rulers. Except for a small period of 14 years from 1192 to 1206, when Qutab-ud-din Aibak was under Ghori (after Ghori's death in 1206, he declared himself sovereign), all Mohammedan kings thereafter were independent and India was not a colony as had been the case under British, when India was colony under English emperor ruled from England.
4. Therefore, in ancient India and upto about 1809, when Delhi was annexed into British territory (Delhi being representative of India at that time) i.e. upto Muslim period, India continued to be an independent state having its sovereign rulers. The tyranny caused to Hindus by Muslim rulers is only an ethnic problem and politically we were one sovereign India.
5. Inspite of the tyranny caused, the Hindus continued to be faithful to Muslim rulers, either out of fear or because they had got used to the Muslim rule, that they did not jointly arose against the Muslim rulers although during the Slave and Khalji rulers, their number was quite insignificant.

In this way, Muslims continued to rule India for over 600 years from 1194 to about 1809, when Btitish took over Delhi rajya. The rulers included Slaves, Khaljis, Tughlaqs, Lodhis, Suri, Mughals. Initially Turks had come and they established the rule in India in 1192. Subsequent rulers were out of the Muslim chiefs settled in India. But each of the kings had to face many rebellious chiefs—Hindus and Muslims—whenever the existing ruler died as after such death, all governors, chiefs under him used to declare themselves independent and the first thing for the enthroned king was to suppress such rebellious chiefs. Even during the reign of such kings, they had to continuously keep on fighting, either to suppress some rebels or to conquer the left over Hindu rulers. Along with the rebellions from within the country, there had always been foreign aggressions from Central Asia and Middle East, particularly the Mangols. The Indian kings during Mohammedan period were, therefore, never in peace, They could, therefore, hardly think of public welfare works as major portion of their revenues went in the maintenance of adequate army.

Mohammedan rule was, however, responsible for destroying Bhartiyata in the Hindus in following manners—

As already indicated Bhartiyata and Hindu dharma were almost synonyms. To kill Bhartiyata from amongst the Indians, the Muslims—

1. Destroyed their religious and literary books. It is said that Taxila, Nalanda and Benaras had huge libraries and they had been burning for years. Hindus thus lost their religious granthas.
2. Converted by force many Hindus to Islam and those who had been converted became more fanatic Muslims so that their bonafides were not questioned. Some of the Muslim rulers, who had born of Hindu mothers caused more agony to Hindus with a view to keep the Muslims Ulemas with them.
3. Muslim rulers like Akbar developed cordiality with Hindu Rajput chiefs and employed many brave Rajputs in their army and then put them to fight against the staunch Hindu rulers and with a view to prove their sincerity to their employer ruler, they were more strict in the battle fields like Man Singh fought with Rana Pratap and during Aurangzeb's rule; Jai Singh negotiated Shivaji's surrender to Mughal emperor and so on. In this way the Muslim rulers' two purposes were served—one they could effectively divide the Rajput rulers and secondly made them fight against each other causing enmity within

themselves. Hindus in such a situation could not think of Bhartiyata or even Hindutva.

4. Destroyed the places of worship as a result of which, their faith in God got reduced slowly and slowly. Also as a result of the temples having been destroyed, the Hindus could not be preached and imbibed with Hinduistic/Bhartiyata element within themselves.
5. Even the worship was prohibited at many places. This finished the Hindutva within Hindus.
6. Hindu schools/pathshalas/gurukuls were destroyed as a result of which again the Hindu children could not know their religion or their past history and the pride for their religion or country. What to speak of pride for Hinduism, the Hindus could not even claim themselves to be Hindus openly. Thus the feeling of Hindutva was killed. On the contrary, the children of Hindus were taught in Muslim madarsas, where they were told of Islamism only. This enabled them to effect many conversions.
7. Government files could be given to Muslim/Muslim converts only. As such government servants caused cruelty on Hindus. The Hindus had always a fear of such cruelty being caused by them to their children etc. e.g. Hakikat Rai on claiming to be a Hindu had been asked to either accept conversion or get killed. He preferred latter. But many would have been converted to Islam under such threats day-in-and-day-out. As a result, from a few thousand Muslims only, who had come from abroad, there were over 12 crore at the time of partition of India.
8. In Mohammedans, Muslim ladies were not entitled to education. They had to remain in 'Purdah ' and whatever they learnt it was by some arrangement at the home itself. So because of fear of being kidnapped, Hindu ladies too could not get out of their houses and thus were deprived of education. There was hardly any Hindu educated lady of that period. In this way fifty per cent of the Hindu population was restricted to their homes only and could not join the main stream of nationalism or Hinduism.

9. Many taxes were imposed on Hindus like Jizia, professional tax, pilgrimage tax etc. which put Hindus to a lot of humiliation and thus their innerself i.e. Hindutva or Bhartiyata was killed.
10. Hindu rulers, who saved themselves from the clutches of Muslim rulers were very few only. Even they always had the fear of being annihilated any time. They, therefore, had always been thinking of saving themselves. They or their subjects could not, therefore, think of Hindustan at all.
11. The Hindus, in this way, having lost their religious books, unaware of Hindu tenets; unaware of their past; unaware of any affinity within themselves; became completely ignorant about Hinduism or what was happeing in India and the universe. They could with great difficulty keep their bodies and souls together. Then how and on what could they have any pride and consequently such people were internally killed. It is the Hindus, who were born and brought up in such a situation that they were quite illiterate, without any knowledge, so/much/so that English could call them barbaric.
12. So during Muslim rule, although Hindus had been able to save their religion, which none in Central Asia or Western Asia or Eastern Europe could save from being converted to Islam on the advent of that religion in 7th centuary A.D., they were berefit of their religious feelings i.e. Hindutva or national feeling i.e. Bhartiyata and this is one reason why many Hindus preferred to be ruled by English than by Muslims, when the former became the rulers of India and did not rise against them in rebellions.
13. Thus although the Indian sovereignty was maintained and India continued as an independent country during Muslim regime, the element of Bhartiyata had gone from these people. For the purpose of this book, therefore, we only have to see that Indian Independence was intact during the Muslim rulers, which had gone during the British period. In fact the wave of colonialism came only from Europe

in 16th or 17th centuary A.D. and they made almost whole of Asia, Africa, America and Australia their colonies. In ancient India and in Muslims' rule such a concept of colonialism was not there and, therefore, they became sovereign kings of the countries they conquered.

14. Still in spite of all the cruelties caused to Hindus, some feeling was left in them about the affinity for their nation and they had been up to find out some leadership/time to express the same. Such a feeling started showing up in Marathas under Shivaji, in Sikhs in Punjab, particularly under the patronage of Maharaja Ranjit Singh, ruler of Punjab. Scindias, Holker, Gaikwad, Rajas of south Indian States and but for suppression by English by their treacherous methods, they might have come up as rulers of India immediately after the decline of Mughals. This would only show that inspite of suppression for 600 years, Hindutva could not be completely killed from the minds of Hindus and this Hindutva subsequently took shape of Bhartiyata in giving a fight to English rulers (combined by people of all states).

And with the fall of Mughal rule, came to an end the sovereignty of India and India became a colony under the British government unheard of in India eversince the Vedic era. The African countries, America and Australia having been new colonies, is understandable as these were the new found lands by Europeans but the most flourishing, developed, educationally advanced and vast country having been made a colony by a small state of Britain is unthinkable. But this is what had happened and became history of this motherland of 40 crore people at that time due to their internal disunity, rivalry for power and treacherous methods adopted by the British.

As already indicated, with the death of a king in India, two things happened—one the war of succession amongst the sons, wards, chiefs of the king and another the declaration of independence by various provinces from central government.

After Aurangzeb's death too, same thing happened. Without considering the position of the country, we may only see the situation leading to the rise of English. The Governor of Bengal declared his independence. At that time Europeans, particularly French and English, started making out their trade centres in Calcutta and since there was rivalry amongst them, they provided small forces and constructed forts. This should have been discouraged by the Nawab as this only subsequently led to the battle of Plassy and fall of Nawab and establishment of British rule in India. The Indian rulers were not with farsight and thought them just small flies, who could be smashed any time. The English too took the Nawab with all reverence saying "their foreheads are on their feet" etc. But Siraj-ud-daula, when he became Nawab, he could sense some mischief in the minds of English. So he cautioned them from building castles etc. But by then it was too late, as English had by then seen—

1. The weakness of the Indian armies.
2. The superiority of their armaments, training of troops and discipline in troops. They had also judged the successful operation of their treacherous designs on Indians, who were after power, particularly the Mohammedans, who always had wars for the succession to throne. The skirmishes led to the battle of Plassy in which, Mir Jafar the commander of the army had been purchased to betray Siraj-ud-daula in consideration of his being made the Nawab of Bengal. It is here that Bhartiyata was lost in the sense that—
   - (i) The central government had been weak and the provincial governments had become independent as a result, the affinity for Bharat had gone and the king and the subjects cared for their kingdom only.
   - (ii) The Bhartiyata, which prescribes absolute devotion to the raja and the motherland had been sacrificed by people like Mir Jafar, who for the sake of becoming Nawab of Bengal, betrayed the ruling Nawab although he too ultimately suffered in the game and had bad

time under the British's domination with their ever increasing demands.

(iii) There were such people like Aminchand, who for the sake of some wealth, worked as a broker between English and Mir Jafar in the treacherous deal putting entire India in the feet of English for which beginning was made in battle of Plassy.

(iv) Lord Clive had brought troops by ship from Madras and the intellegence of the Nawab of Bengal could not know such movements and should have stopped such movements ab-initio, knowing fully well that such movements could be only for the purpose of enforcement of their position by the English. Hindu shastras, particularly Arthashastra, emphasise on the strong net of spies.

(v) Having already seen the armaments used by English, the Indian rulers did not arm themselves commensurately and on the other hand sought British help in fighting with other Indian rulers. As a result of such assistance, English got lot of money as compensation for extending such help and weakened the Indian rulers fighting within themselves vis-a-vis the English.

(vi) The masses were not with the ruler. This again is lack of Bhartiyata as Bhartiyata provides for full devotion of subjects to the king. On the contrary the masses were already pained under the tyranny of Muslim rulers, particularly on Hindus. They, therefore, thought that the change over to British might be better for them compared to that of Muslims.

(vii) Leaving aside the Bhartiyata and working for Hidutava, the Hindus thought that English were only a trading company and would not become rulers of India and once they got rid of Muslim rule and their tyranny, they might eventually be able to establish their own rule. So rather than Bhartiyata, Hindutava prevailed upon them. But they could not get a good leader within themselves to face English and establish their rule.

So whenever, we have lost the affinity for India (Bhartiyata), we have suffered. Whatever had happened at the time of Muslims invasion of India in 1192 (Mohammed Ghori), had been repeated on the advent of English in India by Hindus and Muslims combined. At the time of Muslim, invasion, it was Hindus, who lost Hindutava as also Bhartiyata. and yielded before Muslim invaders, sacrificing all Vedic values and now it was Hindus and Muslims who sacrificed Bhartiyata (if any was available in Muslims by then) on the advent of English. English again won the battle of Buxar by their manipulations and subsequently by enforcing Subsidiary Alliance, Doctrine of Lapse, annexed one kingdom after another in British dominion.They subdued Marathas by creating division within their allies and making them fight against the others. They downed Tipu Sultan same way. They won the Sikh wars by purchasing the commanders.

By 1857, British had brought more than half of India under them. The Indians had already started thinking in terms of uprooting the English from India. There had been skirmishes in rebellions against them right after 1761. There was a rebellion in Bengal by a regiment in 1766; in Vellore in 1806; an organised insubordination by Company's European troops. in 1809; rebellion by high caste sepoys in Barrakpur; deterioration in discipline after Afghan war; in Bengal, regiments refused to march for south India in 1844; two regiments mutineed on Sikh frontiers; resistance against non-payment of battle allowance in Madras; four regiments refused to draw their pay in Punjab in 1849; regiments refused to go to Burma for war in 1852; etc. But these were all on local basis and were easily and successfully subdued by British as per their tactical manipulations in which they were superb. One thing which enabled British to win over

Indian rulers was their discipline and sincerety to motherland (England) which was missing in Indians. Indians too were supreme till they were sincere to Bharat.

In 1857 there was a broader rebellion against the British. It started with the outbreak from Meerut by a regiment, which rebelled and after killing their officers marched to Delhi, killing all Europeons on way. On reaching Delhi, they made Bahadur Shah, their emperor. This was wrong decision as Bahadur Shah, who was a pensioner of British and was their pet but the rebels made him emperor which he may not have been able to refuse but he could not give them a leadership and also many Hindus were against making him the emperor. The rebellion was limited to Meerut, Delhi, Oudh, Jhansi etc. It was not only peaceful in Bengal. Madras and Bombay Presidencies but the army was brought from these provinces to quell the rebellion in Delhi, Oudh etc. Gorkhas and Sikhs also helped British in suppressing the rebellion. The rebellion, therefore, failed in the absence of an able leadership and uprising only in limited area. British also had a plus point with them that the rebels did not disrupt telegraphic lines as a result of which the government could call in the army from other places and monitor the quelling of the rebellion effectively. Here again it was lack of Bhartiyata in Indians in not rising against the English jointly. Although the people of Bengal, Madras, Bombay and other places had rebelled against the English time and again during the last about 80 years but at the time of rebellion in Meerut and Delhi, they remained indifferent, treating it as the cause of other provinces. Even Sikhs, who had just been subdeed by English, helped them suppressing the rebellion. The princes of about all states too had been with the British. Infact right upto 1947, that was the class created by English as of their loyals. So these Rajas/ Nawabs holding about two-fifth of India with the major provinces remaining with English, the rebellion was quelled. Also such rebellions could be effective only with great speed but in the case of this uprising after reaching Delhi, they were all quiet, giving the English a chance to collect army from other places and then had victory over the rebels. Also 25 per cent of population comprising of Muslims did not join the mutineers.

After the mutiny, English became extra careful in dealing with the Indians and for about 30 years it was all peaceful because of the terror created in the minds of Indians by many butcherings etc. after the Mutiny. It was only after the Indian National Congress was founded in 1885, that the Congress created some movement in political circles. Their demand was restricted only to self rule under the British rajya as they did not consider themselves capable of ruling the country themselves. There was, however, no effect as the voice raised was by a limited number of people, who were members of Congress. It was only after the passage of partition of Bengal Act that people of Bengal rose against it and adopted the boycott and swadeshi. It spread to other parts of the country too. It was, therefore, because of the partition of Bengal that Indian leaders came on one common platform, and Bhartiyata started showing its colours. But here too it was a fight of Hindus only against the English and in fact it is from here that the English policy of Divide and Rule started by creating a wedge between the Hindus and Muslims. The very concept of partition of Bengal was to lesson the effect of Congress workers of Bengal by creating half Bengal a Muslim majority state, who would be with the English. At first the Muslims were with the Hindus in demanding estoppel of the creation of partition of Bengal but when the Muslim leaders of Eastern Bengal were briefed by the English, they rose in favour of the partition.This was again a brake in the movements of swadeshi and demand for cancellation of partition of Bengal. Thus English—

1. reduced the effect of the voice of Congress demanding home rule.
2. by partitioning Bengal, wanted to take away at least 50 per cent of Bengal population from any demands.

3. gave effect to their policy of 'Divide and Rule' and created differences between Hindus and Muslims.
4. encouraged Muslims to rise against the demands of Congress, which was said to be Hindu oriented.
5. encouraged Muslim leaders like Syed Ahmed Khan and Mohammed Ali Jinnah not to join the Congress dominated by Hindus as Hindus would treat Muslims in a biased manner because of what they had done to Hindus in 600 years of their rule. Like Kaikayee of Ramayan, Muslims could be brought round in demanding separate electorate for Muslims.
6. This led to 'Two Nation Theory' of Muslims. The Muslims treating themselves as a separate nation within India and had a right to rule the Muslim majority areas and not be subdued by Hindu rulers.
7. Muslims met Viceroy Minto at Simla and put their demands of separate electorate and recognition of Muslims for reservation in government jobs, municipalities, district boards, legislative assemblies of provinces and centre etc. In fact it appears that the conference was arranged by British themselves with a view never to give effect to the self-rule demand under the guise of disunity amongst Congres and Muslim League.
8. Muslims, therefore, had always been against the demand of self-rule unless they were given effective representation and always pleaded for being ruled by English only rather than having self-rule and then being ruled by Hindu dominated government.
9. Hindus and Muslims had come closer during the first world war but again departed and the result was the Act of 1919 based on Minto-Morley reforms, fulfilling the aspirations of Muslim leaders as envisaged in their Simla Conference with Lord Minto.

The struggle for independence had been dealt with in detail in the previous chapter indicating how the Indians were bereft of Bhartiyata and then were two nations created—one formed by Hindus and another composed by Muslims as a result of English diplomacy. Also the constitutional developments have been dealt with separatly how the various Acts passed by British had been with an eye on continuing the British rajya in India by creating different voices of Hindus and Muslims so that the English had an excuse of demanding unity amongst the Hindus and Muslims to enable them to consider the same and at the same time dissuading Muslims from joining Hindu dominated Constituent Assembly and from raising their voice as one 'Bhartiya' rather than that of Hindus and Muslims. Our leaders also had been after the Muslims to join them and did not till end see through the game. They ultimately had to agree to the division of the country on the basis of the religion. Here again the Constituent Assembly had been harping upon secularism when the country itself had been partitioned on the basis of religion and the correct thing should have been, when the Muslims got Pakistan on the basis of Muslim majority areas and they declared Pakistan as Islamic State, India could have been declared as a Hindu State or Aryavrat. But strictly as per vedic tenets, India welcomed all religions and made India a Secular State. The result of all this today is that India being a democracy, have to be governed by the party having majority of seats in Lok Sabha. In the craze for obtaining more votes, the parties have been wooing the Muslim voters promising many concessions to them even at the cost of the majority community Hindus, whereas no such concessions are granted to Hindus in Islamic states. Every action in favour of Hindus is labelled as communal but the same favour for Muslims is secular. Admittedly many of the Muslims are in the main stream of the country but it cannot be said of all and, therefore, there is a constant danger to the country from such people not in the main stream of the country. Let us see where this concept of secularism shall lead this country to. We can judge it from one instance. Recently the atom bomb explosion by India (May, 1998) has been criticised by the countries abroad because they could not tolerate such actions by India, whereas the same actions by themselves are considered justified. Not only this, even our own people have not come out of the party thinkings of criticising the ruling party for criticising sake and do not rise with them as one so that the other countries get shock not of explosions but more of the unity of Indian people. Let us search ourselves and unite at least on national achievements. The fact is that due again to regional thinking as a result of the rising up of regional parties, the ruling party thinks of appeasing their constituents, who only value the development of their own regions and not the country as a whole, the interest of the nation is being sacrificed for regional gains. The result is that out of our total budget, the major portion goes to regional developments, where the states only eat away the resources without actually investing in the purpose for which the money is allotted; then the next draw on the budget is subsidy of thousands of crores of rupees, again to appease a particular class of people; then the next charge is payment of debt and interest thereon and on defence. Thus hardly any amount is left for structural development, without which there cannot be any development of industry without which there cannot be prosperity in the country. So we are getting poorer and poorer as a country without any scope for development. With rising in population and scarce industrial development, we may get into an economic crash any day, if we donot undertake development of the country unitedly as a nation forgetting the regional bias.

Glossary

Abkari : Cess /excise
Adab-i-Alamgiri: History of Aurangzeb
Ahvaniya : Caller in court
Akash : Space
Amantran : Invitation
Amins : Land Revenue Collector
Ananda : Happiness
Anushilan : Constant study
Arya-Niwas : Rajmahal
Aryaputra : Raja
Aryavrat : India
Ashramas : Four stages of life
Ashwamedha yagya : Yagya held by emperor to establish his suzeranity
Asuras : Demons
Aswa : Horse
Aswamedha : A sacrificial ceremony centering in a house, generally performed by independent monarchs.
Ayuktas : Commissioners
Baboos : Office workers
Bakr-Id : The Muslim 'Feast of Sacrifice', celebrating the faith of Abraham who was willing to sacrifice his son at Allah's request.
Bakshi : A military officer-in-charge of payments of salaries or an officer who kept an account of all disbursements connected with military tenures.
Baman Avtar : Incarnation of God
Bande Matram : National song
Bania : Businessman
Banjaras : The nomads who lived with their families in camps. The would also transport or land the goods of bulk, like foodgrains, sugar, butter and salt, etc.
Banprastha : Living in forest in third stage of life
Bapis : Wells with stairs
Barchhi : Spear
Barid-i-Mumalik : Head of Intelligence department
Bazaar : Market
Bhagwad bhakti : Devotion to God
Bhaktas : Devotees
Bhakti : Devotion
Bhandagrika : Officer in charge of the treasury or the royal store-house.
Bhang : Dissolve
Bharat : India
Bharatiyata : Indianism
Bhartiya : Indian
Bhatta : Allowance
Bhogapatis : Mess-Incharge
Bhuktis : Provinces
Brahamrishi : Devotee/seer
Bramhamcharis : First stage in life
Brahmanyans : Religious books of Hindus
Brahmin : First of four castes in Hindus
Brahmvrat : India
Brihaspati : Preceptor of gods
Chakavarty : Emperor
Chandals : Menials
Chauth : In theory one-fourth, share of the revenue granted to or extracted by the Marathas, in practice could be more or less than one-fourth.
Chowkies : Posts

Dak chowkies : Postal posts
Dal ke khane wale : vegetarians
Danda-Samata : Equaliser
Darbar : Court
Daroga : Police Inspector
Daroga-i-Dak : Inspector of Posts
Daroga-i-Dak Chowkies : Inspector of Postal posts
Darshan : To grant an audience, to condescend to meet; also a levy, presents offered to a king or a chief when one meets him.
Darsita visvarupa : World view in God
Dasas : Servants
Dasavtara : Ten incarnations of God
Dasyu : Non-Hindu
Desh : Country
Dev Pooja : Worship of God
Devas : Gods
Devgiri : A mountain
Devi mandir : Temple of Goddess
Devlok : Heaven
Dewan/Diwan : Chief Minister; this title was also applied to the incharge of the finance department of the State.
Dhanyavishnu : A God
Dharma : Religion
Dharma mahamatras : Ecclеisiastical Minister
Dharma Yudh : War based on Laws of war
Dharmadhikama : Eccleesiastical Minister
Dharmashastras : Religious books
Dharmasthan : Religious place
Dharmavidya : Knowledge of Religion
Dharmavijaya : Victory of religion
Diwan-i-riyasat : Minister for Home
Ekamukha : One-mouthed
Faqirs : Hermits
Farman : Notification
Fauj : Army
Faujdar : An officer invested with the charge of the police and had jurisdiction on all criminal matters.
Ganapati : Elephant God
Gandharva : A god
Ghats : Bathing places on river bank
Ghee : Butter oil
Ghusalkhana : Bathroom/A meeting with spier by the King
Gopas : Cowherdsman
Gram bhojaka : Village Head
Granthas : Religious books
Grihapatya : Head of family
Grihasthaashrama : Second of four stages of life
Grithastha : A family man
Gunas : Qualities
Guru : Teacher
Gurukuls : Teaching places
Harkarahas : Messengers
Hindi-Chini bhai bhai : Indo-China brotherhood
Hindushahi : Indian rulers
Hindustan : India
Hindutava : Hinduism
Ishwar : God
Iti : The end
Jagir : A tenure in which the public revenue of a given tract of land was made over to a servant of a state together with the powers required to enable him to collect and appropriate such revenue, and administer the general government of the assigned territory. The assignment could be conditional or unconditional. During the early period of British rule it was also the practice to confer *jagir* as rewards for meritorious services to the state.
Jagirdars : Holder of a jagir.
Jana : Human being
Janpadas : Blocks of villages
Jayapatra : Victory sign
Jharokha : The balcony from which the emperor showed himself to the populace.
Jiziya : Tax levied by Muslim rulers on

non-Muslims
Kahn-e-Saman : A house steward
Karambhoomi : Active place (own country)
Karma : Actions
Kshatriya : Second of four castes in Hindus.
Khalsa : Sikh
Khilawat Khana : A meeting place with ministers by Mughal Kings
Khufiyanavis : Spy
Kotwals : Police Inspector/chief/ official of the town
Krishna Avtar : Incarnation of God
Kumarjiva : Son of the King
Kutsa : A god incharge of vigilance department
Lalit Kala : Fine Arts
Lokas : Various Universes
Madarsas : Schools
Madhya Desha : Central Province
Mahamatras : Ministers
Maharaja : The King
Maharajadhiraj : The Emperor
Mantra : Religious verse
Mantri : Minister
Mariah : A tribe, who robbed and killed travellers
Mir Bakshi : A military officer-in-charge for payments of salaries or an officer who kept an account of all disbursements connected with military tenures.
Mir-i-Adal : Chief of Court
Mirbahari : Chief Collector of land revenue
Munsifs : Magistrates
Musalman : Follower of Islam religion
Nagarasreshti : Municipal Commission
Nagarpati : Municipal Commissioner
Nagrika : A citizen
Narsingh Avtar : An incarnation of God as man and lion
Nazar : Customary presents; a fee, offering, tribute, a fine on transfer of land; the sum paid down to secure a grant of a revenue lease of a village.
Padshah : King
Padshahi : Kingship
Paisacha : Evil spirit
Panchajanab : Five heads
Panchas : Member of village council
Panchayat : Village council
Panchjanya : Five heads of religious body
Pandits : Priests
Parisada : Offering made to idol
Patal : A universe below this universe
Pathashalas : School
Phansidar : A tribe which used to rob and kill people in forests
Pradhan : Head of a village
Pramukhs : Heads of village blocks
Pratitnidhi : Representative
Pucca : Firm
Purdah : Veil
Purohit : Ecclesiastical head
Raajbhag : Share of raja in the produce
Raghuvanshi rajas : Kings of RamaÕs dynasty
Rai : A noble
Raj Guru : Ecclesiastical head in the kingdom.
Raja : The king
Raja-Vyavahara-Kosa : A dictionary of administrative terms
Rajab : A Muslim month
Rajan : King
Rajdharma : Religion of the ruler
Rajgurus : Ecclesiastical head of king
Rajkumars : Sons of the king
Rajya : Kingdom
Rajya Sabha : King's Council of Ministers
Rakshas : Demons
Ram Avtar : Incarnation of god as Rama
Ram rajya : Region of King Rama
Rishis : Hermits
Ryotwari : A settlement made by the

government immediately with the *rayats*, without intermediary renters or zamindars.

Sabha : Council

Sachivas : Secretaries

Sadhu : A hermit

Sadr : Head of the Muslim judiciary and religious patronage

Sadr Diwani Adalat : Highest court of Civil justice

Sadr Nizmat Adalat : Highest criminal court

Sahmarna : Burning of alive wife with husband on same pyre

Saka : Indian year

Samaharta : Collector of land revenues

Samaj : Society

Samghata Kalapa : A tribe who sacrificed human life

Samiti : Council of the king

Samrat : Emperor

Samritis : Religious books

Sangha : One block of villages

Sansad : Parliament

Sanyas : Fourth stage of human life

Sanyasis : One who is in fourth stage of life

Sarais : Lodges

Sardars : Chieftains

Sarkar : Government

Sati : Dying with the husband

Shaharia-mandi : Administrator of market

Sharstras : Religious books

Shehzadas : Sons of the king

Shiqdar : In charge of revenue collection as well as of maintaining law and order in a *pargana*

Shudras : Fourth caste in Hindus.

Slokas : Rhyme/couplet in Sanskrit poetry.

Sramons : Buddhist Monks

Sthanikas : Religious places

Stridhan : Lady's property

Subedars : Governors

Sultan : Muslim rulers

Svayambar : Selection of groom

Swadeshi : Indigenous

Swaraga : Heaven

Swaraj : Swarajya : Independence

Tadi : Liquor

Talwar : Sword

Tamasha : Festivity

Tamgha : A medal

Tapasya : Asceticism

Tarafdars : Holder of a *taraf* or portion of village lands; chief revenue and police anthority in the area of his posting.

Thana : A geographical unit; a watch house; a police station; garrison in a fort; small fortified check-points to protect more settled areas against incursious from predatory tribal people.

Thanedar : Commander of one or more check-points (*thanas*); commander of a small fort; a man who has a management of a district; an incharge of a *thana*.

Thug : A cheat

Thugee : Act of cheating

Unarya : Non-Aryans

Uparika : Governors

Vaisesika : Indian philosophy

Vaish : Third of the four Hindu Castes

Vaish Dharma : Job of the third of Hindu castes

Varanashrama : Four castes and four stages of life in Hindus

Vatika : Garden

Vidyas : Knowledge

Virat Sabha : General assembly

Vis/Vishyas : District

Vishayapati : District Chief

Vyavahara Samata : Equality before Law

Vyvaharikas : Law and legal procedure

Wah-e-Guruji Ka Khalsa : A salutation in Sikhs

Wah-e-Guruji-ke-Fateh : A salutation in Sikhs

Wahabis : A tribe of devotees in Muslim

Waqahanavis : Reporter

Wazir : Minister; head of the fiscal administration of the empire.

Yagya : Religious oblation in Hindus

Yogis : Hermits

Zamindar : Broadly speaking, the holder (of the rights over the produce) of the land. The term implied a range of highly variagated dominant rural classes and was inclusive of the so-called rajas who had an 'autonomous' control over the territories under their jurisdiction.

Zenana : A meeting place between the Mughal king and spies

Zimmis : Protected subjects (under the Muslim rule).

Bibliography

1. Abbas Sarwani (Translation by Elliot & Dowsan), *Tarikh-e-Sher Shahi*
2. Acharya Priya Vrat Ved Vachaspati, *A Study in Vedic Polity*
3. Agnihotri, V.K., *Complete Guide of Indian History*
4. *Atharva Ved Samhita*
5. Awasthi, A.B.C., *Indian Nationalism*
6. *Babar-nama,* The foundation of our knowledge by Babur's history
7. Bana, *Harsh Charita*
8. Basham, A.L., *The Wonder that was India*
9. Chankya (Kautilya), *Arth Shastra*
10. Dutta, M. N., *Ramayan*
11. Edward, Thompson and G.T. Garrot, *Rise and Fulfilment of British Rule in India*
12. Elliot and Dowson, *History of India as told by its own Historians*
13. Elphinston, *History of India*
14. Fuherer, A., *Brihaspati Samriti*
15. Iqbal Narain, *Rajniti Shastra ke Mool Sidhant*
16. Ishwari Prasad and S.K. Subedar, *History of Modern India*
17. Jahangir (Translated by A. Rogers), *Tuzuk - i - Jahangiri*
18. Jain Ram Chander, *The Most Ancient Aryan Society*
19. K.V. Ranga Swami Aiyangar, *A History of India*
20. Kali Das, *Abhigyan Shakuntalam*
21. Mahajan, V.D., *Ancient India*
22. Manjumdar, R.C., *History and Culture of the Indian People* (various volumes)
23. -- *An Advance History of India*
24. -- *History of the Freedom Movement in India*
25. -- *Classical Accounts of India*
26. *Manu Samriti*
27. Michael Edwardes, *British India (1772-1947)* Vol I-II
28. Mirza, Mohammed Khan, *Alamgir-nama*
29. Mushir-ul-Hasan and Narayani Gupta, *Indian Colonial Encounter*

30. *Narad Samriti* Translation by J. Jolly
31. Pradhan, R.G., *Indian Struggle for Swaraj*
32. *The Quran*
33. *Rig Ved Samhita*
34. Sampurnanand, *Aryon Ka Adi Desh*
35. Sethi, R.R. and V.D. Mahajan, *The British Rule in India and After*
36. Shaikh Abu-Ul-Fazl, *Ain-e-Akbari*
37. Shaikh Abul Fazl, *Akbar-nama*
38. Sharma, S.R., *A Bibliography of Mughal India*
39. Smith, V.A., *A History of Fine Arts in India and Ceylon*
40. Srivastava, A.L. *The Sultanate of Delhi*
41. Swami Dayanand, *Rig Ved Adi Bhashya Bhumika*
42. - - *Satyarth Prakash*
43. Swami Vidyanand Saraswati, *Aryon Ka Adi Desh Aur Unki Sabhyata*
44. Tilak, B.G., *Qion*
45. Tulsi Das, *Ramcharit Manas*
46. Ved Vyas, *Shrimad Bhagwat*
47. Vincent A. Smith, *The Early History of India*
48. Vishwa Nath Prasad Verma, *Vedic Rajniti Shastra*
49. *Yajur Ved Samhita.*

Index